FREEDOM OF SPEECH

TWO CONCERNS

1. Types of Protected Speech
2. Speech Regulations

DANGEROUS SPEECH

1. *Unlawful Activity:* The state may prohibit speech advocating unlawful or subversive action.

    a. *Clear and Present Danger:* Words used in a manner and specific context where they would bring about a criminal harm. *Schenck v. United States*, 249 U.S. 47 (1919).

    b. *Overthrow of Government by Force:* Words that may cause harm by influencing others to undertake harmful acts, even those taught as advocacy of a certain doctrine. *Gitlow v. New York*, 268 U.S. 652 (1925).

2. *Incitement:* The urging of a group or person to take immediate action. *Brandenburg v. Ohio*, 395 U.S. 444 (1969).

    a. Likely to cause harmful action;

    b. Speaker intends to incite or produce imminent lawless action and is likely to do so;

    c. Applies only where speaker urges illegal action in opposition to government, government policies, or private parties.

3. *Fighting Words:* Direct personal insults likely to cause a person to react violently. Other injurious insults are not prosecuted. *Chaplinsky v. New Hampshire*, 315 U.S. 568 (1942).

4. *Group Libel:* False and derogatory statements tending to produce hate or prejudice about a particular group. *Example: Statements that a certain race, creed, or religion is depraved.* *Beauharnais v. Illinois*, 343 U.S. 250 (1952).

5. *Defamation:* False and derogatory statements, tending to harm the reputation of the subject discussed. *New York Times v. Sullivan*, 376 U.S. 254 (1964).

    a. *Public Figures:*

    i. *Actual malice required:* statement made with knowledge of falsity or in reckless disregard for the truth. *Milkovich v. Lorain Journal*, 497 U.S. 1 (1990).

    ii. Applies to statements of fact. *Exception: where reasonable person would interpret statement of opinion as based on fact.*

    b. *Private Persons:*

    i. Malice required if private persons voluntarily place themselves into a particular controversy. Private person becomes a "public figure" for a limited range of issues.

    ii. Malice is NOT required for private persons not involved in public issue, or involuntarily involved in a public matter. *Gertz v. Robert Welch, Inc.*, 418 U.S. 323 (1974).

6. *Invasion of Privacy:* Disclosure of true facts that are private or harm to reputation based on false impression created by statement. *Exception:*

    a. Disclosure of private information that is already publicly known because it is:

    i. in public record; *Cox Broadcasting Corp. v. Cohn*, 420 U.S. 469 (1975).

    ii. otherwise publicly apparent. *Zacchini v. Scripps-Howard Broadcasting Co.*, 433 U.S. 562 (1977).

CONTENT REGULATION

First Amendment prevents regulation of ▮▮▮ based on its content or the viewpoint ex▮▮▮ by the speaker. Laws that regulate spee▮▮ basis of content or viewpoint are uncons▮▮

1. *Content Neutral:* A law that doesn't dist▮▮ between types of speech on the basis of what the speech is about, is constitutional.

2. *Viewpoint Neutral:* A law that regulates an entire topic or speech regardless of the opinions or views expressed about that topic is constitutional.

2. *Content-based Regulation:* Government may regulate speech on the basis of content if:

    a. The government has a compelling interest to do so and the means of regulation are necessary to achieve that interest.

    b. The law regulates conduct and not the content of the speech associated with it.

PRIOR RESTRAINT

1. Government regulation of speech before it has taken place is generally unconstitutional.

2. Prior restraint on speech is permissible where:

    a. National security interests are affected by the publication of particular subject matter. *Near v. Minnesota (ex rel. Olson)*, 283 U.S. 697 (1931).

    b. Government interest exists in securing a fair trial. *Nebraska Press Assn. v. Stuart*, 427 U.S. 539 (1976).

VAGUENESS AND OVERBREADTH

Government regulations that are vague or over-broad are unconstitutional as regulating more or less speech than they purport to proscribe.

1. *Vagueness:* A statute is vague if persons of common intelligence cannot guess what type of behavior is being regulated. *Connally v. General Construction Co.*, 269 U.S. 385 (1926).

2. *Overbreadth:* A statute is overbroad if it is worded in such a way that permits a state to regulate both matters that it may constitutionally proscribe, and those that it may not constitutionally regulate or proscribe.

OBSCENE SPEECH

Miller v. California, 413 U.S. 15 (1973)

1. To the average person applying contemporary community standards, the expression is obscene if:

    a. It appeals to the prurient interest;

    b. Work is patently offensive; and

    c. Taken as a whole, lacks serious literary, artistic, political, or scientific value.

INDECENT AND OFFENSIVE SPEECH

Government cannot prohibit the use of specific words in a public place where speech is not legitimately restricted. Words so protected are not obscene; but are merely indecent, vulgar, or offensive. Risk of censorship in specific words is the possibility of a government ban on the expression of an unpopular message. *Cohen v. California*, 403 U.S. 15 (1971).

▮ to uphold
▮▮ regulation incidentally affects expression, or government has important aim unrelated to the expression, balancing test is applied: government interest is weighed against the impact of the law on expression. *United States v. O'Brien*, 391 U.S. 367 (1968).

2. *Discriminatory Conduct:* First Amendment does not protect speech and attendant conduct that is motivated by bias or discrimination.

3. *Time, Place, and Manner Regulations:* The government may regulate the time, place, and manner of access to locations that may be used for expressive purposes. Laws regulating access to property on the basis of the speech that is to be made on such property are generally unconstitutional.

    a. *Public Forums:* Specific types of public property traditionally associated with the act of speech or expression. Laws regulating speech in public forums may by upheld if they are:

    i. content neutral;

    ii. narrowly tailored to serve a compelling governmental interest; and

    iii. allow for alternative channels of communication.

    b. *Nonpublic Forums:* Property that is not traditionally associated with speech, or whose primary use is not for expressive activity. Laws regulating speech in non-public forums may be upheld if they are:

    i. viewpoint neutral; and

    ii. reasonably related to a legitimate government purpose.

    c. *Private Forums:* Property that is not open to the public at large, or otherwise in the hands of private parties. Laws regulating speech in private forums may be upheld if states allow access to shopping centers for expression, but otherwise the Constitution does not apply to private property.

COMMERCIAL SPEECH

Any speech that is economically motivated or which does nothing more than propose a commercial transaction is protected. Commercial speech also provides information helping consumers make choices about products or services. *Exception: Government may regulate commercial speech that is likely to deceive or that is related to an illegal activity.*

FREEDOM OF THE PRESS

IN GENERAL

Press has special rights beyond those conferred by the free speech guarantee. *New York Times Co. v. United States (The Pentagon Papers Case)*, 403 U.S. 713 (1971).

1. *Government Inquiry:* Press not immune from subpoena or search warrants.

2. *Access to Information:*

    a. Government must ensure that places traditionally open to the public remain open unless government has a compelling interest in closing.

    b. Press only has same right of access as the public itself.

THE COMMERCE POWER/CLAUSE
ARTICLE I § 8

Congress has the power to regulate commerce between the states. What may Congress regulate?

1. *"Commerce":* Any activity may be regulated, even if it is not commerce in the traditional sense (the movement of persons or goods), as long as that activity:

   a. Takes place within interstate commerce.

   b. Uses the channels or instrumentalities of interstate commerce.

   c. Affects interstate commerce.

2. *Interstate v. Intrastate:* Congress may clearly regulate any activity that affects interstate commerce. Congress may regulate some activities that take place wholly intrastate, due to their effects on, or relationship to, interstate commerce. *Gibbons v. Ogden*, 22 U.S. 1 (1824).

   a. Any intrastate activity which has a substantial effect on interstate commerce. *United States v. Lopez*, 514 U.S. 549 (1995).

      i. *"Substantial effect":* Currently, an intrastate activity will have a substantial effect on interstate commerce only if the matter regulated is economic or commercial.

   b. Individual activities that have an aggregate effect on interstate commerce.

   c. All parts of an enterprise, even if only a part of the enterprise affects interstate commerce, where the nonregulated part may adversely impact the part affecting commerce.

3. *Scope of Power:* Congress's control over interstate commerce is plenary. Congress can prohibit or condition the movement of persons or goods regardless of its motive, so long as it does not violate any other constitutional provision.

   a. May do so to protect the national economy.

   b. As a means to achieve health, safety, or welfare aims.

      i. To a degree, Congress can regulate what happens after interstate commerce has taken place. *United States v. Sullivan*, 332 U.S. 689 (1948).

      ii. Congress may regulate and protect the instrumentalities of interstate commerce, such as vehicles, transportation terminals, even if the threat comes from intrastate activities. *Southern Railway Co. v. United States*, 222 U.S. 20 (1911).

      iii. Congress's conclusion that an activity affects interstate commerce need only be reasonable. *Hodel v. Virginia Surface Mining & Reclamation Assn.*, 452 U.S. 264 (1981).

      iv. Once Congress finds that a class or aggregate of activities affects commerce, that activity may be regulated regardless of whether any particular instance of that activity affects commerce. *Perez v. United States*, 402 U.S. 146 (1971).

FEDERAL EXECUTIVE POWER

DOMESTIC POWERS

Executive Power: Constitution confers the executive power on the president to administer and carry out the laws, and act in times of national, not domestic, emergencies without authorizing congressional legislation. ARTICLE II § 1

1. Presidential Pardon ARTICLE II § 2: Can pardon individuals or whole classes of persons any time after offense is committed. Effect of pardon is to preclude conviction or to mitigate or remove any penalties that result from conviction. The power to pardon cannot be limited by Congress. *United States v. Klein*, 80 U.S. 128 (1871).

2. Presidential Veto ARTICLE 1 § 7: President has power to disapprove of any legislation passed by Congress. President has power to override, Congress needs a vote of two-thirds of each house.

3. Power of Appointment ARTICLE II § 2: President has the ability to vest executive power in certain government officers through the power of appointment.

   a. *"Officers of the United States":* President can appoint officers who exercise "significant authority under the laws of the United States." Includes persons who formulate government policy, enact rulemaking and adjudication, or otherwise have broad governmental powers. *Buckley v. Valeo*, 424 U.S. 1 (1976).

   b. *Inferior Officers:* Power to appoint belongs to Congress, not President. Includes the heads of departments, or officers whose work is "directed and supervised" by persons appointed by the President. *Edmond v. United States*, 520 U.S. 651 (1997).

   c. *Removal Power:* President has power to terminate at will those officials whose exercise of discretion is essential to the functioning of the executive branch. Congress can create an "independent" executive branch for officials relatively free from presidential control, who may only be removed "for cause." *Morrison v. Olson*, 487 U.S. 654 (1988).

FOREIGN AFFAIRS POWERS

Executive branch has some ability to take action or enter into international commitments on behalf of the United States as a sovereign state among other sovereign states.

1. *Treaties:* President negotiates treaties. For treaty to be effective, Senate must still consent by ratifying it. ARTICLE II § 2

2. *Executive Agreements:* President can enter into international agreements without consent of Senate. To be valid, an executive agreement must be:

   a. Pursuant to the exercise of a presidential power;

   b. Based on authorizing legislation;

   c. Based on a prior treaty;

   d. Adopted by Congress (congressional-executive agreement).

3. *Military Powers and Foreign Affairs:* The President as Commander-in-Chief has the power to take some military actions without authorization by Congress.

PRESIDENTIAL IMMUNITIES AND PRIVILEGES

1. *Executive Liability:* President is absolutely immune from civil damages liability for his official acts. No immunity, or temporary immunity while in office, against civil litigation arising from events that took place before President took office. Criminal proceedings may be brought only after President has been impeached. No immunity from judicial process; court may order the President to comply with a subpoena. *United States v. Nixon*, 418 U.S. 683 (1974).

2. *Executive Privilege:* Communications conducted in exercise of executive function are confidential. Not in Constitution, but inferred by the Supreme Court. Exceptions:

   a. Disclosure to ensure justice. *United States v. Nixon*, 418 U.S. 683 (1974).

   b. Disclosure to ensure preservation of records.

GOVERNMENTAL RELATIONS

TWO TYPES

1. **Federalism**
2. **Separation of Powers**
   (use chart on Page 4)

1. FEDERALISM—DEFINITION

Constitution balances power between dual sovereign governments; one belonging to the states, and the other to a central, federal government.

1. FEDERALISM—LIMITATIONS OF STATE POWER

1. Exclusive Federal Power ARTICLE I § 8:

   a. *Necessary and Proper Clause:* Congress has the power to make all laws "necessary and proper" for executing its powers and all others given by the Constitution to federal government. Congress has broad authority to choose the means for achieving some legitimate aim of the government. *Heart of Atlanta Motel, Inc. v. United States*, 379 U.S. 241 (1964).

   b. *Enumerated Powers:* Congress may use any of its enumerated powers to achieve any result not forbidden by the Constitution. *McCulloch v. Maryland*, 17 U.S. 316 (1819).

2. Concurrent State and Federal Power:

   a. *Supremacy Clause:* When Congress acts within its powers, it may expressly or implicitly enact laws that preempt state law. Congress acts implicitly to preempt state law if:

      i. It regulates a subject matter pervasively; or

      ii. It enacts a law that directly conflicts with a state law.

   b. *Preemption:* Where Congress has not enacted conflicting law and state action does not interfere with the federal structure, states may exercise nonexclusive federal power.

Governmental Relations continues on page 3 ▶

2. SEPARATION OF POWERS

	...TO LEGISLATIVE	...TO JUDICIAL	...TO EXECUTIVE
LEGISLATIVE IN RELATION...	• Delegation of Powers • Bicameralism *INS v. Chadha*, 462 U.S. 919 (1983) • Removal of Legislative Officers	• Assignment of Non-Judiciary Tasks • Article I Legislative Courts • Privilege against Congressional Arrest • Judicial Inquiry into Congressional Doings • Legislative Re-opening of Final Judgments	• Removal of Executive Officers • Presentment • Executive Inquiry into Congressional Doings • Executive Immunities and Privileges
JUDICIAL IN RELATION...	• Will not Re-open Final Judgments • Political Question	• Independence, Impartiality • Life Tenure	• Judicial, not Executive Duties *Marbury v. Madison*, 5 U.S. 137 (1803) • Executive Immunities and Privilege • Political Question
EXECUTIVE IN RELATION...	• Removal of Presidential Officers • Congress cannot override, unless for cause • Veto power (Presentment) • Cannot Inquire into Congressional Doings • Executive Immunities and Privileges	• Executive Immunities and Privileges • Political Question	• Removal of Executive Officers

DUE PROCESS

TWO TYPES

1. **Substantive Due Process**
2. **Procedural Due Process**

▼

1. SUBSTANTIVE DUE PROCESS

1. States cannot act to affect certain rights. *In re Slaughter-House Cases*, 83 U.S. 36 (1976).
2. State legislation affecting fundamental rights subject to review similar to strict scrutiny: regulation must be narrowly tailored to meet a compelling state interest. *Exception: Economic substantive due process legislation that involves governmental regulation of social and economic matters is subject to the rational basis test.*
3. Applies only to fundamental rights (some of which are not expressly stated in the Constitution).

▼

2. PROCEDURAL DUE PROCESS

No taking of life, liberty, or property without adequate procedures. What Procedures are appropriate? To determine "adequate procedures," examine several factors that must be balanced against each other:

1. What private interest is affected? The more important the affected interest, the more careful the applied procedures must be.
2. What risk of error is inherent in procedure? The higher the risk, the more careful and specific the applied procedures must be.
3. Weigh interest of government against alternatives? The greater the government interest, the greater likelihood of using a procedure that will achieve government aims and reduce administrative costs. Interests protected by procedural due process:
   a. Life–criminal procedure for death penalty cases.
   b. Liberty–liberties contained in the Bill of Rights: right to privacy, family relationships, and unlawful incarceration.
   c. Property–usually any property interest.

Fundamental Rights

1. *Right to Privacy:*
   a. Create, maintain, or change family relationships *Zablocki v. Redhail*, 434 U.S. 374 (1978);
   b. Procreate, educate and nurture children *Meyer v. Nebraska*, 262 U.S. 390 (1923);
   c. Maintain parent-child relationship;
   d. Engage in consensual sexual practices within marriage *Bowers v. Hardwick*, 478 U.S. 186 (1986); *Griswold v. Connecticut*, 381 U.S. 479 (1965);
   e. Refuse involuntary medical treatment *Washington v. Harper*, 494 U.S. 210 (1990);
   f. NOT including the right of family members to withdraw life-sustaining treatment for an incapacitated person *Cruzan v. Dir., Missouri Dept. of Health*, 497 U.S. 261 (1990).
   g. *Abortion:* fundamental right of women to terminate a pregnancy without undue state interference. Balance against state interests, formula devised to weigh woman's right against state interests and life of fetus; *Roe v. Wade*, 410 U.S. 113 (1973); *Planned Parenthood v. Casey*, 505 U.S. 833 (1992):
      i. *First trimester:* state cannot interfere; strict scrutiny applied;
      ii. *Second trimester:* state interest in health of mother is compelling; state may regulate to protect mother's health and safety;
      iii. *Third trimester:* fetus is viable and state interest in that life is compelling; may regulate to prevent abortion, except where health or life of mother is at issue.
2. *Right to Vote:*
   a. *Two-part analysis:* Court balances state restriction of voting rights against state's interest in imposing the restriction:
      i. if effect to voting rights outweighs the state's interest, regulation must be narrowly drawn to advance a compelling government interest;
      ii. if state interest outweighs restriction, regulation will be upheld if it is reasonable and nondiscriminatory, and the state interest is important.
   b. *Types of vote regulations:* Qualifying or restricting votes, vote dilution *Reynolds v. Sims*, 377 U.S. 533 (1964), and gerrymandering.

3. *Right to Travel (Interstate):* State imposition of penalties for a nonresident traveling from one state to relocate to another is subject to fundamental rights analysis. Types of travel regulations:
   a. *Deter immigration:* states may not save state funds by preventing nonresidents from receiving state benefits. Cannot deter indigent immigrants in this manner *Shapiro v. Thompson*, 394 U.S. 618 (1969).
   b. *Durational residency requirements:* denial of basic necessities of life is subject to strict scrutiny. May not apportion funds based on length of residency. May not grant preferential treatment based on date of residency. *Exceptions: (no right exists).*
4. *Right to Education:*
   a. There is no fundamental right to education *San Antonio Ind. School District v. Rodriguez*, 411 U.S. 1 (1973).
   b. States are not required to ensure that equivalent financial resources are devoted to the education of each child. *Plyler v. Doe*, 457 U.S. 202 (1982).
5. *Right to Basic Necessities of Life:* Welfare benefits are a matter of social/economic legislation, subject to rational basis review, not strict fundamental rights scrutiny. There is no fundamental constitutional right to the basic necessities of life requiring strict scrutiny review in welfare benefits legislation *Dandridge v. Williams*, 397 U.S. 471 (1970).

▶

Preemption questions generally involve determining Congress's intent:

i. States may not regulate if Congress has "occupied the field";

ii. *Express preemption:* if Congress has not occupied the field, state laws not consistent with the regulatory scheme may still be valid.

iii. *Implicit preemption:* Same issues as to extent of preemption must be court-determined.

iv. *Factors:* In determining the scope of preemption, courts must consider the nature of the subject matter regulated and the comprehensiveness of the regulation in addition to legislative intent and history, plain meaning, and construction.

OTHER LIMITS ON STATE REGULATION

1. *Dormant Commerce Clause:* Not expressly provided for, but implied from Constitution (dormant). Limits state regulation of interstate commerce. While Congress has plenary power over interstate commerce, in the absence of congressional action, states can regulate local matters for health, safety or welfare even if it affects interstate commerce. States may not, however, discriminate against or impose unjustifiable state burdens on interstate commerce. ARTICLE I § 8

   a. If state regulation discriminatory:
      i. *Discriminatory on face:* regulation is unconstitutional.
      ii. *Discriminatory in effect:* will be upheld where:
         a. legitimate state interest.
         b. no other nondiscriminatory alternatives.

   b. If state regulation nondiscriminatory:
      i. Benefit to state must outweigh burden.
      ii. Where substantial burden is to commerce, regulation is unconstitutional. Market Participant exception:
         a. When a state decides to regulate a particular market, it may enter that market as a participant (such as a trader or manufacturer).
         b. Dormant Commerce Clause will not apply to that state's regulatory activities.
         c. It may therefore favor its own citizens over others, subsidize the activities of its citizens and operate a business favoring state citizens. *Exception: Market participant exception only applies to state activities in a particular market, narrowly defined.*
         d. *Privileges of Immunities Exception* ARTICLE IV § 2: *A state cannot treat a noncitizen differently than a citizen with respect to the exercise of a privilege without substantial justification.*

2. *Contract Clause:* Generally prohibits state law from impairing contracts. Financial contracts may be impaired. ARTICLE I § 10
   a. Where impairment reasonable and necessary to important public purpose.

3. *5th Amendment Takings:* No taking of private property for public use without just compensation.
   a. *Public Purpose Nexus:*
      i. Taking is for public use if the means chosen must further a public purpose. *Pennsylvania Coal Co. v. Mahon*, 260 U.S. 393 (1922).

b. *Compensable Takings:* the government must pay compensation for a taking that involves:
   i. Physical invasion/occupation;
   ii. Denial of economically beneficial use *Lucas v. South Carolina Coastal Council*, 505 U.S. 1003 (1992); or
   iii. Public functions.

c. *Non-compensable Takings:* the government is NOT required to pay compensation for takings that involve:
   i. Public harm to be prevented; or
   ii. Economically viable use still exists *Nollan v. California Coastal Commn.*, 483 U.S. 825 (1987).

d. *Temporary Takings:* even if the property taken is returned, the government must pay damages incurred by the property returned.

1. FEDERALISM— INTERGOVERNMENTAL IMMUNITIES

1. *State Taxation/Regulation of Federal Activity:* Supremacy Clause provides that federal government and its properties are immune from state taxation and regulation. *McCulloch v. Maryland*, 17 U.S. 316 (1819). *Exceptions:*

   a. *Indirect Taxation:* Federal government does not have the direct legal obligation to pay the tax, but pays it incidental to another arrangement.

   b. Congress consents to state taxation and regulation. *Cleveland v. United States*, 323 U.S. 329 (1945).

   c. State income taxation of federal employees. *Johnson v. Maryland*, 254 U.S. 51 (1920).

   d. *State Taxation of Interstate Commerce:* A state may impose a direct tax on interstate business where:
      i. tax is on activity having a substantial nexus with the state;
      ii. tax is fairly apportioned between commerce originating in state & commerce from out of state;
      iii. tax must not discriminate against interstate commerce;
      iv. tax is related to some service the state provides (e.g., sales tax).

2. *Federal Regulation of States:* Supreme Court recognizes expansive power of Congress to influence or affect almost any state activity. *Exception: 10th Amendment limits federal power to override state laws concerning traditional governmental "functions essential to the separate and independent existence" of the states.*

3. *Federal Taxation of States:* No state immunity from federal taxation. *Exception: Federal tax which discriminates against a state or unduly interferes with essential state functions is impermissible.*

4. *Relations between States:*

   a. *Full Faith and Credit Clause:* requires that states recognize and give appropriate effect to the legal acts and proceedings of other states. ARTICLE IV § 1

   b. *Interstate Compacts:* states may enter into agreements with other states, including those involving multi-state relationships, without first obtaining the consent of Congress. ARTICLE I § 10 *Exception: Those agreements that might increase the political power of member states in a way that might encroach on the supremacy of the federal government.*

c. *Interstate Privileges and Immunities:* states must accord residents and nonresidents equal treatment with regard to certain interests Essential to a national economy and interstate harmony (i.e., "fundamental rights"). ARTICLE IV § 2

   i. Equal treatment for fundamental interests: states must give nonresidents the same rights as their own residents for "fundamental rights," including:
      a. owning, possessing, or disposing of property;
      b. engaging in employment;
      c. doing business;
      d. traveling through and within a state, including changing state residence;
      e. seeking medical care; and
      f. equal treatment by justice institutions. *Exception: States MAY treat a nonresident differently with respect to those rights that are fundamental, if:*
         • State has a substantial reason for different treatment;
         • nonresidents are the cause of the problem the state is trying to remedy; and
         • there is no alternative that would be less injurious to the exercise of the nonresident's rights. *Supreme Court of New Hampshire v. Piper*, 470 U.S. 274 (1985).

   ii. If rights infringed are nonfundamental, a state need only show that it did not act arbitrarily.
      a. *Unconstitutional discrimination:*
         • State may not impose residency requirement on nonresident women seeking abortions; *Doe v. Bolton*, 410 U.S. 179 (1973).
         • State may not require employers to give state residents preference in hiring; *Hicklin v. Orbeck*, 437 U.S. 518 (1978).
         • State may not condition bar admission on residency *Supreme Court of Virginia v. Friedman*, 487 U.S. 59 (1988).
      b. *Constitutional discrimination:* State may charge nonresident hunters higher fees for hunting licenses than residents. *Baldwin v. Fish and Game Commn. of Montana*, 436 U.S. 371 (1978).

   iii. Clause only applies to "citizens," meaning only natural persons born in or naturalized in the United States. The Clause does not apply to corporations or aliens.

1. FEDERALISM—STATE RELATIONS

1. The Constitution establishes a central federal system of government as well as independent state governments. All citizens are subjects of both governments. Both federal and state governments are sovereign and possess independent governmental power.

2. States' independent powers are defined by:
   a. Prohibition of exercise by the Constitution;
   b. Constitution's delegation of exclusively federal power;
   c. Reservation solely to the states by the 10th Amendment.

Governmental Relations continues on page 4 ▶

CONSTITUTIONAL LAW

FEDERAL JUDICIAL POWER

JUDICIAL REVIEW

Definition: The Supreme Court's authority to review the actions of the legislative and executive branches to determine their constitutionality. The doctrine requires courts to interpret and apply the Constitution to acts to determine their validity. The power a federal court has to adjudicate over claims brought before it. *Marbury v. Madison*, 5 U.S. 137 (1803).

1. *Original Jurisdiction* ARTICLE III § 2: Federal courts have authority to first hear or try cases involving:
   a. Ambassadors
   b. Public ministers and consuls
   c. Cases in which the state is a party
2. *Appellate Jurisdiction* ARTICLE III § 2: Federal courts may also hear other (non-original jurisdictional) cases that come to court by appeal.
3. *Supreme Court Review:*
   a. *Discretionary Review/Writ of Certiorari:* Cases may be petitioned for review by writ of certiorari. Supreme Court has discretion to hear or refuse.
   b. *State Court Review of Federal Issues:* Federal courts may only review final judgments of federal issues made by the highest court in a state.
      Exception: On Adequate Independent State Grounds, Federal court will not review state decision, that is independent of that state's separate ruling on federal law that may otherwise be incorrect.
   c. *State Court Refusal to Hear Federal Claims:* States are generally required to hear appropriately presented federal claims, but the state may refuse. Federal courts may review state court's refusal to hear such claims.

JUDICIAL LIMITS ON JUDICIAL REVIEW

1. *Abstention:* Federal courts will abstain from hearing a case involving an unsettled or unclear state statute on whose construction a federal constitutional issue depends, until a state court interprets it. *Railroad Commn. of Texas v. Pullman Co.*, 312 U.S. 496 (1941).
2. *Equitable Restraint:* Federal courts may enjoin state criminal actions to protect constitutional rights. *Ex parte Young*, 209 U.S. 123 (1908).
3. *Constitutional Question:* A case issue involves the constitutionality of statute. Court will apply rules of statutory construction to avoid passing on constitutional questions:
   a. Alternative (nonconstitutional) ground exists to dispose of case.
   b. Between several possible interpretations, one exists that permits a finding of constitutionality.
   c. Courts will otherwise construe a statute reasonably.
   d. *Racial Challenges:* Challenger must show there is no circumstance under which the legislative act or administrative regulation would be valid.

CONSTITUTIONAL LIMITS ON JUDICIAL REVIEW ARTICLE III § 2

1. *Cases and Controversies: Aetna Life Ins. Co. v. Haworth*, 300 U.S. 227 (1937).
   a. *Justiciability:* A case is justiciable if there is standing to sue, the Constitution permits the issue to be judicially resolvable, and there is no cause for judicial restraint.
   b. *Standing:* To have standing to bring a suit, a plaintiff must meet three criteria:
      i. *Injury:* Plaintiff must show facts demonstrating any injury in fact. Injury can be small or trifling, but must be real. *Sierra Club v. Morton*, 405 U.S. 727 (1972).
      ii. *Causation:* Injury must be proximately and directly traceable to defendant's conduct. *Lujan v. Defenders of Wildlife*, 504 U.S. 555 (1992).
      iii. *Redressibility:* Plaintiff must show facts that demonstrate the relief she is entitled to will substantially eliminate or redress the injury. *Warth v. Seldin*, 422 U.S. 490 (1975).
   c. *Ripeness:* Case must involve concrete disputes between genuine adversaries or will not be heard. A court will not give advisory opinions.
   d. *Mootness:* If underlying controversy is not real or has been resolved/dissolved prior to the adjudication, case is moot and will not be adjudicated. *Exceptions: cases that appear moot but are not.*
      i. Cases involving continuing harm.
      ii. Harms that have ended but may recur.
      iii. Cases capable of repetition but evading review. *Roe v. Wade*, 410 U.S. 113 (1973).
2. *Political Question:* Even if plaintiff has standing, courts may refuse to decide a "political" question.
   a. Constitutionally committed or need exists for deference to another branch of government.
   b. There is a lack of judicially discoverable and manageable standards for resolving it.
3. *11th Amendment:* State sovereign immunity prevents citizens of a state from suing that state in federal court without that state's consent. *Hans v. Louisiana*, 134 U.S. 1 (1890).

STRUCTURE OF THE GOVERNMENT

1. FEDERAL JUDICIAL POWER
2. FEDERAL LEGISLATIVE POWER
3. FEDERAL EXECUTIVE POWER

FEDERAL LEGISLATIVE POWER

THE SPENDING POWER ARTICLE I § 8

Congress has the power to spend for the common defense and general welfare. This includes spending done in order to exercise its other powers or for proper public purpose. Congress by conditioning receipt of funds on compliance with federal regulations is able to indirectly regulate what it cannot regulate directly.

TREATY POWER ARTICLE I § 10

Power co-exists with the President's power to make treaties pursuant to the advice and consent of the Senate. Treaties, once ratified, become the law of the land.

1. Treaties take precedent over conflicting state and federal law but are not equal in authority to the Constitution.
2. Treaties pertaining to matters of international concern are binding in the states even if they regulate an area normally under state control. *Missouri v. Holland*, 252 U.S. 416 (1920).

THE TAXING POWER ARTICLE I § 8

Congress can regulate or limit activities by imposing taxes on them, effectively prohibiting them where the tax is substantial. As long as the tax produces revenue, it may be enacted for any motive, even purely regulatory ones that have no genuine money-raising purpose at all.

THE IMMIGRATION POWER ARTICLE I § 8

Congress has exclusive control over immigration.

1. May admit, expel, exclude, or deport noncitizens of the United States.
2. May not treat naturalized citizens differently from native-born citizens.

WAR AND MILITARY AFFAIRS POWER ARTICLE I § 8

1. *Domestic War Power:* Congress has broad power to enact economic or other regulations during wartime or after war to restore the economy.
2. *Draft:* Congress can enlist men for war and use state militias to fight foreign enemies.
3. *Military Justice/Courts Martial:* Congress may establish a system of military courts and justice. Courts are legislatively created and located in the legislative branch; therefore, the Bill of Rights is inapplicable. Jurisdiction extends to all offenses committed by service personnel while in service.

Federal Legislative Power continues on page 2

EQUAL PROTECTION

EQUAL PROTECTION

Fourteenth Amendment requires that no state shall deny any person the equal protection of the laws. Equal protection analysis determines whether a state is constitutionally permitted to differentiate between persons.

TYPES OF JUDICIAL REVIEW

To determine whether state legislation affecting certain rights in constitutional, a court must examine that state's goals and the means used to achieve its goal.

1. *Rational Basis:* State regulation will be upheld if it is rationally related to achieving a legitimate state purpose. Applies primarily to social and economic regulations. *Dandridge v. Williams*, 397 U.S. 471 (1970).

   a. *Taxation:* States have great latitude in creating taxation schemes as long as the schemes bear a rational relationship to a plausible policy justification. *Williams v. Vermont*, 472 U.S. 14 (1985).

   b. Over-inclusive and under-inclusive classifications are not per se unconstitutional in violation of equal protection. *Williamson v. Lee Optical Co.*, 348 U.S. 483 (1955).

   c. Prohibits arbitrary, unreasonable, and irrational classifications:

      i. Unlikely to lead to any discernable and understandable legitimate purpose.

      ii. Regulates similarly-situated parties differently, without legitimate reason. *City of Cleburne v. Cleburne Living Center*, 473 U.S. 432 (1985).

2. *Intermediate Review (Heightened Scrutiny):* State regulation will be upheld if it is substantially related to an important government purpose. Applies primarily to gender, alienage, and illegitimacy cases.

   a. Gender classifications must fairly and substantially relate to the achievement of an important and articulated government objective. Government must provide an "exceedingly persuasive justification." *United States v. Virginia*, 518 U.S. 515 (1996); *J.E.B. v. Alabama ex rel. T.B.*, 511 U.S. 127 (1994); *Mississippi University for Women v. Hogan*, 458 U.S. 718 (1982). Unconstitutional types of gender-based classifications:

      i. Statutes presuming greater male competency. *Reed v. Reed*, 404 U.S. 71 (1971).

      ii. Statutes presuming women are dependent.

      iii. Statutes presuming gender bias (peremptory challenges). *J.E.B. v. Alabama ex rel. T.B.*, 511 U.S. 127 (1994).

   b. *Alienage Classifications:*

      i. Congress has plenary power to regulate immigration and naturalization and its decisions are subject to rational basis review.

      ii. States do not have constitutional authority to regulate immigration and nationalization; state classifications based on alienage are inherently suspect and subject to strict scrutiny review.

---

   c. *Illegitimacy Classifications:* Classifications of children based on nonmarital status of parents; intermediate scrutiny applies. These include:

      i. Qualification for awards or benefits (wrongful death, workers' compensation, social security survivor's benefits, parental support, paternity suit statutes of limitations).

      ii. Interstate inheritance.

3. *Strict Scrutiny:* State regulation will be upheld if it is necessary to achieve a compelling government interest. Strict scrutiny is applied to:

   a. *Suspect Classifications:*

      i. Suspect Classes—race, national origin, ethnicity. *Katzenbach v. Morgan*, 384 U.S. 641 (1966).

      ii. Proving Discrimination—must show discriminatory intent or purpose. If disproportionate impact, intent to maintain activity is sufficient. *Washington v. Davis*, 426 U.S. 229 (1976).

      iii. Benign Racial Classifications— Affirmative Action:
         a. subject to strict scrutiny;
         b. race is only one factor to show compelling state interest.

   b. *Fundamental Rights:* Strict scrutiny used to uphold laws infringing on rights.

FREEDOM OF ASSOCIATION

IN GENERAL

Definition: The First Amendment provides for the right to associate with others for the advancement of beliefs, ideas and opinions, to communicate and to engage in all activities protected by the First Amendment. *NAACP v. Alabama*, 357 U.S. 449 (1958).

1. *Compelled Disclosure:*

   a. *Lawful associations:* law is unconstitutional if it compels disclosure of membership in a lawful association where disclosure subjects members of the organizations to sanctions, reprisals, or public embarrassment. *NAACP v. Alabama*, 357 U.S. 449 (1958).

   b. *Exception:* If there is a compelling state interest implicated. *Buckley v. Valeo*, 424 U.S. 1 (1976).

2. *Public Employees:*

   a. Inquiry into fitness or competence: inquiry into fitness or competence of applicants for public employment may be unconstitutional because it chills freedom of association.

   b. *Exception: if* inquiry is narrowly tailored to the government interest in fitness or competence.

3. *Freedom not to Associate:* The freedom of association also entails a freedom not to associate.

   a. State cannot require persons to provide for support of organizations or causes with which they disagree. *Abood v. Detroit Board of Educ.*, 431 U.S. 209 (1977); *Keller v. State Bar of California*, 496 U.S. 1 (1990).

   b. *Limitation:* application of rule is limited to political or ideological associations.

FREEDOM OF RELIGION

ESTABLISHMENT CLAUSE

States should not provide aid to religion, favoring any one religion over and above the others. If state statute aids religion, may still be upheld if:

1. It has a secular purpose.

2. Its principal or primary effect neither advances nor inhibits religion.

3. It doesn't promote excessive state entanglement with religion. *Lemon v. Kurtzman*, 403 U.S. 602 (1971). Aid to sectarian or religious schools:

   a. *Impermissible aid:* tuition, building funds.

   b. *Permissible aid:* bus transportation, secular book loans.

FREE EXERCISE CLAUSE

State must permit people to believe and practice their religious beliefs without interference. State may not deny benefits to or burden persons based on their beliefs. *Empl. Div., Dept. of Human Resources of Oregon v. Smith*, 494 U.S. 872 (1990). *Exceptions:*

1. *Unemployment compensation:* denial of compensation following discharge for refusing to work on Sabbath or resigning because of religious beliefs violates strict scrutiny, compelling state interest test, and is an unconstitutional burden. *Sherbert v. Verner*, 374 U.S. 398 (1963).

2. *Religious Freedom Restoration Act [RFRA]:* Congress's attempt to restore the compelling state interest test.

CONSTITUTIONAL ACTION AGAINST PRIVATE PARTIES

STATE ACTION

Cannot bring action against private individuals for constitutional violations unless state action is shown.

A private party will be treated as a state actor, and thus subject to constitutional restrictions, in the following circumstances: *The Civil Rights Cases*, 109 U.S. 3 (1883).

1. *Public Functions:* private party exercises powers traditionally reserved to the state. *Marsh v. Alabama*, 326 U.S. 501 (1946).

2. *State Involvement:* private party has a "close nexus" to state activity that injured plaintiff, such as the use of state courts to enforce a private action, or use of state funds. *Burton v. Wilmington Parking Authority*, 365 U.S. 715 (1961).

   a. Private party's use of state enforcement of racially restrictive covenants constitutes state action. *Shelley v. Kraemer*, 334 U.S. 1 (1948).

3. *State Authorization or Encouragement:* private action pursuant to an affirmative state act designed to encourage private violations of civil rights.

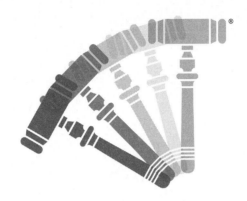

Casenote® Legal Briefs

CONSTITUTIONAL LAW

Keyed to Courses Using

Sullivan and Feldman's
Constitutional Law

Eighteenth Edition

This publication is designed to provide accurate and authoritative information in regard to the subject matter covered. It is sold with the understanding that the publisher is not engaged in rendering legal, accounting, or other professional services. If legal advice or other expert assistance is required, the services of a competent professional person should be sought.

> — From a Declaration of Principles adopted jointly
> by a Committee of the American Bar Association
> and a Committee of Publishers and Associates

Printed in the United States of America.

1 2 3 4 5 6 7 8 9 0

ISBN 978-1-4548-4077-0

About Wolters Kluwer Law & Business

Wolters Kluwer Law & Business is a leading global provider of intelligent information and digital solutions for legal and business professionals in key specialty areas, and respected educational resources for professors and law students. Wolters Kluwer Law & Business connects legal and business professionals as well as those in the education market with timely, specialized authoritative content and information-enabled solutions to support success through productivity, accuracy and mobility.

Serving customers worldwide, Wolters Kluwer Law & Business products include those under the Aspen Publishers, CCH, Kluwer Law International, Loislaw, ftwilliam.com and MediRegs family of products.

CCH products have been a trusted resource since 1913, and are highly regarded resources for legal, securities, antitrust and trade regulation, government contracting, banking, pension, payroll, employment and labor, and healthcare reimbursement and compliance professionals.

Aspen Publishers products provide essential information to attorneys, business professionals and law students. Written by preeminent authorities, the product line offers analytical and practical information in a range of specialty practice areas from securities law and intellectual property to mergers and acquisitions and pension/benefits. Aspen's trusted legal education resources provide professors and students with high-quality, up-to-date and effective resources for successful instruction and study in all areas of the law.

Kluwer Law International products provide the global business community with reliable international legal information in English. Legal practitioners, corporate counsel and business executives around the world rely on Kluwer Law journals, looseleafs, books, and electronic products for comprehensive information in many areas of international legal practice.

Loislaw is a comprehensive online legal research product providing legal content to law firm practitioners of various specializations. Loislaw provides attorneys with the ability to quickly and efficiently find the necessary legal information they need, when and where they need it, by facilitating access to primary law as well as state-specific law, records, forms and treatises.

ftwilliam.com offers employee benefits professionals the highest quality plan documents (retirement, welfare and non-qualified) and government forms (5500/PBGC, 1099 and IRS) software at highly competitive prices.

MediRegs products provide integrated health care compliance content and software solutions for professionals in healthcare, higher education and life sciences, including professionals in accounting, law and consulting.

Wolters Kluwer Law & Business, a division of Wolters Kluwer, is headquartered in New York. Wolters Kluwer is a market-leading global information services company focused on professionals.

Format for the Casenote® Legal Brief

Nature of Case: This section identifies the form of action (e.g., breach of contract, negligence, battery), the type of proceeding (e.g., demurrer, appeal from trial court's jury instructions), or the relief sought (e.g., damages, injunction, criminal sanctions).

Fact Summary: This is included to refresh your memory and can be used as a quick reminder of the facts.

Rule of Law: Summarizes the general principle of law that the case illustrates. It may be used for instant recall of the court's holding and for classroom discussion or home review.

Facts: This section contains all relevant facts of the case, including the contentions of the parties and the lower court holdings. It is written in a logical order to give the student a clear understanding of the case. The plaintiff and defendant are identified by their proper names throughout and are always labeled with a (P) or (D).

Palsgraf v. Long Island R.R. Co.

Injured bystander (P) v. Railroad company (D)

N.Y. Ct. App., 248 N.Y. 339, 162 N.E. 99 (1928).

NATURE OF CASE: Appeal from judgment affirming verdict for plaintiff seeking damages for personal injury.

FACT SUMMARY: Helen Palsgraf (P) was injured on R.R.'s (D) train platform when R.R.'s (D) guard helped a passenger aboard a moving train, causing his package to fall on the tracks. The package contained fireworks which exploded, creating a shock that tipped a scale onto Palsgraf (P).

RULE OF LAW
The risk reasonably to be perceived defines the duty to be obeyed.

FACTS: Helen Palsgraf (P) purchased a ticket to Rockaway Beach from R.R. (D) and was waiting on the train platform. As she waited, two men ran to catch a train that was pulling out from the platform. The first man jumped aboard, but the second man, who appeared as if he might fall, was helped aboard by the guard on the train who had kept the door open so they could jump aboard. A guard on the platform also helped by pushing him onto the train. The man was carrying a package wrapped in newspaper. In the process, the man dropped his package, which fell on the tracks. The package contained fireworks and exploded. The shock of the explosion was apparently of great enough strength to tip over some scales at the other end of the platform, which fell on Palsgraf (P) and injured her. A jury awarded her damages, and R.R. (D) appealed.

ISSUE: Does the risk reasonably to be perceived define the duty to be obeyed?

HOLDING AND DECISION: (Cardozo, C.J.) Yes. The risk reasonably to be perceived defines the duty to be obeyed. If there is no foreseeable hazard to the injured party as the result of a seemingly innocent act, the act does not become a tort because it happened to be a wrong as to another. If the wrong was not willful, the plaintiff must show that the act as to her had such great and apparent possibilities of danger as to entitle her to protection. Negligence in the abstract is not enough upon which to base liability. Negligence is a relative concept, evolving out of the common law doctrine of trespass on the case. To establish liability, the defendant must owe a legal duty of reasonable care to the injured party. A cause of action in tort will lie where harm,

though unintended, could have been averted or avoided by observance of such a duty. The scope of the duty is limited by the range of danger that a reasonable person could foresee. In this case, there was nothing to suggest from the appearance of the parcel or otherwise that the parcel contained fireworks. The guard could not reasonably have had any warning of a threat to Palsgraf (P), and R.R. (D) therefore cannot be held liable. Judgment is reversed in favor of R.R. (D).

DISSENT: (Andrews, J.) The concept that there is no negligence unless R.R. (D) owes a legal duty to take care as to Palsgraf (P) herself is too narrow. Everyone owes to the world at large the duty of refraining from those acts that may unreasonably threaten the safety of others. If the guard's action was negligent as to those nearby, it was also negligent as to those outside what might be termed the "danger zone." For Palsgraf (P) to recover, R.R.'s (D) negligence must have been the proximate cause of her injury, a question of fact for the jury.

ANALYSIS
The majority defined the limit of the defendant's liability in terms of the danger that a reasonable person in defendant's situation would have perceived. The dissent argued that the limitation should not be placed on liability, but rather on damages. Judge Andrews suggested that only injuries that would not have happened but for R.R.'s (D) negligence should be compensable. Both the majority and dissent recognized the policy-driven need to limit liability for negligent acts, seeking, in the words of Judge Andrews, to define a framework "that will be practical and in keeping with the general understanding of mankind." The Restatement (Second) of Torts has accepted Judge Cardozo's view.

Quicknotes
FORESEEABILITY A reasonable expectation that change is the probable result of certain acts or omissions.

NEGLIGENCE Conduct falling below the standard of care that a reasonable person would demonstrate under similar conditions.

PROXIMATE CAUSE The natural sequence of events without which an injury would not have been sustained.

Party ID: Quick identification of the relationship between the parties.

Concurrence/Dissent: All concurrences and dissents are briefed whenever they are included by the casebook editor.

Analysis: This last paragraph gives you a broad understanding of where the case "fits in" with other cases in the section of the book and with the entire course. It is a hornbook-style discussion indicating whether the case is a majority or minority opinion and comparing the principal case with other cases in the casebook. It may also provide analysis from restatements, uniform codes, and law review articles. The analysis will prove to be invaluable to classroom discussion.

Issue: The issue is a concise question that brings out the essence of the opinion as it relates to the section of the casebook in which the case appears. Both substantive and procedural issues are included if relevant to the decision.

Holding and Decision: This section offers a clear and in-depth discussion of the rule of the case and the court's rationale. It is written in easy-to-understand language and answers the issue presented by applying the law to the facts of the case. When relevant, it includes a thorough discussion of the exceptions to the case as listed by the court, any major cites to the other cases on point, and the names of the judges who wrote the decisions.

Quicknotes: Conveniently defines legal terms found in the case and summarizes the nature of any statutes, codes, or rules referred to in the text.

Note to Students

Wolters Kluwer Law & Business is proud to offer *Casenote® Legal Briefs*—continuing thirty years of publishing America's best-selling legal briefs.

Casenote® Legal Briefs are designed to help you save time when briefing assigned cases. Organized under convenient headings, they show you how to abstract the basic facts and holdings from the text of the actual opinions handed down by the courts. Used as part of a rigorous study regimen, they can help you spend more time analyzing and critiquing points of law than on copying bits and pieces of judicial opinions into your notebook or outline.

Casenote® Legal Briefs should never be used as a substitute for assigned casebook readings. They work best when read as a follow-up to reviewing the underlying opinions themselves. Students who try to avoid reading and digesting the judicial opinions in their casebooks or online sources will end up shortchanging themselves in the long run. The ability to absorb, critique, and restate the dynamic and complex elements of case law decisions is crucial to your success in law school and beyond. It cannot be developed vicariously.

Casenote® Legal Briefs represents but one of the many offerings in Legal Education's Study Aid Timeline, which includes:

- *Casenote® Legal Briefs*
- *Emanuel® Law Outlines*
- Emanuel® *Law in a Flash* Flash Cards
- Emanuel® *CrunchTime®* Series
- *Siegel's Essay and Multiple-Choice Questions and Answers Series*

Each of these series is designed to provide you with easy-to-understand explanations of complex points of law. Each volume offers guidance on the principles of legal analysis and, consulted regularly, will hone your ability to spot relevant issues. We have titles that will help you prepare for class, prepare for your exams, and enhance your general comprehension of the law along the way.

To find out more about Wolters Kluwer Law & Business' study aid publications, visit us online at *www.wolterskluwerlb.com* or email us at *legaledu@wolterskluwer.com*. We'll be happy to assist you.

A. Decide on a Format and Stick to It

Structure is essential to a good brief. It enables you to arrange systematically the related parts that are scattered throughout most cases, thus making manageable and understandable what might otherwise seem to be an endless and unfathomable sea of information. There are, of course, an unlimited number of formats that can be utilized. However, it is best to find one that suits your needs and stick to it. Consistency breeds both efficiency and the security that when called upon you will know where to look in your brief for the information you are asked to give.

Any format, as long as it presents the essential elements of a case in an organized fashion, can be used. Experience, however, has led *Casenote® Legal Briefs* to develop and utilize the following format because of its logical flow and universal applicability.

NATURE OF CASE: This is a brief statement of the legal character and procedural status of the case (e.g., "Appeal of a burglary conviction").

There are many different alternatives open to a litigant dissatisfied with a court ruling. The key to determining which one has been used is to discover *who is asking this court for what.*

This first entry in the brief should be kept as *short as possible.* Use the court's terminology if you understand it. But since jurisdictions vary as to the titles of pleadings, the best entry is the one that addresses who wants what in this proceeding, not the one that sounds most like the court's language.

RULE OF LAW: A statement of the general principle of law that the case illustrates (e.g., "An acceptance that varies any term of the offer is considered a rejection and counteroffer").

Determining the rule of law of a case is a procedure similar to determining the issue of the case. Avoid being fooled by red herrings; there may be a few rules of law mentioned in the case excerpt, but usually only one is *the* rule with which the casebook editor is concerned. The techniques used to locate the issue, described below, may also be utilized to find the rule of law. Generally, your best guide is simply the chapter heading. It is a clue to the point the casebook editor seeks to make and should be kept in mind when reading every case in the respective section.

FACTS: A synopsis of only the essential facts of the case, i.e., those bearing upon or leading up to the issue.

The facts entry should be a short statement of the events and transactions that led one party to initiate legal proceedings against another in the first place. While some cases conveniently state the salient facts at the beginning of the decision, in other instances they will have to be culled from hiding places throughout the text, even from concurring and dissenting opinions. Some of the "facts" will often be in dispute and should be so noted. Conflicting evidence may be briefly pointed up. "Hard" facts must be included. Both must be *relevant* in order to be listed in the facts entry. It is impossible to tell what is relevant until the entire case is read, as the ultimate determination of the rights and liabilities of the parties may turn on something buried deep in the opinion.

Generally, the facts entry should not be longer than three to five *short* sentences.

It is often helpful to identify the role played by a party in a given context. For example, in a construction contract case the identification of a party as the "contractor" or "builder" alleviates the need to tell that that party was the one who was supposed to have built the house.

It is always helpful, and a good general practice, to identify the "plaintiff" and the "defendant." This may seem elementary and uncomplicated, but, especially in view of the creative editing practiced by some casebook editors, it is sometimes a difficult or even impossible task. Bear in mind that the *party presently* seeking something from this court may not be the plaintiff, and that sometimes only the cross-claim of a defendant is treated in the excerpt. Confusing or misaligning the parties can ruin your analysis and understanding of the case.

ISSUE: A statement of the general legal question answered by or illustrated in the case. For clarity, the issue is best put in the form of a question capable of a "yes" or "no" answer. In reality, the issue is simply the Rule of Law put in the form of a question (e.g., "May an offer be accepted by performance?").

The major problem presented in discerning what is *the* issue in the case is that an opinion usually purports to raise and answer several questions. However, except for rare cases, only one such question is really the issue in the case. Collateral issues not necessary to the resolution of the matter in controversy are handled by the court by language known as "*obiter dictum*" or merely "*dictum.*" While dicta may be included later in the brief, they have no place under the issue heading.

To find the issue, ask *who wants what* and then go on to ask *why did that party succeed or fail in getting it.* Once this is determined, the "why" should be turned into a question.

The complexity of the issues in the cases will vary, but in all cases a single-sentence question should sum up the issue. *In a few cases,* there will be two, or even more rarely, three issues of equal importance to the resolution of the case. Each should be expressed in a single-sentence question.

Since many issues are resolved by a court in coming to a final disposition of a case, the casebook editor will reproduce the portion of the opinion containing the issue or issues most relevant to the area of law under scrutiny. A noted law professor gave this advice: "Close the book; look at the title on the cover." Chances are, if it is Property, you need not concern yourself with whether, for example, the federal government's treatment of the plaintiff's land really raises a federal question sufficient to support jurisdiction on this ground in federal court.

The same rule applies to chapter headings designating sub-areas within the subjects. They tip you off as to what the text is designed to teach. The cases are arranged in a casebook to show a progression or development of the law, so that the preceding cases may also help.

It is also most important to remember to *read the notes and questions* at the end of a case to determine what the editors wanted you to have gleaned from it.

HOLDING AND DECISION: This section should succinctly explain the rationale of the court in arriving at its decision. In capsulizing the "reasoning" of the court, it should always include an application of the general rule or rules of law to the specific facts of the case. Hidden justifications come to light in this entry: the reasons for the state of the law, the public policies, the biases and prejudices, those considerations that influence the justices' thinking and, ultimately, the outcome of the case. At the end, there should be a short indication of the disposition or procedural resolution of the case (e.g., "Decision of the trial court for Mr. Smith (P) reversed").

The foregoing format is designed to help you "digest" the reams of case material with which you will be faced in your law school career. Once mastered by practice, it will place at your fingertips the information the authors of your casebooks have sought to impart to you in case-by-case illustration and analysis.

B. Be as Economical as Possible in Briefing Cases

Once armed with a format that encourages succinctness, it is as important to be economical with regard to the time spent on the actual reading of the case as it is to be economical in the writing of the brief itself. This does not mean "skimming" a case. Rather, it means reading the case with an "eye" trained to recognize into which "section" of your brief a particular passage or line fits and having a system for quickly and precisely marking the case so that the passages fitting any one particular part of

the brief can be easily identified and brought together in a concise and accurate manner when the brief is actually written.

It is of no use to simply repeat everything in the opinion of the court; record only enough information to trigger your recollection of what the court said. Nevertheless, an accurate statement of the "law of the case," i.e., the legal principle applied to the facts, is absolutely essential to class preparation and to learning the law under the case method.

To that end, it is important to develop a "shorthand" that you can use to make marginal notations. These notations will tell you at a glance in which section of the brief you will be placing that particular passage or portion of the opinion.

Some students prefer to underline all the salient portions of the opinion (with a pencil or colored underliner marker), making marginal notations as they go along. Others prefer the color-coded method of underlining, utilizing different colors of markers to underline the salient portions of the case, each separate color being used to represent a different section of the brief. For example, blue underlining could be used for passages relating to the rule of law, yellow for those relating to the issue, and green for those relating to the holding and decision, etc. While it has its advocates, the color-coded method can be confusing and time-consuming (all that time spent on changing colored markers). Furthermore, it can interfere with the continuity and concentration many students deem essential to the reading of a case for maximum comprehension. In the end, however, it is a matter of personal preference and style. Just remember, whatever method you use, underlining must be used sparingly or its value is lost.

If you take the marginal notation route, an efficient and easy method is to go along underlining the key portions of the case and placing in the margin alongside them the following "markers" to indicate where a particular passage or line "belongs" in the brief you will write:

N   (NATURE OF CASE)
RL   (RULE OF LAW)
I   (ISSUE)
HL   (HOLDING AND DECISION, relates to the RULE OF LAW behind the decision)
HR   (HOLDING AND DECISION, gives the RATIONALE or reasoning behind the decision)
HA   (HOLDING AND DECISION, applies the general principle(s) of law to the facts of the case to arrive at the decision)

Remember that a particular passage may well contain information necessary to more than one part of your brief, in which case you simply note that in the margin. If you are using the color-coded underlining method instead of marginal notation, simply make asterisks or checks in the margin next to the passage in question in the colors that indicate the additional sections of the brief where it might be utilized.

The economy of utilizing "shorthand" in marking cases for briefing can be maintained in the actual brief writing process itself by utilizing "law student shorthand" within the brief. There are many commonly used words and phrases for which abbreviations can be substituted in your briefs (and in your class notes also). You can develop abbreviations that are personal to you and which will save you a lot of time. A reference list of briefing abbreviations can be found on page x of this book.

C. Use Both the Briefing Process and the Brief as a Learning Tool

Now that you have a format and the tools for briefing cases efficiently, the most important thing is to make the time spent in briefing profitable to you and to make the most advantageous use of the briefs you create. Of course, the briefs are invaluable for classroom reference when you are called upon to explain or analyze a particular case. However, they are also useful in reviewing for exams. A quick glance at the fact summary should bring the case to mind, and a rereading of the rule of law should enable you to go over the underlying legal concept in your mind, how it was applied in that particular case, and how it might apply in other factual settings.

As to the value to be derived from engaging in the briefing process itself, there is an immediate benefit that arises from being forced to sift through the essential facts and reasoning from the court's opinion and to succinctly express them in your own words in your brief. The process ensures that you understand the case and the point that it illustrates, and that means you will be ready to absorb further analysis and information brought forth in class. It also ensures you will have something to say when called upon in class. The briefing process helps develop a mental agility for getting to the *gist* of a case and for identifying, expounding on, and applying the legal concepts and issues found there. The briefing process is the mental process on which you must rely in taking law school examinations; it is also the mental process upon which a lawyer relies in serving his clients and in making his living.

Abbreviations for Briefs

acceptance	acp	offer	O
affirmed	aff	offeree	OE
answer	ans	offeror	OR
assumption of risk	a/r	ordinance	ord
attorney	atty	pain and suffering	p/s
beyond a reasonable doubt	b/r/d	parol evidence	p/e
bona fide purchaser	BFP	plaintiff	P
breach of contract	br/k	prima facie	p/f
cause of action	c/a	probable cause	p/c
common law	c/l	proximate cause	px/c
Constitution	Con	real property	r/p
constitutional	con	reasonable doubt	r/d
contract	K	reasonable man	r/m
contributory negligence	c/n	rebuttable presumption	rb/p
cross	x	remanded	rem
cross-complaint	x/c	res ipsa loquitur	RIL
cross-examination	x/ex	respondeat superior	r/s
cruel and unusual punishment	c/u/p	Restatement	RS
defendant	D	reversed	rev
dismissed	dis	Rule Against Perpetuities	RAP
double jeopardy	d/j	search and seizure	s/s
due process	d/p	search warrant	s/w
equal protection	e/p	self-defense	s/d
equity	eq	specific performance	s/p
evidence	ev	statute	S
exclude	exc	statute of frauds	S/F
exclusionary rule	exc/r	statute of limitations	S/L
felony	f/n	summary judgment	s/j
freedom of speech	f/s	tenancy at will	t/w
good faith	g/f	tenancy in common	t/c
habeas corpus	h/c	tenant	t
hearsay	hr	third party	TP
husband	H	third party beneficiary	TPB
injunction	inj	transferred intent	TI
in loco parentis	ILP	unconscionable	uncon
inter vivos	I/v	unconstitutional	unconst
joint tenancy	j/t	undue influence	u/e
judgment	judgt	Uniform Commercial Code	UCC
jurisdiction	jur	unilateral	uni
last clear chance	LCC	vendee	VE
long-arm statute	LAS	vendor	VR
majority view	maj	versus	v
meeting of minds	MOM	void for vagueness	VFV
minority view	min	weight of authority	w/a
Miranda rule	Mir/r	weight of the evidence	w/e
Miranda warnings	Mir/w	wife	W
negligence	neg	with	w/
notice	ntc	within	w/i
nuisance	nus	without	w/o
obligation	ob	without prejudice	w/o/p
obscene	obs	wrongful death	wr/d

Table of Cases

The Supreme Court's Authority and Role

Quick Reference Rules of Law

Marbury v. Madison

Justice (P) v. Secretary of State (D)

5 U.S. (1 Cranch) 137 (1803).

NATURE OF CASE: Writ of mandamus to compel delivery of commission.

FACT SUMMARY: President Jefferson's Secretary of State, James Madison (D), refused to deliver a commission granted to William Marbury (P) by former President Adams.

🏛 RULE OF LAW
The Supreme Court has the power, implied from Article VI, § 2, of the Constitution, to review acts of Congress and if they are found repugnant to the Constitution, to declare them void.

FACTS: On March 2, 1801, the outgoing President of the United States, John Adams, named forty-two justices of the peace for the District of Columbia under the Organic Act passed the same day by Congress. William Marbury (P) was one of the justices named. The commissions of Marbury (P) and other named justices were signed by Adams on his last day in office, March 3, and signed and sealed by the Acting Secretary of State, John Marshall. However, the formal commissions were not delivered by the end of the day. The new President, Thomas Jefferson, treated those appointments that were not formalized by delivery of the papers of commission prior to Adams's leaving office as a nullity. Marbury (P) and other affected colleagues brought this writ of mandamus to the Supreme Court to compel Jefferson's Secretary of State, James Madison (D), to deliver the commissions. John Marshall, the current Chief Justice of the Supreme Court, delivered the opinion.

ISSUE: Does the Constitution give the Supreme Court the authority to review acts of Congress and declare them, if repugnant to the Constitution, to be void?

HOLDING AND DECISION: (Marshall, C.J.) Yes. The Supreme Court has the power, implied from Article VI, § 2, of the Constitution, to review acts of Congress and if they are found repugnant to the Constitution, to declare them void. The government of the United States is a government of laws, not of men. The President, bound by these laws, is given certain political powers by the Constitution which he may use at his discretion. To aid him in his duties, he is authorized to appoint certain officers to carry out his orders. Their acts as officers are his acts and are never subject to examination by the courts. However, where these officers are given by law specific duties on which individual rights depend, any individual injured by breach of such duty may resort to his country's laws for a remedy. Here, Marbury (P) had a right to the commission, and Madison's (D) refusal to deliver it violat-

ed that right. The present case is clearly one for mandamus. However, should the Supreme Court be the court to issue it? The Judiciary Act of 1789 established and authorized United States courts to issue writs of mandamus to courts or persons holding office under U.S. authority. Secretary of State Madison (D) comes within the Act. If the Supreme Court is powerless to issue the writ of mandamus to him, it must be because the Act is unconstitutional. Article III of the Constitution provides that the Supreme Court shall have original jurisdiction in all cases affecting ambassadors, other public ministers and consuls, and where a state is a party. In all other cases, the Supreme Court shall have appellate jurisdiction. Marbury (P) urged that since Article III contains no restrictive words, the power to assign original jurisdiction to the courts remains in the legislature. But if Congress is allowed to distribute the original and appellate jurisdiction of the Supreme Court, as in the Judiciary Act, then the constitutional grant of Article III is form without substance. But no clause in the Constitution is presumed to be without effect. For the Court to issue a mandamus, it must be an exercise of appellate jurisdiction. The grant of appellate jurisdiction is the power to revise and correct proceedings already instituted; it does not create the cause. To issue a writ of mandamus ordering an executive officer to deliver a paper is to create the original action for that paper. This would be an unconstitutional exercise of original jurisdiction beyond the power of the court. It is the province and duty of the judicial department to say what the law is. And any law, including acts of the legislature that is repugnant to the Constitution is void. Mandamus denied.

▶ ANALYSIS

Judicial review of legislative acts was a controversial subject even before the Constitution was ratified and adopted. Alexander Hamilton upheld the theory of judicial review in the Federalist Papers. He argued that the judiciary, being the most vulnerable branch of the government, was designed to be an intermediary between the people and the legislature. Since the interpretation of laws was the responsibility of the judiciary, and the Constitution the supreme law of the land, any conflict between legislative acts and the Constitution was to be resolved by the court in favor of the Constitution. But other authorities have attacked this position. In the case of *Eakin v. Raub*, 12 Serg. & Rawle 330 (1825), Justice Gibson dissented, stating that the judiciary's function was limited to interpreting the

Continued on next page.

laws and should not extend to scrutinizing the legislature's authority to enact them. Judge Learned Hand felt that judicial review was inconsistent with the separation of powers. But history has supported the authority of judicial review of legislative acts. The United States survives on a tripartite government. Theoretically, the three branches should be strong enough to check and balance the others. To limit the judiciary to the passive task of interpretation would be to limit its strength in the tripartite structure. Marbury served to buttress the judiciary branch making it equal to the executive and legislative branches.

Quicknotes

APPELLATE JURISDICTION The power of a higher court to review the decisions of lower courts.

JUDICIAL REVIEW Authority of the courts to review decisions, actions or omissions committed by another agency or branch of government.

ORIGINAL JURISDICTION The power of a court to hear an action upon its commencement.

WRIT OF MANDAMUS A court order issued commanding a public or private entity, or an official thereof, to perform a duty required by law.

Martin v. Hunter's Lessee

Heir to land (P) v. Lessee (D)

14 U.S. (1 Wheat.) 304 (1816).

NATURE OF CASE: Appeal from an action of ejectment.

FACT SUMMARY: After the Supreme Court reversed a Virginia Court of Appeals ruling that had held that Martin (P) had lost title to land in favor of the state, the Virginia court ruled that since the Federal Judiciary Act extended the Supreme Court's appellate jurisdiction to state courts, the Judiciary Act was unconstitutional.

🏛 RULE OF LAW
Federal courts may hear appeals brought from state court decisions.

FACTS: Martin (P), a British subject resident in England, inherited vast Virginia landholdings from his uncle, Lord Fairfax. In 1789, Virginia, pursuant to state laws confiscating land owned by British subjects, purported to grant a land patent to Hunter. Martin (P) sought to eject Hunter's lessee (D) from the land. The Virginia District Court ruled for Martin (P) on the basis of anti-confiscation clauses in the treaties of 1783 and 1794 with Great Britain. The Virginia Court of Appeals reversed on grounds that the 1796 act of compromise between the Fairfax claimants and the state settled the matter against Martin (P) and that the state's title had been perfected before the treaties. The Supreme Court, relied on the treaty of 1794 and without discussing the compromise, reversed and remanded. On remand, the Virginia court ruled that insofar as the Judiciary Act extended the Supreme Court's appellate jurisdiction to state courts, the Act was unconstitutional. Martin (P) appealed.

ISSUE: May federal courts hear appeals brought from state court decisions?

HOLDING AND DECISION: (Story, J.) Yes. Federal courts may hear appeals brought from state court decisions. The third article of the Constitution grants appellate jurisdiction to the Supreme Court where it does not have original jurisdiction except in those instances where Congress has limited federal appellate jurisdiction. The Framers anticipated federal courts would not have original jurisdiction over cases that arose in state court, but provided for appellate jurisdiction. Some argue that the federal courts cannot interfere with state sovereignty by taking jurisdiction over state cases, but the Constitution provides in several other instances for state obligations and intrusions into state sovereignty. State judges are not entitled to independence from the federal judicial system but are in fact subject to it pursuant to the Constitution. Federal appellate power over state cases is a necessity for uniformity because of the possibility of different state courts interpreting the same statute or treaty differently. The Supreme Court's job is not to inquire into the reasons the Framers provided for federal appellate jurisdiction but to construe the Constitution as written. The Constitution expressly provides for federal appellate jurisdiction over cases arising in state courts. Reversed (judgment of the district court affirmed).

▶ ANALYSIS

As a historical note, Chief Justice Marshall disqualified himself in the first, remanded case, *Fairfax's Devisee v. Hunter's Lessee*, 7 Cranch 603 (1813), and in the case above. Marshall, as a member of the Virginia legislature, had negotiated the 1796 act of compromise while acting for the purchasers of the Fairfax estate. Marshall also had a great financial interest in the outcome because he and his brother had organized a syndicate which had purchased, from Martin (P), 160,000 acres of the land in question.

Quicknotes

APPELLATE JURISDICTION The power of a higher court to review the decisions of lower courts.

EJECTMENT An action to oust someone in unlawful possession of real property and to restore possession to the party lawfully entitled to it.

FEDERAL JUDICIARY ACT § 34 The laws of the states shall be regarded as rules of decisions in trials at common law in the federal courts.

Cooper v. Aaron

Government officials (P) v. Court (D)

358 U.S. 1 (1958).

NATURE OF CASE: Certiorari for review of suspension of plan to desegregate public schools.

FACT SUMMARY: The Governor and Legislature of Arkansas refused to obey a federal court order to desegregate the public schools in Little Rock based on the *Brown v. Board of Education*, 344 U.S. 1 (1952), case, pending further challenges to the *Brown* decision.

🏛 RULE OF LAW
State officials may not refuse to obey federal court orders resting on constitutional grounds.

FACTS: The Governor and Legislature of the State of Arkansas acted upon the premise that there was no duty on state officials to obey federal court orders resting upon Supreme Court's interpretations of the Constitution. The actions consisted of the suspension of a desegregation plan for the public schools in Little Rock. The state officials claimed that they had the right to disobey the order until the decision in *Brown v. Board of Education* was further challenged. The Supreme Court reviewed the actions.

ISSUE: May state officials refuse to obey federal court orders resting on constitutional grounds?

HOLDING AND DECISION: (Warren, C.J.) No. State officials may not refuse to obey federal court orders resting on constitutional grounds. The Constitution of the United States is the "supreme law of the land." The federal judiciary is supreme in the exposition of the law of the Constitution. No state legislator or executive or judicial officer can refuse to obey a federal court order based upon a federal interpretation of the Constitution without violating the duty to support the Constitution. If such refusal was permitted, the fiat of the official would be the supreme law instead of the Constitution. [Decision not stated in casebook excerpt.]

▌ *ANALYSIS*

The Supremacy Clause of the Constitution, Article VI, § 2, requires that federal court decisions based on Supreme Court's interpretations of constitutional language govern the states' legislative, judicial, and executive branches. However, where the federal court asserts power based on anything other than the Constitution or constitutional interpretations, the doctrine announced in *Erie v. Tompkins*, 304 U.S. 64, 58 S. Ct. 817, 82 L. Ed. 1188 (1937), may permit the state law, if applicable, to govern.

Quicknotes

***ERIE* DOCTRINE** Federal courts must apply state substantive law and federal procedural law.

FEDERALISM A scheme of government whereby the power to govern is divided between central and localized governments.

SUPREMACY CLAUSE Art. VI, § 2, of the Constitution, which provides that federal action must prevail over inconsistent state action.

■=■

Lujan v. Defenders of Wildlife

Secretary of the Interior (D) v. Environmental organizations (P)

504 U.S. 555 (1992).

NATURE OF CASE: Appeal of injunction requiring the Secretary of the Interior to promulgate a regulation.

FACT SUMMARY: Defenders of Wildlife (P) sued for an injunction ordering the Secretary of the Interior (D) to apply the Endangered Species Act to actions taken in foreign countries.

RULE OF LAW

To establish standing, a plaintiff must show injury-in-fact, causation, and redressability, and Congress may not create a right of standing based on a generalized grievance against government.

FACTS: The Endangered Species Act § 7(a)(2) required federal agencies to consult with the Interior Department (D) to ensure that federal actions do not jeopardize endangered species. Interior (D) reinterpreted § 7(a)(2) to apply only in the United States or at sea. Defenders of Wildlife (Defenders) (P) sued for an injunction requiring Secretary of the Interior Lujan (D) to issue a regulation restoring the interpretation that § 7(a)(2) applies worldwide. To support standing, two of the Department's (D) members, who claimed to have observed certain endangered animals on trips to Egypt and Sri Lanka, averred that they would suffer harm from federal programs overseeing and funding projects in Egypt and Sri Lanka that threatened the animals. They also presented three novel standing theories whereby anyone anywhere with a vocational, educational, or aesthetic interest in an endangered species or "contiguous ecosystem" harmed by a federal activity would have standing. They also cited the "citizen suit" provision of the Act which grants "any person" the right to sue to enforce any of its provisions. The Secretary (D) moved for summary judgment, claiming Defenders (P) lacked standing. The district court instead issued Defenders (P) the injunction it sought. The court of appeals affirmed, and the Secretary (D) appealed.

ISSUE: Can Congress create a right of standing based on a generalized grievance against government, allowing a plaintiff to establish standing without showing injury-in-fact, causation, and redressability?

HOLDING AND DECISION: (Scalia, J.) No. To establish standing a plaintiff must show injury-in-fact, causation, and redressability. Congress may not create a right of standing based on a generalized grievance against government. Defenders (P) failed to establish injury-in-fact. "Someday" future intentions to observe animals do not establish "actual or imminent" injury. The novel theories

establish harm to the ecosystem or animals but fail to establish injury to a plaintiff. It is pure speculation that anyone anywhere is harmed by a single project affecting some portion of a species without a specific connection. They also failed to establish redressability. Other agencies, not being parties, would not be bound by an injunction. Moreover, there was no evidence Egypt, Sri Lanka, or any other country would reduce a project or harm to endangered species if minimal U.S. support were stopped. The Act's "citizen-suit" provision is unconstitutional. Under Article III, federal courts may not hear cases where the plaintiff merely has a generalized grievance against government. Congress may not give power to the courts which the Constitution says the courts do not have. Congress may create rights which establish injury-in-fact to satisfy Article III, but those rights must be individualized or there is no "case or controversy." Reversed.

CONCURRENCE: (Kennedy, J.) The Court must be sensitive to Congress's ability to create new standing rights. At a minimum, though, Congress must identify the injury it wishes to vindicate and relate the injury to a class of persons who can sue. The "citizen-suit" provision fails to do either.

CONCURRENCE: (Stevens, J.) While I do not agree with the Court's conclusion that the threatened injury is not imminent nor with the plurality additional conclusion that the injury is not redressable in this litigation, I concur in the reversal because I am not persuaded Congress intended the consultation requirement of § 7(a)(2) to apply to activities in foreign countries.

DISSENT: (Blackmun, J.) On summary judgment a plaintiff need show only a genuine issue of material fact as to standing. Many environmental injuries cause harm far from the challenged activity. The funding agencies would be bound by an injunction based on their involvement in this case. Congress imposes procedural restraints on executive power. Surely the courts do not violate separation of powers by enforcing these procedures at the mandate of Congress.

ANALYSIS

The precedential value of *Lujan* is questionable. Only four justices found that the plaintiffs had not established redressability. Only three justices agreed that there was

Continued on next page.

no injury-in-fact and that the "citizen-suit" provision was invalid.

■═■

Quicknotes

CAUSATION The aggregate effect of preceding events that brings about a tortious result; the causal connection between the actions of a tortfeasor and the injury that follows.

GENERALIZED GRIEVANCE It refers to a class of actions that does not have standing because it does not represent a controversy for the particular plaintiff but is something that affects the general public.

INJURY IN FACT An injury that gives rise to standing to sue.

REDRESSABILITY Requirement that in order for a court to hear a case there must be an injury that is redressable or capable of being remedied.

STANDING Whether a party possesses the right to commence suit against another party by having a personal stake in the resolution of the controversy.

■═■

Massachusetts v. Environmental Protection Agency

State (P) v. Federal agency (D)

549 U.S. 497 (2007).

NATURE OF CASE: Appeal challenging a federal agency's alleged refusal to enforce the federal Clean Air Act against motor-vehicle emissions.

FACT SUMMARY: A state and several other parties challenged the Environmental Protection Agency's (EPA) (D) failure to enforce the Clean Air Act against motor-vehicle emissions.

🏛 RULE OF LAW
A plaintiff has standing if it demonstrates a concrete injury that is both fairly traceable to the defendant and redressable by judicial relief.

FACTS: The Environmental Protection Agency (EPA) (D) refused to enforce the Clean Air Act against motor-vehicle emissions. Massachusetts (P) and several other parties appealed the EPA's (D) refusal [by petitioning the Court of Appeals for the District of Columbia Circuit to review the Agency's (D) decision. The appellate court did not affirmatively hold that Massachusetts (P) had standing, but a majority of that court did uphold the EPA's (D) decision. Massachusetts (P) petitioned the Supreme Court for further review.]

ISSUE: Does a plaintiff have standing if it demonstrates a concrete injury that is both fairly traceable to the defendant and redressable by judicial relief?

HOLDING AND DECISION: (Stevens, J.) Yes. A plaintiff has standing if it demonstrates a concrete injury that is both fairly traceable to the defendant and redressable by judicial relief. A well-documented rise in global temperatures has coincided with an increase in carbon dioxide in the atmosphere, and scientists believe that the two trends are related. Calling global warming "the most pressing environmental challenge of our time," a group of states, including Massachusetts (P), alleges that the EPA has abdicated its responsibility in protecting the nation. The jurisdiction of federal courts is limited to "cases" and "controversies," and Massachusetts (P) has satisfied that threshold hurdle here. It is important to note that only one of the petitioners needs to have standing in order to permit this Court to consider the petition for review. As a state, Massachusetts (P) proceeds in its quasi-sovereign capacity, and case law supports applying different standards of justiciability for such litigants. The particularized injury for Massachusetts (P) in this case is the damage to the State's (P) coastline that will, and will continue to, occur. Further, the injury to that coastline is fairly traceable to the EPA's (D) inaction; even small effects on an injury in fact satisfy the causation requirement in federal standing analysis.

Finally, Massachusetts's (P) injury can be redressed judicially, even though the outcome of a judicial remedy might be delayed while new motor-vehicle emissions are implemented. Accordingly, Massachusetts (P) has standing. [Reversed.]

DISSENT: (Roberts, C.J.) Any redress of the injuries in this case should be left to the political branches. Relaxing standing requirements for a State exists nowhere in this Court's precedents. Under normal standing analysis, Massachusetts's (P) injury fails to satisfy the requirement of a "concrete and particularized" injury; injuries to "humanity at large" do not suffice. Also, any causal connection between the EPA's (D) inaction and damage to the coastlines is so tenuous and speculative that it cannot support a finding of standing. Further, Massachusetts (P) cannot satisfy the redressability factor because emissions from other countries are likely to dwarf any reduction in emissions that might result from the EPA's (D) enforcement of the Clean Air Act. Diluting the appropriate standing requirements only permits courts to encroach upon authority that is properly committed to Congress and the President.

▌ANALYSIS

The three factors in the standing analysis announced by *Lujan v. Defenders of Wildlife*, 504 U.S. 555 (1992), are very clear: the complaining party must have suffered (1) an injury in fact (2) that is fairly traceable to the defendant and (3) that can be redressed by judicial relief. As the Court's five-to-four decision in this case shows, however, what is not so clear is how those three factors should apply to any specific dispute. The fundamental importance of justiciability, as Chief Justice Roberts notes in dissent, resides in the most basic questions about the kinds of disputes that courts should—and should not—hear.

■▬■

Quicknotes

REDRESSABILITY Requirement that in order for a court to hear a case there must be an injury that is redressable or capable of being remedied.

STANDING Whether a party possesses the right to commence suit against another party by having a personal stake in the resolution of the controversy.

■▬■

Baker v. Carr

Resident (P) v. State (D)

369 U.S. 186 (1962).

NATURE OF CASE: Certiorari granted to review unconstitutionality of a state political reapportionment law.

FACT SUMMARY: Baker (P) alleged that because of population changes since 1901, the 1901 State Apportionment Act was obsolete and unconstitutional, and that the state legislature refused to reapportion itself.

🏛 RULE OF LAW
The fact that a suit seeks protection of a political right does not mean it necessarily presents a political question.

FACTS: Between 1901 and 1961, Tennessee's population had grown substantially and had been redistributed. Baker (P) alleged that because of the population changes and the state legislature's failure to reapportion voting districts by itself, the 1901 Apportionment Act was unconstitutional, as violating equal protection, and obsolete. Baker (P) also alleged that because of the makeup of the legislature resulting from the 1901 Act, redress in the form of a state constitutional amendment was difficult or impossible. Baker (P) sought an injunction against further elections under the 1901 system and reapportionment, but the lower court denied relief.

ISSUE: Does a constitutional challenge to a state apportionment act present a political question?

HOLDING AND DECISION: (Brennan, J.) No. The fact that a suit seeks protection of a political right does not mean it necessarily presents a political question. The primary reason that political questions have been held to be nonjusticiable is the separation of powers. An analysis of any case held to involve a political question will reveal: (1) a history of the issue's management by another governmental branch; (2) a lack of judicially manageable standards for resolving it; (3) the impossibility of deciding the case without an initial policy determination calling for nonjudicial discretion; (4) the impossibility of resolving it without expressing lack of respect due other government branches; (5) an unusual need for unquestioning adherence to a political decision already made; or (6) the potentiality of embarrassment from a variety of announcements by different governmental departments on one question. The mere fact that a suit seeks protection of a political right does not mean that it involves a political question. The Court cannot reject as involving a political question a real controversy as to whether a certain action exceeded constitutional limits. Here, Baker (P) alleges that a state's actions violate his right to equal protection. None of the above-mentioned characteristics of a political question are present. Further, the nonjusticiability of claims arising under the Guaranty Clause can have no bearing on the justiciability of the equal protection claim presented here. The judgment of dismissal is reversed, and the case is remanded.

DISSENT: (Frankfurter, J.) A long line of cases has held that the Guaranty Clause is not enforceable through the courts. The present case involves all of the elements that have made the Guaranty Clause cases nonjusticiable. The Equal Protection Clause provides no clearer guide for judicial examination of apportionment statutes than would the Guaranty Clause. What is actually asked here is for the Court to choose among competing theories of representation, and ultimately, among competing political philosophies, to establish an appropriate frame of government for Tennessee. To find the Court's power to make such a choice in the broad guarantee of the Equal Protection Clause is to rewrite the Constitution.

▶ ANALYSIS

Baker v. Carr is the most important case on political questions. Traditionally, the Court refused to review cases arising from state apportionment statutes, since they were all said to present political questions. In *Colegrove v. Green*, 328 U.S. 549 (1946), it was contended that the fact that apportioned districts were not of approximate equality in population rendered the state apportionment act unconstitutional. The Court held that a political question was presented and so the case was nonjusticiable. However, in *Gomillion v. Lightfoot*, 364 U.S. 339 (1960), the Court showed some willingness to enter the area of apportionment. There, a statute apportioned a district with the obvious purpose of excluding black votes. The Court held that a justiciable violation of equal protection had been alleged. In distinguishing *Colegrove*, it stated that there the complaint alleged only a dilution of the strength of the appellants' votes as a result of legislative inaction over a number of years, whereas in *Gomillion*, the petitioners complained that affirmative legislative action had deprived them of their votes.

■==■

Quicknotes

JUSTICIABILITY An actual controversy that is capable of determination by the court.

POLITICAL QUESTION An issue more appropriately left to the determination of another governmental branch and which the court declines to hear.

■==■

Federalism: History and Principles

Quick Reference Rules of Law

McCulloch v. Maryland

Bank cashier (D) v. State (P)

17 U.S. (4 Wheat.) 316 (1819).

NATURE OF CASE: Action arising out of violation of a state statute.

FACT SUMMARY: McCulloch (D), the cashier of the Baltimore branch of the U.S. Bank, issued bank notes in violation of a Maryland (P) statute providing that no bank, without authority from the state, could issue bank notes except on stamped paper issued by the state.

RULE OF LAW

(1) Certain federal powers, which give Congress the discretion and power to choose and enact the means to perform the duties imposed upon it, are to be implied from the Necessary and Proper Clause.
(2) The federal Constitution and the laws made pursuant to it are supreme and control the constitutions and the laws of the states.

FACTS: A Maryland (P) statute prohibited any bank operating in the state without state authority from issuing bank notes except upon stamped paper issued by the state. The law specified the fees payable for the paper, and provided for penalties for violators. An act of Congress established a U.S. Bank. McCulloch (D), the U.S. Bank's cashier for its Baltimore branch, issued bank notes without complying with the Maryland (P) law.

ISSUE:
(1) Does Congress have the power to incorporate a bank?
(2) Does a state have the power to impose fees on the operation of an institution created by Congress pursuant to its constitutional powers?

HOLDING AND DECISION: (Marshall, C.J.)
(1) Yes. Certain federal powers, which give Congress the discretion and power to choose and enact the means to perform the duties imposed upon it, are to be implied from the Necessary and Proper Clause. It is true that this government is one of enumerated powers. However, the Constitution does not exclude incidental or implied powers. It does not require that everything be granted expressly and minutely described. To have so required would have entirely changed the character of the Constitution and made it into a legal code. The enumerated powers given to the government imply the ordinary means of execution. The power of creating a corporation may be implied as incidental to other powers, or used as a means of executing them. The Necessary and Proper Clause gives Congress the power to make "all laws which shall be necessary and proper, for carrying into execution" the powers vested by the Constitution in the U.S. Government. Maryland (P) argues that the word "necessary" limits the right to pass laws for the execution of the granted powers to those which are indispensable. However, in common usage, "necessary" frequently means convenient, useful, or essential. Considering the word's common usage, its usage in another part of the Constitution (Article 1, § 10), and its inclusion among the powers given to Congress, rather than among the limitations upon Congress, it cannot be held to restrain Congress. The sound construction of the Constitution must allow Congress the discretion to choose the means to perform the duties imposed upon it. As long as the end is legitimate and within the scope of the Constitution, any means that are appropriate, are plainly adapted to that end, and that are not prohibited by the Constitution, but are consistent with its spirit, are constitutional. A bank is a convenient, useful, and essential instrument for handling national finances. Hence, it is within Congress's power to enact a law incorporating a U.S. bank.

(2) No. The federal Constitution and the laws made pursuant to it are supreme and control the constitutions and the laws of the states. The federal Constitution and the laws made in pursuance thereof are supreme. They control the constitutions and laws of the states and cannot be controlled by them. Maryland (P) is incorrect in its contention that the powers of the federal government are delegated by the states, which alone are truly sovereign. The Constitution derives its authority from the people, not from the states. Here, Maryland's (P) statute in effect taxes the operation of the U.S. Bank, a bank properly created within Congress's power. The power to tax involves the power to destroy. Here it is in opposition to the supreme congressional power to create a bank. Also, when a state taxes an organization created by the U.S. Government, it acts upon an institution created by people over whom it claims no control. The states have no power, by taxation or otherwise, to impede, burden, or in any manner control the operations of constitutional laws enacted by Congress. The Maryland (P) statute is, therefore, unconstitutional and void. Reversed.

ANALYSIS

Federalism is the basis of the Constitution's response to the problem of governing large geographical areas with diverse local needs. The success of federalism depends upon maintaining the balance between the need for the

Continued on next page.

supremacy and sovereignty of the federal government and the interest in maintaining independent state government and curtailing national intrusion into intrastate affairs. The U.S. federal structure allocates powers between the nation and the states by enumerating the powers delegated to the national government and acknowledging the retention by the states of the remainder. The Articles of Confederation followed a similar scheme. The Constitution expanded the enumerated national powers to remedy weaknesses of the Articles. The move from the Articles to the Constitution was a shift from a central government with fewer powers to one with more powers.

■▬■

Quicknotes

FEDERALISM A scheme of government whereby the power to govern is divided between central and localized governments.

NECESSARY AND PROPER CLAUSE, ART I, § 8 OF THE CONSTITUTION Enables Congress to make all laws that may be "necessary and proper" to execute its other, enumerated powers.

■▬■

U.S. Term Limits, Inc. v. Thornton

Proponents of term limits (D) v. League of Women Voters (P)

514 U.S. 779 (1995).

NATURE OF CASE: Review of summary judgment striking down state term limits.

FACT SUMMARY: Arkansas' (D) congressional term limitation law was challenged as unconstitutional.

🏛 RULE OF LAW
States may not limit the terms of members of Congress.

FACTS: In 1992, Arkansas (D) adopted by initiative a state constitutional amendment limiting the tenure of both state and federal elected officials. With respect to the United States congressional and senatorial delegations, the amendment provided that an incumbent could not have his name placed on a ballot after a set number of terms. The League of Women Voters (P) challenged this provision as contrary to the Constitution. The Arkansas Supreme Court held the amendment unconstitutional, and the U.S. Supreme Court granted review.

ISSUE: May states limit the terms of members of Congress?

HOLDING AND DECISION: (Stevens, J.) No. States may not limit the terms of members of Congress. The qualifications for sitting in the U.S. Congress are stated in Article I of the Constitution. The Supreme Court has already held that Congress itself cannot add to, subtract from, or otherwise change these qualifications. The issue here is whether the states can do so. First, states do not have a Tenth Amendment power in this area. The Tenth Amendment reserved to the states those powers that predated the Constitution and were not delegated to the federal government. State governments never had any powers over national elections prior to the Constitution, because there were none. Consequently, the Tenth Amendment gives the states no powers here. Second, the historical record is quite clear that the notion of term limits was vigorously debated prior to adoption of the Constitution, and to add such a requirement now would violate the Framers' intent. Finally, to allow states to impose term limits would violate a fundamental principle of our system of representative democracy, to wit, that people should be free to choose those whom they please to govern them. For these reasons, term limits violate the Constitution. U.S. Term Limits, Inc. (D), however, contends that the amendment in question does not truly limit terms but only restricts ballot access. The Constitution allows states to regulate the time, manner and place of elections. U.S. Term Limits (D) contends that the amendment constitutes such a regulation. It does not. The amendment tries to do indirectly what it cannot do in a direct manner, and this sort of form over substance argument will not be endorsed by the Court. [Affirmed.]

CONCURRENCE: (Kennedy, J.) The federal character of congressional elections flows from the political reality that our national government is republican in form and that national citizenship has privileges and immunities protected from state abridgement by the force of the Constitution itself.

DISSENT: (Thomas, J.) [Nothing] in the Constitution deprives the people of each state of the power to prescribe eligibility requirements for congressional candidates; it is silent in that area. "Where the Constitution is silent, it raises no bar to action by the states or the people." The Court's analysis is wrong on several counts. The Tenth Amendment protects not only those powers that predate the Constitution. All power flows from consent of the people; when the people have spoken, as they did here, and the Constitution does not countermand the will of the people, the Tenth Amendment applies. When selecting members of Congress, the people of each state have retained their independent political identity, which would allow them to determine eligibility requirements. Also, the Qualifications Clause is a bare recitation of the minimum qualifications necessary to hold office; it says nothing to the effect that these are the only qualifications that can be imposed. Finally, the Court incorrectly equates limitations on ballot access with limits on tenure.

▶ ANALYSIS

The present case is a good illustration of two different and competing theories of constitutional interpretation. The majority's approach can be called "structural." While the Constitution did not specifically prohibit term limits, the Court invalidated them as contrary to our governmental structure. Justice Thomas, in his dissent, took a strict constructionist/literalist approach, looking to the text and nothing more.

■=■

Quicknotes

TENTH AMENDMENT The Tenth Amendment to the United States Constitution reserves those powers therein, not expressly delegated to the federal government or prohibited to the states, to the states or to the people.

■=■

United States v. Comstock

Federal government (P) v. Sexually violent prisoner (D)

560 U.S. 126 (2010).

NATURE OF CASE: Appeal in action challenging as beyond Congress's power under the Necessary and Proper Clause a federal civil-commitment statute authorizing the federal government to civilly commit "sexually dangerous persons" beyond the date it lawfully could hold them on a charge or conviction for a federal crime. [The procedural posture of the case is not presented in the casebook extract.]

FACT SUMMARY: Congress enacted § 4248, which authorizes the federal government to civilly commit "sexually dangerous persons" beyond the date it lawfully could hold them on a charge or conviction for a federal crime. The statute was challenged as beyond Congress's power under the Necessary and Proper Clause.

RULE OF LAW
Congress has power under the Necessary and Proper Clause to enact a law authorizing the federal government to civilly commit "sexually dangerous persons" beyond the date it lawfully could hold them on a charge or conviction for a federal crime.

FACTS: Congress enacted § 4248, which authorizes the federal government to civilly commit "sexually dangerous persons" beyond the date it lawfully could hold them on a charge or conviction for a federal crime. The statute was challenged as beyond Congress's power under the Necessary and Proper Clause. [The procedural posture of the case is not presented in the casebook extract.]

ISSUE: Does Congress have power under the Necessary and Proper Clause to enact a law authorizing the federal government to civilly commit "sexually dangerous persons" beyond the date it lawfully could hold them on a charge or conviction for a federal crime?

HOLDING AND DECISION: (Breyer, J.) Yes. Congress has power under the Necessary and Proper Clause to enact a law authorizing the federal government to civilly commit "sexually dangerous persons" beyond the date it lawfully could hold them on a charge or conviction for a federal crime. This conclusion rests on five principal conclusions. First, the Clause grants Congress broad authority to pass laws in furtherance of its constitutionally enumerated powers. It makes clear that grants of specific federal legislative authority are accompanied by broad power to enact laws that are "convenient, or useful" or "conducive" to the enumerated power's "beneficial exercise." In determining whether the Clause authorizes a particular federal statute, there must be "means-ends rationality" between the enacted statute and the source of

federal power. Although the Constitution nowhere grants Congress express power to create federal crimes beyond those specifically enumerated, to punish their violation, to imprison violators, or to provide appropriately for those imprisoned, Congress possesses broad authority to do each of those things under the Clause. Second, the statute is a modest addition to a longstanding federal statutory framework. Third, the Government (P), as custodian of its prisoners, has the constitutional power to act in order to protect nearby (and other) communities from the danger such prisoners may pose. Moreover, § 4248 is reasonably adapted to Congress's power to act as a responsible federal custodian. Congress could have reasonably concluded that federal inmates who suffer from a mental illness that causes them to have serious difficulty in refraining from sexually violent conduct would pose an especially high danger to the public if released, since Congress could have reasonably concluded that a reasonable number of such individuals would likely not be detained by the states if released from federal custody. Fourth, § 4248 does not invade state sovereignty but seeks to accommodate state interests, since it requires the Attorney General to encourage the relevant states to take custody of the individual without inquiring into the "suitability" of their intended care or treatment, and to relinquish federal authority whenever a state asserts its own. Fifth, § 4248 is narrow in scope and does not result in Congress having a general police power, given that it has been applied to only a small fraction of federal prisoners, and its reach is limited to individuals already in the Government's (P) custody. Taken together, these five considerations lead to the conclusion that the statute is a "necessary and proper" means of exercising the federal authority that permits Congress to create federal criminal laws, to punish their violation, to imprison violators, to provide appropriately for those imprisoned, and to maintain the security of those who are not imprisoned but who may be affected by the federal imprisonment of others. [The procedural outcome of the case is not presented in the casebook extract.]

CONCURRENCE: (Kennedy, J.) Under the Necessary and Proper Clause, application of a "rational basis" test should be at least as exacting as it has been in the Commerce Clause cases, which require a tangible link to commerce, not a mere conceivable rational relation. Thus, the link must be an empirically demonstrated link in fact. Also, while it is logically correct to say that if the federal Government (P) has a given power to act under the Necessary and Proper Clause then that power is not one reserved

Continued on next page.

to the States, it is essential in determining whether the Government (P) has authority to exercise a given power in the first place to consider whether state sovereignty is compromised by the federal Government's (P) assertion of that power. If state sovereignty is compromised, that suggests that the power is not one properly within the reach of federal power.

CONCURRENCE: (Alito, J.) It is necessary and proper for Congress to protect the public from dangers created by the federal criminal justice and prison systems. Given that it is necessary and proper for Congress to provide for the apprehension of escaped federal prisoners, it is similarly necessary and proper for Congress to provide for the civil commitment of dangerous federal prisoners who would otherwise escape civil commitment as a result of federal imprisonment.

DISSENT: (Thomas, J.) The Government (P) identifies no specific enumerated power or powers as a constitutional predicate for § 4248, and none are readily discernible; and not even the Commerce Clause can justify federal civil detention of sex offenders. Moreover, the Court has long recognized that the power to care for the mentally ill and, where necessary, the power to protect the community from the dangerous tendencies of some mentally ill persons, are among the numerous powers that remain with the States. Notwithstanding that a majority of the states argue that § 4248 is constitutional—because the cost of detaining such sexually dangerous persons is expensive and they would rather the federal Government (P) bear this expense—Congress's power is fixed by the Constitution; it does not depend on the states' policy preferences, or on considerations of the states' allocation of their funds. Thus, the majority's decision comes perilously close to transforming the Necessary and Proper Clause into a basis for the federal police power that the Court has always rejected.

▶ ANALYSIS

One of the constitutional principles that the Court elaborated in this decision is that congressional authority under the Necessary and Proper Clause can be more than one step removed from an enumerated power. When the inquiry is whether a federal law has sufficient links to an enumerated power to be within the scope of federal authority, the analysis depends not on the number of links in the congressional-power chain but on the strength of the chain. Thus, concluding that a relation can be put into a verbal formulation that fits somewhere along a causal chain of federal powers is merely the beginning, not the end, of the constitutional inquiry.

Quicknotes

ENUMERATED POWERS Those powers expressly delegated by the U.S. Constitution to a particular branch of government.

NECESSARY AND PROPER CLAUSE, ART. I, § 8 OF THE CONSTITUTION Enables Congress to make all laws that may be "necessary and proper" to execute its other, enumerated powers.

POLICE POWER The power of a government to impose restrictions on the rights of private persons, so long as those restrictions are reasonably related to the promotion and protection of public health, safety, morals, and the general welfare.

CHAPTER 3

The Commerce Power and Its Federalism-Based Limits

Quick Reference Rules of Law

Gibbons v. Ogden

Ship operator (D) v. Ship operator (P)

22 U.S. (9 Wheat.) 1 (1824).

NATURE OF CASE: Certiorari to review interpretation of federal commerce power in underlying action seeking an injunction to protect an exclusive right to operate ships between New York and New Jersey.

FACT SUMMARY: [Ogden (P), after acquiring a monopoly right from the State of New York to operate ships between New York City and New Jersey, sought to enjoin Gibbons (D) from operating his ships, licensed by the federal government, between the same points.]

🏛 RULE OF LAW
If a state law conflicts with a congressional act regulating commerce, the congressional act is controlling.

FACTS: [The New York legislature granted an exclusive right to Robert Livingston and Robert Fulton to operate ships powered by fire or steam in New York waters for twenty years, which right was subsequently extended for another ten years. Ogden (P) obtained an assignment from Livingston and Fulton to operate his ships between Elizabethtown, New Jersey, and New York City. Gibbons (D) was also running two boats between these points, and his boats had been enrolled and licensed under the laws of the United States for employment in the coasting trade. Ogden (P) obtained an injunction stopping Gibbons (D) from operating his ships between the points for which Ogden (P) had received an exclusive right to operate his own ships. The case was appealed to the Supreme Court.] Ogden (P) claimed the federal government did not have exclusive jurisdiction over commerce, but that the states had retained power by which they could regulate commerce within their own states and that the exclusive right to operate his ships only concerned intrastate commerce. Gibbons (D) contended that Congress had exclusive power to regulate interstate commerce and that New York had attempted to regulate interstate commerce by granting the exclusive right and enforcing it with the injunction.

ISSUE: If a state law conflicts with a congressional act regulating commerce, is the congressional act controlling?

HOLDING AND DECISION: (Marshall, C.J.) Yes. If a state law conflicts with a congressional act regulating commerce, the congressional act is controlling. The appellee Ogden (P) seeks to limit the meaning of the word commerce and have it apply only to traffic, or the buying or selling of commodities. Commerce certainly includes those meanings but is not limited to them. Commerce is the commercial intercourse between nations. If commerce does not embrace navigation, the government of

the Union would have no direct power over this subject, but the fact is that this power over navigation has been exercised by the government from the beginning and it is understood as a commercial regulation. The subject to which the power is applied is commerce "among the several states." Commerce among the states cannot stop at the external boundary line of each state, but applies to the interior as well. The government thus has the power to regulate navigation within states as part of its general commerce power. [The Court dismissed Ogden's (P) suit to obtain an injunction against Gibbons (D)].

▶ ANALYSIS

The federal commerce power is concurrent with state power over commerce within the state. Hence, the Court has been asked many times to define the line between federal and state power to regulate commerce. During the early history of the United States, the Court was not often called upon to determine the scope of federal power under the Commerce Clause. Instead, the early cases generally involved some state action which was claimed to discriminate against or burden interstate commerce. Hence, the Commerce Clause operated as a restraint upon state powers. Most of these cases did not involve any exercise of the commerce power by Congress at all. *Gibbons v. Ogden* stands for the important principle that even where Congress has not acted under its commerce power, state regulation affecting interstate commerce will often be foreclosed. This is called Congress's negative or dormant commerce power. Large-scale regulatory action by Congress began with the Interstate Commerce Act in 1887 and the Sherman Anti-Trust Act in 1890. Challenges to these statutes initiated the major modern confrontations between the Court and congressional authority regarding commerce.

■≡■

Quicknotes

COMMERCE POWER The power delegated to Congress by the Constitution to regulate interstate commerce.

DORMANT COMMERCE CLAUSE The regulatory effect of the Commerce Clause on state activity affecting interstate commerce, where Congress itself has not acted to control the activity; a provision inferred from, but not expressly present in, the language of the Commerce Clause.

INJUNCTION A court order requiring a person to do, or prohibiting that person from doing, a specific act.

■≡■

Hammer v. Dagenhart (The Child Labor Case)

U.S. Attorney General (D) v. Parent of child laborers (P)

247 U.S. 251 (1918).

NATURE OF CASE: Certiorari review of judgment enjoining enforcement of the Child Labor Act.

FACT SUMMARY: Congress passed a law prohibiting the shipment in interstate commerce of any products of any mills, mines, or factories which employed children.

> 🏛 **RULE OF LAW**
> The making of goods and the mining of coal are not commerce, even if afterwards shipped or used in interstate commerce.

FACTS: Congress passed a law prohibiting the shipment in interstate commerce of any products of any mills, mines, or factories which employed children.

ISSUE: Is the making of goods and the mining of coal commerce if afterwards shipped or used in interstate commerce?

HOLDING AND DECISION: (Day, J.) No. The making of goods and the mining of coal are not commerce, even if afterwards shipped or used in interstate commerce. It is argued that the power of Congress to regulate commerce includes the power to prohibit the transportation of ordinary products in commerce. However, in cases such as *The Lottery Case*, 188 U.S. 321 (1903), the power to prohibit the carrying of lottery tickets is as to those particular objects the same as the exertion of the power to regulate. In those cases, the use of interstate commerce was necessary to the accomplishment of harmful results. Regulation over commerce could be accomplished only by prohibiting the use of interstate commerce to affect the evil intended. Here, the thing intended to be accomplished by this act is the denial of interstate commerce facilities to those employing children within the prohibited ages. The goods shipped are of themselves harmless. The production of articles intended for interstate commerce is a matter of local regulation. The making of goods and the refining of coal are not commerce, nor does the fact that these things are to be afterwards shipped or used in interstate commerce make their production a part thereof. It is also argued that congressional regulation is necessary because of the unfair advantage possessed by manufacturers in states which have less stringent child labor laws. However, Congress has no power to require states to exercise their police powers to prevent possible unfair competition. The act is unconstitutional and the decree enjoining its enforcement is affirmed.

DISSENT: (Holmes, J.) *The Lottery Case* and others following it establish that a law is not beyond Congress's commerce power merely because it prohibits certain trans-

portation. There is no legal distinction between the evils sought to be controlled in those cases and the evil of premature and excessive child labor. The court has no right to substitute its judgment of which evils may be controlled.

▶ *ANALYSIS*

After the *Hammer* decision, Congress sought to regulate child labor through the taxing power. The law was invalidated in *Bailey v. Drexel Furnishing Co.*, 259 U.S. 20 (1922). Subsequently, Congress submitted a proposed constitutional amendment to the states that authorized a national child labor law. The amendment has not been ratified, but the need for it has largely disappeared in view of *U.S. v. Darby*, 312 U.S. 100 (1941), which overruled *Hammer*.

◼️▭◼️

Quicknotes

COMMERCE POWER The power delegated to Congress by the Constitution to regulate interstate commerce.

◼️▭◼️

NLRB v. Jones & Laughlin Steel Corp.

Federal agency (P) v. Steel company (D)

301 U.S. 1 (1937).

NATURE OF CASE: Certiorari review of alleged unfair labor practice under the National Labor Relations Act.

FACT SUMMARY: Jones & Laughlin Steel Corp. (Jones & Laughlin) (D), a manufacturing company with subsidiaries in several states and nationwide sales, was charged with an unfair labor practice under the National Labor Relations Act. In defense, Jones & Laughlin (D) claimed that the Act was an unconstitutional attempt to regulate intrastate production.

RULE OF LAW
Under the Commerce Clause, Congress has the power to regulate any activity, even intrastate production, if the activity has an appreciable effect, either direct or indirect, on interstate commerce.

FACTS: Pursuant to a complaint filed by a labor union, the National Labor Relations Board (the "Board") (P) found that Jones & Laughlin Steel Corp. (Jones & Laughlin) (D) had engaged in "unfair labor practices." The Board (P) issued a cease and desist order to Jones & Laughlin (D) to stop using discriminatory and coercive practices to prevent union organization at two steel plants in and around Pittsburgh. The company refused to comply, and the Board (P) went to court for judicial enforcement of its order under the authority of the National Labor Relations Act of 1935. Jones & Laughlin (D) contended that the order was an unconstitutional exercise of the Board's (P) authority since the plants were not engaged in interstate commerce, being totally manufacturing facilities. The court of appeals upheld the company's position and refused enforcement of the order on the ground that "the order lay beyond the range of federal power."

ISSUE: Under the Commerce Clause, does Congress have the power to regulate any activity, even intrastate production, if the activity has an appreciable effect, either direct or indirect, on interstate commerce?

HOLDING AND DECISION: (Hughes, C.J.) Yes. Under the Commerce Clause, Congress has the power to regulate any activity, even intrastate production, if the activity has an appreciable effect, either direct or indirect, on interstate commerce. The act of the Board (P) in ordering Jones & Laughlin (D) to cease interfering with its employees' rights of self-organization and collective bargaining is an exercise of the congressional power to regulate interstate commerce. The definitions in the Act restrict the Board's (P) actions to protecting interstate commerce in the constitutional sense, and the Board (P) is given the power to determine if the practice in question affects commerce in such a way as to be subject to federal control. Congress has the power to protect interstate commerce by all appropriate types of legislation, and the controlling question is the effect on interstate commerce, not the source of the interference. Although such legislation may result in the regulation of acts that are intrastate in character, Congress still has the power to regulate if the intrastate acts bear such a close and substantial relation to interstate commerce that control is appropriate for the protection of commerce. Congress is forbidden only from regulating acts that have a remote and indirect effect on interstate commerce. Here, even though the application of the National Labor Relations Act results in the regulation of labor practices at Jones & Laughlin's (D) manufacturing plants, the circumstances indicate the required substantial effect on interstate commerce. If production were interrupted at one of the plants due to a labor dispute, the extensive nationwide operations of Jones & Laughlin (D) indicate that there would necessarily be an immediate effect on interstate commerce. Therefore, the National Labor Relations Act as applied to the facts of this case is a proper exercise of Congress's power to regulate interstate commerce. Reversed.

DISSENT: (McReynolds, J.) The majority reasons that there is an effect on interstate commerce in the following manner: if the employer discharges a few employees for union activities, this will create discontent among the remaining employees which will lead to a strike which may result in reduced production which may decrease the volume of goods in interstate commerce. This is obviously only a remote and indirect effect on interstate commerce and not subject to federal regulation. Manufacturing and production are purely local activities, even if the raw materials come from another state and the finished goods are shipped across state lines.

ANALYSIS

With this case the Supreme Court retreated from its strict geographical definition of interstate commerce and the direct/indirect approach which it used in *Schecter*, 295 U.S. 495 (1935), and *Carter*, 298 U.S. 238 (1936). *Jones & Laughlin* states that under the Commerce Clause, Congress has the power to regulate any activity that has a significant effect on interstate commerce, regardless of whether that effect is direct or indirect. This new concept is often called the "affectation doctrine." Although the Court cited prior

Continued on next page.

cases in its opinion and said it was not creating new law, *Jones & Laughlin* is, in effect, a reversal of the *Schecter* line of cases. The Court now bases its opinions on a combination of the Commerce Clause and the Necessary and Proper Clause: the power to regulate interstate commerce extends to control over intrastate activities when necessary and appropriate to make regulation of interstate commerce effective.

∎▬∎

Quicknotes

INTRASTATE Any activity that takes place entirely within a single state and thus does not trigger regulation under the Commerce Clause.

∎▬∎

United States v. Darby

Federal government (P) v. Lumber manufacturer (D)

312 U.S. 100 (1941).

NATURE OF CASE: Appeal from denial to quash indictment for violation of Fair Labor Standards Act.

FACT SUMMARY: Darby (D) was a lumber manufacturer, some of whose goods were later shipped in interstate commerce. He was indicted for violation of the wage and hour provisions of the Fair Labor Standards Act, and defended on the ground that as an intrastate producer he was not subject to federal regulation.

🏛 RULE OF LAW
Congress has the power to regulate the hours and wages of workers who are engaged in the production of goods destined for interstate commerce and can prohibit the shipment in interstate commerce of goods manufactured in violation of the wage and hour provisions.

FACTS: Darby (D) was a manufacturer of finished lumber, and a large part of the lumber he produced was shipped in interstate commerce. The purpose of the Fair Labor Standards Act (the "Act") was to prevent the shipment in interstate commerce of certain products produced under substandard labor conditions. The Act set up minimum wages and maximum hours and punished the shipment in interstate commerce of goods produced in violation of the wage/hour requirements and also punished the employment of persons in violation of those requirements. Darby (D) was arrested for both shipment of goods in violation of the Act and employment of workers in violation of the Act. The trial court dismissed the indictment on the ground that the Act was an unconstitutional regulation of manufacturing within the states.

ISSUE: Does Congress have the power to prohibit shipment in interstate commerce of goods produced in violation of the wage/hour provisions of the Fair Labor Standards Act and the power to prohibit employment of workers involved in the production of goods for interstate shipment in violation of the wage/hour provisions of the Fair Labor Standards Act?

HOLDING AND DECISION: (Stone, J.) Yes. Congress has the power to regulate the hours and wages of workers who are engaged in the production of goods destined for interstate commerce and can prohibit the shipment in interstate commerce of goods manufactured in violation of the wage and hour provisions. Both prohibitions are a constitutional exercise of Congress's commerce power. Although manufacturing itself is not interstate commerce, the shipment of goods across state lines is interstate commerce and the prohibition of such shipment is a regulation of commerce. Congress has plenary power to exclude from interstate commerce any article which it determines to be injurious to public welfare, subject only to the specific prohibitions of the Constitution. In the Fair Labor Standards Act, Congress has determined that the shipment of goods produced under substandard labor conditions is injurious to commerce, and therefore has the power to prohibit the shipment of such goods, independent of the indirect effect of such prohibition on the states. The prohibition of employment of workers engaged in the production of goods for interstate commerce at substandard conditions is also sustainable, independent of the power to exclude the shipment of the goods so produced. The power over interstate commerce is not confined to the regulation of commerce among the states, but includes regulation of intrastate activities that so affect interstate commerce as to make regulation of them an appropriate means to the end of regulating interstate commerce. Here, Congress has determined that the employment of workers in substandard conditions is a form of unfair competition injurious to interstate commerce, since the goods so produced will be lower priced than the goods produced under adequate conditions. Such a form of competition would hasten the spread of substandard conditions and produce a dislocation of commerce and the destruction of many businesses. Since Congress has the power to suppress this form of unfair competition, and the Act is an appropriate means to that end, the wage/hour provisions are within Congress's power. It is irrelevant that only part of the goods produced will be shipped in interstate commerce; Congress has the power to regulate the whole factory even though only a part of the products will have an effect on interstate commerce. Reversed.

▶ ANALYSIS

Darby, like the preceding case of *Jones & Laughlin*, 301 U.S. 1 (1937), is an example of the application of the affectation doctrine. It had long been the law that Congress had the power to exclude from interstate commerce harmful objects or immoral activities, such as mismarked goods or lottery tickets. This case extends the power to exclude articles produced under conditions that Congress considered harmful to the national welfare. Even though production of lumber was an entirely intrastate activity, it was a part of an economic process that led to the eventual sale of lumber across state limits, affecting interstate commerce. The federal commerce power extends to purely intrastate transactions; the effect on commerce, not the

Continued on next page.

location of the regulated act, is the basis for the exercise of the federal power. This case overruled the earlier case of *Hammer v. Dagenhart*, 247 U.S. 251 (1918), which held unconstitutional an attempt by Congress to exclude articles made by child labor from interstate commerce.

Quicknotes

COMMERCE POWER The power delegated to Congress by the Constitution to regulate interstate commerce.

PLENARY Unlimited and open; as broad as a given situation may require.

Wickard v. Filburn

Department of Agriculture (P) v. Farmer (D)

317 U.S. 111 (1942).

NATURE OF CASE: Action to enjoin enforcement of penalty provisions of the Agricultural Adjustment Act.

FACT SUMMARY: Filburn (D) was ordered to pay a penalty imposed by the Agriculture Adjustment Act for producing wheat in excess of his assigned quota. He argued that the federal regulations could not be constitutionally applied to his crops because part of his crop was intended for his own consumption, not for interstate commerce.

🏛 RULE OF LAW
Farm production that is intended for consumption on the farm is subject to Congress's commerce power, since it may have a substantial economic effect on interstate commerce.

FACTS: The purpose of the Agriculture Adjustment Act (the "Act") was to control the volume of wheat moving in interstate commerce to avoid surpluses and shortages that would result in abnormally high or low prices and thereby obstruct commerce. Under the Act, the Secretary of Agriculture would set a national acreage allotment for wheat production, which would be divided into allotments for individual farms. Filburn (D) was the owner and operator of a small farm. In the past he had grown a small amount of wheat of which he sold part, fed part to poultry and livestock (some of the livestock were later sold), used part in making flour for home consumption, and kept the rest for seeding the next year. In 1940, his wheat production exceeded the maximum he was allowed under the Act and he was assessed a penalty for the excess. Filburn (D) refused to pay on the ground the Act was unconstitutional in that it attempted to regulate purely local production and consumption, which at most, had an indirect effect on interstate commerce. The Government (P) argued the Act regulated not production and consumption, but only marketing (which was defined in the Act to include the feeding of the wheat to livestock that was later sold), and even if interpreted to include production and consumption, it was a legitimate exercise of the Commerce Clause and the Necessary and Proper Clause.

ISSUE: Does Congress, under the Commerce Clause, have the power to regulate the production of wheat that is grown for home consumption purposes rather than for sale in interstate commerce?

HOLDING AND DECISION: (Jackson, J.) Yes. Farm production that is intended for consumption on the farm is subject to Congress's commerce power, since it may have a substantial economic effect on interstate commerce.

A local activity, such as production, may be reached under the Commerce Clause if it exerts a substantial economic effect on interstate commerce. The Act was enacted because of the problems of the wheat market: there had been a decrease in export in recent years, causing surpluses that in turn caused congestion in the market and lower prices. It has been repeatedly held that the commerce power of Congress includes the power to regulate prices and practices affecting prices. Wheat destined for home consumption has an effect on the interstate price of wheat and is, therefore, subject to regulation. As the market price of wheat climbs, farmers will sell more of their crop that was intended for home consumption on the market causing a decrease in prices. Even if the wheat is never sold, there still is a substantial effect on interstate commerce because it reduces demand for wheat; that wheat which Filburn (D) produces for his own use means he will buy less wheat on the market. Although the actual effect of Filburn's (D) overproduction will be small, the combination of all such producers does cause a substantial effect on commerce. Reversed.

▶ ANALYSIS

Wickard is yet another application of the "affectation doctrine." The Court focuses not on the nature of the regulated activity (e.g., whether it is local) but on the final economic effect of that activity. Here, although the effect of Filburn's (D) excess wheat production was insignificant on the national market, there still was some effect, at least in theory, so regulation was allowed. The Court in *Wickard* expressly rejected the old formulas for determining the extent of the commerce power such as direct/indirect and production/commerce.

■▬■

Quicknotes

LOCAL ACTIVITY An activity such as mining or manufacturing that has only an indirect effect in interstate commerce because it can be conducted entirely within the boundaries of the state.

NECESSARY AND PROPER CLAUSE, ART. I, § 8 OF THE CONSTITUTION Enables Congress to make all laws that may be "necessary and proper" to execute its other, enumerated powers.

■▬■

United States v. Lopez

Federal government (P) v. Student (D)

514 U.S. 549 (1995).

NATURE OF CASE: Appeal from order reversing federal firearms law violation conviction.

FACT SUMMARY: Lopez (D) was convicted under the 1990 federal Gun-Free School Zones Act, which prohibited guns near schools.

RULE OF LAW
The 1990 federal Gun-Free School Zones Act exceeded Congress's Commerce Clause regulatory powers.

FACTS: The 1990 federal Gun-Free School Zones Act made it a federal offense for a student to carry a gun onto campus. Lopez (D) was charged and convicted under the Act. On appeal, he contended that the Act was beyond Congress's powers under the Commerce Clause. The Fifth Circuit agreed and reversed. The Supreme Court granted review.

ISSUE: Did the 1990 Federal Gun-Free School Zones Act exceed Congress's Commerce Clause regulatory powers?

HOLDING AND DECISION: (Rehnquist, C.J.) Yes. The 1990 federal Gun-Free School Zones Act exceeded Congress's Commerce Clause regulatory powers. It must be remembered that the federal government is one of limited, enumerated powers. For Congress to legislate, it must do so under an express constitutional provision. Since the 1930s, the Commerce Clause has been the source of most of Congress's legislative power. However, this clause is not a general grant of police power. A law passed under this Clause must relate to: (1) a channel of interstate commerce; (2) an instrumentality of interstate commerce; or (3) an activity having a substantial effect on interstate commerce. In this case, the regulated activity, carrying a gun to school, has no such effect. It is a purely local matter. Granted, if one is willing to accept a lengthy series of interferences and assumptions, such an activity may affect interstate commerce. Any activity can do so. However, if the concept of limited federal government is to have any meaning, Congress's legislative power must be cut off somewhere. That somewhere is the point at which a regulated activity does not substantially affect interstate commerce, and that point has been passed here. Affirmed.

CONCURRENCE: (Kennedy, J.) It is only with great care that this Court should intervene in matters relating to the Commerce Clause, as it is a matter best left to the political sectors of government. However, when an exercise of power under the Clause unduly upsets the balance of power between the states and the national government, as does the law at issue here, it is proper for the Court to intervene.

CONCURRENCE: (Thomas, J.) The substantial effects test is a New Deal innovation that goes far beyond the original intent of the Framers, who had a much narrower view of what was regulatable commerce. In fact, it grants Congress something approaching a general police power, a result clearly at odds with the Tenth Amendment.

DISSENT: (Breyer, J.) The education of our youth has a major impact on the national economy and is a proper subject for Commerce Clause regulation. In determining whether a regulated activity has a significant impact on interstate commerce, it is necessary to consider not a single example of the regulated activity, but rather the cumulative effects of all similar instances of that conduct. Here, it is clear that the cumulative impact of the possession of weapons by students on campus will, over time, have a significant impact on the national economy.

DISSENT: (Souter, J.) The Court's approach today constitutes a step backward toward the excessive judicial activism that characterized judicial review of congressional enactments during the first third of this century.

DISSENT: (Stevens, J.) Congressional power to regulate commerce in firearms incorporates power to prohibit the possession of guns at any locations based on their potentially harmful use. It therefore follows that Congress also may prohibit their possession in specific markets. In this regard, the market for handgun possession by school-age children is substantial.

ANALYSIS

Since 1937, the scope of congressional regulatory power under the Commerce Clause has grown enormously. By the 1960s, Congress's power under the Clause had increased to a level approaching a general police power. The present case represents the first significant break in this pattern and may signal a states' rights trend.

■=■

Quicknotes

COMMERCE CLAUSE Article 1, section 8, clause 3 of the United States Constitution, granting Congress the power to regulate commerce with foreign countries and between the states.

Continued on next page.

ENUMERATED POWERS Specific powers mentioned in, and granted by, the U.S. Constitution, e.g., the taxing power.

POLICE POWER The power of a government to impose restrictions on the rights of private persons, as long as those restrictions are reasonably related to the promotion and protection of public health, morals, safety, and the general welfare.

REGULATORY POWER Power granted pursuant to statute granting a particular government agency or body the authority to govern a particular area.

United States v. Morrison

Federal government (P) v. Students (D)

529 U.S. 598 (2000).

NATURE OF CASE: Certiorari to review constitutionality of Violence Against Women Act.

FACT SUMMARY: [Brzonkala (P) brought suit against two football-playing male students (D) and Virginia Polytechnic University under the Violence Against Women Act.]

RULE OF LAW

Commerce Clause regulation of intrastate activity may only be upheld where the regulated activity is economic in nature.

FACTS: [Brzonkala (P), a student at Virginia Polytechnic Institute, complained that two male football-playing students raped her. Virginia Tech's Judicial Committee found insufficient evidence to punish one and then set aside the other's punishment. Brzonkala (P) then dropped out of the university and brought suit against the school and the male students (D) under the Violence Against Women Act, 42 U.S.C. § 13981, providing a federal cause of action of a crime of violence motivated by gender.]

ISSUE: May Commerce Clause regulation of intrastate activity only be upheld where the regulated activity is economic in nature?

HOLDING AND DECISION: (Rehnquist, C.J.) Yes. Commerce Clause regulation of intrastate activity may only be upheld where the regulated activity is economic in nature. The Court considered whether either the Commerce Clause or the Fourteenth Amendment authorized Congress to create this new cause of action. There are three main categories of activity Congress may regulate under its Commerce Clause power: (1) the use of channels of interstate commerce; (2) regulation or protection of the instrumentalities of interstate commerce or persons or things in interstate commerce, though the threat may come from intrastate activities; and (3) the power to regulate those activities having a substantial relation to interstate commerce. Brzonkala (P) argued that § 13981 falls under the third category. In *Lopez*, 514 U.S. 549 (1995), this Court concluded that those cases in which federal regulation of intrastate activity (based on the activity's substantial effects on interstate commerce) has been sustained have included some type of economic endeavor. Gender-motivated crimes of violence are not economic activities. While § 13981 is supported by numerous findings regarding the serious impact that gender-motivated violence has on victims and their families, the existence of congressional findings is not sufficient in itself to sustain the constitutionality of Commerce Clause legislation.

Whether a particular activity affects interstate commerce sufficiently to come under the constitutional power of Congress to regulate is a judicial question. The Court also rejects the argument that Congress may regulate non-economic, violent criminal conduct based solely on that conduct's aggregate effect on interstate commerce. The regulation and punishment of intrastate violence that is not directed at the instrumentalities of interstate commerce is reserved to the states. Brzonkala (P) also argued that § 5 of the Fourteenth Amendment authorized the statutory cause of action. This argument is based on the assertion that there is pervasive bias in various state justice systems against victims of gender-motivated violence. While sex discrimination is one of the objects of the Fourteenth Amendment, the amendment prohibits only state action.

CONCURRENCE: (Thomas, J.) The notion of a substantial effects test is inconsistent with Congress's powers and early Commerce Clause jurisprudence, perpetuating the federal government's (P) view that the Commerce Clause has no limits.

DISSENT: (Souter, J.) Congress has the power to legislate with regard to activities that in the aggregate have a substantial effect on interstate commerce. The fact of the substantial effect is a question for Congress in the first instance and not the courts. Here, Congress assembled a mountain of data demonstrating the effects of violence against women on interstate commerce.

DISSENT: (Breyer, J.) Congress, in enacting the statute, followed procedures that work to protect the federalism issues at stake. After considering alternatives, Congress developed the federal law with the intent of compensating for documented deficiencies in state legal systems, and tailored federal law to prevent its use in areas traditionally reserved to the states. This law represents the result of state and federal efforts to cooperate in order to resolve a national problem.

ANALYSIS

The primary issue here is that the federal government is seeking to regulate areas that have been traditionally regulated by the states alone. The majority concludes that the regulation and punishment of intrastate violence that is not directed to the instrumentalities of interstate commerce is the exclusive jurisdiction of local government. What the dissent argues here is that Congress in this case has amassed substantial findings to demonstrate that such

Continued on next page.

intrastate violence does have an effect on the instrumentalities of commerce.

■━━■

Quicknotes

COMMERCE CLAUSE Article 1, section 8, clause 3 of the United States Constitution, granting Congress the power to regulate commerce with foreign countries and between the states.

FOURTEENTH AMENDMENT Declares that no state shall make or enforce any law which shall abridge the privileges and immunities of citizens of the United States.

VIOLENCE AGAINST WOMEN ACT Legislation passed in 1994 that provides harsh federal penalties for sexual assaults commonly perpetrated against women, and authorizes funding for training, counseling and treatment programs for victims of these specific forms of violence, including battered women's shelters and projects serving victims of domestic violence and child abuse.

■━━■

Gonzales v. Raich

Attorney General (D) v. Medicinal user of marijuana (P)

545 U.S. 1 (2005).

NATURE OF CASE: Certiorari review of challenge to the validity of the federal Controlled Substances Act as applied to the medicinal use of marijuana.

FACT SUMMARY: Two sufferers of serious physical ailments sought to grow and use marijuana for medicinal purposes as permitted by California law.

🏛 RULE OF LAW
The Commerce Clause permits Congress to criminalize local cultivation and medicinal use of marijuana even if those uses otherwise comply with a state's laws.

FACTS: Congress enacted the Controlled Substances Act (CSA), which could be interpreted to proscribe possessing, obtaining, or manufacturing marijuana for personal medicinal use. Angel Raich (P) and Diane Monson (P), California residents who suffered from serious medical conditions, wanted to use marijuana for medicinal purposes, a use permitted by California law. Raich (P) and Monson (P) sued the Government (D) for injunctive and declaratory relief to prohibit the CSA from being enforced against them.

ISSUE: Does the Commerce Clause permit Congress to criminalize local cultivation and medicinal use of marijuana even if those uses otherwise comply with a state's laws?

HOLDING AND DECISION: (Stevens, J.) Yes. The Commerce Clause permits Congress to criminalize local cultivation and medicinal use of marijuana even if those uses otherwise comply with a state's laws. Congress may regulate local economic activities that substantially affect interstate commerce. As applied to Angel Raich (P) and Diane Monson (P), the CSA would comply with that standard: the statute would regulate home-grown, home-used marijuana, an activity that would substantially affect the nationwide market for marijuana. The decisions in *United States v. Morrison*, 529 U.S. 598 (2000), and *Lopez v. United States*, 514 U.S. 549 (1995), are inapposite because those cases decided challenges to entire statutes, and they involved no economic activity; the proposed use here seeks only to invalidate local enforcement of the CSA for a very specific purpose, and the use is also an economic activity. Vacated and remanded.

CONCURRENCE: (Scalia, J.) By itself the Commerce Clause is not sufficient to support the CSA's application against Raich (P) and Monson (P). The CSA has the essential additional support, however, in the Necessary and Proper Clause, which permits Congress to regulate local, noneconomic activity if the regulation is necessary to effectuate valid legislation enacted pursuant

to the Commerce Clause. Here, congressional regulation of Raich's (P) and Monson's (P) proposed use of marijuana should be permitted as a necessary part of the CSA's overall regulatory scheme.

DISSENT: (O'Connor, J.) The Court today denies California citizens the ability to serve as a national laboratory on the question of medicinal use of marijuana. Contrary to precedent, the majority has upheld federal law under the Commerce Clause without any proof that the proposed use of marijuana constitutes economic activity or that the use substantially affects interstate commerce even if it is economic activity. Today's definition of "economic activity" is effectively unlimited because the marijuana at issue here was never remotely involved in interstate commerce. Moreover, there was no evidence that in-home medicinal use of marijuana makes up a large enough proportion of the national market for marijuana to be detected at all, let alone to be seen as "substantially affecting" the national market. Regardless of how this Court might assess the wisdom of California's laws, that state's citizens should be permitted to conduct the local experiment that they chose.

DISSENT: (Thomas, J.) This decision means that Congress can regulate almost anything under the Commerce Clause. Today's decision is wrong because merely possessing an item for personal use is not economic activity within the meaning of the Commerce Clause. The CSA fares no better under the Necessary and Proper Clause because regulating these proposed uses is not "necessary" based on some failure of California's law. The regulation also is not "proper" because it would undermine federalism and states' rights.

▶ ANALYSIS

The majority in *Raich* uses contemporary Commerce Clause analysis, as it must do, in distinguishing *Morrison* and *Lopez*. By grounding this decision in *Wickard v. Filburn*, 317 U.S. 111 (1942), though, the *Raich* majority seems to have restored much of the gigantic breadth of the Commerce Clause power that existed before *Lopez* was handed down in 1995.

■=■

Quicknotes

INJUNCTIVE RELIEF A court order issued as a remedy, requiring a person to do, or prohibiting that person from doing, a specific act.

■=■

National Federation of Independent Business v. Sebelius

Business group (P) v. Government official (D)

132 S. Ct. 2566 (2012).

NATURE OF CASE: Appeal from judgment in action challenging the constitutionality of the "individual mandate" provision of the 2010 Patient Protection and Affordable Care Act. [The procedural posture of the case is not presented in the casebook extract.]

FACT SUMMARY: A coalition of plaintiffs (P) challenged the constitutionality of the "individual mandate" provision of the 2010 Patient Protection and Affordable Care Act (Act). The Government (D) contended that the individual mandate was a valid exercise of Congress's authority under the Commerce Clause and the Necessary and Proper Clause.

RULE OF LAW

(1) The "individual mandate" provision of the Patient Protection and Affordable Care Act, which requires individuals to purchase health care insurance under certain circumstances, is not a valid exercise of Congress's power under the Commerce Clause.

(2) The "individual mandate" provision of the Patient Protection and Affordable Care Act, which requires individuals to purchase health care insurance under certain circumstances, is not a valid exercise of Congress's power under the Necessary and Proper Clause.

FACTS: In 2010, Congress enacted the Patient Protection and Affordable Care Act (the "Act") in order to increase the number of Americans covered by health insurance and decrease the cost of health care. A key provision of the Act is the individual mandate, which requires most Americans to maintain "minimum essential" health insurance coverage. For individuals who are not exempt, and who do not receive health insurance through an employer or government program, the means of satisfying the requirement is to purchase insurance from a private company. Those who do not comply with the mandate must make a "shared responsibility payment" to the federal government based on income and subject to a statutory cap. A coalition of plaintiffs (P) challenged the individual mandate as unconstitutional. The Government (D) contended the individual mandate was a valid exercise of Congress's authority under the Commerce Clause and the Necessary and Proper Clause. The Government (D) asserted the health care market is characterized by a significant cost-shifting problem. This problem arises because, according to the Government (D), everyone will eventually need health care at a time and to an extent they cannot predict, but if they do not have insurance, they often will

not be able to pay for it. Because state and federal laws nonetheless require hospitals to provide a certain degree of care to individuals without regard to their ability to pay, hospitals end up receiving compensation for only a portion of the services they provide. To recoup the losses, hospitals pass on the cost to insurers through higher rates, and insurers, in turn, pass on the cost to policy holders in the form of higher premiums. Congress estimated that the cost of uncompensated care raises family health insurance premiums, on average, by over $1,000 per year. To address this problem, at least in part, Congress included "guaranteed-issue" and "community-rating" provisions in the Act. These provisions together prohibit insurance companies from denying coverage to those with preexisting conditions or charging unhealthy individuals higher premiums than healthy individuals. The guaranteed-issue and community-rating reforms do not, however, address the issue of healthy individuals who choose not to purchase insurance to cover potential health care needs. In fact, the reforms sharply exacerbate that problem, by providing an incentive for individuals to delay purchasing health insurance until they become sick, relying on the promise of guaranteed and affordable coverage. The reforms also threaten to impose massive new costs on insurers, who are required to accept unhealthy individuals but prohibited from charging them rates necessary to pay for their coverage. This will lead insurers to significantly increase premiums on everyone. The individual mandate was Congress's solution to these problems. By requiring that individuals purchase health insurance, the mandate prevents cost-shifting by those who would otherwise go without it. In addition, the mandate forces into the insurance risk pool more healthy individuals, whose premiums on average will be higher than their health care expenses. This allows insurers to subsidize the costs of covering the unhealthy individuals the reforms require them to accept. The Government (D) contended the individual mandate is within Congress's power because the failure to purchase insurance "has a substantial and deleterious effect on interstate commerce" by creating the cost-shifting problem. The Government (D) also contended the mandate is an "integral part of a comprehensive scheme of economic regulation"—the guaranteed-issue and community-rating insurance reforms—so Congress has the authority to enact the individual mandate under the Necessary and Proper Clause. The Supreme Court granted certiorari. [The procedural posture of the case is not presented in the casebook extract.]

Continued on next page.

ISSUE:

(1) Is the "individual mandate" provision of the Patient Protection and Affordable Care Act, which requires individuals to purchase health care insurance under certain circumstances, a valid exercise of Congress's power under the Commerce Clause?

(2) Is the "individual mandate" provision of the Patient Protection and Affordable Care Act, which requires individuals to purchase health care insurance under certain circumstances, a valid exercise of Congress's power under the Necessary and Proper Clause?

HOLDING AND DECISION: (Roberts, C.J.)

(1) No. The "individual mandate" provision of the Patient Protection and Affordable Care Act, which requires individuals to purchase health care insurance under certain circumstances, is not a valid exercise of Congress's power under the Commerce Clause. Congress has never attempted to rely on the commerce power to compel individuals not engaged in commerce to purchase an unwanted product—and with good reason. Congress is empowered to regulate commerce, which presupposes the existence of commercial activity to be regulated. If the power to "regulate" something included the power to create it, many of the provisions in the Constitution would be superfluous. The Constitution's language supports such a conclusion, as does the Court's precedent, which uniformly describes the commerce power as reaching "activity." The individual mandate, however, does not regulate existing commercial activity. It instead compels individuals to become active in commerce by purchasing a product, on the ground their failure to do so affects interstate commerce. Construing the Commerce Clause to permit Congress to regulate individuals precisely because they are doing nothing would open a new and potentially vast domain to congressional authority, as the Government's (D) logic would justify a mandatory purchase to solve almost any problem. People, for reasons of their own, often fail to do things that would be good for them or good for society. Those failures—joined with the similar failures of others—can readily have a substantial effect on interstate commerce. Under the Government's (D) logic, that authorizes Congress to use its commerce power to compel citizens to act as the Government (D) would have them act. Congress already possesses expansive power to regulate what people do. Upholding the Act under the Commerce Clause would give Congress the same license to regulate what people do not do. The Framers knew the difference between doing something and doing nothing. They gave Congress the power to regulate commerce, not to compel it. Ignoring that distinction would undermine the principle the federal government is a government of limited and enumerated powers. Contrary to the Government's (D) contention, the uninsured to be affected by the individual are not "active in the market

for health care." In fact, the individual mandate's regulation of the uninsured as a class is particularly divorced from any link to existing commercial activity. The mandate primarily affects healthy, often young adults who are less likely to need significant health care and have other priorities for spending their money. It is precisely because these individuals, as an actuarial class, incur relatively low health care costs that the mandate helps counter the effect of forcing insurance companies to cover others who impose greater costs than their premiums are allowed to reflect. If the individual mandate is targeted at a class, it is a class whose commercial inactivity rather than activity is its defining feature. The Commerce Clause is not a general license to regulate an individual from cradle to grave, simply because he will predictably engage in particular transactions. Any police power to regulate individuals as such, as opposed to their activities, remains vested in the States. The individual mandate thus cannot be sustained under Congress's power to "regulate Commerce."

(2) No. The "individual mandate" provision of the Patient Protection and Affordable Care Act, which requires individuals to purchase health care insurance under certain circumstances, is not a valid exercise of Congress's power under the Necessary and Proper Clause. Each of this Court's prior cases upholding laws under that Clause involved exercises of authority derivative of, and in service to, a granted power. The individual mandate, by contrast, vests Congress with the extraordinary ability to create the necessary predicate to the exercise of an enumerated power and draw within its regulatory scope those who would otherwise be outside of it. This is in no way an authority that is "narrow in scope," or "incidental" to the exercise of the commerce power, as required by precedent. Rather, the Government's (D) conception of the Necessary and Proper Clause would work a substantial expansion of federal authority. No longer would Congress be limited to regulating under the Commerce Clause those who by some preexisting activity bring themselves within the sphere of federal regulation. Instead, Congress could reach beyond the natural limit of its authority and draw within its regulatory scope those who otherwise would be outside of it. Thus, even if the individual mandate is "necessary" to the Act's other reforms, such an expansion of federal power is not a "proper" means for making those reforms effective. Accordingly, the individual mandate cannot be upheld as a "necessary and proper" component of the insurance reforms. Affirmed in part and reversed in part. [The procedural posture of the case is not presented in the casebook extract.]

DISSENT: (Scalia, J.)

It is manifestly clear there are structural limitations on the commerce power and on what

Continued on next page.

Congress can prescribe with respect to private conduct, and upon what it can impose upon the states. To say Congress's commerce power reaches inactivity would be to permit Congress to regulate virtually every aspect of human activity and inactivity. If the individual mandate regulates anything it is the failure to maintain minimum essential coverage. That failure is abstention from commerce, not commerce. One does not regulate commerce that does not exist by compelling its existence. The meaning of "regulate" at the time the Constitution was written was "[t]o adjust by rule, method or established mode." It can mean to direct the manner of something but it has never been understood to mean to direct that something come into being. When Congress provides citizens must buy an insurance contract, it goes beyond "adjust[ing] by rule or method," or "direct[ing] according to rule;" it directs the creation of commerce. The fact the proposed regulations will impose great costs on the health insurance industry does not justify pressing into service healthy individuals who could be but are not customers of the relevant industry, to offset the undesirable consequences of the regulation. Congress's desire to force these individuals to purchase insurance is motivated by the fact they are further removed from the market than unhealthy individuals with preexisting conditions, because they are less likely to need extensive care in the near future. If Congress can reach out and command even those furthest removed from an interstate market to participate in the market, then the Commerce Clause becomes a font of unlimited power. Precedent makes clear the Commerce Clause, even when supplemented by the Necessary and Proper Clause, is not carte blanche for doing whatever will help achieve the ends Congress seeks by the regulation of commerce. The precedent on which the Government (D) relies to support the individual mandate is also distinguishable, as that precedent did not represent the expansion of the federal power to direct into a broad new field. The mandating of economic activity does, and since it is a field so limitless that it converts the Commerce Clause into a general authority to direct the economy, that mandating is inconsistent with the letter and spirit of the Constitution. Moreover, in that precedent, the prohibition was the only practicable way of achieving the desired outcome. Here, in contrast, there are many ways other than the individual mandate by which the regulatory scheme's goals of reducing insurance premiums and ensuring the profitability of insurers could be achieved. For example, those who did not purchase insurance could be subjected to a surcharge when they do enter the health insurance system, or they could be denied a full income tax credit given to those who do purchase the insurance. Also, the Government's (D) argument the individual mandate regulates activities having a substantial relation to interstate commerce must be rejected. The Government (D) argues the provision directs the manner in which individuals purchase health care services and related goods, but the primary problem with this argument is it does not apply only to persons who purchase all, or most, or even any, of the health care services or goods the mandated insurance covers. Those persons—generally healthy and young—are not participants in the health care market the individual mandate purports to regulate. Because the decision to forgo participation in an interstate market is not itself commercial activity within Congress's power to regulate, the individual mandate cannot be justified by claiming it regulates such decisions because they have a substantial and deleterious effect on interstate commerce. If the Government (D) is permitted to regulate everyone who may at some point engage in commerce, there no longer will be any limits on the Government's (D) powers. Although Justice Ginsburg is correct in pointing out that Congress needs only a rational basis for concluding regulated activity substantially affects interstate commerce, she disregards the premise this test contains, which is that what is regulated is activity, not merely the failure to engage in commerce. If all inactivity affecting commerce is commerce, commerce is everything. The constitutional order is threatened by such an expansive reading of the commerce power, by which all private conduct (including failure to act) becomes subject to federal control, effectively destroying the Constitution's division of governmental powers. Contrary to Justice Ginsburg's treatment of the Constitution as an enumeration of problems Congress can address, the Constitution is not an enumeration of federally soluble problems, but federally available powers. Accordingly, the individual mandate is unconstitutional, and because it is not severable from the Act's other provisions, the Act in its entirety must be struck down.

CONCURRENCE AND DISSENT: (Ginsburg, J.) Beyond question, Congress could have provided a single-payer federal health care scheme similar to Social Security, whereby the federal government would be the only health care insurer. However, it chose to preserve a central role for private insurers and state governments. According to the majority opinion on this issue, authored by the Chief Justice, the Commerce Clause does not permit that preservation. This rigid reading of the Clause makes scant sense and is stunningly retrogressive. The problem the Act seeks to remedy with the individual mandate is that the uninsured heavily burden the national health-care market. Those with health insurance subsidize the medical care of those without it, or, in the words of economists, the uninsured "free ride" on those who pay for health insurance. States cannot resolve the problem of the uninsured on their own. A state offering universal health care would place itself in a position of economic disadvantage as compared with neighbors or competitors, because it would have to raise taxes, private health-insurance companies would have to increase premiums, and higher taxes and increased insurance costs would, in turn, encourage businesses and healthy individuals to leave the state. Because

Continued on next page.

the states cannot resolve this problem on their own, Congress stepped in with the Act to provide a national solution. However, Congress comprehended guaranteed-issue and community-rating laws alone will not work. When insurance companies are required to insure the sick at affordable prices, individuals can wait until they become ill to buy insurance. The result is those in need of immediate medical care—i.e., those who cost insurers the most—become the insurance companies' main customers. This "adverse selection" problem leaves insurers with two choices: They can either raise premiums dramatically to cover their ever-increasing costs or they can exit the market. This, in fact, is what happened in those states that implemented guaranteed-issue and community-rating laws without requiring universal acquisition of insurance coverage, and the results were disastrous. In the one state—Massachusetts—that succeeded, almost all residents were required to obtain a minimum level of health insurance. Congress passed the minimum coverage provision as a key component of the Act to address an economic and social problem that has plagued the country for decades: the large number of U.S. residents who are unable or unwilling to obtain health insurance. Congress had the prerogative to make this policy decision, which passes muster under the Commerce Clause and the Necessary and Proper Clause. As to the Commerce Clause, precedent holds Congress's authority under the Commerce Clause is dependent upon "practical" considerations, including "actual experience," and Congress is afforded the leeway "to undertake to solve national problems directly and realistically." When appraising Congress's social and economic legislation, the Court asks only (1) whether Congress had a "rational basis" for concluding the regulated activity substantially affects interstate commerce, and (2) whether there is a "reasonable connection between the regulatory means selected and the asserted ends." In answering these questions, it is presumed the statute under review is constitutional, and the Court may strike it down only on a "plain showing" Congress acted irrationally. Here, Congress had a rational basis for concluding the uninsured, as a class, substantially affect interstate commerce. The individual mandate, furthermore, bears a "reasonable connection" to Congress's goal of protecting the health-care market from the disruption caused by individuals who fail to obtain insurance. By requiring those who do not carry insurance to pay a toll, the minimum coverage provision gives individuals a strong incentive to insure. This incentive, Congress had good reason to believe, would reduce the number of uninsured and, correspondingly, mitigate the adverse impact the uninsured have on the national health-care market. Further, Congress also acted reasonably in requiring uninsured individuals, whether sick or healthy, either to obtain insurance or to pay the specified penalty. Because it is not disputed all U.S. residents participate in the market for health services over the course of their lives, contrary to the Chief Justice's position, Congress is not compelling individuals not engaged in commerce to purchase an unwanted product, even

assuming the Chief Justice is correct that it is beyond Congress's power to compel individuals that way. Also contrary to the Chief Justice's position, the facts show an uninsured's consumption of health care is thus quite proximate: It is virtually certain to occur in the next five years and more likely than not to occur this year. It is Congress's role, not the Court's, to delineate the boundaries of the market Congress seeks to regulate. The Chief Justice defines the health-care market as including only those transactions that will occur either in the next instant or within some (unspecified) proximity to the next instant. However, Congress could reasonably have viewed the market from a long-term perspective, encompassing all transactions virtually certain to occur over the next decade, not just those occurring here and now. Moreover, precedent directs that Congress may dictate the conduct of an individual today because of prophesied future activity. Congress's actions in this case are rational, where the future activity (the consumption of medical care) is certain to occur, the sole uncertainty being the time the activity will take place. Thus, upholding the individual mandate on the ground that all are participants or will be participants in the health-care market does not imply that Congress may use its commerce power to mandate individuals to buy products and services other than the ones they do or will buy at some point. Further, it is inaccurate to say, as does the Chief Justice, that the individual mandate compels individuals to purchase an unwanted product, given that virtually everyone will at some point or another seek medical care. In requiring individuals to obtain health insurance, Congress is therefore not mandating the purchase of a discrete, unwanted product. Rather, Congress is merely defining the terms on which individuals pay for an interstate good they consume. Additionally, contrary to the Chief Justice's view, the individual mandate is not an effort to have the young and healthy subsidize the health care of the unhealthy or infirm. Under the current health-care system, healthy persons who lack insurance receive a benefit for which they do not pay: They are assured that, if they need it, emergency medical care will be available, although they cannot afford it. Those who have insurance bear the cost of this guarantee. By requiring the healthy uninsured to obtain insurance or pay a penalty structured as a tax, the minimum coverage provision ends the free ride these individuals currently enjoy. Viewed over a lifespan, the costs and benefits may even out, and everyone will be covered for catastrophic loss, even if not everyone will need to use that coverage; that is the nature of insurance. The Constitution's language and precedent also do not support the Chief Justice's interpretation that by enacting the individual mandate, Congress is not regulating something already in existence, but rather is bringing the subject of the regulation into existence. Requiring individuals to obtain insurance unquestionably regulates the interstate health-

Continued on next page.

insurance and health-care markets, both of them in existence well before the Act's enactment. Thus, the "something to be regulated" was surely there when Congress created the minimum coverage provision. A long line of precedent also rejects the Chief Justice's formalistic distinction between activity and inactivity as a measure of the subject of Congress's commerce power. The fear the commerce power would be unlimited unless limited to regulating active participants in a commercial market is unfounded. Given the unique attributes of the health care market, upholding the individual mandate would not give Congress carte blanche to enact any and all purchase mandates. Nor would the commerce power be unbridled, absent an "activity" limitation, as Congress would remain unable to regulate noneconomic conduct that has only an attenuated effect on interstate commerce and is traditionally left to state law. The choice to self-insure, however, does not have an attenuated effect on commerce, but is an economic act with the requisite connection to interstate commerce. Also, the democratic process serves as another check on Congress's purchase-mandating behavior. Finally, merely because the individual mandate is a novelty is not a reason to override it. To the contrary, and as the Court has recognized for decades, Congress must be permitted to adapt to the changing "economic and financial realities."

The individual mandate is also a valid exercise of Congress's commerce power under the Necessary and Proper Clause. That Clause empowers Congress to enact laws in effectuation of its commerce power that are not within its authority to enact in isolation. It is undisputed the Congress has the power to eliminate the insurance industry's practice of charging higher prices or denying coverage to individuals with preexisting medical conditions. Without the individual mandate, however, this goal would be undercut and would lead to an adverse-selection death-spiral in the health-insurance market. Therefore, the individual mandate is an essential part of a larger regulation of economic activity that may be upheld under the Necessary and Proper Clause. Additionally, it is spurious to suggest, as does the Chief Justice, that the individual mandate improperly intrudes on "essential attributes of state sovereignty." First, the Act does not operate in an area such as criminal law enforcement or education where states historically have been sovereign. Second, and more importantly, the minimum coverage provision, along with the Act's other provisions, addresses the very sort of interstate problem that made the commerce power essential in our federal system. Instead of intruding on state's rights, the Act is an attempt to solve a problem the states cannot solve separately, on their own; the Act serves the general welfare of the people of the United States while retaining a prominent role for the states.

New Deal cases, the Court attempted to cabin Congress's Commerce Clause authority by distinguishing "commerce" from activity once conceived to be noncommercial, notably, "production," "mining," and "manufacturing." The Court also sought to distinguish activities having a "direct" effect on interstate commerce, and for that reason, subject to federal regulation, from those having only an "indirect" effect, and therefore not amenable to federal control. These line-drawing exercises were untenable, and the Court long ago abandoned them. Accordingly, Justice Ginsburg opines the Chief Justice has failed to learn from history and instead "plows ahead" with his formalistic distinction between those who are "active in commerce," and those who are not. She also, therefore, warns hindering Congress's ability to address the health care problem is shortsighted, and predicts that if history is any guide, the Court's constriction of the Commerce Clause will not endure.

■■■

Quicknotes

COMMERCE CLAUSE Article 1, section 8, clause 3 of the Constitution, granting Congress the power to regulate commerce with foreign countries and among the states.

NECESSARY AND PROPER CLAUSE, ART. I, § 8 OF THE CONSTITUTION Enables Congress to make all laws that may be "necessary and proper" to execute its other, enumerated powers.

■■■

▶ **ANALYSIS**

The Court's former endeavors to impose categorical limits on the commerce power did not fare well. In several pre-

New York v. United States

State (P) v. Federal government (D)

505 U.S. 144 (1992).

NATURE OF CASE: Appeal of dismissal of suit for declaratory judgment.

FACT SUMMARY: New York (P) sought a declaration that the Low-Level Radioactive Waste Policy Amendments Act (1985 Act) was unconstitutional.

🏛 RULE OF LAW
The federal government may not order a state government to enact particular legislation.

FACTS: Three states had disposal sites for radioactive waste. After study and negotiation, the National Governors' Association (NGA) devised a plan that became the 1985 Act. The 1985 Act set deadlines for every state to join a regional waste compact, develop instate disposal, or find another way to dispose of its own waste. The 1985 Act assured the sited states they would not have the entire nation's waste burden, and gave the other 47 states seven more years of access to active sites. The 1985 Act provided three incentives for state compliance: (1) Congress authorized sited states to impose a surcharge, part of which would go into federal escrow, with funds to be returned to complying states; (2) Congress empowered sited states to deny access to states not in compliance; and (3) any state not in compliance by 1992 had to either take title to all waste generated in their state or else become liable to instate waste generators for all damages. As of 1990 New York (P) had not joined a regional waste compact. Unable to settle on an instate site, New York (P) sought to invalidate the 1985 Act as violative of state sovereignty principles of the Tenth Amendment. The sited states intervened as defendants. The district court dismissed, the court of appeals affirmed, and New York (P) appealed.

ISSUE: May the federal government order a state government to enact particular legislation?

HOLDING AND DECISION: (O'Connor, J.) No. The federal government may not order a state government to enact particular legislation. The federal government may provide incentives for states to regulate in a certain way by tying funding to acceptance of a federal plan or by giving states a choice between enacting a federal plan or having state law preempted by federal law. Here, the first incentive is a congressional exercise of Commerce Clause power (allowing sited states to impose a surcharge on interstate commerce and imposing a federal tax on that surcharge) combined with an exercise of Spending Clause power (making return of surcharges contingent on compliance with the federal plan). The second incentive is a routine exercise of the commerce power. If a state chooses not to

follow the federal plan, generators of waste within that state become subject to federal regulation authorizing states with waste sites to deny access. The burden would fall on the waste generators, not on the state, and the state would not be forced to spend funds or accede to federal direction. The third incentive, however, crossed the line to coercion. Whether a state "chooses" to take title to waste or to accept liability for disposal, the burden of not enacting the federal plan falls on the state. The strength of the federal interest is irrelevant. Federal courts may issue directives to state officials, but the Constitution expressly grants that authority. Such authority is outside Congress's enumerated powers and, for that reason, also infringes on state sovereignty reserved by the Tenth Amendment. While the 1985 Act was a creation of and compromise among the states, the states may not constitutionally consent to give up their sovereignty. Affirmed as to the first two incentives, reversed as to the third.

DISSENT: (White, J.) The Acts were the product of cooperative federalism. The states bargained among themselves to solve an imminent crisis and achieve compromises for Congress to sanction. New York (P) reaped the benefits of the 1985 Act, an agreement which it helped formulate, and should not be able to sue now. The majority wrongly finds that states cannot consent to relinquish some sovereignty. Tenth Amendment restrictions on the commerce power are procedural limits, designed to prevent federal destruction of state governments, not to protect substantive areas of state autonomy.

CONCURRENCE AND DISSENT: (Stevens, J.) The notion that Congress may not order states to implement federal legislation is incorrect and unsound. The federal government regulates state railroads, schools, prisons, and elections, and in time of war, Congress undoubtedly could command states to supply soldiers.

▶ ANALYSIS

Under the Articles of Confederation, the federal government could act only by ordering states to enact legislation. The Framers decided that the federal government needed power to regulate citizens directly and so drafted the Constitution. The Court interpreted the Framers' decision as a rejection of federal power to order states to enact legislation.

■=■

Continued on next page.

Quicknotes

ENUMERATED POWERS Specific powers mentioned in, and granted by, the U.S. Constitution, e.g., the taxing power.

STATE SOVEREIGNTY The absolute power of self-government possessed by a state.

■━━■

CHAPTER 4

The National Taxing and Spending Powers and Their Federalism-Based Limits

Quick Reference Rules of Law

Child Labor Tax Case (Bailey v. Drexel Furniture Co.)

Collector of internal revenue (D) v. Furniture company (P)

259 U.S. 20 (1922).

NATURE OF CASE: Certiorari review of the constitutionality of the Child Labor Tax Law.

FACT SUMMARY: The Child Labor Tax Law imposes a tax upon persons employing children under certain ages.

🏛 RULE OF LAW
A law passed by Congress under the pretext of executing its powers, but which is for the accomplishment of objects not within congressional power, is unconstitutional.

FACTS: The Child Labor Act provides that any company employing children in violation of its provisions shall pay a tax equal to 10 percent of its net profits. The Act provides that mines and quarries shall not employ children under the age of 16; mills, canneries, and factories shall not employ children under the age of 14; and children under the age of 16 shall not work more than eight hours a day, more than six days a week, or before 6 a.m. or after 7 p.m. Anyone employing children believing them to be of the proper age is relieved of liability. Both the Internal Revenue Service (IRS) and the Labor Department are given the authority to enter and inspect any mine, quarry, mill, cannery, or factory. [Drexel Furniture Co. (P) paid an approximately $6000 tax under protest, and after rejection of its claim for a refund, brought this suit.]

ISSUE: Is a law passed by Congress under the pretext of executing its powers, but which is for the accomplishment of objects not within congressional power constitutional?

HOLDING AND DECISION: (Taft, C.J.) No. A law passed by Congress under the pretext of executing its powers, but which is for the accomplishment of objects not within congressional power, is unconstitutional. The principle announced by Marshall in *McCulloch v. Maryland*, 17 U.S. 316 (1819), is applicable here. "Should Congress, under the pretext of executing its powers, pass laws for the accomplishment of objects not entrusted to the government, it would be the painful duty of this tribunal . . . to say that such an act was not the law of the land." The Child Labor Tax Law concerns the regulation of the employment of children in the states, an exclusively state function under the Constitution. It provides a heavy extraction for a departure from a detailed and specified course of conduct in business. The amount of the tax is not to be proportioned to the degree or the frequency of the violation. Moreover, only employers who knew that the children were underage will be taxed. Scienter is associated with penalties, not taxes. Further, factories, etc., are to be subject to inspection by the Secretary of Labor as well as the IRS, the department normally charged with tax collection. In light of these features, "A court must be blind not to see that the so-called tax is imposed to stop the employment of children within the age limits prescribed." It is true that taxes imposed with the primary motive of obtaining revenue may have an incidental motive of discouraging the taxed activity. These taxes do not lose their character as taxes because of the incidental motives. But there is a point in the extension of the penalizing features of the tax when it loses its character as a tax and becomes a mere penalty with the characteristics of regulation and punishment. Such is the case with the Child Labor Tax Law, and for these reasons it is invalid. Affirmed.

▎*ANALYSIS*

The taxing and spending powers have close functional and doctrinal ties to the commerce power, since the manner in which taxes are imposed can have significant regulatory impacts. As with commerce laws, taxing measures have been used to deal with "police" as well as economic problems. The Court in *Drexel* noted the clear analogy between that case and *Hammer*, 247 U.S. 251 (1918), the child labor case. Regulations through taxing have been resorted to when the need for legislation seemed great and the direct regulatory authority through the Commerce Clause was "under constitutional clouds," such as in the cases of child labor and of New Deal legislation in the 1930s.

■▬■

Quicknotes

SCIENTER Knowledge of certain facts; often refers to "guilty knowledge," which implicates liability.

TAXING POWER The authority delegated to Congress by the Constitution to impose taxes.

■▬■

National Federation of Independent Business v. Sebelius

Business group (P) v. Government official (D)

132 S. Ct. 2566 (2012).

NATURE OF CASE: Appeal from judgment in action challenging the constitutionality of the "individual mandate" provision of the 2010 Patient Protection and Affordable Care Act. [The procedural posture of the case is not presented in the casebook extract.]

FACT SUMMARY: A coalition of plaintiffs (P) challenged the constitutionality of the "individual mandate" provision of the 2010 Patient Protection and Affordable Care Act (Act). The Government (D) contended, inter alia, that the individual mandate was a valid exercise of Congress's taxing power, since it provided that individuals who did not purchase health care insurance would pay a penalty in the form of a tax.

🏛 RULE OF LAW
The "individual mandate" provision of the Patient Protection and Affordable Care Act, which requires that individuals who do not purchase health care insurance under certain circumstances must pay a penalty in the form of a tax, is a valid exercise of Congress's taxing power.

FACTS: In 2010, Congress enacted the Patient Protection and Affordable Care Act (the "Act") in order to increase the number of Americans covered by health insurance and decrease the cost of health care. A key provision of the Act is the individual mandate, which requires most Americans to maintain "minimum essential" health insurance coverage. For individuals who are not exempt, and who do not receive health insurance through an employer or government program, the means of satisfying the requirement is to purchase insurance from a private company. Those who do not comply with the mandate must make a "shared responsibility payment" to the Internal Revenue Service (IRS) based on factors such as income, number of dependents, and joint filing status, and is subject to a statutory cap. A coalition of plaintiffs (P) challenged the individual mandate as unconstitutional. The Government (D) contended, inter alia, the individual mandate was a valid exercise of Congress's taxing power, since the Act provided the penalty would be paid to the IRS with an individual's taxes, and "shall be assessed and collected in the same manner" as tax penalties. The imposition of the individual mandate was expected to raise $4 billion per year by its third year. The Supreme Court granted certiorari. [The procedural posture of the case is not presented in the casebook extract.]

ISSUE: Is the "individual mandate" provision of the Patient Protection and Affordable Care Act, which requires that individuals who do not purchase health care insurance under certain circumstances must pay a penalty in the form of a tax, a valid exercise of Congress's taxing power?

HOLDING AND DECISION: (Roberts, C.J.) Yes. The "individual mandate" provision of the Patient Protection and Affordable Care Act, which requires that individuals who do not purchase health care insurance under certain circumstances must pay a penalty in the form of a tax, is a valid exercise of Congress's taxing power. The individual mandate must be construed as imposing a tax on those who do not have health insurance, if such a construction is reasonable. The most straightforward reading of the individual mandate is it commands individuals to purchase insurance. However, the Government's (D) alternative argument is that the mandate may be upheld as within Congress's power to "lay and collect Taxes." In pressing its taxing power argument, the Government (D) asks the Court to view the mandate as imposing a tax on those who do not buy a health insurance product. Granting the Act the full measure of deference owed to federal statutes, it can be so read, for the following reasons. First, the exaction imposed by the Act has many of the features of a tax, and is functionally like a tax, and it has the essential feature of a tax insofar as it raises revenue for the Government (D). Taking such a functional approach is confirmed by precedent. Second, taking such an approach, the exaction functions more like a tax than a penalty. For most Americans, the amount due will be far less than the price of insurance, and, by statute, it can never be more. Also, the individual mandate contains no scienter requirement. Further, the payment is collected solely by the IRS through the normal means of taxation—except the IRS is not allowed to use those means most suggestive of a punitive sanction, such as criminal prosecution. For these reasons, the exaction may be viewed as a tax and not as a penalty. Additionally, merely because the individual mandate is designed to regulate individual conduct and encourage the purchasing of health insurance does not mean it cannot be a valid exercise of the taxing power. To some extent, all taxes are regulatory in nature. Because it is estimated four million people each year will choose to pay the IRS rather than buy insurance, and because Congress apparently regards such extensive failure to comply with the mandate as tolerable, it seems Congress did not think it was creating four million outlaws. It suggests instead the shared responsibility payment merely imposes a tax citizens may lawfully choose to pay in lieu of buying health insurance. Contrary to the joint dissenters' opinion, the individual mandate may be upheld as a tax notwith-

Continued on next page.

standing Congress did not frame it as a tax. The mandate's substance is in the form of a tax, and that conclusion should not change simply because Congress used the word "penalty" to describe the payment. Thus, interpreting such a law to be a tax would not impose a tax through judicial legislation, but instead would give practical effect to Congress's enactment. The individual mandate also complies with the other requirements for taxes under the Constitution, as it is not a capitation, and is not a direct tax that is required to be apportioned among the states. A more fundamental objection to a tax on those who lack health insurance—similar to the objection to the individual mandate as exceeding the commerce power—is that it should be troubling to permit Congress to impose a tax for not doing something. There are three reasons why such a tax passes constitutional scrutiny. First, the Constitution does not guarantee that individuals may avoid taxation through inactivity, so that upholding the individual mandate under the Taxing Clause does not recognize any new federal power, but is a determination Congress has used an existing one. Second, while Congress's taxing power has limits, so exactions cannot become punitive, it has already been explained the individual mandate passes muster as a tax and not as a punitive penalty. Accordingly, it comes within the strict limits within which Congress can tax. Third, Congress's authority under the taxing power is limited to requiring an individual to pay money to the federal government; the individual retains the choice whether to do or not do a certain act, so long as he is willing to pay a tax levied on that choice. The individual mandate also imposes a cost on the choice not to obtain health care insurance. Accordingly, the individual mandate comes within the Constitution's requirements. [The procedural outcome of the case is not presented in the casebook extract.]

DISSENT: (Scalia, J) The individual mandate cannot be characterized as a tax. Therefore, there is no need to reach the issue of whether it comes within Congress's permissible taxing power.

▶ ANALYSIS

The issue of whether the individual mandate comes within Congress's taxing power was reached only because the majority determined the Commerce Clause did not authorize the individual mandate's command to purchase insurance. Because the statute reads more naturally as a command to buy insurance than as a tax, and because the Court held the statute was unconstitutional as a command, the Court exercised its duty to construe the statute to save it, if fairly possible, if it could be interpreted as a tax. Without deciding the Commerce Clause question, the Court would have found no basis to adopt such a saving construction. Through the exercise of its duty of statutory construction, the Court upheld the individual mandate's

constitutionality, but only because the Court determined the statute could reasonably be read as a tax.

■=■

Quicknotes

TAXING POWER The authority delegated to Congress by the Constitution to impose taxes.

■=■

United States v. Butler

Federal government (D) v. Receivers (P)

297 U.S. 1 (1936).

NATURE OF CASE: Certiorari review of the constitutionality of the Agricultural Adjustment Act of 1933.

FACT SUMMARY: [The Agricultural Adjustment Act of 1933 stated that there was a national economic emergency arising from the low price of agricultural products in comparison with other commodities. To remedy this situation, a tax would be collected from processors of an agricultural product. The revenue raised would be paid to farmers who curtailed their production of that product.]

> ## 🏛 RULE OF LAW
> Congress may not, under the pretext of exercising the taxing power, accomplish prohibited ends, such as the regulation of matters of purely state concern and clearly beyond its national powers.

FACTS: [The Agricultural Adjustment Act of 1933 declared that a national economic emergency had arisen due to the disparity between the prices of agricultural and other commodities, resulting in the destruction of farmers' purchasing power. To remedy this situation, a tax would be collected from processors of agricultural products. The revenue raised thereby would be paid to farmers who voluntarily curtailed their production of those crops used by the processors. The Secretary of Agriculture was to determine the crops to which the Act's plan would apply. In July 1933, the Secretary determined that the Act's plan should be applied to cotton. A tax claim was presented to Butler (P) as receivers of the Hoosac Mills Corp., as cotton processors.] The district court held the tax to be valid.

ISSUE: May Congress, under the pretext of exercising the taxing power, accomplish prohibited ends, such as the regulation of matters of purely state concern and clearly beyond its national powers?

HOLDING AND DECISION: (Roberts, J.) No. Congress may not, under the pretext of exercising the taxing power, accomplish prohibited ends, such as the regulation of matters of purely state concern and clearly beyond its national powers. First, Butler (P) has standing to question the validity of the tax because it is but a part of the unconstitutional plan of the Agricultural Adjustment Act. A tax, as the term is used by the Constitution, is an exaction for the support of the government. It has never been thought to mean the expropriation of money from one group for the benefit of another, as is attempted by the Act in question here. The Act is unconstitutional in that it invades the rights of the states. It is a statutory plan to regulate and control agriculture production, a matter be-

yond the power of the federal government. The Government (D), in attempting to defend the Act, places great reliance on the fact that the Act's plan is voluntary. However, the farmer who chooses not to comply with the plan loses benefits. "The power to confer or withhold unlimited benefits is the power to coerce or destroy." Even if the plan were truly voluntary, it would not be valid. "At best, it is a scheme for purchasing with federal funds submission to federal regulation of a subject reserved to the states." Contracts for the reduction of acreage and the control of production are not within Congress's power. Congress has no power to enforce the ends sought by this Act onto the farmer. Hence, it may not indirectly accomplish those ends by taxing and spending to enforce them. If this Act is valid, Congress could exercise its power to regulate all industry. It could extract money from one branch of an industry and pay it to another branch. Congress may not, under the pretext of exercising the taxing power, accomplish prohibited ends. Affirmed.

DISSENT: (Stone, J.) Courts are to be concerned only with the power to enact statutes, not with their wisdom. The constitutional power of Congress to tax the processing of agricultural products is not questioned. The present tax is held to be invalid because the use to which its proceeds are to be put is disapproved. The tax is held to be invalid because it is a step in a plan to regulate agricultural production. The Court states that state powers are infringed by the expenditure of the proceeds of the tax to compensate farmers for the curtailment of their crop production. Such a limitation is contradictory and destructive of the power to appropriate for the public welfare, and is incapable of practical application. Congress's spending power is not subordinate to its legislative powers. This independent grant of power presupposes freedom of selection among diverse ends and aims and the capacity to impose such conditions as will render the choice effective. It is contradictory to say that there is a power to spend for the national welfare, while rejecting any power to impose conditions reasonably adapted to the end which justifies the expenditure. "If appropriation in aid of a program of curtailment is constitutional, and it is not denied that it is, payment to farmers on condition that they reduce their crop acreage is constitutional."

▶ ANALYSIS

The *Butler* decision contributed greatly to the pressure that produced the court-packing plan a few months later. It is called the landmark case in the area of federal regulation

Continued on next page.

of local matters through taxation. However, if the tax and the appropriation provisions had not been so closely tied together, it is doubtful that the Court would have invalidated the tax. The tax appeared to have a valid revenue-raising purpose, and once separated from the taxing provisions, there would have been no one with standing to attack the appropriation.

■═■

Quicknotes

COURT PACKING PLAN An attempt to alter the composition of a court to maximize concurrence with the appointing officer's views.

SPENDING POWER The power delegated to Congress by the Constitution to spend money in providing for the nation's welfare.

■═■

South Dakota v. Dole

State (P) v. Federal government (D)

483 U.S. 203 (1987).

NATURE OF CASE: Certiorari review of decisions upholding federal highway funding requirement.

FACT SUMMARY: Congress passed a law withholding federal highway funds to states with a minimum drinking age of less than 21 years.

RULE OF LAW

Congress may withhold federal highway funds to states with a minimum drinking age of less than 21 years.

FACTS: [In 1984, Congress enacted 23 U.S.C. § 158, which directed the Secretary of Transportation to withhold 5 percent of federal highway funds to states with a drinking age of less than 21 years of age. This was based on the perception border-states, with drinking ages of less than 21, encouraged drinking and driving. South Dakota (P) sought a declaration that the law was unconstitutional.] The district and circuit courts upheld the law, and the Supreme Court granted review.

ISSUE: May Congress withhold federal highway funds to states with a minimum drinking age of less than 21 years?

HOLDING AND DECISION: (Rehnquist, C.J.) Yes. Congress may withhold federal highway funds to states with a minimum drinking age of less than 21 years. It is well recognized that Congress may use its spending power to induce cooperation by states in areas which it cannot necessarily regulate directly. Therefore, even if Congress could not directly legislate state drinking ages, it can use the threat of withheld funds to achieve its regulatory goal. South Dakota (P) argued that alcohol is a special case, as the Twenty-first Amendment specifically leaves the regulation of drinking to the states. However, this leads the analysis back to its point of origin, namely, that Congress can indirectly regulate through its spending power. That is all it has done here. Affirmed.

DISSENT: (O'Connor, J.) Section 158 cannot be justified as reasonably related to the federal highway system. It is an attempt to regulate alcoholic beverages, something Congress may not do. When Congress appropriates money to build a highway, it is entitled to insist that the highway be a safe one, but it cannot insist as a condition of the funding that the state change its regulations in other areas of the state's social and economic life because of a tangential or attenuated relationship to highway use or safety. Congress has no power under the Spending Clause to impose requirements on a grant that go beyond specifying how the money should be spent. A requirement that is not such a specification is not a condition, but a regulation, which is valid only if it falls within one of Congress's delegated regulatory powers.

▶ ANALYSIS

It is not uncommon for Congress to attempt to regulate "with a carrot" rather than by direct regulation. The present case is one such action. Probably the most controversial area where this has been subject to constitutional consideration is in the area of abortions. Cases such as *Maher v. Roe*, 432 U.S. 464 (1977) and *Rust v. Sullivan*, 500 U.S. 173 (1991) have established Congress's right in this area.

Quicknotes

DECLARATORY JUDGMENT A judgment of the rights between opposing parties in a justiciable controversy that does not grant coercive relief (i.e., damages), but is binding.

GENERAL WELFARE Governmental interest or concern for the public's health, safety, morals, and well-being.

SPENDING POWER The power delegated to Congress by the Constitution to spend money in providing for the nation's welfare.

National Federation of Independent Business v. Sebelius

Business group (P) v. Government official (D)

132 S. Ct. 2566 (2012).

NATURE OF CASE: Appeal from judgment in action challenging the constitutionality of the "Medicaid expansion" provision of the 2010 Patient Protection and Affordable Care Act. [The procedural posture of the case is not presented in the casebook extract.]

FACT SUMMARY: A coalition of plaintiffs (P) challenged the constitutionality of the "Medicaid expansion" provision of the 2010 Patient Protection and Affordable Care Act, which expanded certain Medicaid benefits, but also threatened the states, which administer Medicaid, with the loss not only of funding for the increased coverage, but also the loss of all federal Medicaid funds.

RULE OF LAW

That part of the "Medicaid expansion" provision of the Patient Protection and Affordable Care Act that threatens the states with a loss of all federal Medicaid funding for failing to comply with the Act's expansion of Medicaid benefits and coverage, is not a valid exercise of Congress's power under the Spending Clause.

FACTS: In 2010, Congress enacted the Patient Protection and Affordable Care Act (the "Act") in order to increase the number of Americans covered by health insurance and decrease the cost of health care. A key provision of the Act is the "Medicaid expansion." The current Medicaid program offers federal funding to states to assist pregnant women, children, needy families, the blind, the elderly, and the disabled in obtaining medical care. The Act would expand the scope of the Medicaid program and increases the number of individuals the states must cover. For example, the Act requires state programs to provide Medicaid coverage by 2014 to adults with incomes up to 133 percent of the federal poverty level, whereas many states now cover adults with children only if their income is considerably lower, and do not cover childless adults at all. The Act increases federal funding to cover the states' costs in expanding Medicaid coverage, but if a state does not comply with the Act's new coverage requirements, it may lose not only the federal funding for those requirements, but all of its federal Medicaid funds. A coalition of plaintiffs (P), including some states, challenged the Medicaid expansion as unconstitutionally exceeding Congress's spending power under the Spending Clause by coercing the states to enact the statute. The Supreme Court granted certiorari. [The procedural posture of the case is not presented in the casebook extract.]

ISSUE: Is that part of the "Medicaid expansion" provision of the Patient Protection and Affordable Care Act that

threatens the states with a loss of all federal Medicaid funding for failing to comply with the Act's expansion of Medicaid benefits and coverage, a valid exercise of Congress's power under the Spending Clause?

HOLDING AND DECISION: (Roberts, C.J.) No. That part of the "Medicaid expansion" provision of the Patient Protection and Affordable Care Act that threatens the states with a loss of all federal Medicaid funding for failing to comply with the Act's expansion of Medicaid benefits and coverage, is not a valid exercise of Congress's power under the Spending Clause. There is no doubt the Act dramatically increases state obligations under Medicaid. In light of the expansion in coverage mandated by the Act, the Government (D) estimates its Medicaid spending will increase by approximately $100 billion per year, nearly 40 percent above current levels. To be constitutional, Congress's power under the Spending Clause to secure state compliance with federal objectives rests on whether the state voluntarily and knowingly accepts the terms of the "contract" offered by the federal Government (D). The Constitution has never been understood to confer upon Congress the ability to require the states to govern according to Congress' instructions. Otherwise the two-government system established by the Framers would give way to a system that vests power in one central government, and individual liberty would suffer. Thus, Congress may use its spending power to create incentives for states to act in accordance with federal policies, but when pressure turns into compulsion, the legislation runs contrary to our system of federalism. That is true whether Congress directly commands a state to regulate or indirectly coerces a state to adopt a federal regulatory system as its own. Here, the plaintiffs (P) claim Congress has crossed the line from encouragement to coercion by structuring the Medicaid expansion so states that refuse the new conditions not only will not receive new funding, but will lose all existing funding. The plaintiffs (P) claim this threat serves no purpose other than to force unwilling states to sign up for the dramatic expansion in health care coverage affected by the Act. Under the circumstances presented by the case, the plaintiffs (P) are correct—the Government's (D) "inducement" to participate is tantamount to a gun to the head. Respecting some states, the loss of all Medicaid funding represents a loss of as much as 10 percent of the state's entire budget. This is economic coercion that leaves the states with no real option but to acquiesce in the Medicaid expansion. The states contend the expansion is in reality a new program and Congress is forcing them to

Continued on next page.

accept it by threatening the funds for the existing Medicaid program. The Government (D) counters the Medicaid expansion is properly viewed merely as a modification of the existing program, and emphasizes the states agreed Congress could change the terms of Medicaid when they signed on in the first place. The issue is one of substance, not merely what Congress has labeled the program. Here, the Medicaid expansion accomplishes a shift in kind, not merely degree. The original program was designed to cover medical services for four particular categories of the needy. Previous amendments to Medicaid eligibility merely altered and expanded the boundaries of these categories. Under the Act, however, Medicaid is transformed into a program to meet the health care needs of the entire non-elderly population with income below 133 percent of the poverty level. It is no longer a program to care for the neediest among us, but rather an element of a comprehensive national plan to provide universal health insurance coverage. A state could hardly have anticipated when it signed on to the Medicaid program that Congress's reservation of the right to "alter" or "amend" the Medicaid program included the power to transform it so dramatically. The constitutional violation is fully remedied by precluding the Government (D) from withdrawing existing Medicaid funds for failure to comply with the requirements set out in the expansion. The other provisions of the Act are not affected. Congress would have wanted the rest of the Act to stand, had it known that states would have a genuine choice whether to participate in the Medicaid expansion. [The procedural outcome of the case is not presented in the casebook extract.]

CONCURRENCE AND DISSENT: (Ginsburg, J.) Congress could have recalled the existing Medicaid legislation, and replaced it with a new law making Medicaid as embracive of the poor as Congress chose. Congress should not have to take that route. Instead, Congress may expand by amendment the classes of needy persons entitled to Medicaid benefits. A ritualistic requirement that Congress repeals and reenacts spending legislation in order to enlarge the population served by a federally funded program would advance no constitutional principle and would scarcely serve the interests of federalism. Here, Medicaid, and Medicaid as amended by the Act, are not two separate programs, but just one with a constant aim—to enable poor persons to receive basic health care when they need it. Moreover, the states are not entitled to Medicaid funding, and if they accept such funding, they must do so on Congress's terms. Here, there are no coercion concerns, because the expansion relates solely to the federally funded Medicaid program; if states choose not to comply, Congress has not threatened to withhold funds earmarked for any other program. Nor does the Act use Medicaid funding to induce states to take action Congress itself could not undertake. The Government (D) undoubtedly could operate its own health-care program for poor persons, just as it operates Medicare for seniors' health care. Contrary to the

Chief Justice's opinion, the Act does not affect a new program; it merely expands the number of people covered by the existing program. The aspects of the expansion cited by the Chief Justice as supporting his premise that the expansion creates a new program do not, in fact, support his premise. The Chief Justice's finding the expansion took states by surprise is also unfounded. The precedent on which he relies merely requires conditions on federal funds be unambiguously clear at the time a state receives and uses the money—not at the time, perhaps years earlier, when Congress passed the law establishing the program. In any event, from the start, the Medicaid Act put states on notice the program could be changed, or even repealed. Thus, the states were on notice of the Act's proposed changes. Further, the Chief Justice does not announce a workable judicial standard for determining when a state is being coerced by the federal government. The coercion inquiry appears to involve political judgments that defy judicial calculation, and conceptions of when a state has been "coerced" are too amorphous to be judicially administrable. In sum, the Chief Justice and the joint-dissenters position is that the states' reliance on federal funds limits Congress's authority to alter its spending programs. This gets things backwards: Congress, not the states, is tasked with spending federal money in service of the general welfare, and each successive Congress is empowered to appropriate funds as it sees fit. For all these reasons, the Medicaid expansion is within Congress's spending power.

DISSENT: (Scalia, J.) Contrary to the Government's (D) argument, it is not enough to meet the anticoercion rule if states are free as a matter of law to turn down federal funds. This argument ignores the reality that when a heavy federal tax is levied to support a federal program that offers large grants to the states, states may, as a practical matter, be unable to refuse to participate in the federal program and to substitute a state alternative. This is because, as a practical matter, states would have to impose a huge tax on top of the heavy tax imposed by the federal government. Acceptance of the Government's (D) interpretation of the anticoercion rule would permit Congress to dictate policy in areas traditionally governed primarily at the state or local level. Further, the record shows Congress anticipated 100 percent state participation. The Government (D) asserts this expectation arose because the Act's offer to the states was a generous gift. If, however, that was true, why did more than half the states file this suit claiming the Medicaid expansion was coercive? Also, if the "gift" was so generous, Congress could have made just the new funding provided under the Act contingent on acceptance of the terms of the Medicaid expansion. Accordingly, the Medicaid expansion must fall, as it is not severable from the Medicaid extension.

Continued on next page.

▶ *ANALYSIS*

It should be noted that the Court's decision does not strike down any provision of the Act. It prohibits only the "application" of the Secretary of Health and Human Service's authority to withhold Medicaid funds from states that decline to conform their Medicaid plans to the Act's requirements. Thus the Act's authorization of funds to finance the expansion remains intact, and the Secretary's authority to withhold funds for reasons other than non-compliance with the expansion remains unaffected. The joint dissenters would have held the expansion was not severable from the Medicaid extension, and would have consequently held the entire expansion was invalid. Justice Ginsburg agreed with the Chief Justice the Medicaid Act's severability clause determined the appropriate remedy. That clause provides that "[i]f any provision of [the Medicaid Act], or the application thereof to any person or circumstance, is held invalid, the remainder of the chapter, and the application of such provision to other persons or circumstances shall not be affected thereby." 42 U.S.C. § 1303.

■=■

Quicknotes

FEDERALISM A scheme of government whereby the power to govern is among central and localized governments.

SPENDING CLAUSE The power delegated to Congress by the Constitution to spend money in providing for the nation's welfare.

SPENDING POWER The power delegated to Congress by the Constitution to spend money in providing for the nation's welfare.

■=■

CHAPTER 5

Federal Limits on State Regulation of Interstate Commerce

Quick Reference Rules of Law

Gibbons v. Ogden

Ship operator (D) v. Ship operator (P)

22 U.S. (9 Wheat.) 1 (1824).

NATURE OF CASE: Certiorari to review interpretation of federal commerce power in underlying action seeking an injunction to protect an exclusive right to operate ships between New York and New Jersey.

FACT SUMMARY: [Ogden (P), after acquiring a monopoly right from the State of New York to operate ships between New York City and New Jersey, sought to enjoin Gibbons (D) from operating his ships, licensed by the federal government, between the same points.]

RULE OF LAW
If a state law conflicts with a congressional act regulating commerce, the congressional act is controlling.

FACTS: [The New York legislature granted an exclusive right to Robert Livingston and Robert Fulton to operate ships powered by fire or steam in New York waters for twenty years which was subsequently extended for another ten years. Ogden (P) obtained an assignment from Livingston and Fulton to operate his ships between Elizabethtown, New Jersey, and New York City. Gibbons (D) was also running two boats between these points, and his boats had been enrolled and licensed under the laws of the United States for employment in the coasting trade. Ogden (P) obtained an injunction stopping Gibbons (D) from operating his ships between the points for which Ogden (P) had received an exclusive right to operate his own ships. The case was appealed to the Supreme Court.]

ISSUE: If a state law conflicts with a congressional act regulating commerce, is the congressional act controlling?

HOLDING AND DECISION: (Marshall, C.J.) Yes. If a state law conflicts with a congressional act regulating commerce, the congressional act is controlling. Congress has the power to regulate navigation within the limits of every state, and therefore, the regulations which Congress passed controlling navigation within the boundaries of New York were valid. Ogden's (P) argument that the states through the Tenth Amendment have the power to regulate commerce with foreign nations and among the states because the power which the states gave up to Congress to regulate commerce was not absolute and the residue of that power remained with the states. But Congress was given all the power to regulate interstate commerce, although it is possible for the states to pass regulations which may affect some activity associated with interstate commerce. In that case, states must base such regulations on some other source of power than the commerce power (such as the police power of the state).

Regardless of the source of the state power, any time a state regulation conflicts with a federal regulation, the state regulation must yield to the federal law. Since in this case the law of New York conflicted with a federal regulation dealing with interstate commerce, the New York law is not valid. Accordingly, the Court dismissed Ogden's (P) suit to obtain an injunction against Gibbons (D).

ANALYSIS

The federal commerce power is concurrent with state power over commerce within the state. Hence, the Court has been asked many times to define the line between federal and state power to regulate commerce. During the early history of the United States, the court was not often called upon to determine the scope of federal power under the Commerce Clause. Instead, the early cases generally involved some state action which was claimed to discriminate against or burden interstate commerce. Hence, the Commerce Clause operated as a restraint upon state powers. Most of these cases did not involve any exercise of the commerce power by Congress at all. *Gibbons v. Ogden* stands for the important principle that even where Congress has not acted under its commerce power, state regulation affecting interstate commerce will often be foreclosed. This is called Congress's negative or dormant commerce power. Large-scale regulatory action by Congress began with the Interstate Commerce Act in 1887 and the Sherman Anti-Trust Act in 1890. Challenges to these statutes initiated the major modern confrontations between the Court and congressional authority regarding commerce.

Quicknotes

COMMERCE POWER The power delegated to Congress by the Constitution to regulate interstate commerce.

DORMANT COMMERCE CLAUSE The regulatory effect of the Commerce Clause on state activity affecting interstate commerce, where Congress itself has not acted to control the activity; a provision inferred from, but not expressly present in, the language of the Commerce Clause.

INJUNCTION A court order requiring a person to do, or prohibiting that person from doing, a specific act.

Cooley v. Board of Wardens

Shipper (D) v. State board (P)

53 U.S. (12 How.) 299 (1851).

NATURE OF CASE: Certiorari review of state regulatory law in appeal from state agency penalty assessment.

FACT SUMMARY: Cooley (D) violated a Pennsylvania law requiring all ships using the port of Philadelphia to engage a local pilot for navigation through the harbor. Congress also enacted a 1789 statute requiring all pilots to be regulated in conformity with existing laws of the state in which the pilot is located until Congress acts further.

RULE OF LAW

The states may regulate those areas of interstate commerce that are local in nature and do not demand one national system of regulation by Congress.

FACTS: In 1803, Pennsylvania passed a law that required every ship entering or leaving the port of Philadelphia to use a local pilot for navigating the harbor. The law imposed a penalty of half the pilotage fee, which was paid to the Board of Wardens (P) and put in a fund for retired pilots and their dependents. An act of Congress in 1789 stated all pilots in the rivers, harbors, and ports of the United States shall continue to be regulated in conformity with the existing laws of the states and such laws as the states shall enact for that purpose, until Congress enacts legislation to the contrary.

ISSUE: May the states regulate those areas of interstate commerce that are local in nature and do not demand one national system of regulation by Congress?

HOLDING AND DECISION: (Curtis, J.) Yes. The states may regulate those areas of interstate commerce that are local in nature and do not demand one national system of regulation by Congress. It is evident from the Congressional Act of 1789 that Congress recognized that the states can, in some areas, enact regulations that have an effect on interstate commerce. Some subjects of commerce demand a single uniform national rule and therefore Congress has exclusive jurisdiction over those areas. However, there are some subjects that are primarily local in nature and therefore require many different rules to meet the local necessities. The problem concerning pilots is local in nature and therefore Congress does not have exclusive power over this area. In the Act that Congress passed allowing the states to regulate pilots, Congress has recognized that the problems involved with pilots do not demand one uniform rule and thus allowed the states to regulate pilots. The Court held that the grant of the power over commerce to Congress did not imply a prohibition on the states to exercise the same power, but it is the exercise of the power by Congress that may make the exercise of the same power by the states unlawful. The Court noted that its decision in this case applied only to its facts and did not attempt to delineate the dividing line between those subjects of commerce that were primarily local and those which were primarily national in scope. Affirmed.

ANALYSIS

The local interest versus the national interest test is still used by the Court today. In applying this test the Court balances the national interest against the local interest and also determines if the local regulation discriminates against interstate commerce. If the local interest outweighs the national interest and the regulation does not discriminate against interstate commerce, the states are allowed to regulate that subject of commerce. If it appears that the state regulation has placed a burden on interstate commerce, the Court has drawn the line and refused to hold the state regulations valid even though a local subject may be involved.

Quicknotes

COMMERCE CLAUSE Article 1, section 8, clause 3 of the United States Constitution, granting Congress the power to regulate commerce with foreign countries and between the states.

CONSIGNEE A person to whom goods are delivered or shipped.

INTERSTATE COMMERCE Commercial dealings between two parties located in different states or located in one state and accomplished through a point in another state or a foreign country; commercial dealings transacted between two states.

Philadelphia v. New Jersey

State (P) v. State (D)

437 U.S. 617 (1978).

NATURE OF CASE: Certiorari review of constitutionality of state commerce statute.

FACT SUMMARY: The New Jersey Supreme Court upheld a New Jersey law prohibiting the importation of waste originating in another state into New Jersey (D) on the basis that it protected a legitimate health interest of the state of New Jersey (D).

🏛 RULE OF LAW
State laws that are basically protectionist in nature unduly burden interstate commerce and thus are unconstitutional.

FACTS: New Jersey enacted a statute which prohibited the importation of solid or liquid waste which was collected or originated in another state. The law was challenged by private landfill owners in New Jersey (D), and the trial court held that it unduly burdened interstate commerce by discriminating against products from other states. The New Jersey Supreme Court reversed, holding the law advanced legitimate health and safety concerns and thus did not unduly burden interstate commerce. The United States Supreme Court granted certiorari.

ISSUE: Do state laws that are basically protectionist in nature unduly burden interstate commerce?

HOLDING AND DECISION: (Stewart, J.) Yes. State laws that are basically protectionist in nature unduly burden interstate commerce and are unconstitutional. Even if New Jersey's (D) ultimate purpose was to protect the health and safety of its citizens, it may not accomplish this by discriminating against articles of commerce coming from outside the state. Discrimination must be based on some property of the goods other than geographic origin. This law treats inherently similar products differently based solely on place of origin. As a result, it improperly discriminates against out-of-state production and unduly burdens interstate commerce. Reversed.

DISSENT: (Rehnquist, J.) The fact that New Jersey (D) must somehow dispose of its own noxious items does not mean that it must serve as a depository for those of every other state. New Jersey (D) should be free under our past precedents to prohibit the importation of solid waste because of the health and safety problems that such waste poses to its citizens.

▶ ANALYSIS

This case reaffirms the Court's holding in *Dean Milk Co. v. Madison*, 340 U.S. 349 (1951). It recognizes that waste is an element of commerce, and its disposal must be regulated as is all commerce. Because no federal regulation exists on the interstate transport and disposition of waste, states may regulate it only if done in a way which is not unduly burdensome. Since the *Dean Milk* decision, discrimination based on point of origin has been held unduly burdensome.

Quicknotes

CERTIORARI The informing of a higher court by a lower court through the examination of a certified copy of the case enabling the higher court to determine whether any irregularities occurred in the lower court's proceedings.

INTERSTATE COMMERCE Commercial dealings between two parties located in different states or located in one state and accomplished through a point in another state or a foreign country; commercial dealings transacted between two states.

POLICE POWER The power of a government to impose restrictions on the rights of private persons, so long as those restrictions are reasonably related to the promotion and protection of public health, safety, morals and the general welfare.

Dean Milk Co. v. Madison

Milk products distributor (P) v. Municipality (D)

340 U.S. 349 (1951).

NATURE OF CASE: Certiorari review of validity of a city ordinance regulating the sale of milk and milk products within the municipality's jurisdiction.

FACT SUMMARY: [A Madison (D) ordinance made it unlawful to sell any milk as pasteurized unless it had been processed and bottled at an approved pasteurization plant located within five miles of the city.]

🏛 RULE OF LAW
A locality may not discriminate against interstate commerce, even to protect the health and safety of its people, if reasonable alternatives exist that do not discriminate and are adequate to conserve legitimate local interests.

FACTS: [Dean Milk Co. (P) was an Illinois corporation engaged in distributing milk products in Illinois and Wisconsin. Madison (D) is a city in Wisconsin. A Madison (D) ordinance prohibited the sale of any milk as pasteurized unless it had been processed and bottled at an approved pasteurization plant located within five miles of the city. Dean Milk (P) had pasteurization plants located 65 and 85 miles from Madison (D). Dean Milk (P) was denied a license to sell its milk products within Madison (D) solely because its pasteurization plants were more than five miles away. Dean Milk (P) contended that the ordinance imposed an undue burden on interstate commerce.]

ISSUE: May a locality discriminate against interstate commerce, even to protect the health and safety of its people, if reasonable alternatives exist that do not discriminate and are adequate to conserve legitimate local interests?

HOLDING AND DECISION: (Clark, J.) No. A locality may not discriminate against interstate commerce, even to protect the health and safety of its people, if reasonable alternatives exist that do not discriminate and are adequate to conserve legitimate local interests. The Madison (D) ordinance erects an economic barrier protecting a major local industry against competition from without the state. Hence, it plainly discriminates against interstate commerce. It must be decided whether the ordinance can be justified in view of the local interest and the available methods for protecting those interests. Reasonable and adequate alternatives do exist. Madison (D) could send its inspectors to the distant plants, or it could exclude from its city all milk not produced in conformity with standards as high as those enforced by Madison (D). It could use the local ratings checked by the U.S. Public Health Service to enforce such a provision. The Madison (D) ordinance must

yield to the principle that "one State, in its dealings with another, may not place itself in a position of economic isolation." Reversed.

DISSENT: (Black, J.) Dean Milk's (P) personal preference not to pasteurize within five miles of Madison (D), not the ordinance, keeps its milk out of Madison (D). The lower court found the ordinance to be a good faith attempt to safeguard public health. Never has a bona fide health law been struck down on the ground that equally good or better alternatives exist. At the very least the ordinance should not be invalidated without having the parties present evidence on the relative merits of the Madison (D) ordinance and the alternatives suggested by the court. The court can, on the basis of judicial knowledge, guarantee that the substitute methods it proposes would not lower health standards.

▶ ANALYSIS

In *Nebbia v. New York*, 291 U.S. 502 (1934), the Court sustained the state regulation of minimum milk prices to be paid by dealers to local producers. However, in *Baldwin v. G.A.F. Seelig, Inc.*, 294 U.S. 511 (1935), the same law was challenged as applied to out-of-state producers. The Supreme Court held that application to be an unconstitutional burden on commerce since it "set a barrier to traffic between one state and another as effective as if custom duties, equal to the price differential (between the out-of-state price and the minimum price set by New York) had been laid upon the thing transported." *Baldwin* was heavily relied upon in *Dean Milk*.

Quicknotes

INTERSTATE COMMERCE Commercial dealings between two parties located in different states or located in one state and accomplished through a point in another state or a foreign country; commercial dealings transacted between two states.

UNDUE BURDEN Unlawfully oppressive or troublesome.

C & A Carbone, Inc. v. Clarkstown

Recycling center (D) v. Municipality (P)

511 U.S. 383 (1994).

NATURE OF CASE: Certiorari review of municipal ordinance regulating solid waste disposal.

FACT SUMMARY: The Town of Clarkstown (P) mandated that all solid waste leaving the city be processed through a particular transfer station.

RULE OF LAW
Discrimination against interstate commerce in favor of local businesses is per se invalid unless the municipality can demonstrate under rigorous scrutiny that it has no other means to advance a legitimate local interest.

FACTS: The Town of Clarkstown (P) entered an arrangement with a local contractor that the latter would build and operate a solid waste transfer station, which, in five years, would be sold back to the Town (P). In order to amortize the cost of the facility, the Town (P), by ordinance, mandated that all solid waste leaving the Town (P) be processed through that station. When C & A Carbone (Carbone) (D), a recycling center in town, attempted to ship its nonrecyclable waste to another state in order to save money, the Town (P) sought an injunction to force Carbone (D) to comply with the ordinance. Carbone (D) challenged the ordinance as contrary to the Commerce Clause. The state courts rejected the challenge, and the Supreme Court granted review.

ISSUE: Is discrimination against interstate commerce in favor of local businesses per se invalid unless the municipality can demonstrate under rigorous scrutiny that it has no other means to advance a legitimate local interest?

HOLDING AND DECISION: (Kennedy, J.) Yes. Discrimination against interstate commerce in favor of local businesses is per se invalid unless the municipality can demonstrate under rigorous scrutiny that it has no other means to advance a legitimate local interest. Any ordinance that deprives nonlocal businesses from access to local markets discriminates against interstate commerce and is invalid under the [dormant] Commerce Clause. When a city designates a particular commercial entity as the sole provider of such services, nonlocal providers of the service are effectively shut out. Local governments may not use their regulatory power to favor local businesses by prohibiting patronage of out-of-state competitors. Here, the Town (P) has shut out nonlocal solid waste operators, although it has a number of nondiscriminatory alternatives that would satisfy its environmental and fiscal concerns, and thus its ordinance is unconstitutional.

CONCURRENCE: (O'Connor, J.) The local law here differs from prior invalidated processing laws in one key respect: it favors a local business to the exclusion of all competitors, not simply all nonlocal competitors. Even with that distinction, however, the local law here violates the Commerce Clause.

DISSENT: (Souter, J.) Clarkstown's (P) local law conforms with the Commerce Clause because the town (P) may legitimately subject local and out-of-state investors to the same economic constraints. The town (P) here is regulating a traditional government function, something it may legitimately do.

ANALYSIS

The essential vice in discriminatory ordinances that mandate local processing is that they bar the import of the processing service. These laws hoard a local resource, whether shrimp, milk, or solid waste, for the benefit of local businesses that treat it. Clarkstown's (P) ordinance was even more egregiously protectionist than most such laws since it favored a single local proprietor.

━■═■

Quicknotes

INJUNCTION A court order requiring a person to do, or prohibiting that person from doing, a specific act.

PER SE An activity that is so inherently obvious that it is unnecessary to examine its underlying validity.

━■═■

United Haulers Assn. v. Oneida-Herkimer Solid Waste Management Authority

Private hauler of trash (P) v. County waste authority (D)

550 U.S. 330 (2007).

NATURE OF CASE: Certiorari review of a county's "flow control" ordinance under the dormant Commerce Clause.

FACT SUMMARY: A county's "flow control" ordinance required haulers of trash to deliver the trash to facilities owned and operated by a state-created public benefit corporation.

🏛 RULE OF LAW
An ordinance requiring that trash be delivered to a state-created public benefit corporation does not violate the dormant Commerce Clause.

FACTS: The Oneida-Herkimer Solid Waste Management Authority (WMA) (D) adopted an ordinance requiring that all trash be delivered to a state-created public benefit corporation. [United Haulers Association (P) sued the WMA (D), alleging that it could deliver trash to out-of-state facilities at lower costs than those required by the WMA's (D) ordinance. The trial court agreed with United Haulers' (P) Commerce Clause argument and enjoined the WMA (D) from enforcing the ordinance. The intermediate appellate court reversed, reasoning that the ordinance was permissible because it benefited a public entity instead of private businesses.] United Haulers (P) petitioned the Supreme Court for further review.

ISSUE: Does an ordinance requiring that trash be delivered to a state-created public benefit corporation violate the dormant Commerce Clause?

HOLDING AND DECISION: (Roberts, C.J.) No. An ordinance requiring that trash be delivered to a state-created public benefit corporation does not violate the dormant Commerce Clause. The distinction between private and public facilities is constitutionally significant because laws benefiting local government may serve several legitimate purposes instead of economic protectionism. To hold otherwise—that is, to treat public and private facilities equally under the dormant Commerce Clause—would lead to much interference by federal courts in state and local affairs. Also worth noting is that the injury alleged by United Haulers (P)—more expensive waste disposal—will be borne by local citizens, not by citizens of other states. Typically, the dormant Commerce Clause is enforced to prohibit shifting expenses out of state instead of keeping them at home. United Haulers' (P) proper remedy is therefore through the local political process, not through the federal courts. [Affirmed.]

DISSENT: (Alito, J.) Benefiting public facilities does not meaningfully distinguish this ordinance from the ordinance struck down in *C & A Carbone, Inc. v. Clarkstown*, 511 U.S. 383 (1994). The difference is merely formal because the waste facility in Carbone was "private" only in the most technical sense of the term: when that suit was filed, the facility's title was in the process of transferring to the town of Clarkstown. Further, the WMA's (D) ordinance here violates the market-participant doctrine, which prohibits local governments from discriminatorily regulating markets in which they participate. The ordinance here also fails to serve "legitimate goals unrelated to protectionism" because it clearly benefits local employees of the public facilities and local businesses who supply those facilities. Such preference is economic protectionism by any other name and thus deserves strict scrutiny. Finally, the fact that the WMA's (D) ordinance applies equally to in-state and out-of-state private businesses is not persuasive because case law squarely provides that such an equality of burdens cannot save legislation under the dormant Commerce Clause.

▶ ANALYSIS

The dormant Commerce Clause usually prohibits state and local regulations that impose relatively direct, overt burdens on interstate commerce. Here, the WMA's (D) ordinance clearly imposed direct, overt burdens on interstate commerce, but it did so for public benefit. That distinction with cases that bar interstate commerce to protect local private businesses saved the WMA's (D) ordinance under the dormant Commerce Clause.

■▬■

Quicknotes

DORMANT COMMERCE CLAUSE The regulatory effect of the Commerce Clause on state activity affecting interstate commerce, where Congress itself has not acted to control the activity; a provision inferred from, but not expressly present in, the language of the Commerce Clause.

INTERSTATE COMMERCE Commercial dealings between two parties located in different states or located in one state and accomplished through a point in another state or a foreign country; commercial dealings transacted between two states.

Continued on next page.

MARKET PARTICIPANT DOCTRINE Allows states acting as market participants (i.e., businesses) to be exempted from the dormant Commerce Clause.

STRICT SCRUTINY Method by which courts determine the constitutionality of a law, when a law affects a fundamental right; under the test, the legislature must have had a compelling interest to enact the law and measures prescribed by the law must be the least restrictive means possible to accomplish its goal.

South-Central Timber Development, Inc. v. Wunnicke

Timber company (P) v. State (D)

467 U.S. 82 (1984).

NATURE OF CASE: Certiorari review of congressional authorization of state regulation.

FACT SUMMARY: Alaska offered to sell large amounts of state-owned timber if the buyers, including South-Central Timber Development, Inc. (P), agreed to process it within state boundaries, but South-Central Timber (P) wanted to buy the timber and ship it to Japan for processing.

> **🏛 RULE OF LAW**
> If a state imposes burdens on commerce within a market in which it is a participant, but which have a substantial regulatory effect outside of that particular market, they are per se invalid under the federal Commerce Clause.

FACTS: Alaska offered for sale a large quantity of state-owned timber. However, it required potential purchasers to agree to process the timber within state boundaries before shipment out of Alaska. This law was enacted to protect existing timber-processing industries within the state and to obtain further revenue from the timber beyond its sale. South-Central Timber Development, Inc. (P) wanted to buy Alaska timber and also wanted to ship it beyond Alaskan borders to Japan for processing. South-Central Timber (P) challenged the constitutional validity of the Alaska requirement on Commerce Clause grounds. Alaska responded by asserting that the in-state processing requirement was exempt from invalidation under the Commerce Clause under the "market participant" doctrine. The court of appeals found that Congress had authorized Alaska's processing requirement, and the Supreme Court granted certiorari.

ISSUE: If a state imposes burdens on commerce within a market in which it is a participant, but those burdens have a substantial regulatory effect outside of that particular market, are they per se invalid under the Federal Commerce Clause?

HOLDING AND DECISION: (White, J.) Yes. If a state imposes burdens on commerce within a market in which it is a participant, but which have a substantial regulatory effect outside of that particular market, they are per se invalid under the federal Commerce Clause. The market-participant doctrine allows a state to impose burdens on interstate commerce within the market in which it is a participant but allows it to go no further. The state may not impose conditions whether by statute, regulation or contract that have a substantial regulatory effect outside of that particular market. "Market" for Com-

merce Clause purposes is narrowly defined and precludes a state's exercise of leverage in the market in which it is directly participating in order to regulate a "downstream" market. Here, Alaska is a direct participant in the timber market but not in the processing market. Although Alaska may legitimately prefer its own residents in the initial disposition of goods, in other words, when it is a "private trader" in the immediate transaction, it may not attach restrictions on dispositions subsequent to the goods coming to rest in private hands after Alaska no longer has a proprietary interest in them. Alaska may not govern the private, separate economic relationships of its trading partners downstream; as a typical seller, it has no say over how the product is used after sale. Reversed and remanded.

DISSENT: (Rehnquist, J.) The distinction drawn in the plurality opinion between market participation and market regulation is unconvincing and artificial. Alaska could have chosen a number of constitutionally valid ways of requiring the buyers of its timber to process it within the state, all of which in substance are the same as the contractual provisions the plurality found violative of the Commerce Clause. For instance, Alaska could have chosen to sell its timber only to those companies that own and operate processing plants in Alaska, or the statute itself could have paid to have the logs processed and then sold only processed, rather than unprocessed. The plurality approach is unduly formalistic.

▶ ANALYSIS

The facts of this case closely resemble the facts of an earlier Supreme Court case, in which the court struck down a Louisiana law prohibiting export from the state of any shrimp from which the heads and hulls had not been removed. See *Foster-Fountain Packing Co. v. Haydel*, 278 U.S. 1 (1928). The Court rejected the claim that the fact that the shrimp were owned by the state authorized the state to impose such limitations. The case, as here, involved a natural resource which the court noted could have been retained for use and consumption within its borders, but because Louisiana permitted its shrimp to be taken and sold in interstate commerce, it released its right to and terminated its control of the shrimp so taken.

━■━

Quicknotes

DISPOSITION A transferring of property; conveyance.

Continued on next page.

MARKET PARTICIPANT DOCTRINE Allows states acting as market participants (i.e., businesses) to be exempted from the dormant Commerce Clause.

PER SE An activity that is so inherently obvious that it is unnecessary to examine its underlying validity.

PROPRIETARY INTEREST Any interest that is exclusively owned or controlled.

Baldwin v. G.A.F. Seelig, Inc.

State agency (D) v. Milk dealer (P)

294 U.S. 511 (1935).

NATURE OF CASE: Certiorari review of action to enjoin enforcement of a state milk price support statute.

FACT SUMMARY: [G.A.F. Seelig, Inc. (P), a New York milk dealer, sought to enjoin a New York statute establishing minimum producer-to-dealer prices on milk and prohibiting the sale in New York of milk purchased out of state at lower than the minimum price for a similar in-state purchase.]

RULE OF LAW

It is a violation of the Commerce Clause for a state to regulate intrastate prices by prohibiting the importation of less expensive goods in interstate commerce.

FACTS: [In addition to setting up minimum producer-to-dealer prices for the in-state sale of milk, a New York statute prohibited the sale in New York of milk bought out of state for lower prices. G.A.F. Seelig, Inc. (Seelig) (P), a New York milk dealer, bought milk in Vermont in 40-quart cans at prices below the minimums for similar in-state purchases. When New York then refused to license him to sell it, Seelig (P) brought an action seeking injunctive relief and charging an unconstitutional interference with interstate commerce. An injunction was granted as to the milk Seelig (P) wanted to sell in the original containers but not as to that milk which had been subsequently placed into bottles for sale in the New York market. The latter was deemed to have passed outside the stream of interstate commerce, thereby being subject to state regulation.]

ISSUE: Is it a violation of the Commerce Clause for a state to regulate intrastate prices by prohibiting the importation of less expensive goods in interstate commerce?

HOLDING AND DECISION: (Cardozo, J.) Yes. A state violates the Commerce Clause when it attempts to regulate intrastate prices by prohibiting the importation of less expensive goods in interstate commerce. Neither the power to tax nor the police power may be used by the state of destination with the aim and effect of establishing an economic barrier against competition with the products of another state or the labor of its residents. Such is a violation of the theory upon which the Constitution was framed, that the peoples of the several states must sink or swim together and that the mutual jealousies of the states cannot be permitted to result in customs barriers and other economic retaliation. Here, the argument is made that the purpose of the regulation is to advance the health of the state's citizens, and not to securing an economic advantage over rival states. "This would be to eat up the rule under the guise of an exception. Economic welfare is always related to health, for there can be no health if men are starving."

ANALYSIS

The underlying principle in this case is that one state may not, in its dealings with another, place itself in a position of economic isolation. Such a tenet is essential to maintenance of a union of states, which is why *Baldwin* is still recognized as authority.

Quicknotes

COMMERCE CLAUSE Article 1, § 8, cl. 3 of the United States Constitution, granting Congress the power to regulate commerce with foreign countries and between the states.

INJUNCTION A court order requiring a person to do or prohibiting that person from doing a specific act.

INTERFERENCE WITH INTERSTATE COMMERCE Interference with commercial dealings between two parties located in different states or located in one state and accomplished through a point in another state or a foreign country.

H.P. Hood & Sons v. Du Mond

Milk distributor (P) v. Milk commissioner (D)

336 U.S. 525 (1949).

NATURE OF CASE: Certiorari review of constitutionality of a New York milk dealer licensing law.

FACT SUMMARY: H.P. Hood & Sons (P), a Boston milk distributor, obtained milk from New York. He was denied a license to establish a receiving depot in New York on the basis of a New York law which makes a condition of the issuance of a license that such issuance will not tend to be destructive of competition in a market already "adequately served."

RULE OF LAW
A state may not constitutionally enact restrictions with the purpose and effect of curtailing the volume of interstate commerce for the benefit of local economic interests.

FACTS: H.P. Hood & Sons (P) was a Boston milk distributor who obtained his supply of milk from producers in New York State. He had established three milk receiving and processing depots in New York under licenses from that state. When he applied for a license to open a fourth depot, he was denied. The basis for the denial was that issuance would tend to creative destructive competition in an area already adequately served. In his denial, the milk commissioner (D) stated that the fourth depot would draw milk supplies away from other existing processing plants and would tend to deprive the local market of an adequate supply of milk.

ISSUE: May a state constitutionally enact restrictions with the purpose and effect of curtailing the volume of interstate commerce for the benefit of local economic interests?

HOLDING AND DECISION: (Jackson, J.) No. A state may not constitutionally enact restrictions with the purpose and effect of curtailing the volume of interstate commerce for the benefit of local economic interests. This Court has previously denied states' attempts to advance their own economic interests by curtailing the movement of articles of commerce, while it has generally supported their right to impose restrictions in the interests of health and safety. While the State insists that the denial of a license for Hood (P) does not restrict interstate commerce, we can hardly be asked to assume that the denial of the license will not deny petitioner access to such added supplies. Since the statute, as applied to Hood (P), violates the Commerce Clause and is not authorized by federal legislation pursuant to that Clause, it cannot stand. Reversed and remanded.

DISSENT: (Black, J.) The question here is whether all local phases of interstate business are to be judicially immunized from state laws against destructive competitive business practices. The language of the state act is not discriminatory, nor does the legislative history show such intent. While I have doubt about the wisdom of this New York law, I do not conceive it to be the function of this Court to revise that state's economic judgments.

DISSENT: (Frankfurter, J.) In effect, the majority holds that no matter how important the prevention of destructive competition may be to the internal economy of a state and no matter how unimportant the interstate commerce affected, a state cannot, as a means of preventing such competition, deny an applicant access to a market within the state if that applicant intends to ship out of state.

ANALYSIS

In *Milk Control Board v. Eisenberg*, 306 U.S. 346 (1939), a New York milk dealer who bought milk from Pennsylvania producers challenged a Pennsylvania law. The law set the minimum price to be paid by dealers to milk producers. The Supreme Court upheld the law, stating that it did not attempt to regulate shipment to or sale in New York. It also found that the activity affected was essentially local in Pennsylvania, since only a fraction of the milk produced in that state is shipped out of state. The effect on interstate commerce was found to be incidental. *Baldwin* was not controlling. The Court stated that that decision "condemned an enactment aimed solely at interstate commerce, attempting to affect and regulate the price of milk in a sister state" and amounted, in effect, to a tariff.

Quicknotes

PAROCHIAL Regional or narrow in scope.

POLICE POWER The power of a government to impose restrictions on the rights of private persons, so long as those restrictions are reasonably related to the promotion and protection of public health, safety, morals and the general welfare.

Kassel v. Consolidated Freightways Corp.

State (D) v. Common carrier (P)

450 U.S. 662 (1981).

NATURE OF CASE: Certiorari review of constitutionality of state statute prohibiting specific vehicles.

FACT SUMMARY: Consolidated Freightways Corp. (P) challenged the constitutionality of an Iowa statute which prohibited the use of certain large trucks within the state boundaries.

🏛 RULE OF LAW
A state safety regulation will be unconstitutional if its asserted safety purpose is outweighed by its degree of interference with interstate commerce.

FACTS: Iowa (D) passed a statute restricting the length of vehicles that may use its highways. The state law set a general length limit of 55 feet for most vehicles, and 60 feet for trucks pulling two trailers (doubles). Iowa was the only state in the western or midwestern United States to outlaw the use of 65-foot doubles. Consolidated Freightways Corp. (P), one of the largest common carriers in the country, alleged that the Iowa statute unconstitutionally burdened interstate commerce. The district court and the court of appeals found the statute unconstitutional and Kassel (D), on behalf of the state, appealed.

ISSUE: Will a state safety regulation be held to be unconstitutional if its asserted safety purpose is outweighed by the degree of interference with interstate commerce?

HOLDING AND DECISION: (Powell, J.) Yes. A state safety regulation will be unconstitutional if its asserted safety purpose is outweighed by its degree of interference with interstate commerce. While bona fide state safety regulations are entitled to a strong presumption of validity, the asserted safety purpose must be weighed against the degree of interference with interstate commerce. Less deference will be given to the findings of state legislators where the local regulation has a disproportionate effect on out-of-state residents and businesses. Here, Iowa (D) failed to present any persuasive evidence that 65-foot doubles are less safe than 55-foot single trailers. Consolidated Freightways Corp. (P) demonstrated that Iowa's law substantially burdens interstate commerce by compelling trucking companies either to route 65-foot doubles around Iowa or use the smaller trucks allowed by the state statute. Thus the Iowa statute is in violation of the Commerce Clause. Affirmed.

CONCURRENCE: (Brennan, J.) In ruling on the constitutionality of state safety regulations, the burdens imposed on commerce must be balanced against the regulatory purposes identified by the state's lawmakers. In its analysis, a court should focus ultimately on the regulatory purposes identified by the lawmakers. The only relevant evidence concerns whether the lawmakers "could rationally have believed that the challenged regulation would foster those purposes." Iowa's (D) actual rationale for the regulation had nothing to do with the alleged safety differences in the lengths of trucks, but had to do with discouraging interstate truck traffic on its highways. Protectionist legislation is unconstitutional under the Commerce Clause, even if its purpose is to promote safety rather than economic purposes.

DISSENT: (Rehnquist, J.) A sensitive consideration must be made when weighing the safety purposes of a statute against the burden on interstate commerce. A state safety regulation is invalid if its asserted safety justification is merely a pretext for discrimination against interstate commerce. The Iowa statute is a valid highway safety regulation and is entitled to the strongest presumption of validity.

▶ ANALYSIS

Traditionally, states have been free to pass public safety regulations restricting the use of highways and railway facilities. However, state safety regulations have been struck down when only a marginal increase in safety causes a substantial burden on interstate commerce. This case simply follows this rationale.

■≡■

Quicknotes

COMMERCE CLAUSE Article 1, section 8, clause 3 of the United States Constitution, granting Congress the power to regulate commerce with foreign countries and between the states.

INTERSTATE COMMERCE Commercial dealings between two parties located in different states or located in one state and accomplished through a point in another state or a foreign country; commercial dealings transacted between two states.

SALUTARY Remedial or beneficial.

■≡■

United Building & Construction Trades Council v. Mayor and Council of Camden

Trade council (P) v. City (D)

465 U.S. 208 (1984).

NATURE OF CASE: Certiorari review of constitutionality of a municipal residency ordinance.

FACT SUMMARY: [The New Jersey Supreme Court held that a municipal ordinance, which required that 40 percent of all workers on city construction projects be residents of the city, was not covered by the Privileges and Immunities Clause.]

🏛 RULE OF LAW
The Privileges and Immunities Clause applies to municipal ordinances that discriminate on the basis of municipal residence.

FACTS: [The City of Camden (D), New Jersey, enacted an ordinance requiring that contractors and subcontractors working on city construction projects employ a workforce of 40 percent Camden (D) residents. The United Building & Construction Trades Council (P) sued, contending the ordinance discriminated against non-city residents in violation of the Privileges and Immunities Clause. The Supreme Court of New Jersey upheld the ordinance, holding that the Privileges and Immunities Clause did not apply to municipal ordinances which discriminate on the basis of municipal residence because the discrimination applies to both New Jersey residents outside Camden (D) as well as out-of-state residents.] The United States Supreme Court granted certiorari to review the application of the Privileges and Immunities Clause to the particular ordinance.

ISSUE: Does the Privileges and Immunities Clause apply to municipal ordinances that discriminate on the basis of municipal rather than state citizenship?

HOLDING AND DECISION: (Rehnquist, J.) Yes. The Privileges and Immunities Clause applies to municipal ordinances that discriminate on the basis of municipal residence. Ordinances are enacted under the municipality's power derived from the state. Thus, ordinances are not outside the Clause merely because they are enacted by a municipality. Further, although New Jersey residents living outside of Camden (D) were affected by the ordinance along with out-of-state residents, New Jersey residents had the opportunity to expand or contract municipal power by voting in state elections. Out-of-state residents had no such power. Therefore, the Clause applies. The ordinance affected the rights of non-residents to pursue a livelihood of their choosing. This is clearly a fundamental privilege protected by the Clause. Because no trial was held, it is necessary that the decision of the Supreme Court of New Jersey be reversed and the case remanded to determine whether Camden's (D) economic problems were sufficient to justify the discrimination placed on non-residents by the ordinance. Reversed and remanded.

DISSENT: (Blackmun, J.) The Court erroneously extends the scope of the Privileges and Immunities Clause without textual or historical support. Historically, the meaning of the Clause is well settled: absent some substantial noninvidious justification, a state cannot discriminate between its own residents and those of other states on the basis of state citizenship. Now, this Court holds that the Clause applies to laws "that discriminate among state residents on the basis of municipal residence. . . ."

▶ ANALYSIS

In this case, the court points out that although the ordinance may have been valid under the Commerce Clause, as the City (D) was acting as a market participant, such an analysis does not apply under the Privileges and Immunities Clause. That Clause imposes a direct restraint on state action in the interest of interstate harmony.

■=■

Quicknotes

PRIVILEGES AND IMMUNITIES CLAUSE Article IV, section 2, clause 1 of the U.S. Constitution, which states that a state cannot favor its own citizens by discriminating against other states' citizens who may come within its borders.

■=■

Pacific Gas & Elec. Co. v. State Energy Resources Conservation & Development Commn.

Electric utility company (P) v. State agency (D)

461 U.S. 190 (1983).

NATURE OF CASE: Certiorari review of federal law preemption of state law energy act.

FACT SUMMARY: Pacific Gas & Elec. Co. (P) maintained that certain provisions of California's Warren-Alquist Act were invalid because it was preempted by Congress's passage of the Atomic Energy Act of 1954.

🏛 RULE OF LAW

In passing the Atomic Energy Act of 1954, Congress preempted state regulation of the radiological safety aspects involved in the construction and operation of nuclear plants but intended for the states to retain their traditional responsibility in the field of regulating electrical utilities for determining questions of need, reliability, cost, and other related state concerns.

FACTS: In challenging the validity of various provisions of California's Warren-Alquist State Energy Resources Conservation and Development Act, Pacific Gas & Elec. Co. (P) claimed in its declaratory judgment action that such regulation as it attempted was preempted by the Atomic Energy Act, which Congress enacted in 1954. Of particular concern was a provision imposing a moratorium on the certification of new nuclear plants until the State Energy Resources and Conservation Commission (Energy Commission) (D) "finds that there has been developed and that the United States through its authorized agency has approved and there exists a demonstrated technology or means for the disposal of high-level nuclear waste." Disposal was defined as a "method for the permanent and terminal disposition of high-level nuclear waste," a goal which was not even close to being reached. The district court held that the aforementioned nuclear moratorium provision was not preempted because it saw in certain sections of the Atomic Energy Act congressional authorization for states to regulate nuclear power plants "for purposes other than protection against radiation hazards."

ISSUE: In passing the Atomic Energy Act of 1954, has Congress preempted state regulation of the radiological safety aspects involved in the construction and operation of nuclear plants but intended for the states to retain their traditional responsibility in the field of regulating electrical utilities for determining questions of need, reliability, cost, and other related state concerns?

HOLDING AND DECISION: (White, J.) Yes. In passing the Atomic Energy Act of 1954, Congress preempted state regulation of the radiological safety aspects involved in the construction and operation of nuclear

plants but intended for the states to retain their traditional responsibility in the field of regulating electrical utilities for determining questions of need, reliability, cost, and other related state concerns. The intent of Congress in passing the Atomic Energy Act of 1954 was to give the federal government exclusive regulatory power over the radiological safety aspects involved in the construction and operation of a nuclear plant. It did not intend to preempt the states from exercising their traditional responsibility in the field of regulating electrical utilities (nuclear or otherwise) for determining questions of need, reliability, cost, and other related state concerns. California has maintained that its moratorium provisions are aimed at economic problems, arguing that without a permanent nuclear waste disposal system the nuclear waste problem could become critical and lead to unpredictably high costs to either contain the problem or shut down reactors. Accepting this avowed economic purpose as the rationale for enacting the moratorium provision, the statute lies outside the occupied field of nuclear safety regulation. It does not conflict with federal regulation of nuclear waste disposal. In fact, its very words accept that it is the federal responsibility to develop and license such technology and it nowhere seeks to impose its own state standards on nuclear waste disposal. It does not conflict with the Nuclear Regulatory Commission's (NRC's) decision to continue licensing reactors despite the uncertainty surrounding the waste disposal problem nor with Congress's recent passage of legislation directed at that problem. The NRC's imprimatur indicates only that it is safe to proceed with such plants, not that it is economically wise to do so. Since the NRC order does not and could not compel a utility to develop a nuclear plant, compliance with both it and California's challenged statutory provision is possible. Furthermore, because the NRC's regulations are aimed at insuring that plants are safe, not necessarily that they are economical, California's statutory provision does not interfere with the objective of the federal regulation. Finally, there is little doubt that a primary purpose of the Atomic Energy Act was and is the promotion of nuclear power. But, as the court of appeals noted, the promotion of nuclear power was not intended by Congress to be accomplished "at all costs." The elaborate licensing and safety provisions and the continued preservation of state regulation in traditional areas belie that. Thus, it cannot be said that California's statutory provision "frustrates" the Atomic Energy Act's purpose of developing the commercial use of nuclear power. Quite simply, there has

Continued on next page.

been no preemption with regard to the type of provision California enacted. Affirmed.

CONCURRENCE: (Blackmun, J.) It is unnecessary for the majority to rule that a state may not prohibit the construction of nuclear power plants if the state is motivated by concerns about the safety of such plants.

▶ *ANALYSIS*

There are instances in which Congress explicitly preempts state authority by so stating in express terms in the federal statute itself. More often, however, Congress's intent to supersede state law altogether is to be found: (1) from a "scheme of federal regulation so pervasive as to make reasonable the inference that Congress left no room to supplement it;" or (2) because "the Act of Congress touches a field in which the federal interest is so dominant that the federal system will be assumed to preclude enforcement of state laws on the same subject;" or (3) because "the object sought to be obtained by the federal law and the character of obligations imposed by it may reveal the same purpose." *Fidelity Federal Savings & Loan Assn. v. de la Cuesta*, 458 U.S. 141 (1982).

Quicknotes

DECLARATORY JUDGMENT A judgment of the rights between opposing parties in a justiciable controversy that does not grant coercive relief (i.e., damages), but is binding.

PREEMPTION Judicial preference recognizing the procedure of federal legislation over state legislation of the same subject matter.

CHAPTER 6

Separation of Powers

Quick Reference Rules of Law

Youngstown Sheet & Tube Co. v. Sawyer (The Steel Seizure Case)

Steel companies (P) v. Federal government (D)

343 U.S. 579 (1952).

NATURE OF CASE: Certiorari review of underlying suit for declaratory and injunctive relief from a presidential order.

FACT SUMMARY: Faced with an imminent steel strike during the Korean War, the President ordered governmental seizure of the steel companies to prevent the strike. The companies challenged his power to take such action as being without constitutional authority or prior congressional approval.

🏛 RULE OF LAW
The President, relying on a concept of inherent powers, and in his capacity as Commander-in-Chief, may not make an order that usurps the lawmaking authority of Congress on the basis of a compelling need to protect the national security.

FACTS: As a result of long, but unsuccessful, negotiations with various steel companies, the United Steelworkers of America served notice of intent to strike in April 1952. Through the last months of the negotiations the President had utilized every available administrative remedy to effect a settlement and avert a strike. Congress had engaged in extensive debate on solutions but had passed no legislation on the issue. By order of the President, the Secretary of Commerce seized the steel companies so that steel production would not be interrupted during the Korean War. The steel companies sued in federal district court to have the seizure order declared invalid and to enjoin its enforcement. The government asserted that the President had "inherent power" to make the order and that it was "supported by the Constitution, historical precedent and court decisions." The district court granted a preliminary injunction which was stayed the same day by the court of appeals. The Supreme Court granted certiorari and ordered immediate argument.

ISSUE: May the President, relying on a concept of inherent powers, and in his capacity as Commander-in-Chief, make an order that usurps the lawmaking authority of Congress on the basis of a compelling need to protect the national security?

HOLDING AND DECISION: (Black, J.) No. The President, relying on a concept of inherent powers, and in his capacity as Commander-in-Chief, may not make an order that usurps the lawmaking authority of Congress on the basis of a compelling need to protect the national security. There is, admittedly, no express congressional authority for these seizures, and so, if any authority for the President's act can be found, it must come from the Constitution. In the absence of express authority for the President's act, it is argued that the power can be implied from the aggregate of his express powers granted by the Constitution. This order cannot be justified by reliance on the President's role as Commander-in-Chief. Even though the term "theater of war" has enjoyed an expanding definition, it cannot embrace the taking of private property to prevent a strike. The President's powers in the area of legislation are limited to proposing new laws to Congress or vetoing laws which he deems inadvisable. This order is not executive implementation of a congressional act but a legislative act performed by the President. Only Congress may do what the President has attempted here. The Constitution is specific in vesting the lawmaking powers in Congress. Affirmed.

CONCURRENCE: (Frankfurter, J.) This decision does not attempt to define the limits of presidential authority. The President cannot act in contravention of an express congressional act, nor may he act where Congress has done nothing. Were this a case of a long history of congressional acquiescence to presidential practice our decision might be different, but no such showing has been made.

CONCURRENCE: (Jackson, J.) The power of the President to act can be viewed as three separate categories of circumstances. First, the President's power is at its maximum when he acts pursuant to express or implied congressional authority. Second, in the absence of a congressional grant of power, the President acts solely on the basis of his powers as specified in the Constitution. Third, when the President acts in contravention of congressional action, he may do so only where it can be shown that Congress has exceeded its constitutional powers and the President is acting in his own sphere of authority. It is in this last area where presidential acts are subject to the closest scrutiny. This order is clearly not in the first category. His act cannot be justified in the second category since Congress has limited seizure powers to specific instances not embracing this order. The constitutional grant of powers to the President is in specific terms that do not permit any loose aggregation to create powers not specified. There is little question that Congress could have authorized those seizures and this very power denies the same authority to the President. Finally, the President's act is justified by arguing it is the result of powers accruing to his office by custom and practice of previous administrations. Present unconstitutional acts cannot be justified by

Continued on next page.

the prior unconstitutional acts of others. Presidential power may, in fact, enlarge due to congressional inaction, but the courts will not assist or approve this process.

DISSENT: (Vinson, C.J.) The majority's opinion has left the President powerless to act at the very time the need for his independent and immediate action is greatest. From Washington to Roosevelt, history is replete with examples of needed presidential action in the face of congressional inaction. Jefferson's Louisiana Purchase, Lincoln's Emancipation Proclamation, Wilson's War Labor Board with accompanying industrial seizures, and Roosevelt's seizure of an aircraft plant to avert a strike are but a few examples of presidential action that received subsequent, not prior, congressional or judicial authorization. The President's seizure in this case is in accord with congressional intent to support the resistance of aggression in the world and is in furtherance of his duty to execute the laws of this nation. The executive is the only branch of government that may, by design, act swiftly to meet national emergencies. This decision emasculates that necessary power.

▶ *ANALYSIS*

Justice Black's broad language was criticized by many scholars as being overly expansive for the case presented. However, other authorities pointed out that the broad arguments advanced by the government required a broad response. During oral argument before the court, the government counsel stated that while the Constitution imposed limits on congressional and judicial powers, no such limits were imposed on the presidency. While supplemental briefs were filed modifying this position, the damage may already have been done. The Court was faced with a paucity of judicial precedents. The President and Congress have traditionally preferred political rather than judicial solutions to their conflicts. This practice avoids the limitations imposed on future actions by binding judicial precedents. And, as can be seen by the cases of *Marbury v. Madison*, 5 U.S. 137 (1803), and *United States v. Nixon*, 418 U.S. 683 (1974), the executive branch has not fared well when it has submitted to judicial jurisdiction.

■═■

Quicknotes

EXECUTIVE ORDER An order issued by the President, or another executive of government, which has the force of law.

PRELIMINARY INJUNCTION A judicial mandate issued to require or restrain a party from certain conduct; used to preserve a trial's subject matter or to prevent threatened injury.

■═■

Dames & Moore v. Regan

Creditor (P) v. Federal government (D)

453 U.S. 654 (1981).

NATURE OF CASE: Certiorari review of appeal of decision issuing an order of attachment pursuant to a breach of contract.

FACT SUMMARY: Dames & Moore (P) filed suit to recover funds owed on a contract with the government of Iran, but the order of attachment was voided by an Executive Agreement.

🏛 RULE OF LAW
The President lacks the plenary power to settle claims against foreign governments through an Executive Agreement; however, where Congress at least acquiesces in the President's actions, the President can settle such claims.

FACTS: In November of 1979 President Carter, acting pursuant to the International Emergency Economic Powers Act (IEEPA), froze Iranian assets in the United States after Americans were taken hostage in Tehran. The Americans held hostage were subsequently released on January 20, 1981, pursuant to an Executive Agreement entered into the day before. The agreement included a promise to settle all claims and litigation between the countries through arbitration. Dames & Moore (P), holders of an attachment order against Iranian assets, took exception with this agreement and filed suit. The litigation eventually reached the Supreme Court.

ISSUE: Does the President possess plenary powers to settle claims against foreign governments through an Executive Agreement?

HOLDING AND DECISION: (Rehnquist, J.) No. The President lacks the plenary power to settle claims against foreign governments through an Executive Agreement; however, where Congress at least acquiesces in the President's actions, the President can settle such claims. When Congress implicitly or explicitly authorizes presidential action, the action is given the greatest presumption of validity. Here, while the President's exact decision was not contemplated in the IEEPA, substantial powers to seize and handle foreign assets was conferred in the President by Congress. Dames & Moore (P) would have to show that the government as a whole lacks the power to settle claims with foreign entities when it is in the interest of the United States to do so; such a heavy burden has not been met. There is a long history of congressional acquiescence to international agreements settling claims between citizens of the United States and nationals of other countries. However, there is no independent source of presidential authority to settle such claims. Had Congress not implicitly approved of the action, the President would have been beyond his bounds. But, in this case, he acted under the implied authority of Congress.

▶ ANALYSIS

Justice Rehnquist cites the concurring opinion of Justice Jackson in the case of *Youngstown Sheet & Tube Co. v. Sawyer*, 343 U.S. 579 (1952). In that case, Justice Jackson divided presidential authority into three categories: express or implied grants of power from Congress, actions in the face of congressional silence, and actions in direct contravention to congressional legislation. When acting against the wishes of Congress, the President's power was limited to express constitutional grants in Article II. At the other extreme, presidential power was at its greatest when acting with congressional approval, as Justice Rehnquist found to be the case here.

■=■

Quicknotes

EXECUTIVE AGREEMENT An agreement with a foreign nation that is binding on the country, entered into by the President without Senate approval.

ORDER OF ATTACHMENT An order mandating the seizing of the property of one party in anticipation of, or in order to satisfy, a favorable judgment obtained by another party.

PLENARY Unlimited and open; as broad as a given situation may require.

■=■

Ex parte Quirin

Federal government (P) v. Third Reich sabotage agents (D)

317 U.S. 1 (1942).

NATURE OF CASE: Petition for habeas corpus to Supreme Court.

FACT SUMMARY: When Third Reich sabotage agents (D) were apprehended within the United States during World War II, they argued it would be unconstitutional for them to be tried before a military tribunal. The agents (D) sought trial by jury in the civil courts.

🏛 RULE OF LAW
The detention and trial of foreign espionage and sabotage agents within the United States during time of war, by a military commission appointed by the President, is constitutional.

FACTS: During World War II, citizens of the German Reich, with which the United States was at war, after being trained at a sabotage school near Berlin, entered the United States by submarine, with explosives and plans to disrupt a variety of military targets throughout the United States. All were to receive salary payments from the German government for this operation. Prior to being able to carry our their mission, they were apprehended by the Federal Bureau of Investigation (FBI) and were to be tried by a military tribunal according to the Articles of War enacted by Congress for violations of the law of war and of the Articles of Law. The federal district court denied the German sabotage agents' (D) argument that their trial before a military tribunal would be unconstitutional, and the sabotage agents (D) petitioned for habeas corpus to the Supreme Court.

ISSUE: Is the detention and trial of foreign espionage and sabotage agents within the United States during time of war, by a military commission appointed by the President, constitutional?

HOLDING AND DECISION: (Stone, C.J.) Yes. The detention and trial of foreign espionage and sabotage agents within the United States during time of war, by a military commission appointed by the President, is constitutional. By universal agreement and practice, the law of war draws a distinction between the armed forces and the peaceful populations of belligerent nations and also between those who are lawful and unlawful combatants. Lawful combatants are subject to capture and detention as prisoners of war by opposing military forces. Unlawful combatants are likewise subject to capture and detention, but in addition they are subject to trial and punishment by military tribunals for acts which render their belligerency unlawful. The latter, such as spies and those who seek to wage war through destruction of life or property, as here, are familiar examples of belligerents who are deemed not to be entitled to the status of prisoners of war, but rather are offenders against the law of war subject to trial and punishment by military tribunals. Furthermore, even citizenship in the United States of an enemy belligerent does not relieve such person from the consequences of a belligerency which is unlawful because in violation of the law of war. This Court cannot say that Congress in preparing the Fifth and Sixth Amendments intended to extend trial by jury to the cases of alien or citizen offenders against the law of war otherwise triable by a military commission. Writ of habeas corpus denied.

▶ ANALYSIS

As explained in the *Quirin* decision, by the Articles of War, Congress had explicitly provided that military tribunals had jurisdiction to try offenders or offenses against the law of war in appropriate cases. It made no difference that the unlawful combatants in the *Quirin* case were apprehended before they had the opportunity to actually commit the espionage and sabotage which was their goal.

■=■

Quicknotes

FIFTH AMENDMENT Provides that no person shall be compelled to serve as a witness against himself, or be subject to trial for the same offense twice, or be deprived of life, liberty, or property without due process of law.

SIXTH AMENDMENT Provides the right to a speedy trial by impartial jury, the right to be informed of the accusation, to confront witnesses, and to have the assistance of counsel in all criminal prosecutions.

WRIT OF HABEAS CORPUS A proceeding in which a defendant brings a writ to compel a judicial determination of whether he is lawfully being held in custody.

■=■

Hamdi v. Rumsfeld

Alleged enemy combatant (P) v. Secretary of Defense (D)

542 U.S. 507 (2004).

NATURE OF CASE: Certiorari review from the denial of right to challenge enemy-combatant status.

FACT SUMMARY: Hamdi (P), an American citizen designated as an enemy combatant, argued that he was entitled to contest such designation in court.

🏛 RULE OF LAW
Due process requires that a citizen held in the United States as an enemy combatant be given a meaningful opportunity to contest the factual basis for that detention before a neutral decisionmaker.

FACTS: Hamdi (P), an American citizen, was designated by the Government (D) an "enemy combatant" and placed into indefinite detainment. The Federal Court of Appeals held the detention to be legally authorized and that Hamdi (P) was entitled to no further opportunity to challenge his enemy-combatant label. Hamdi (P) appealed to the Supreme Court.

ISSUE: Does due process require that a citizen held in the United States as an enemy combatant be given a meaningful opportunity to contest the factual basis for that detention before a neutral decisionmaker?

HOLDING AND DECISION: (O'Connor, J.) Yes. Due process requires that a citizen held in the United States as an enemy combatant be given a meaningful opportunity to contest the factual basis for that detention before a neutral decisionmaker. This Court understands Congress's statutory grant of authority for the use of "necessary and appropriate force" to include the authority to detain for the duration of the relevant conflict, and our understanding is based on long-standing law-of-war principles. If the practical circumstances of a given conflict are entirely unlike those of the conflicts that informed the development of the law of war, that understanding may unravel. But that is not the situation that we face as of this date. The United States may, therefore, detain, for the duration of these hostilities, Hamdi (P) and other individuals legitimately determined to be Taliban combatants who "engaged in an armed conflict against the United States." Nevertheless, the writ of habeas corpus remains available to every individual detained within the United States; the writ remains a critical check on the Executive, ensuring that Hamdi (P) was properly brought before an Article III court to challenge his detention by this writ. On the evidence presented below, the circumstances surrounding Hamdi's (P) seizure cannot in any way be characterized as "undisputed." He may—or may not—in fact be an "enemy combatant" such as to justify his detention without trial or ultimate trial before a military tribunal. It is vital that this Court not give short shrift to the values that this country holds dear or to the privilege that is American citizenship. Accordingly, a citizen-detainee seeking to challenge his or her classification as an enemy combatant must receive notice of the factual basis for the classification, and a fair opportunity to rebut the Government's (D) factual assertions before a neutral decisionmaker. These essential constitutional promises may not be eroded. Vacated and remanded.

CONCURRENCE AND DISSENT: (Souter, J.) The Government (D) has failed to demonstrate that the Force Resolution authorizes the detention complained of here even on the facts the Government (D) claims. If the Government (D) raises nothing further than the record now shows, the Non-Detention Act entitles Hamdi (P) to be released. The branch of government asked to counter a serious threat is not the branch on which to rest the Nation's entire reliance in striking the balance between the will to win and "the cost in liberty on the way to victory."

DISSENT: (Scalia, J.) The very core of liberty secured by our Anglo-Saxon system of separated powers has been freedom from indefinite imprisonment at the will of the executive. The gist of the Due Process Clause was to force the Government (D) to follow those common-law procedures traditionally deemed necessary before depriving a person of life, liberty, or property. Hamdi (P) is entitled to a habeas decree requiring his release unless (1) criminal proceedings are promptly brought, or (2) Congress has suspended the writ of habeas corpus. Neither has here occurred. Rather than remand, the decision below should be reversed.

DISSENT: (Thomas, J.) The executive branch, acting pursuant to powers vested in the President by the Constitution and by explicit congressional approval, has determined that Hamdi (P) is an enemy combatant and should be detained. This Court lacks the expertise and capacity to second-guess that decision. As such, Hamdi's (P) habeas challenge should fail, and there is no reason to remand the case.

▶ ANALYSIS

As made clear in the *Hamdi* decision, in cases of this type the court must balance two vital yet competing interests: on the one hand, respect for separation of powers and the

Continued on next page.

fundamental importance of the nation to be able to protect itself during time of war; on the other hand, the critical and deep-seated individual constitutional interests at stake.

■═■

Quicknotes

DUE PROCESS CLAUSE Clauses found in the Fifth and Fourteenth Amendments to the United States Constitution providing that no person shall be deprived of "life, liberty, or property, without due process of law."

WRIT OF HABEAS CORPUS A proceeding in which a defendant brings a writ to compel a judicial determination of whether he is lawfully being held in custody.

■═■

Hamdan v. Rumsfeld

Guantanamo Bay detainee (P) v. Secretary of Defense (D)

548 U.S. 557 (2006).

NATURE OF CASE: Petition for writ of habeas corpus filed by a Guantanamo Bay detainee.

FACT SUMMARY: A Yemeni national detained by U.S. military forces at Guantanamo Bay, Cuba was charged with conspiracy "to commit offenses triable by military commission."

🏛 RULE OF LAW

A military commission does not have jurisdiction to hear a case if the commission's structures and procedures violate the Uniform Code of Military Justice and the Geneva Conventions.

FACTS: A Yemeni national, Salim Ahmed Hamdan (P), was captured by U.S. military forces in Afghanistan in November 2001; he was transported to an American prison at Guantanamo Bay, Cuba, in June 2002. At some time after June 2003, President Bush (D) declared Hamdan (P) subject to trial by military commission for crimes that the President (D) did not specify at that time. More than a year later, Hamdan (P) was charged with conspiring, from 1996 to November 2001, "to commit . . . offenses triable by military commission." Hamdan (P) sued the Government (D), filing a petition for writ of habeas corpus to challenge the validity of his detention. [The trial court agreed with Hamdan (P) that the military commission convened to hear his case lacked authority because it failed to comply with the Uniform Code of Military Justice and the Geneva Conventions.] The intermediate appellate court reversed, and Hamdan (P) petitioned the Supreme Court for further review.

ISSUE: Does a military commission have jurisdiction to hear a case if the commission's structures and procedures violate the Uniform Code of Military Justice and the Geneva Conventions?

HOLDING AND DECISION: (Stevens, J.) No. A military commission does not have jurisdiction to hear a case if the commission's structures and procedures violate the Uniform Code of Military Justice and the Geneva Conventions. Congress generally approved military commissions in 1916, but only on the express condition that the President (D) follows the law of war. But more recent congressional action—the joint resolution authorizing use of military force ("AUMF") and the Detainee Treatment Act (DTA)—did not expand executive power to create military commissions. Such commissions generally are permitted in three circumstances: (1) to substitute for civilian law after martial law has been declared; (2) to substitute for civilian law during times of temporary military government, whether the territory in question is or is not occupied by an enemy; and (3) in a situation usually occurring on the battlefield, to decide whether the defendant has violated the law of war. Only the third situation applies here because Guantanamo Bay is not under martial law and is not territory occupied by the enemy. That holding in turn leads to the conclusion that the military commission convened to hear Hamdan's (P) conspiracy charge lacks jurisdiction. Conspiracy has almost never, if ever, been tried by a law-of-war military commission, and conspiracy is not seen internationally as violating the law of war. Moreover, the procedures to be used by the commission hearing Hamdan's (P) trial undermine the commission's authority by failing to comply with the Uniform Code of Military Justice (UCMJ) and the Geneva Conventions. The commission in this case would be permitted to try Hamdan (P) while preventing him from knowing what evidence was introduced against him. The rules of courts-martial, however, apply to military commissions unless such application is impracticable, and those rules grant an accused the right to be present. Here, the Government (D) has made no showing that the rules of courts-martial would be impracticable in this case. Those rules therefore must apply to Hamdan's (P) trial. Further, Article 3 of the Geneva Conventions provides that military commissions are permitted only if some demonstrated practical need to deviate from normal courts-martial exists. Again, the Government (D) has failed to make the requisite showing of need, and the military commission here thus also fails under the Geneva Conventions. The right to be present, which is guaranteed by the Conventions, therefore applies in this case under international law, too. Reversed.

CONCURRENCE: (Breyer, J.) Congress did not grant the President (D) unlimited authority to fight the war on terror. If no emergency warrants the President's (D) failure to consult with Congress, then the Court's insistence on such consultation does not undermine the war effort.

CONCURRENCE: (Kennedy, J.) Congressional action establishes boundaries in this case that the President (D) has exceeded. The military commission's structure and procedure in this case raises severe separation-of-powers issues: the executive branch can define, prosecute, and hear the charges against Hamdan (P) without any oversight or review from the other two branches of government. Additionally, this record shows no special urgency to justify trial by military commission because Hamdan (P) now has been detained for approximately four years. For all these reasons, the military commission in this case is not regularly

Continued on next page.

constituted under U.S. law as required by the UCMJ. There is therefore no reason to decide whether the commission complies with the Geneva Conventions or whether (as the dissent undertakes) Hamdan's (P) conspiracy charge is valid.

DISSENT: (Thomas, J.) This decision substitutes the Court's discretion for the President's (D), contrary to our constitutional order. In the AUMF, Congress authorized the President (D) to use his discretion in using force to combat international terrorism. The military commission convened here easily complies with that authorization, and with the requirement that such commissions hear charges of offenses "committed within the field of the command of the convening commander." The President (D) has deemed this conflict to have roots stretching back into the 1990s, and this Court cannot question that conclusion. But whether the Court applies the correct, flexible approach to military commissions or today's more rigid analysis, Hamdan (P) can be tried by military commission because he is an alleged member of a criminal enterprise and he allegedly conspired to commit war crimes. Countering these clear grounds for upholding the military commission in this case, the plurality can only substitute its own impression of "military necessity" for the President's (D) own discretionary judgment. The UCMJ does not support this decision, and the Geneva Conventions are not judicially enforceable. Even if they were, though, Hamdan (P) should not prevail on his petition because, consistent with the Conventions, the Government (D) may not deprive him of the right to be present if doing so would subject him to an unfair trial.

DISSENT: (Alito, J.) Hamdan's (P) military commission is a "regularly constituted court," and it therefore complies with the laws applied by the plurality to invalidate the commission. The commission here provides trial procedures, administrative review, and even opportunity for formal appellate review. Contrary to today's decision, such a procedure affords an accused much more than "summary justice."

▶ *ANALYSIS*

Justice Kennedy's concurrence highlights the grave separation-of-powers issues generated by the military commission in Hamdan. Here the executive branch tried (1) to perform legislative functions by creating a previously unknown crime subject to hearing by military commission; (2) to perform executive functions by prosecuting the alleged violation of the new crime, and (3) to perform judicial functions by adjudicating the prosecution of the alleged violation of the new crime in a forum over which the executive branch held great control. Such goals are the classic ingredients for violations of the doctrine of the separation of powers.

Quicknotes

CONSPIRACY Concerted action by two or more persons to accomplish some unlawful purpose.

GENEVA CONVENTION International agreement that governs the conduct of warring nations.

SEPARATION OF POWERS The system of checks and balances preventing one branch of government from infringing upon exercising the powers of another branch of government.

WRIT OF HABEAS CORPUS A proceeding in which a defendant brings a writ to compel a judicial determination of whether he is lawfully being held in custody.

■═■

Boumediene v. Bush

Guantanamo detainees (P) v. Federal government (D)

553 U.S. 723 (2008).

NATURE OF CASE: Review of federal appeals court judgment.

FACT SUMMARY: Lakhdar Boumediene (P) and other detainees (P) held at Guantanamo Bay, Cuba, petitioned the court for a writ of habeas corpus. The federal appeals court ruled in favor of the U.S. government (D).

RULE OF LAW

(1) The Military Commissions Act of 2006 strips federal courts of jurisdiction over habeas petitions filed by foreign citizens detained at Guantanamo Bay.

(2) Detainees are not barred from seeking habeas or invoking the Suspension Clause simply because they had been designated as enemy combatants or held at Guantanamo Bay.

(3) The Military Commissions Act of 2006 is a violation of the Suspension Clause of the Constitution.

FACTS: Bosnian police captured Lakhdar Boumediene (P) and five other Algerian natives after U.S. intelligence officers suspected them of plotting to attack the U.S. embassy there. The U.S. government (D) classified the men as enemy combatants in the war on terror and held them at the Guantanamo Bay. Boumediene (P) filed a petition for a writ of habeas corpus, claiming that the U.S. government (D) violated the Due Process Clause of the U.S. Constitution, various statutes and treaties, the common law, and international law. A district court judge granted the government's (D) motion to have all of the claims dismissed on the ground that Boumediene (P), as an alien held at an overseas military base, had no right to a habeas petition. The Court of Appeals for the D.C. Circuit affirmed, but the Supreme Court reversed in *Rasul v. Bush*, 542 U.S. 466 (2004), holding that the habeas statute extends to noncitizen detainees at Guantanamo. In 2006, Congress passed the Military Commissions Act of 2006 (MCA), which withdrew the jurisdiction of federal courts to hear habeas applications from detainees classified as enemy combatants under the Detainee Treatment Act of 2005. The case was appealed to the D.C. Circuit for the second time, and this time the detainees (P) argued that the MCA did not apply to their petitions, and that if it did, it was unconstitutional under the Suspension Clause. The D.C. Circuit ruled in favor of the government (D) on both points, holding that the MCA applied to "all cases, without exception," that pertain to aspects of detention. One of the purposes of the MCA, according to the court, was to overrule the Supreme

Court's opinion in *Hamdan v. Rumsfeld*, 548 U.S. 557 (2006), which had allowed petitions like Boumediene's (P) to go forward. The D.C. Circuit held that the Suspension Clause protects only the writ of habeas corpus as it existed in 1789, and that the writ would not have been understood in 1789 to apply to an overseas military base leased from a foreign government. Constitutional rights do not apply to aliens outside of the United States, the court held, and the leased military base in Cuba does not qualify as inside the geographic borders of the United States. The Supreme Court granted certiorari after initially denying review, three months earlier.

ISSUE:

(1) Does the Military Commissions Act of 2006 strip federal courts of jurisdiction over habeas petitions filed by foreign citizens detained at Guantanamo Bay?

(2) Are detainees barred from seeking habeas or invoking the Suspension Clause simply because they had been designated as enemy combatants or held at Guantanamo Bay?

(3) Is the Military Commissions Act of 2006 a violation of the Suspension Clause of the Constitution?

HOLDING AND DECISION: (Kennedy, J.)

(1) Yes. The Military Commissions Act of 2006 strips federal courts of jurisdiction over habeas petitions filed by foreign citizens detained at Guantanamo Bay. If the MCA is considered valid, its legislative history requires that the detainees' cases be dismissed.

(2) No. Detainees are not barred from seeking habeas or invoking the Suspension Clause simply because they had been designated as enemy combatants or held at Guantanamo Bay. The Suspension Clause provides that the "Privilege of the Writ of Habeas Corpus shall not be suspended, unless when in Cases of Rebellion or Invasion the public Safety may require it." The Framers thought the writ was an essential mechanism in the separation-of-powers scheme. Moreover, the Suspension Clause applies to Guantanamo, despite the fact that the United States (D) does not claim sovereignty over the place of detention. Even when the United States (D) acts outside its borders, its powers are subject to the Constitution.

(3) Yes. The Military Commissions Act of 2006 is a violation of the Suspension Clause of the Constitution. Because the procedures laid out in the Detainee Treatment Act are not adequate substitutes for the

Continued on next page.

habeas writ, the MCA operates as an unconstitutional suspension of that writ. Reversed.

CONCURRENCE: (Souter, J.) Two additional points are worth mentioning: First, the jurisdictional question answered in this case would be answered in the same way in purely constitutional cases. Second, the prisoners involved in this case have been held at Guantanamo for six years, without habeas scrutiny, and while the military should handle such cases within some reasonable period of time, it was appropriate for the courts to step in where the military had failed after six years.

DISSENT: (Roberts, C.J.) The procedural protections offered aliens who are detained by this country as enemy combatants were generous under the Detainee Treatment Act, and the court rejects them out of hand without stating what due process rights the detainees hold. The majority also fails to delineate the procedures that should be followed by the judiciary in reviewing cases deemed appropriate. The majority's opinion is not really about the detainees, but about control of federal policy regarding enemy combatants.

DISSENT: (Scalia, J.) The Court's grant of constitutional right to habeas corpus to alien enemies detained abroad by military forces occurs in the course of an ongoing war, but the writ of habeas corpus does not, and never has, run in favor of aliens abroad. The Suspension Clause has no application, and the court's intervention is ultra vires.

▶ ANALYSIS

President Bush agreed to honor the ruling. At a June 2008 town hall meeting, then-Republican presidential nominee John McCain said the ruling was "one of the worst decisions in the history of this country." He said that "[t]hese are people who are not citizens. They do not and never have been given the rights that citizens in this country have." Then-Democratic presidential nominee Barack Obama described the ruling as "a rejection of the Bush administration's attempt to create a legal black hole at Guantanamo" and "an important step toward re-establishing our credibility as a nation committed to the rule of law."

■■■

Quicknotes

DUE PROCESS The constitutional mandate requiring the courts to protect and enforce individuals' rights and liberties consistent with prevailing principles of fairness and justice and prohibiting the federal and state governments from such activities that deprive its citizens of life, liberty, or property interest.

DUE PROCESS CLAUSE Clauses, found in the Fifth and Fourteenth Amendments to the U.S. Constitution, providing that no person shall be deprived of "life, liberty, or property, without due process of law."

HABEAS CORPUS A proceeding in which a defendant brings a writ to compel a judicial determination of whether he is lawfully being held in custody.

SUSPENSION CLAUSE A clause found in Article I of the U.S. Constitution that protects against arbitrary suspensions of the writ of habeas corpus.

■■■

INS v. Chadha

Federal agency (D) v. Deportable alien (P)

462 U.S. 919 (1983).

NATURE OF CASE: Consolidated actions challenging the constitutionality of a federal statute.

FACT SUMMARY: Chadha (P) and others challenged the constitutionality of a federal statute that purported to authorize one House of Congress, by resolution, to invalidate the decision of the Attorney General (made under authority delegated by Congress) to allow a particular deportable illegal immigrant to remain in the United States.

🏛 RULE OF LAW
The Constitution does not permit Congress to statutorily authorize a one-house veto of a decision the Attorney General makes, pursuant to authority delegated to him by Congress, to allow a particular deportable alien to remain in the United States.

FACTS: Three cases consolidated on appeal all presented the question of the constitutionality of a federal statute that authorized either House of Congress, by resolution, to invalidate the decision of the Attorney General (made pursuant to authority delegated by Congress) to allow a particular deportable alien to remain in the United States. After such a one-house veto effectively overturned the Attorney General's decision to let Chadha (P) and certain other individuals remain in the United States, each instituted action challenging the constitutionality of the aforesaid statute. Chadha (P) filed a petition for a review of his deportation order, with the Immigration and Naturalization Service (INS) (D) actually agreeing with his contention that the statute was unconstitutional. The court of appeals held that the statute violated the doctrine of separation of powers.

ISSUE: Is it constitutional for Congress to statutorily authorize a one-house veto of a decision the Attorney General makes, pursuant to authority delegated to him by Congress, to allow a particular deportable alien to remain in the United States?

HOLDING AND DECISION: (Burger, C.J.) No. The Constitution does not permit Congress to statutorily authorize a one-house veto of a decision the Attorney General makes, pursuant to authority delegated to him by Congress, to allow a particular deportable alien to remain in the United States. Such an action is clearly an exercise of legislative power, which makes it subject to the bicameralism and presentment requirements of Article I of the Constitution unless one of the express constitutional exceptions authorizing one House to act alone applies. None of them apply. Thus, to accomplish what has been

attempted by one House of Congress in this case requires action in conformity with the express procedures of the Constitution's prescription for legislative action, passage by a majority of both Houses, and presentment to the President (for his signing or his veto). Such requirements were built into the Constitution to act as enduring checks on each branch and to protect the people from the improvident exercise of power by mandating certain prescribed steps. In attempting to bypass those steps, Congress has acted unconstitutionally. Affirmed.

CONCURRENCE: (Powell, J.) This case should be decided on the narrower ground that Congress assumes a judicial function in violation of the principle of separation of powers when it finds that a particular person does not satisfy the statutory criteria for permanent residence in this country. The Framers were concerned that a trial by the legislature lacks the safeguards necessary to prevent the abuse of power. The legislature here has undertaken the type of decision that has normally been left to other branches.

DISSENT: (White, J.) Today's decision sounds the death knell for nearly two hundred statutory provisions in which Congress has reserved a "legislative veto," which has become a central means by which Congress secures the accountability of executive and independent agencies. Without this particular tool, Congress faces a Hobson's choice: either to refrain from delegating the necessary authority, leaving itself with a hopeless task of writing laws with the requisite specificity to cover endless special circumstances across the entire policy landscape, or, in the alternative, to abdicate its lawmaking function to the executive branch and independent agencies. Thus, the apparent sweep of the Court's decision today, which appears to invalidate all legislative vetoes irrespective of form or subject, is regrettable. Furthermore, the Court's decision fails to recognize that the legislative veto is not the type of action subject to the bicameralism and presentment requirements of Article I. Only bills and their equivalent are subject to such requirements. The initial legislation delegating to the Attorney General the power to make a decision on the deportation of a particular alien complied with the Article I requirements. Congress's power to exercise a legislative veto over that decision cannot be viewed, then, as the power to write new law without bicameral approval or presidential consideration. If Congress can delegate lawmaking power to executive agencies, it is most difficult to understand Article I as forbidding

Continued on next page.

Congress from simply reserving a check on legislative power for itself. Without the veto, agencies to whom power has been delegated may issue regulations having the force of law without bicameral approval and without the President's signature. It is thus not apparent why the reservation of a veto over the exercise of that legislative power must be subject to a more exacting test. In both cases, it is enough that the initial statutory authorizations comply with the Article I requirements.

▶ ANALYSIS

It is only within the past 50 years that the legislative veto has come into widespread use. When the federal government began its massive growth in response to the Depression, the legislative veto was "invented" as one means of keeping a check on the sprawling new structure. While many commentators, upon the Court's announcement of this decision, opined that the result was a major shift of power from the legislative branch to the executive branch, Congress, through more restrictive draftsmanship, should actually see a minimal diminishment of its control over those areas in which it desires to retain control.

■▬■

Quicknotes

BICAMERALISM The necessity for approval by a majority of both houses of Congress when ratifying legislation, or approving other legislative action.

LEGISLATIVE VETO A statutory provision that contemplates the congressional ability to require the President or another part of the executive branch to act, or to refrain from taking action.

PRESENTMENT Act of bringing a congressional decision before the President for his approval or veto.

■▬■

Clinton v. New York

President of the United States (D) v. City government et al. (P)

524 U.S. 417 (1998).

NATURE OF CASE: Challenge to the constitutionality of new presidential powers.

FACT SUMMARY: The Line Item Veto Act of 1996 allowed the President to cancel provisions that have been signed into law. Parties affected by President Clinton's cancellation of a provision of the Balanced Budget Act of 1997 challenged the constitutionality of the Act.

> ## 🏛 RULE OF LAW
> The cancellation provisions authorized by the Line Item Veto Act are not constitutional.

FACTS: [President Clinton used his authority under the Line Item Veto Act of 1996 to cancel a provision of the Balanced Budget Act of 1997. This forced New York to repay certain funds to the federal government under the Medicaid program and removed a tax benefit to food processors acquired by farmers' cooperatives. New York City and several private organizations challenged the constitutionality of the Medicaid cancellation, and the Snake River Potato Growers (a farmers' cooperative) challenged the food processors provision.]

ISSUE: Are the cancellation provisions authorized by the Line Item Veto Act constitutional?

HOLDING AND DECISION: (Stevens, J.) No. The cancellation provisions authorized by the Line Item Veto Act are not constitutional. The Line Item Veto Act gives the President the power to "cancel in whole" three types of provisions that have already been signed into law: (1) any dollar amount of discretionary budget authority; (2) any item of new direct spending; or (3) any limited tax benefit. With respect to each cancellation, the President must determine that it will (i) reduce the federal budget deficit; (ii) not impair any essential government functions; and (iii) not harm the national interest. A cancellation takes effect upon receipt by Congress of the notification of the cancellation. However, a majority vote of both Houses is sufficient to make the cancellation null and void. Although the Constitution expressly authorizes the President to veto a bill under Article I, § 7, it is silent on the subject of unilateral Presidential action that repeals or amends parts of duly enacted statues as authorized under the Line Item Veto Act. Constitutional silence should be construed as express prohibition. If there is to be a new role for the President in the procedure to determine the final text of a law, such a change must come through the amendment procedures and not by legislation. Affirmed.

CONCURRENCE: (Kennedy, J.) Separation of powers was designed to protect liberty, because the concentration of power in any single branch is a threat to liberty.

CONCURRENCE AND DISSENT: (Scalia, J.) If the Line Item Veto Act authorized the President to "decline to spend" any item of spending rather than "canceling" it, it would have been constitutional. Given that there is only a technical difference between the two actions and that it is no different from what Congress has permitted the President to do since the formation of the Union, the Line Item Veto does not offend Article I, § 7.

DISSENT: (Breyer, J.) Given how complex our nation has become, Congress cannot divide bills into thousands or tens of thousands of separate appropriations bills, each of which the President would have to veto or sign separately. Therefore, the Line Item Veto may help representative government work better.

▶ ANALYSIS

The majority did not comment on the wisdom of the Line Item Veto Act, because they found this step unnecessary given their finding that the Act was unconstitutional. Justice Kennedy did not let that stop him, since he felt that the Line Item Veto Act affected the separation of powers which in turn threatened liberty.

■■■

Quicknotes

LINE ITEM VETO ACT Act authorizes a governor to veto specified items in appropriation bills.

SEPARATION OF POWERS The system of checks and balances preventing one branch of government from infringing upon exercising the powers of another branch of government.

■■■

Bowsher v. Synar

Federal government (D) v. Challenger to legislation (P)

478 U.S. 714 (1986).

NATURE OF CASE: Direct appeal to consider constitutionality of "Gramm-Rudman-Hollings Act" reporting provisions.

FACT SUMMARY: Bowsher (D) took a direct appeal to the Supreme Court from a district court ruling invalidating the reporting provisions of the "Gramm-Rudman-Hollings" deficit control act, finding the assignment of certain functions under the Act to the Comptroller General violated the doctrine of separation of powers.

🏛 RULE OF LAW
The assignment of executive powers to an agent or officer of the legislative branch violates the doctrine of separation of powers.

FACTS: [In 1985, the President signed into law the Gramm-Rudman-Hollings Deficit Control Act (the "Act"). The Act called for automatic reductions through the implementation of the so-called reporting provisions of the Act. Under these provisions, deficits are estimated, and if excessive, the Directors of the Office of Management and Budget and the congressional Budget Office were to calculate necessary, program-by-program reductions, which are reported to the Comptroller General. After reviewing these figures, the Comptroller General reports his conclusions to the President, who is required to implement the reductions specified in the report. Anticipating constitutional challenge, the Act contained a fall-back reporting provision, whereby the Directors would report to a specially created Committee on Deficit Reduction, which in turn would report a joint resolution to both houses, which would then be voted on and amended. If the resolution were passed and signed by the President, the resolution would become the basis of the mandated reductions. Hours after the Act was signed, Synar (P) filed a complaint seeking declaratory relief that the Act was unconstitutional. The district court invalidated the reporting provisions, and a direct appeal was taken to the Supreme Court.]

ISSUE: Does the assignment of executive powers to an agent or officer of the legislative branch violate the doctrine of separation of powers?

HOLDING AND DECISION: (Burger, C.J.) Yes. The assignment of executive powers to an agent or officer of the legislative branch violates the doctrine of separation of powers. [The Court quickly disposed of standing issues.] The Constitution does not contemplate an active role for Congress in the supervision of officers charged with the execution of the laws. Congress would thereby retain a sort of congressional veto. The Comptroller General is subject to removal by Congress, and these removal powers dictate that he will be subservient to congressional control. Further, Congress has consistently viewed the Comptroller General as an officer of the legislative branch. There is no question that the Comptroller General acts in an executive capacity by executing the Act's reduction reporting provisions. By law, the President is required to implement the reductions of the Comptroller General. By placing the execution of the Act in the hands of an officer controlled by Congress, the doctrine of separation of powers is violated. Affirmed.

DISSENT: (White, J.) The majority's conclusion rests on the premise that any direct involvement of Congress in the removal of officers charged with the execution of laws violates the separation of powers. It is unrealistic to think that the Comptroller General is subservient to Congress. The Act itself represents a congressional choice as to how to execute the Act, and the President has chosen not to upset the choice. Since there is no threat to the balance of authority, the Act need not be struck down.

▶ ANALYSIS

One of the alternatives posited by the dissent ignores the 60-year evolution of the office of the Comptroller General. To invalidate the congressional removal provisions would presumably leave removal in the hands of the executive branch and would wreak havoc with the office as to any number of legislative functions the Comptroller General's office performs.

▬═▬

Quicknotes

CONGRESSIONAL VETO The effort deemed unconstitutional exercised by Congress to engage in decision-making ability over the executive branch of government.

DECLARATORY RELIEF A judgment of the rights between opposing parties that does not grant coercive relief (i.e., damages) but is binding.

SEPARATION OF POWERS The system of checks and balances preventing one branch of government from infringing upon exercising the powers of another branch of government.

▬═▬

Morrison v. Olson

Federal government (D) v. Subject of special prosecutor investigation (P)

487 U.S. 654 (1988).

NATURE OF CASE: Certiorari review of invalidation of the Ethics in Government Act.

FACT SUMMARY: The Ethics in Government Act, which created the independent counsel/special prosecutor, was challenged as unconstitutional.

> **RULE OF LAW**
> Congress's creation of the independent counsel was not an unconstitutional usurpation of power.

FACTS: In 1978, Congress passed the Ethics in Government Act (the "Act"). One facet of this legislation was the creation of the office of the independent counsel. The pertinent provisions mandated that, upon receipt of certain information, the Attorney General may determine whether evidence of official wrongdoing warrants appointment of a special prosecutor. The results are reported to a special court. The court is empowered to appoint a special prosecutor, who would be given broad investigative powers. The only power to remove the prosecutor lay in impeachment or by the Attorney General, after a showing of good cause. The Act contained certain requirements of reporting to Congress. Olson (P), a subject of an inquiry by a special prosecutor, challenged the Act as violative of the Appointments Clause and separation of powers. The district court upheld the law, but the court of appeals reversed. The Supreme Court granted review.

ISSUE: Was Congress's creation of the independent counsel an unconstitutional usurpation of power?

HOLDING AND DECISION: (Rehnquist, C.J.) No. Congress's creation of the independent counsel was not an unconstitutional usurpation of power. The Appointments Clause mandates only the President may appoint "principal" United States officers. However, Congress may invest in the judiciary the power to appoint inferior officers. This Court is of the opinion that independent counsels are inferior officers. He is subordinate to the Attorney General, his role is restricted to the investigation and possible prosecution of a number of federal crimes, and his tenure is limited. Also, this Court rejects the argument that the Appointments Clause does not permit "inter-branch" appointments, exemplified by the Act's provision of a judicial body appointing an executive officer. No restriction is to be found in the Appointments Clause. This Court further rejects the argument that the Act violates the longstanding prohibition on vesting in courts' executive powers. The special court does have certain supervisory powers, but it is the special prosecutor, not the special court, that carries out executive functions. Finally, this Court rejects the argument that the Act violates separation of powers. Congress, in passing the Act, did not attempt to usurp executive or judicial authority. Rather than take such authority unto itself, it created an executive and judicial office not unduly beholden to itself. This was not a violation of separation of powers. This being so, the Act is valid. Reversed.

DISSENT: (Scalia, J.) The Act is a clear violation of the concept of separation of powers. The only relevant questions are: (1) Is the investigation/prosecution of a federal crime an exercise of purely executive power and (2) Does the statute deprive the President of exclusive control over the exercise of that power? The Constitution and precedent mandate an affirmative answer to the former question, and any reasonable reading of the act requires a similar answer to the latter. This being so, the Act violates separation of powers.

▶ ANALYSIS

The Court has made some important separation of powers decisions in recent years. Probably the most important other decision was *INS v. Chadha*, 462 U.S. 919 (1983). This decision struck down legislation review of executive actions. In the present case, the Court distinguished *Chadha* by holding that the Ethics Act did not directly give Congress more power.

▬▬

Quicknotes

APPOINTMENTS CLAUSE Article II, § 2, clause 2 of the United States Constitution conferring power upon the president to appoint ambassadors, public ministers and consuls, judges of the Supreme Court and all other officers of the United States with the advice and consent of the Senate.

ETHICS IN GOVERNMENT ACT Allows for the appointment of special independent counsel to investigate high ranking government officials.

INDEPENDENT COUNSEL An officer, whose appointment is authorized by the Ethics in Government Act, who is charged with the investigation of possible criminal activity by high level government officials.

INFERIOR OFFICERS Members of the executive branch having less power or authority in relation to others.

SEPARATION OF POWERS The system of checks and balances preventing one branch of government from infringing upon exercising the powers of another branch of government.

▬▬

Woods v. Cloyd W. Miller Co.

Federal government (P) v. Landlord (D)

333 U.S. 138 (1948).

NATURE OF CASE: Certiorari review of constitutionality of Housing and Rental Act of 1947.

FACT SUMMARY: When World War II ended and Congress enacted rent control regulation based upon its war power, a federal district court held the legislation unconstitutional on grounds that a Presidential Proclamation had terminated hostilities.

> ## 🏛 RULE OF LAW
> Congress has the power pursuant to its war power to attempt to remedy situations caused by a war and continuing to exist after hostilities have ceased.

FACTS: A federal district court held unconstitutional Title II of the Housing and Rent Act of 1947, which regulated rents by virtue of the war power, reasoning that congressional authority to impose rent controls ended with the Presidential Proclamation terminating hostilities on December 31, 1946. The district court noted that the Proclamation announced "peace-in-fact." The court also stated that, even if the war power continued, Congress did not act under it because Congress did not specifically say so. Direct appeal was taken to the Supreme Court.

ISSUE: Does Congress have the power pursuant to the war power to attempt to remedy situations caused by a war and continuing to exist after hostilities have ceased?

HOLDING AND DECISION: (Douglas, J.) Yes. Congress has the power pursuant to its war power to attempt to remedy situations caused by a war and continuing to exist after hostilities have ceased. The war power includes the power to remedy evils that have arisen due to a war, and, "whatever may be the consequences when war is officially terminated, the war power does not necessarily end with the cessation of hostilities." The war power is adequate to support the preservation of rights created by wartime legislation. And it has an even broader sweep. In *Hamilton v. Kentucky Distilleries Co.*, 251 U.S. 146 (1919), and *Ruppert v. Caffey*, 251 U.S. 264 (1920), prohibition laws enacted after the World War I armistice were sustained as exercises of the war power because they conserved labor and increased efficiency of production in the critical days of demobilization and helped conserve the supply of grains and cereals depleted by the war. Following these cases, the war power sustains the Housing and Rental Act. The legislative history of the Act makes it clear that the housing shortage resulting from the war has not been eliminated. The legislative history also makes it clear that Congress is invoking the war power to sustain the Act.

"The question of the constitutionality of action taken by Congress does not depend on its recitals of the power which it undertakes to exercise." Reversed.

CONCURRENCE: (Jackson, J.) The United States is still technically in a state of war. Hence the war power is a valid ground for federal rent control. However, "I would not be willing to hold that war powers last as long as the effects and consequences of war, for if so they are permanent."

▌*ANALYSIS*

Article I, § 8 of the Constitution gives Congress the power to declare war, to raise and support armies, to provide and maintain a navy, to make rules for the government and regulation of the land and naval forces, and to provide for organizing, arming, disciplining, and calling forth the militia. Under this power, Congress's enactment of comprehensive legislation regulating the national economy during a war has been sustained. The Emergency Price Control Act of 1942 was sustained as applying to rents in *Bowies v. Willingham*, 321 U.S. 503 (1944), and as to prices in *Yakus v. U.S.*, 321 U.S. 414 (1944). The Renegotiation Act was sustained in *Lichter v. U.S.*, 334 U.S. 742 (1948). It provided for recapture of excessive profits realized on war contracts where the ultimate source of payment was the U.S. government.

■=■

Quicknotes

WAR POWERS CLAUSE Article I, § 8 of the United States Constitution granting Congress the power to declare war.

■=■

Missouri v. Holland

State (P) v. Federal game warden (D)

252 U.S. 416 (1920).

NATURE OF CASE: Certiorari review of constitutionality of Migratory Bird Treaty Act (the "Bird Treaty Act").

FACT SUMMARY: Missouri (P) claimed that the Bird Treaty Act was an unconstitutional interference with the rights reserved to the states by the Tenth Amendment.

RULE OF LAW
Congress may validly enact a statute to enforce a treaty even if the statute standing by itself would be unconstitutional because it interfered with the rights reserved to the states by the Tenth Amendment.

FACTS: On December 8, 1916, the United States entered into a treaty with Great Britain to protect birds that migrated between Canada and the United States. Congress passed a statute to enforce the Migratory Bird Treaty, which allowed the Secretary of Agriculture to formulate regulations to enforce the treaty. The State of Missouri (P) filed a bill in equity to prevent Holland (D), the game warden of the United States, from enforcing the treaty. Missouri (P) claimed the statute was an unconstitutional interference with the rights reserved to the states by the Tenth Amendment and it had a pecuniary interest as owner of the wild birds that was being interfered with. Before the treaty had been entered into, Congress had attempted to regulate the killing of migratory birds within the states and that statute, standing by itself, had been declared unconstitutional. The United States contended that Congress had the power to enact the statute to enforce the treaty and that the statute and treaty were the supreme law of the land.

ISSUE: Can Congress validly enact a statute to enforce a treaty if the statute standing by itself would be unconstitutional because it interfered with the rights reserved to the states by the Tenth Amendment?

HOLDING AND DECISION: (Holmes, J.) Yes. Congress may validly enact a statute to enforce a treaty even if the statute standing by itself would be unconstitutional because it interfered with the rights reserved to the states by the Tenth Amendment. Article II, § 2, grants the President the power to make treaties and Article VI, § 2, declares that treaties shall be part of the supreme law of the land. If a treaty is a valid one, Article I, § 8, gives Congress the power to enact legislation that is a necessary and proper means to enforce the treaty. While acts of Congress are the supreme law of the land only when they are made in pursuance of the Constitution, treaties are valid when made under the authority of the United States. The Court stated that there were qualifications to the treaty-making

power, but felt that the qualifications must be determined by looking at the facts of each case. There are situations that require national action, which an act of Congress could not deal with, but which a treaty enforced with a congressional act could. Affirmed.

▶ ANALYSIS

Many people were upset with the decision in this case because they feared that the Court had interpreted the treaty power so broadly that all constitutional limitations could be overridden by the use of treaties and accompanying congressional legislation. In 1954, the Bricker Amendment, which required that a treaty could become effective as internal law in the United States only through legislation that would be valid in the absence of the treaty, was narrowly defeated. This would have, in effect, overruled the decision in this case, because the congressional act was not valid when standing by itself. Several other similar proposals were made during the following three years, which also failed.

Quicknotes

PECUNIARY Monetary, relating to money.

TENTH AMENDMENT The Tenth Amendment to the United States Constitution reserving those powers therein, not expressly delegated to the federal government or prohibited to the states, to the states or to the people.

TREATY An agreement made between two or more independent nations; once a treaty is made into law, it becomes applicable to the states under Article IV, § 2, of the Constitution.

United States v. Nixon

Federal government (P) v. President of the United States (D)

418 U.S. 683 (1974).

NATURE OF CASE: Certiorari granted after denial of a motion to quash a third-party subpoena duces tecum.

FACT SUMMARY: Nixon (D) challenges a subpoena served on him as a third party requiring the production of tapes and documents for use in a criminal prosecution.

🏛 **RULE OF LAW**
Absent a claim of need to protect military, diplomatic, or sensitive national security secrets, an absolute, unqualified presidential privilege of immunity from judicial process under all circumstances does not exist.

FACTS: After the grand jury returned an indictment charging seven defendants with various offenses relating to Watergate, Special Prosecutor Jaworski moved for the issuance of a subpoena duces tecum to obtain Watergate-related tapes and documents from Nixon (D). Jaworski claimed that the materials were important to the government's proof at the criminal proceeding against the seven defendants. The subpoena was issued, and Nixon (D) turned over some materials. His lawyer then moved to quash the subpoena. Nixon (D) contended that the separation of powers doctrine precludes judicial review of a presidential claim of privilege and that the need for confidentiality of high-level communication requires an absolute privilege as against a subpoena.

ISSUE: Absent a claim of need to protect military, diplomatic, or sensitive national security secrets, does the President possess an absolute executive privilege that is immune from judicial review?

HOLDING AND DECISION: (Burger, C.J.) No. Absent a claim of need to protect military, diplomatic, or sensitive national security secrets, an absolute, unqualified presidential privilege of immunity from judicial process under all circumstances does not exist. First of all, Nixon (D) claimed the court lacks jurisdiction to issue the subpoena because the matter was an intra-branch dispute within the executive branch. However, courts must look behind names that symbolize the parties to determine whether a justiciable case or controversy exists. Here, the Special Prosecutor, with his asserted need for the subpoenaed material, was opposed by the President with his assertion of privilege against disclosure. This setting assures that there is the necessary concreteness and adversity to sharpen the presentation of the issues. Against Nixon's (D) claim of absolute privilege immune from judicial review, this court reaffirms the holding of *Marbury v. Madison*, 5

U.S. 137 (1803), that "it is emphatically the province . . . of the Judicial Department to say what the law is," and this is true with respect to a claim of executive privilege. Absent a claim of need to protect military, diplomatic, or sensitive national security secrets, neither the doctrine of the separation of powers nor the generalized need for the confidentiality of high-level communications, without more, can sustain an absolute unqualified presidential privilege. Now that the court has decided that legitimate needs of judicial process may outweigh presidential privilege, it is necessary to resolve those competing interests in this case. It is true that the need for confidentiality justifies a presumptive privilege for presidential communications. However, our criminal justice system depends on a complete presentation of all relevant facts. To ensure this presentation, compulsory process must be available. Here, Jaworski has demonstrated a specific need at a criminal trial for the material sought. Nixon (D) has not based his claim of privilege on the military or diplomatic content of the materials but rather on a generalized interest in confidentiality. The allowance of this privilege based on only a generalized interest in confidentiality to withhold relevant evidence in a criminal trial would cut deeply into the guarantee of due process and cannot prevail. Affirmed.

▌ *ANALYSIS*

On July 16, 1973, Alexander Butterfield testified before the Senate Select Committee on presidential campaign activities that conversations in President Nixon's offices had been recorded automatically at Nixon's (D) direction. Nixon (D) declined to comply with requests for the tapes from Special Prosecutor Cox and the Senate Select Committee. Nixon (D) maintained that the tapes would remain under his personal control. When a subpoena for the tapes was issued, Nixon (D) replied that he asserted executive privilege and that the President is not subject to compulsory process from the courts. The grand jury then instructed the Special Prosecutor to seek an order for the production of the tapes. It was that enforcement proceeding which produced the first ruling in the case. Judge Sirica ordered the President to produce the items for in-camera inspection. The court of appeals affirmed. *Nixon v. Sirica*, 487 F.2d 700 (1973).

■■▬■

Quicknotes

ABSOLUTE PRIVILEGE Unconditional or unqualified immunity enjoyed by a person.

Continued on next page.

EXECUTIVE PRIVILEGE The right of the executive branch to refuse to disclose confidential communications if such exemption is necessary for the effective discharge of its official duties.

SUBPOENA DUCES TECUM A court mandate compelling the production of documents under a witness's control.

■≡■

Clinton v. Jones

President of the United States (D) v. Female state employee (P)

520 U.S. 681 (1997).

NATURE OF CASE: Review of judgment denying presidential immunity and request to postpone trial in sexual harassment case.

FACT SUMMARY: Jones (P) claimed Clinton (D) sexually harassed her during events that took place prior to Clinton (D) assuming the presidency.

🏛 RULE OF LAW
Presidential immunity does not apply to civil damages litigation arising out of unofficial events occurring prior to the assumption of office.

FACTS: In May of 1991, Jones (P) worked as a state employee at a conference for which Clinton (D) gave a speech. Jones (P) claimed that a state police officer persuaded her to go to Clinton's (D) hotel room, where Clinton (D) proceeded to make sexual advances toward her. Jones (P) allegedly experienced on-the-job retaliation because she rejected these advances. When Clinton (D) was elected President in 1992, Jones (P) claimed she was defamed when spokesmen for Clinton (D) denied her allegations, branding Jones (P) a liar. On May 6, 1994, Jones (P) filed suit in district court, and Clinton (D) filed a motion to dismiss based on presidential immunity. The district court denied the motion to dismiss, but delayed the trial until after Clinton (D) left office. Both parties appealed and the court of appeals affirmed the denial of the motion to dismiss, but reversed the delay in the trial. Clinton (D) appealed.

ISSUE: Does presidential immunity apply to civil damages litigation arising out of unofficial events occurring prior to the assumption of office?

HOLDING AND DECISION: (Stevens, J.) No. Presidential immunity does not apply to civil damages litigation arising out of unofficial events occurring prior to the assumption of office. Here, Clinton (D) cannot claim presidential immunity because his actions occurred in an unofficial capacity during a time prior to his assuming the presidency. Because the conduct occurred in an unofficial capacity, this ruling will not make any president unduly cautious in the discharge of his official duties. With respect to the separation of powers, the litigation of questions that relate entirely to the unofficial conduct of the individual who happens to be President poses no perceptible risk of misallocation of either judicial power or executive power. Affirmed.

CONCURRENCE: (Breyer, J.) Although the Constitution does not automatically grant Clinton (D) an immunity from civil lawsuits, a federal judge may not interfere with Clinton's (D) discharge of his public duties once Clinton (D) sets forth and explains how they conflict with judicial proceedings.

▶ ANALYSIS

Intergovernmental immunity generally applies in situations where states attempt to regulate and tax the property and activities of the federal government. The federal government's power is derived from the Supremacy Clause and, generally, the federal government is given greater immunity than state governments. This case brings up an unexplored area where the limits of presidential immunity extend as it relates to the private, unofficial acts of the President.

◼▬◼

Quicknotes

EXECUTIVE PRIVILEGE The right of the executive branch to refuse to disclose confidential communications if such exemption is necessary for the effective discharge of its official duties.

◼▬◼

CHAPTER 7

The Post-Civil War Amendments and the "Incorporation" of Fundamental Rights

Quick Reference Rules of Law

Barron v. Mayor and City Council of Baltimore

Wharf owner (P) v. Municipality (D)

32 U.S. (7 Pet.) 243 (1833).

NATURE OF CASE: Certiorari review of underlying action to recover damages.

FACT SUMMARY: Barron (P) claimed that the City (D) made his wharf useless by diverting the streams during its construction work.

🏛 RULE OF LAW
State legislation is not subject to the limitations imposed by the amendments to the United States Constitution.

FACTS: Barron (P) sued the City (D) for making his wharf in Baltimore Harbor useless. He claimed that the City (D) had diverted the flow of streams during its street construction and that this diversion had deposited earth near the wharf, causing the water to become too shallow for most vessels. Barron (P) claimed that the action violated the Fifth Amendment guarantee that property will not be taken without just compensation.

ISSUE: Is state legislation subject to the limitations imposed by the amendments to the United States Constitution?

HOLDING AND DECISION: (Marshall, C.J.) No. State legislation is not subject to the limitations imposed by the amendments to the United States Constitution. The amendments to the Constitution were intended as limitations solely on the exercise of power by the U.S. Government and are not applicable to the legislation of the states. The Constitution and its amendments were established by the people of the United States for themselves, for their own government, and not for the governments of the states. The people and each state established their own constitution. The constitutional amendments restrain only the power of the federal government and are not applicable to the actions of the state governments. Article I, § 10 expressly lists the restrictions upon the state governments. We find no reason why if the amendments were to apply to the states, there are not express words so stating. The amendments contain no expression indicating intent to apply them to the states. Hence, because there is no conflict here between the City (D) and state's action and the federal Constitution, this court has no jurisdiction over this action. Dismissed.

▶ ANALYSIS

There were relatively few references to individual rights in the original Constitution. Its major concern was with governmental structures and relationships. The most important limitation on state power protective of individual rights was the Contract Clause. Nor was there a significant broader spectrum of individual rights restrictions on the national government. In response to the demand for additional constitutional protection of individual as well as states' rights, the first ten amendments were proposed and ratified. Since federal criminal decisions were not ordinarily reviewable by the Supreme Court, it had little occasion for interpretation of the Bill of Rights prior to the Civil War.

Quicknotes

CONTRACT CLAUSE Article 1, section 10 of the Constitution prohibiting states from passing any "law impairing the Obligation of Contracts."

JUST COMPENSATION The right guaranteed by the Fifth Amendment to the United States Constitution of a person, when his property is taken for public use by the state, to receive adequate compensation in order to restore him to the position he enjoyed prior to the appropriation.

TAKING Governmental use or dispossession of private property.

Dred Scott v. Sanford

Former slave (P) v. Administrator (D)

60 U.S. (19 How.) 393 (1857).

NATURE OF CASE: Action in trespass.

FACT SUMMARY: Dred Scott (P) claimed to have been freed from his slave status by his travels to free-states with his master, but Sanford (D) insisted Scott (P) could not bring a federal court action pressing the point because former slaves and their descendants are not "citizens."

🏛 RULE OF LAW
Since they are not "citizens" in the sense in which that word is used in the Constitution, blacks who were slaves in this country, or who are the descendants of such slaves, cannot bring suit in federal court.

FACTS: Dred Scott (P), a slave, was taken along on his master's sojourns to the free state of Illinois and the free part of the Missouri Territory (according to the Missouri Compromise). It was after they returned to the slave state of Missouri that the master died, and Sanford (D) became the administrator of his estate. Scott (P) attempted to bring a diversity action in federal court based on his claim that his "residence" in the aforementioned free jurisdictions had liberated him from his status as a slave. He was, he insisted, thus properly considered a "citizen" of Missouri and was therefore entitled to bring suit in federal court against Sanford (D), who was a citizen of another state (New York). Sanford (D) argued that a former slave could not be considered a citizen of the United States or of Missouri. The lower court agreed with him. Scott (P) appealed.

ISSUE: Can a former slave be a "citizen" so as to qualify to bring an action in federal court?

HOLDING AND DECISION: (Taney, C.J.) No. Blacks who were slaves in this country, or who are the descendants of such slaves are, not "citizens" in the sense in which that word is used in the Constitution and are thus not entitled to maintain an action in federal court. A review of history reveals quite readily that neither class of persons who had been imported as slaves nor their descendants, whether they had become free or not, were acknowledged as part of the "people" but were rather considered as mere property. They simply were not among those who were "citizens" of the several states when the Constitution was adopted, and that is the time frame that must be utilized in determining who was included as a "citizen" in the Constitution. Because he is not a "citizen," Scott (P) cannot maintain this action.

DISSENT: (Curtis, J.) To determine whether individuals who were free when the Constitution was adopted were citizens, even though those individuals were the descendants of slaves, the only necessary inquiry is whether those free individuals were citizens of any of the States under the Confederation at the time of the Constitution's adoption. It is a fact that at the time the Articles of Confederation were ratified, all free native-born inhabitants of five States were citizens of those States, notwithstanding that they were descended from African slaves. There is nothing in the Constitution that deprived those who were citizens of the United States at the time of its adoption of their citizenship, especially given that those citizens established the Constitution. The Constitution also contains nothing that deprives native-born citizens of any State of their citizenship. Finally, there is nothing in the Constitution that empowers Congress to disenfranchise any State citizen of that citizenship. Therefore, every free person born on the soil of a State, who is a citizen of that State by force of its Constitution or laws, is also a citizen of the United States. This is also true of States that came into being after the Constitution was adopted. When the Constitution was framed, it was expected that some of the States would cede their claims to what were then their territories, and that those territories, and new States formed therefrom, would be subject to the Constitution. Slavery itself is regulated by municipal law, and the Framers, who recognized this, and who knew that a slave was property only in those States where laws so provided, intended that Congress in its discretion would determine what regulations, if any, should be made concerning slavery. This intent can be gleaned from the fact the Constitution is silent as to the regulation of slavery, and expresses no intent to interfere with or to displace these principles. Finally, there is nothing in the Constitution that supports the proposition that prohibiting slave owners from bringing their slaves into a Territory deprives the owners of their property without due process of law.

▶ ANALYSIS

The justices all knew this was a historically important case; each one took the time to write an opinion. Besides the primary opinion by Chief Justice Taney, there were six concurring and two dissenting opinions. No longer doctrinally important because of subsequent amendments to the Constitution resolving of the slavery issues, this case still serves as a prime example of the view that the Constitution, as Chief Justice Taney put it, forever speaks "not only in the same words, but with the same meaning and intent with which it spoke when it came from the hands of the Framers." It is a view that has been roundly criticized as

Continued on next page.

too rigid and formalistic an approach to take toward a document that must be flexible enough to provide effective and operable guidelines and governing principles for an ever-evolving society.

■══■

Quicknotes

ACTION OF TRESPASS An action to recover damages resulting from the wrongful interference with a party's person, property or rights.

DIVERSITY ACTION An action commenced by a citizen of one state against a citizen of another state or against an alien, involving an amount in controversy set by statute, over which the federal court has jurisdiction.

■══■

Slaughter-House Cases

Butchers (P) v. State (D)

83 U.S. (16 Wall.) 36 (1873).

NATURE OF CASE: Certiorari review of state enforcement of a monopoly.

FACT SUMMARY: Louisiana created a 25-year slaughter-house monopoly to which several butchers (P) who were not included objected.

🏛 RULE OF LAW
The Fourteenth Amendment protects the privileges and immunities of national, not state, citizenship; and neither the Equal Protection, Due Process, nor Privileges and Immunities Clauses of that amendment may be used to interfere with state control of the privileges and immunities of state citizenship.

FACTS: [A Louisiana law of 1869 granted a monopoly to a slaughter-house company created by the legislature for the three largest parishes in that state. Butchers (P), who were not included in the monopoly, challenged the law creating it on the grounds that it violated the Thirteenth Amendment ban on involuntary servitude and the Fourteenth Amendment protections of the privileges and immunities of national citizenship and equal protection and due process of law. From a judgment sustaining the law, the butchers (P) appealed.]

ISSUE: Does the Fourteenth Amendment Privileges and Immunities Clause make all privileges and immunities of citizenship federal rights subject to federal enforcement?

HOLDING AND DECISION: (Miller, J.) No. The Fourteenth Amendment protects the privileges and immunities of national, not state, citizenship; and neither the Equal Protection, nor Due Process, nor Privileges and Immunities Clauses of that Amendment may be used to interfere with state control of the privileges and immunities of state citizenship. The underlying purpose of all three of the post-Civil War amendments was to eliminate the remnants of African slavery, not to effect any fundamental change in the relations of the government. The Fourteenth Amendment expressly was adopted to assure only that states would not "abridge the privileges and immunities of citizens of the United States" (i.e., black citizens in their pursuit of national rights such as the right to protection on the high seas). Similarly, the Equal Protection and Due Process Clauses of that Amendment were drawn to protect former slaves from state denial of federal rights. No interpretation of this Amendment (or the Thirteenth, which is an even clearer case) may be used to prevent Louisiana from exercising its police power here (to promote public health in slaughter houses) to define particular privileges and immunities of its citizens. Affirmed.

DISSENT: (Field, J.) The Fourteenth Amendment is protection for all citizens of the fundamental rights of free government from abridgment by the states. Among such rights clearly is the right to an equal opportunity to pursue employment.

DISSENT: (Bradley, J.) The Fourteenth Amendment is a ban upon state deprivation of life, liberty, or property without due process of law. The purpose of its passage was preventing future insubordination to government by law which fostered the Civil War.

▶ *ANALYSIS*

The effect of this decision was to render the Fourteenth Amendment Privileges or Immunities Clause a nullity for the purpose of protecting individual rights from state abridgment. In addition, it ruled out the possibility that the Bill of Rights could be enforced upon the states as privileges and immunities of national citizenship. Subsequently, of course, the Court adopted the position of Justice Bradley and began selectively incorporating parts of those Amendments into the Fourteenth Amendment Due Process Clause. In addition, the Equal Protection Clause has been used extensively to prohibit state action which is discriminatory in any irrational way (i.e., the rational basis test). Note, finally, that even the Thirteenth Amendment, summarily treated above, has been expanded to bar private discriminatory action which can be identified as a badge of slavery.

■=■

Quicknotes

EQUAL PROTECTION CLAUSE A constitutional guarantee that no person should be denied the same protection of the laws enjoyed by other persons in like circumstances.

INVOLUNTARY SERVITUDE Being in a state of forced labor for the benefit of another person.

MONOPOLY A privilege or right conferred upon an individual or entity granting it the exclusive power to manufacture, sell and distribute a particular service or commodity; a market condition in which one or a few companies control the sale of a product or service thereby restraining competition in respect to that article or service.

PRIVILEGES OR IMMUNITIES CLAUSE Section 1 of the Fourteenth Amendment of the U.S. Constitution; prohibits state laws that abridge the privileges or immunities of U.S. citizens.

■=■

Saenz v. Roe

[Parties not identified.]

526 U.S. 489 (1999).

NATURE OF CASE: Certiorari review of a state statute.

FACT SUMMARY: When California (D) discriminated against citizens who had resided in the state for less than one year in distributing welfare benefits, the state statute was challenged and held to be unconstitutional.

🏛 RULE OF LAW
Durational residency requirements violate the fundamental right to travel by denying a newly arrived citizen the same privileges and immunities enjoyed by other citizens in the same state.

FACTS: In 1992, California (D) enacted a statute limiting the maximum first-year welfare benefits available to newly arrived residents to the amount they would have received in the state of their prior residence. California residents who were eligible for such benefits challenged the constitutionality of the durational residency requirement, alleging their right to travel was violated. The district court preliminarily enjoined implementation of the statute and the court of appeals affirmed. Congress enacted the Personal Responsibility and Work Opportunity Reconciliation Act of 1996, which expressly authorized states to apply the rules (including benefit amounts) of another state if the family has resided in the state for less than twelve months. California (D) appealed, alleging that the statute should be upheld if it has a rational basis, and that the state's (D) legitimate interest in saving over $10 million a year satisfied that test.

ISSUE: Do durational residency requirements violate the fundamental right to travel by denying a newly arrived citizen the same privileges and immunities enjoyed by other citizens in the same state?

HOLDING AND DECISION: (Stevens, J.) Yes. Durational residency requirements violate the fundamental right to travel by denying a newly arrived citizen the same privileges and immunities enjoyed by other citizens in the same state. The first sentence of Article IV, § 2, provides that the citizens of each state shall be entitled to all privileges and immunities of citizens in the several states. The right of a newly arrived citizen to the same privileges and immunities enjoyed by other citizens of the same state is protected not only by the new arrival's status as a state citizen, but also by her status as a citizen of the United States. The Citizenship Clause of the Fourteenth Amendment protects all citizens' right to choose to be citizens of the state wherein they reside. Neither mere rationality nor some intermediate standard of review should be used to

judge the constitutionality of a state rule that discriminates against some of its citizens because they have been domiciled in the state for less than a year. The state's legitimate interest in saving money provides no justification for its decision to discriminate among equally eligible citizens. Affirmed.

DISSENT: (Rehnquist, C.J.) If states can require an individual to reside in-state for a year before exercising the right to educational benefits, the right to terminate a marriage, or the right to vote in primary elections that all other state citizens enjoy, then they may surely do the same for welfare benefits. California has reasonably exercised its power to protect state resources through an objective, narrowly tailored residence requirement. There is nothing in the Constitution that should prevent the enforcement of that requirement.

DISSENT: (Thomas, J.) The majority attributes a meaning to the Privileges or Immunities Clause that likely was unintended when the Fourteenth Amendment was enacted and ratified. At that time, people understood "privileges or immunities of citizens" to be their fundamental right, rather than every public benefit established by positive law.

❚ ANALYSIS

The Court in this case found that a state violated the Privileges or Immunities Clause when it discriminated against citizens who had been residents for less than one year. The Thomas dissent alleged that this was contrary to the original understanding at the time the Fourteenth Amendment was enacted. The Rehnquist dissent went on to point out that a welfare subsidy is as much an investment in human capital as is a tuition subsidy and their attendant benefits are just as portable.

■▭▭■

Quicknotes

FOURTEENTH AMENDMENT Declares that no state shall make or enforce any law which shall abridge the privileges and immunities of citizens of the United States.

FUNDAMENTAL RIGHT A liberty that is either expressly or implicitly provided for in the United States Constitution, the deprivation or burdening of which is subject to a heightened standard of review.

Continued on next page.

PRIVILEGES OR IMMUNITIES CLAUSE   Section 1 of the Fourteenth Amendment of the U.S. Constitution; prohibits state laws that abridge the privileges or immunities of U.S. citizens.

RATIONAL BASIS REVIEW   A test employed by the court to determine the validity of a statute in equal protection actions, whereby the court determines whether the challenged statute is rationally related to the achievement of a legitimate state interest.

STRICT SCRUTINY   Method by which courts determine the constitutionality of a law when a law affects a fundamental right. Under the test, the legislature must have a compelling interest to enact law and measures prescribed by the law must be the least restrictive means possible to accomplish its goal.

Duncan v. Louisiana

Criminal defendant (D) v. State (P)

391 U.S. 145 (1968).

NATURE OF CASE: Appeal from conviction of battery and sentence of 60 days with a $150 fine.

FACT SUMMARY: Louisiana's constitution granted jury trials only in cases in which capital punishment or imprisonment at hard labor may be granted.

🏛 RULE OF LAW
The Fourteenth Amendment guarantees a right of jury trial in all criminal cases that would, were they to be tried in a federal court, come within the Sixth Amendment's guarantee.

FACTS: Duncan (D) was charged with simple battery, which in Louisiana was punishable by a maximum of two years' imprisonment and a $300 fine. His request for a jury trial was denied by the trial court because the Louisiana (P) constitution granted jury trials only in cases in which capital punishment or imprisonment at hard labor may be imposed.

ISSUE: Does the Fourteenth Amendment guarantee a right of jury trial in all criminal cases that would, were they to be tried in a federal court, come within the Sixth Amendment's guarantee?

HOLDING AND DECISION: (White, J.) Yes. The Fourteenth Amendment guarantees a right of jury trial in all criminal cases that would—were they to be tried in a federal court—come within the Sixth Amendment's guarantee. The right to a jury trial in serious criminal cases punishable by at least two years in prison is a fundamental right that must be recognized by the states as part of their obligation to extend due process of law to all persons within their jurisdiction. A right to jury trial is granted to a criminal defendant in order to guard against an overzealous or corrupt prosecutor and the compliant, biased, or eccentric judge. A holding that due process assures a right to jury trial will not cast doubt on the integrity of every trial conducted without a jury. Thus, there is no constitutional problem with accepting waivers, and prosecuting petty crimes without extending the right where defendants are satisfied with bench trials, judicial or prosecutorial unfairness is less likely. What controls will be the maximum possible sentence and not the punishment actually meted out. The exact line between petty and serious crimes need not be settled here. Reversed and remanded.

CONCURRENCE: (Black, J.) Both total and selective incorporation of the Bill of Rights are to be preferred to assigning no settled meaning to the term "due process" as this will shift from time to time in accordance with changing theories.

DISSENT: (Harlan, J.) The Due Process Clause requires only that state procedures be fundamentally fair in all respects. There is no historical support for the total incorporation theory. The Framers of the Fourteenth Amendment intended that the meaning of "due process" will change as does the experience and conscience of the American people. Selective incorporation lacks guiding standards. The definition of "fundamental" used by the majority is circular, since it means "old," "much praised," and "found in the Bill of Rights." Here, there was no indication that Duncan's (D) trial was not a fair one.

▶ ANALYSIS

One commentator has suggested that after *Duncan*, the Court, although describing its test as a "fundamental rights" approach, has actually embraced "selective incorporation," in which all of the Bill of Rights, one provision at a time, has been incorporated in fact. Nevertheless, it is still unclear whether by "specific" provisions the Court means only the text of the actual amendments or judicial interpretations in decisions involving those rights.

Quicknotes

DUE PROCESS Fundamental fairness; the laws fairly administered through the court of justice.

FUNDAMENTAL RIGHT A basic and essential right; freedoms expressed in the Bill of Rights and implied freedoms not expressly stated in the Constitution.

RIGHT TO JURY TRIAL The right guaranteed by the Sixth Amendment to the federal constitution that in all criminal prosecutions the accused has a right to a trial by an impartial jury of the state and district in which the crime was allegedly committed.

SELECTIVE INCORPORATION Doctrine providing that the Bill of Rights is incorporated by the Due Process Clause only to the extent that the Supreme Court decides that the privileges and immunities therein are so essential to fundamental principles of due process to be preserved against both state and federal action.

SIXTH AMENDMENT Provides the right to a speedy trial by impartial jury, the right to be informed of the accusation, to confront witnesses, and to have the assistance of counsel in all criminal prosecutions.

McDonald v. City of Chicago

Citizens (P) v. State (D)

561 U.S. 3025 (2010).

NATURE OF CASE: Appeal from affirmance of judgment that the Second Amendment does not apply to the states.

FACT SUMMARY: [Several plaintiffs (P) challenged a ban on handguns in Chicago, contending the ban was unconstitutional because the Second Amendment applies to the states.]

🏛 RULE OF LAW
The Second Amendment applies to the states by incorporation through the Due Process Clause.

FACTS: [The cities of Chicago (D) and Oak Park (D) in Illinois had gun bans. Several lawsuits were filed against the cities challenging those bans after the Supreme Court decided *District of Columbia v. Heller*, 554 U.S. 570 (2008), where the Court held a District of Columbia handgun ban violated the Second Amendment because the D.C. law was enacted under the authority of the federal government and, therefore, the Second Amendment was applicable. The plaintiffs (P) in this case argued the Second Amendment also applies to the states, and because it does, the Chicago (D) handgun bans were unconstitutional. The district court dismissed the suits and on appeal, the U.S. Court of Appeals for the Seventh Circuit affirmed. The Supreme Court granted certiorari.]

ISSUE: Does the Second Amendment apply to the states by incorporation through the Due Process Clause?

HOLDING AND DECISION: (Alito, J.) Yes. The Second Amendment applies to the states by incorporation through the Due Process Clause. As a threshold matter, the privileges or immunities clause does not incorporate the Second Amendment. Also, under the Court's "selective incorporation" approach, once a right under the Bill of Rights is incorporated, it applies fully to the states. In *Heller*, it was decided the right to self-defense is a right that is "fundamental to the Nation's scheme of ordered liberty" and "deeply rooted in this Nation's history and tradition." Throughout the nation's history, Congress has upheld the right to bear arms as a fundamental right, and arguments to the contrary are not supported by history. The question is not whether a civilized society can exist without recognizing this particular right; it's whether our civilized society must recognize the right. If this were not so, for example, many of the criminal protections of the Bill of Rights, which are unique to our country, would not be incorporated against the states. The Due Process Clause of the Fourteenth Amendment incorporates the Second Amendment right recognized in *Heller*, a fundamental, deeply rooted right. Reversed and remanded.

CONCURRENCE: (Scalia, J.) Justice Stevens's dissent is wrong and premised on a subjective standard. Essentially, he advocates disregarding precedent and Due Process principles, and relying exclusively on what judges believe is correct. Under this approach, judges get to pick the rights they want to protect and discard those they don't. Justice Stevens asserts his standard is not subjective because it provides sufficient constraints on judges' subjectivity. The first constraint he offers is that he would avoid attempts to provide any all-purpose, top-down, totalizing theory of liberty. The notion the absence of a coherent theory of the Due Process Clause will somehow curtail judicial subjectivity makes no sense. To the contrary, indeterminacy means opportunity for courts to impose whatever rule they like; it is the problem, not the solution. Another constraint he offers is requiring judges to show respect for the democratic process. While that serves as a constraint on subjectivity, the manner in which Justice Stevens would apply that constraint is extraordinary, as it would give rights the states are considering restricting— such as the right to bear arms—less protection, while giving a privilege the political branches (instruments of the democratic process) have withheld entirely and continue to withhold more protection. This is a topsy-turvy approach that insults rather than respects the democratic process. The next constraint Justice Stevens suggests is more difficult to assess. He advocates judges have "sensitivity to the interaction between the intrinsic aspects of liberty and the practical realities of contemporary society." It is unclear what this means. Is it some sixth sense instilled in judges when they ascend to the bench? Or does it mean judges are more constrained when they agonize about the cosmic conflict between liberty and its potentially harmful consequences? In any event, the historically focused approach is significantly better than the "living Constitution," subjective, approach recommended by Justice Stevens. The historical approach is much less subjective, and intrudes much less upon the democratic process because it depends upon a body of evidence susceptible of reasoned analysis rather than a variety of vague ethicopolitical "First Principles" whose combined conclusion can be found to point in any direction the judges favor. Moreover, the latter approach would not eliminate, but multiply, the hard questions courts must confront, since it would not replace history with moral philosophy, but would have courts consider both.

DISSENT: (Stevens, J.) The core issue to be resolved here is whether the Second Amendment guarantees individuals a fundamental right, enforceable against the states,

Continued on next page.

to possess a functional, personal firearm, including a handgun, within the home. That is a different question than the incorporation question, which was already decided in the late 19th century. This is a substantive due process case. The rights protected by the Due Process Clause are not principally procedural in nature, and substantive due process is fundamentally a matter of personal liberty. Regardless of whether a substantive due process interest is expressly identified in the Constitution, the key inquiry is whether that interest is comprised within the term liberty. Flowing from these principles is the notion that the rights protected against state infringement by the Fourteenth Amendment's Due Process Clause need not be identical in shape or scope to the rights protected against Federal Government infringement by the various provisions of the Bill of Rights. Substantive due process claims that are based on purely local or particular interests, rather than more universal liberty interests, are not constitutionally protected. Such a liberty test undeniably requires judges to apply their own reasoned judgment, but that does not mean it involves an exercise in abstract philosophy. In addition, historical and empirical data of various kinds ground the analysis. A rigid historical test is inappropriate because substantive due process doctrine has never evaluated substantive rights in purely, or even predominantly, historical terms. If it were really the case that the Fourteenth Amendment's guarantee of liberty embraces only those rights "so rooted in our history, tradition, and practice as to require special protection," then the guarantee would serve little function, except to ratify those rights that states and municipalities have already been according the most extensive protection. A purely historical approach would be unfaithful to the expansive principles inherent in the Fourteenth Amendment and to the level of generality in its language. To find otherwise, would mean we would have to countenance the most revolting injustices in the name of continuity, and not be responsive to newly recognized injustices, such as the subjugation of women and other rank forms of discrimination. To adhere to the purely historical approach would in effect be judicial abdication in the guise of judicial modesty. The question then arises how to avoid injecting too much subjectivity when determining substantive due process liberty claims. In addition to grounding the analysis in historical experience and reasoned judgment, there are several constraints that militate against subjectivity. First, the courts must eschew attempts to provide any all-purpose, top-down, totalizing theory of "liberty," which was not defined by the Framers, and which by its very nature cannot be reduced to a formula or otherwise pigeonholed. Nevertheless, the parameters of liberty have been elucidated by a conceptual core that refines and delimits the notion of liberty. The clause safeguards, most basically, "the ability independently to define one's identity," "the individual's right to make certain unusually important decisions that will affect his own, or his family's, destiny," and the right to be respected as a human being. Self-determination, bodily integrity, freedom of conscience,

intimate relationships, political equality, dignity and respect—these are the central values implicit in the concept of ordered liberty. A second constraint is respect for the democratic process, so that where the states have already carefully considered a particular liberty interest, judicial intervention may not be appropriate. The real issue here, then, is not whether the Second Amendment applies to the states merely because it has been incorporated by the Fourteenth Amendment—it has not—but whether the Second Amendment applies because of the Fourteenth Amendment's mandate to protect liberty. Understood as a liberty question, the plea of homeowners to keep arms in their home has real force, founded on a desire for self-defense and to protect their liberty and property. While the individual's interest in firearm possession is thus heightened in the home, the state's corresponding interest in regulation is somewhat weaker. However, under a substantive due process analysis, precedent supports Chicago's (D) ban. First, firearms have a fundamentally ambivalent relationship to liberty. Just as they can help homeowners defend their families and property from intruders, they can help thugs and insurrectionists murder innocent victims. Second, owning a handgun or any particular type of firearm is not critical to leading a life of autonomy, dignity, or political equality. Further, the experience of other advanced democracies, including those that share our British heritage, undercuts the notion an expansive right to keep and bear arms is intrinsic to ordered liberty, as those countries place stricter restrictions on firearms than does the U.S. Finally, Justice Scalia's historically focused approach does not lead to an objective approach. To the contrary, numerous threshold questions that frame the analysis arise before one ever gets to the history—and there is no neutral, objective answer to these questions. Even then, it is hardly a novel insight that history is not an objective science, and that its use can therefore "point in any direction the judges favor." His method invites not only bad history, but also bad constitutional law. While history must be a factor in the analysis, it should not be the determinative factor, and the net result of Justice Scalia's approach is to give federal judges unprecedented lawmaking powers in an area in which they have no special qualifications, and where the political process has handled the issue for decades.

DISSENT: (Breyer, J.) Nothing in our history shows a consensus the right to private-armed defense is deeply rooted in history or tradition, or is otherwise fundamental. To incorporate the right in *Heller* may change the law in many of the states. In addition, incorporation will not necessarily further any other constitutional objective. It does not comprise a necessary part of the democratic process, and does not significantly protect individuals who might otherwise suffer unfair or inhumane treatment at the hands of a majority. The state legislature is in a much better position to assess any particular gun law,

Continued on next page.

and incorporation will impose on every, or nearly every, state a different right to bear arms than they currently recognize—a right that threatens to destabilize settled state legal principles.

▶ *ANALYSIS*

Most scholars agree that when the Bill of Rights was adopted, it was intended to limit the federal, not state, government. After the adoption of the Fourteenth Amendment in 1868, the Supreme Court held that rights from the Bill of Rights may be selectively applied, or "incorporated," through the Due Process Clause. In *McDonald*, the Court stated that provisions of the Bill of Rights may be incorporated only if they are "fundamental to *our* scheme of ordered liberty," or "deeply rooted in this Nation's history and tradition." The case therefore represents a restriction on the application of the Due Process Clause.

■═■

Quicknotes

DUE PROCESS CLAUSE Clauses, found in the Fifth and Fourteenth Amendments to the United States Constitution, providing that no person shall be deprived of "life, liberty, or property, without due process of law."

FOURTEENTH AMENDMENT Declares that no state shall make or enforce any law that shall abridge the privileges and immunities of citizens of the United States. No state shall deny to any person within its jurisdiction the equal protection of the laws.

PRIVILEGES AND IMMUNITIES CLAUSE Refers to the guarantee set forth in the Fourteenth Amendment to the United States Constitution recognizing that any individual born in any of the United States is entitled to both state and national citizenship and guaranteeing such citizens the privileges and immunities thereof.

■═■

Due Process

Quick Reference Rules of Law

Lochner v. New York

Employer bakery (D) v. State (P)

198 U.S. 45 (1905).

NATURE OF CASE: Certiorari review of labor law and underlying conviction for violation.

FACT SUMMARY: A state labor law prohibited employment in bakeries for more than 60 hours a week or more than 10 hours a day. Lochner (D) permitted an employee in his bakery to work over 60 hours in one week.

🏛 RULE OF LAW
To be a fair, reasonable, and appropriate use of a state's police power, an act must have a direct relation, as a means to an end, to an appropriate and legitimate state objective.

FACTS: [Lochner (D) was fined for violating a state labor law. The law prohibited employment in bakeries for more than 60 hours a week or more than 10 hours a day. Lochner (D) permitted an employee to work in his bakery for more than 60 hours in one week.]

ISSUE: To be a fair, reasonable, and appropriate use of a state's police power, must an act have a direct relation, as a means to an end, to an appropriate and legitimate state objective?

HOLDING AND DECISION: (Peckham, J.) Yes. To be a fair, reasonable, and appropriate use of a state's police power, an act must have a direct relation, as a means to an end, to an appropriate and legitimate state objective. The general right to make a contract in relation to one's business is part of the liberty of the individual protected by the Fourteenth Amendment. The right to purchase or sell labor is part of the liberty protected by this Amendment. However, the states do possess certain police powers relating to the safety, health, morals, and general welfare of the public. If the contract is one which the state in the exercise of its police power has the right to prohibit, the Fourteenth Amendment will not prevent the state's prohibition. When, as here, the state acts to limit the right to labor or the right to contract, it is necessary to determine whether the rights of the state or the individual shall prevail. The Fourteenth Amendment limits the state's exercise of its police power; otherwise the state would have unbounded power once it stated that legislation was to conserve the health, morals, or safety of its people. It is not sufficient to assert that the act relates to public health. Rather, it must have a more direct relation, as a means to an end, to an appropriate state goal, before an act can interfere with an individual's right to contract in relation to his labor. In this case, there is no reasonable foundation for holding the act to be necessary to the health of the public or of bakery officials. Statutes such as this one are merely meddlesome interferences with the rights of the individual. They are invalid unless there is some fair ground to say that there is material danger to the public health or to the employees' health if the labor hours are not curtailed. It cannot be said that the production of healthy bread depends upon the hours that the employees work. Nor is the trade of a baker an unhealthy one to the degree which would authorize the legislature to interfere with the rights to labor and of free contract. Lochner's (D) conviction is reversed.

DISSENT: (Harlan, J.) Whether or not this is wise legislation is not a question for this Court. It is impossible to say that there is not substantial or real regulation between the statute and the state's legitimate goals. This decision brings under the Court's supervision matters which supposedly belonged exclusively to state legislatures.

DISSENT: (Holmes, J.) The word "liberty" in the Fourteenth Amendment should not invalidate a statute unless it can be said that a reasonable person would say that the statute infringes fundamental principles of our people and our law. A reasonable person might think this statute valid. Citizens' liberty is regulated by many state laws which have been held to be valid, i.e., the Sunday laws, the lottery laws, laws requiring vaccination.

▶ ANALYSIS

From the *Lochner* decision in 1905 to the 1930s the Court invalidated a considerable number of laws on substantive due process grounds, such as laws fixing minimum wages, maximum hours, prices, and law regulating business activities. The modern Court claims to have rejected the *Lochner* doctrine. It has withdrawn careful scrutiny in most economic areas but has maintained and increased intervention with respect to a variety of non-economic liberties. However, not only economic regulations were struck down under *Lochner*. That doctrine formed the basis for absorbing rights such as those in the First Amendment into the Fourteenth Amendment's concept of liberty. *Lochner* also helped justify other non-economic rights such as the right to teach in a foreign language, *Meyers v. Nebraska*, 262 U.S. 390 (1923). *Meyers* was to be relied upon in the birth control decision, *Griswold v. Connecticut*, 381 U.S. 479 (1965).

Quicknotes

POLICE POWERS The power of a state or local government to regulate private conduct for the health, safety and welfare of the general public.

Continued on next page.

SUBSTANTIVE DUE PROCESS A constitutional safeguard limiting the power of the state, irrespective of how fair its procedures may be; substantive limits placed on the power of the state.

Nebbia v. New York

Grocery store proprietor (D) v. State (P)

291 U.S. 502 (1934).

NATURE OF CASE: Certiorari review of Milk Board order and underlying conviction for violation of the order.

FACT SUMMARY: The State Milk Board fixed nine cents as the price to be charged for a quart of milk. Nebbia (D) sold two quarts of milk and a loaf of bread for eighteen cents.

▥ RULE OF LAW
When the occasion is proper and by appropriate measures, a state may regulate a business in any of its aspects, including fixing prices.

FACTS: In 1933, the New York legislature established a Milk Control Board (the "Board"). The Board was given the power to fix minimum and maximum retail prices to be charged by stores to consumers. The Board fixed the price of a quart of milk at nine cents. Nebbia (D), a grocery store proprietor, charged eighteen cents for two quarts of milk and a five-cent loaf of bread. The law establishing the Board was based on a legislative finding that, "Milk is an essential item of diet. Failure of producers to receive a reasonable return threatens a relaxation of vigilance against contamination. The production of milk is a paramount industry of the state, and largely affects the health and prosperity of its people."

ISSUE: When the occasion is proper and by appropriate measures, may a state regulate a business in any of its aspects, including fixing prices?

HOLDING AND DECISION: (Roberts, J.) Yes. When the occasion is proper and by appropriate measures, a state may regulate a business in any of its aspects, including fixing prices. The general rule is that both the use of property and the making of contracts shall be free from government interference. However, neither property rights nor contract rights are absolute. Equally fundamental with the private interest is the public's right to regulate it in the common interest. The Fifth and Fourteenth Amendments do not prohibit governmental regulation for the public welfare. They guarantee only that regulation shall be consistent with due process. The guarantee of due process demands only that the law shall not be unreasonable, arbitrary, or capricious and that the means selected shall have a real and substantial relation to the object sought to be attained. If an industry is subject to regulation in the public interest, its prices may be regulated. An industry that is "affected with a public industry" is one which is subject to police powers. A state is free to adopt whatever economic policy may be reasonably deemed to promote the public welfare. The courts are without authority to override such policies. If the laws passed have a rational relation to a

legitimate purpose and are neither arbitrary nor discriminatory, the requirements of due process are satisfied. Price control may fulfill these requirements as well as any other type of regulation. The New York law creating the Milk Board and giving it power to fix prices does not conflict with the due process guarantees and is constitutionally valid. Nebbia's (D) conviction is affirmed.

DISSENT: (McReynolds, J.) The Legislative Committee pointed out as the cause of decreased consumption of milk the consumer's reduced buying power. Higher store prices will not enlarge this power, nor will they increase production. This statute arbitrarily interferes with citizens' liberty since the means adopted do not reasonably relate to the end sought, the promotion of the public welfare.

▐ ANALYSIS

The early attitude of the Court had been that the states could regulate selling prices only for industries that affect the public interest. Regulation of prices and rates charged by public utilities, dairies, grain elevators, etc., were upheld, but regulation of the prices of theater tickets or ice was not. *Nebbia* held that price control regulation was to be treated the same as other police powers and a rational relation to a legitimate goal was all that was necessary. The dissent, representing the Court's earlier position, does not want to treat the legislation with the deference exercised by the majority. In its judgment, the method adopted by New York does not rationally relate to its goal. *Nebbia* represents the modern position of the Court, which is to presume the propriety of the legislation.

━■━

Quicknotes

DUE PROCESS The constitutional mandate requiring the courts to protect and enforce individuals' rights and liberties consistent with prevailing principles of fairness and justice and prohibiting the federal and state governments from such activities that deprive its citizens of a life, liberty or property interest.

PRICE FIXING A collaboration by competing companies to uniformly set price levels.

RATIONAL BASIS REVIEW A test employed by the court to determine the validity of a statute in equal protection actions, whereby the court determines whether the challenged statute is rationally related to the achievement of a legitimate state interest.

━■━

Williamson v. Lee Optical Co.

State (P) v. Optical company (D)

348 U.S. 483 (1955).

NATURE OF CASE: Certiorari review of constitutionality of state ophthalmology law.

FACT SUMMARY: A state law prohibited any person from fitting or duplicating lenses without a prescription from an ophthalmologist or optometrist. It also prohibited soliciting the sale of frames and the renting of space in a retail store to any person purporting to do eye examinations.

🏛 RULE OF LAW
The Due Process Clause will no longer be used to strike down state laws regulating business and industrial conditions because they may be unwise, improvident, or out of harmony with a particular school of thought.

FACTS: A state law prohibited any person who was not a licensed ophthalmologist or optometrist from fitting or duplicating lenses without a prescription from a licensed optometrist or ophthalmologist. Opticians are artisans qualified to grind lenses, fill prescriptions, and fit frames. The effect of the provision was to prevent opticians from fitting old glasses into new frames or duplicating a lost or broken lens without a prescription. Two other sections of the law prohibited soliciting the sale of frames, mountings, or other optical appliances and the renting of space in a retail store to one purporting to do eye examinations.

ISSUE: May the Due Process Clause be used to strike down state laws regulating business and industrial conditions because they may be unwise, improvident, or out of harmony with a particular school of thought?

HOLDING AND DECISION: (Douglas, J.) No. The Due Process Clause will no longer be used to strike down state laws, regulating business or industrial conditions, because they may be unwise, improvident, or out of harmony with a particular school of thought. For protection against abuses by the legislature, the people must resort to the polls, not the courts. The state law in question here may exact needless wasteful requirements in many cases. But it is for the legislatures, not the courts, to balance the advantages and disadvantages of the new requirement. The legislature may have concluded that the cases in which prescriptions are essential are frequent enough to justify requiring one in every case. Since frames and mountings are used only in conjunction with lenses, and lenses enter the field of health, the legislature might have concluded that to regulate one it had to regulate the other. Finally, the last provision appeared to be an attempt to rid the profession of commercialism. Hence, it cannot be said that the

regulation had no rational relation to legitimate objectives. Reversed.

▶ ANALYSIS

An example of the Court's deference to legislative judgments is *Ferguson v. Skrupa*, 372 U.S. 726 (1963), where the Court reversed the invalidation of a state statute regulating the business of debt-adjusting. The law prohibited that business except as an incident to the practice of law. The Supreme Court spoke of its abandonment of the use of the vague contours of the Due Process Clause to nullify laws that a majority of the Court believed to be economically unwise. "We refuse to sit as a super legislature to weigh the wisdom of legislation," the Court stated.

Quicknotes

COMMERCIALISM Relating to advertisement or profit.

DUE PROCESS CLAUSE Clauses found in the Fifth and Fourteenth Amendments to the United States Constitution providing that no person shall be deprived of "life, liberty, or property, without due process of law."

LEGISLATIVE OBJECTIVES The goal or purpose motivating the legislature in enacting a particular law.

Griswold v. Connecticut

Doctor/director (D) v. State (P)

381 U.S. 479 (1965).

NATURE OF CASE: Certiorari review of state statute prohibiting the counseling of married persons to take contraceptives.

FACT SUMMARY: Doctor (D) and layman (D) were prosecuted for advising married persons on the means of preventing conception.

🏛 RULE OF LAW
The right to mental privacy, although not explicitly stated in the Bill of Rights, is one of the penumbras emanating from those amendments, formed by certain other explicit guarantees, and it is protected against state regulation that sweeps unnecessarily broad.

FACTS: Griswold (D), the Executive Director of the Planned Parenthood League of Connecticut, and Dr. Buxton (D) were convicted under a Connecticut law that made counseling of married persons to take contraceptives a criminal offense.

ISSUE: Is the right to mental privacy, although not explicitly stated in the Bill of Rights, one of the penumbras emanating from those amendments, formed by certain other explicit guarantees, and is it protected against state regulation that sweeps unnecessarily broad?

HOLDING AND DECISION: (Douglas, J.) Yes. The right to mental privacy, although not explicitly stated in the Bill of Rights, is one of the penumbras emanating from those amendments, formed by certain other explicit guarantees, and it is protected against state regulation that sweeps unnecessarily broad. The various guarantees that create penumbras, or zones, of privacy include the First Amendment's right of association, the Third Amendment's prohibition against the peacetime quartering of soldiers, the Fourth Amendment's prohibition against unreasonable searches and seizures, the Fifth Amendment's Self-Incrimination Clause, and the Ninth Amendment's reservation to the people of unenumerated rights. The Connecticut law, by forbidding the use of contraceptives rather than regulating their manner or sale, seeks to achieve its goals by means having a maximum destructive impact upon that relationship. Reversed.

CONCURRENCE: (Goldberg, J.) The Ninth Amendment, while not constituting an independent source of rights, suggests that the list of rights in the first eight amendments is not exhaustive. This right is a "fundamental" one that cannot be infringed on the state's slender justification in protecting marital fidelity.

CONCURRENCE: (Harlan, J.) The Court, instead of approaching the issue as if the Due Process Clause of the Fourteenth Amendment does not touch this statute unless the enactment is found to violate some penumbra of the Bill of Rights, should have instead relied on the Due Process Clause in finding this law violative of basic values "implicit in the concept of ordered liberty." Doing this would prevent judges from interpolating into the Constitution an "artificial and largely illusory restriction on the content of due process."

CONCURRENCE: (White, J.) The Due Process Clause should be the test in determining whether such laws are reasonably necessary for the effectuation of a legitimate and substantial state interest and are not arbitrary or capricious in application. Here, the causal connection between married persons engaging in extramarital sex and contraceptives is too tenuous.

DISSENT: (Black, J.) While the law is offensive, neither the Ninth Amendment nor the Due Process Clause invalidates it. Both lead the Court into imposing its own notions as to what are wise or unwise laws. What constitutes "fundamental" values this court is incapable of determining. Keeping the Constitution "in tune with the times" is accomplished only through the amendment process. Similarly, the Due Process Clause is too imprecise and lends itself to subjective interpretation.

DISSENT: (Stewart, J.) The Due Process Clause is not the "guide" because there was no claim here that the statute is unconstitutionally vague or that the defendants were denied any of the elements of procedural due process at their trial. The Ninth Amendment simply restricts the federal government to a government of express and limited powers. Finally, the Constitution is silent on the "right to privacy."

▶ ANALYSIS

Although the theory of "substantive due process" has declined as a means to review state economic regulation—at least since 1937—the Court, as here, has freely applied strict scrutiny when dealing with state laws that affect social areas.

◼▬◼

Quicknotes

NINTH AMENDMENT The Ninth Amendment to the United States Constitution provides that the enumeration of any

Continued on next page.

rights contained therein is not to be construed as denying or disparaging other rights retained by the people.

PENUMBRA A doctrine whereby authority of the federal
government is implied pursuant to the Necessary and
Proper Clause; one implied power may be inferred from
the conferring of another implied power.

RIGHT TO PRIVACY The violation of an individual's right to
be protected against unwarranted interference in his
personal affairs, falling into one of four categories:
(1) appropriating the individual's likeness or name for
commercial benefit; (2) intrusion into the individual's
seclusion; (3) public disclosure of private facts regarding
the individual; and (4) disclosure of facts placing the
individual in a false light.

SUBSTANTIVE DUE PROCESS A constitutional safeguard
limiting the power of the state, irrespective of how fair
its procedures may be; substantive limits placed on the
power of the state.

Roe v. Wade

Single pregnant woman (P) v. State (D)

410 U.S. 113 (1973).

NATURE OF CASE: Certiorari review of state laws making it a crime to procure an abortion except by medical advice to save the life of the mother.

FACT SUMMARY: Roe (P), a single woman, wished to have her pregnancy terminated by an abortion.

🏛 RULE OF LAW
The right of privacy found in the Fourteenth Amendment's concept of personal liberty and restrictions upon state action are broad enough to encompass a woman's decision to terminate her pregnancy.

FACTS: The Texas abortion laws challenged here were typical of those adopted by most states. The challengers were Roe (P), a single pregnant woman, a childless couple with the wife not pregnant (J and M Doe), and a licensed physician with two criminal charges pending (Halford). Only Roe (P) was found to be entitled to maintain the action. Although her 1970 pregnancy had been terminated, her case was not found moot since pregnancy "truly could be capable of repetition, yet evading review."

ISSUE: Does the constitutional right of privacy include a woman's right to choose to terminate her pregnancy?

HOLDING AND DECISION: (Blackmun, J.) Yes. The right of privacy found in the Fourteenth Amendment's concept of personal liberty and restrictions upon state action are broad enough to encompass a woman's decision to terminate her pregnancy. While the Constitution does not explicitly mention any right of privacy, such a right has been recognized. This right of privacy, whether founded in the Fourteenth Amendment's concept of personal liberty and restrictions upon state action, as this court feels it is, or in the Ninth Amendment's reservation of rights to the people, is broad enough to encompass a woman's decision to terminate her pregnancy. A statute regulating a fundamental right, such as the right to privacy, may be justified only by a compelling state interest and such statutes must be narrowly drawn. Here, Texas (D) argued that the fetus is a person within the meaning of the Fourteenth Amendment, whose right to life is guaranteed by that Amendment. However, there are no decisions indicating such a definition for "fetus." The unborn have never been recognized in the law as persons in the whole sense. Texas (D) may not, by adopting one theory of life, override the rights of the pregnant woman that are at stake. However, neither are the woman's rights to privacy absolute. The state does have a legitimate interest in preserving the health of the pregnant woman and in protecting the po-

tentiality of life. Each of these interests grows in substantiality as the woman approaches term, and, at a point, each becomes compelling. During the first trimester, mortality in abortion is less than mortality in childbirth. After that point, in promoting its interest in the mother's health, the state may regulate the abortion procedure in ways related to maternal health (i.e., licensing of physicians, facilities, etc.). Prior to viability, the physician, in consultation with the pregnant woman, is free to decide that a pregnancy should be terminated without interference by the state. Subsequent to viability, the state, in promoting its interest in the potentiality of life, may regulate, and even prescribe abortion, except where necessary to save the mother's life. Because the Texas (D) statute makes no distinction between abortions performed in early pregnancy and those performed later, it sweeps too broadly and is, therefore, invalid.

CONCURRENCE: (Stewart, J.) The Texas statute invaded "liberty" protected by the Fourteenth Amendment's Due Process Clause. Substantive due process has been resurrected.

DISSENT: (White, J.) This issue, for the most part, should be left with the people. There is nothing in the language or history of the Constitution to support the Court's opinion. The Texas statute is not constitutionally infirm because it denies abortions to those who seek to serve only their own convenience rather than to protect their life or health.

DISSENT: (Rehnquist, J.) The test to be applied is whether the abortion law has a rational relation to a valid state objective. Here, the court applies the compelling state interest test. The application of this test requires the court to examine the legislative policies and pass on the wisdom of those policies, tasks better left to the legislature.

▶ ANALYSIS

Doe v. Bolton, 401 U.S. 179 (1973), was the companion case to *Roe v. Wade.* The Georgia laws attacked in Doe were more modern than the Texas laws. They allowed a physician to perform an abortion when the mother's life was in danger or the fetus would likely be born with birth defects or the pregnancy had resulted from rape. The Court held that a physician could consider all attendant circumstances in deciding whether an abortion should be performed. No longer could only the three situations specified be considered. The Court also struck down the

Continued on next page.

requirements of prior approval for an abortion by the hospital staff committee and of confirmation by two physicians. They concluded that the attending physician's judgment was sufficient. Lastly, the Court struck down the requirement that the woman be a Georgia resident.

■━■

Quicknotes

MOOTNESS Judgment on the particular issue would not resolve the controversy.

■━■

Planned Parenthood of Southeastern Pa. v. Casey

Clinics/doctors (P) v. State (D)

505 U.S. 833 (1992).

NATURE OF CASE: Certiorari review of state abortion statutes.

FACT SUMMARY: Planned Parenthood (P) challenged the constitutionality of Pennsylvania's (D) abortion law.

RULE OF LAW
A law is unconstitutional as an undue burden on a woman's right to choose an abortion before fetal viability if the law places a substantial obstacle in the path of a woman seeking to exercise that right.

FACTS: The Pennsylvania Abortion Control Act (the "Act") required (a) a doctor to provide a woman seeking an abortion with information designed to persuade her against abortion and imposed a waiting period of at least 24 hours between provision of the information and the abortion; (b) a minor to obtain consent of one parent or a judge's order before having an abortion; (c) a married woman to sign a statement averring that her husband had been notified, her husband was not the father, her husband forcibly had impregnated her, or that she would be physically harmed if she notified her husband; and (d) a public report on every abortion, detailing information on the facility, physician, patient, and steps taken to comply with the Act. The name of the patient was confidential. It provided the first three provisions would not apply in a "medical emergency," i.e., a condition a doctor determines to require immediate abortion to avert death or serious risk of substantial, irreversible impairment of a major bodily function. Five clinics (P), including Planned Parenthood (P), and five doctors (P) sued Pennsylvania (D), including Governor Casey (D), claiming the Act was unconstitutional on its face. The district court held the entire Act invalid under *Roe v. Wade*, 410 U.S. 113 (1973). The court of appeals reversed, upholding the entire Act except the husband-notification requirement. Planned Parenthood et al. (P) appealed.

ISSUE: Is a law an unconstitutionally undue burden on a woman's right to choose an abortion before fetal viability if the law places a substantial obstacle in the path of a woman seeking to exercise that right?

HOLDING AND DECISION: (O'Connor, J.) Yes. A law is unconstitutional as an undue burden on a woman's right to choose an abortion before fetal viability if the law places a substantial obstacle in the path of a woman seeking to exercise that right. For two decades people have organized lives relying on the availability of abortion. The Court rarely resolves a controversy as intensely divisive as

in *Roe*. Such a decision should be overturned only if it proves unworkable or if new information arise that renders the decision unjustified in the present. *Roe* is neither unworkable nor based on outdated assumptions. Medical technology has altered the age of viability, but that does not affect the validity of viability as a dividing line. Viability is the point at which a fetus can be said to be an independent life, so that the state's interest in protecting it then outweighs the mother's decision-making interest. The Court and the nation would be seriously damaged if the Court were to overturn *Roe* simply on the basis of a philosophical disagreement with the 1973 Court, or as surrender to political pressure. The liberty rights of women and the personal, intimate nature of childbearing sharply limit state power to insist a woman carry a child to term or accept the state's vision of her role in society. Thus, the integrity of the Court, stare decisis, and substantive due process require the central principle of *Roe* to be reaffirmed: a state may not prevent a woman from making the ultimate decision to terminate her pregnancy before viability. *Roe* also recognized the state interest in maternal health and in protecting potential life. Application of the rigid trimester framework often ignored state interests, leading to striking down abortion regulations that in no real sense deprived women of the ultimate decision. Therefore, the trimester framework must be rejected and undue burden analysis put in its place. Here, the information requirement is not an undue burden. Truthful, non-misleading information on the nature of abortion procedure, health risks, and consequences to the fetus is reasonable to ensure informed choice, one that might cause a woman to choose childbirth. The 24-hour waiting period does not create a health risk and reasonably furthers the state interest in protecting the unborn. Requiring a period of reflection to make an informed decision is reasonable. A waiting period may increase cost and risk of delay, but on a facial challenge it cannot be called a substantial obstacle. Prior cases establish that a state may require parental consent before abortions by minors, provided there is a judicial bypass procedure. On its face, the statute's definition of "medical emergency" is not too narrow. The reporting requirement is reasonably directed to the preservation of maternal health, providing a vital element of medical research, and the statute protects patient confidentiality. The husband-notification requirement imposes an undue burden on abortion rights of the abused women who fear for their safety and the safety of their children and are likely to be deterred from procuring an abortion as surely as if the

Continued on next page.

state outlawed abortion. A husband has a strong interest in his wife's pregnancy, but before birth it is a biological fact that regulation of the fetus has a far greater impact on the woman. The husband-notification requirement is unconstitutional, and the rest of the statute is valid. Affirmed.

CONCURRENCE AND DISSENT: (Stevens, J.) The Court is correct in determining that stare decisis should have controlling significance in a case like this. *Roe* is an integral part of a "correct understanding of both the concept of liberty and the basic equality of men and women." States must not interfere with the decisional autonomy of the woman to choose, even where it thinks that it acts in the best interests of all.

CONCURRENCE AND DISSENT: (Blackmun, J.) The Court correctly reaffirms a woman's right to abortion. However, that right should remain fundamental, and any state-imposed burden upon it should be subjected to the strictest judicial scrutiny. Categorizing a woman's right to abortion as merely a "liberty interest" is not sufficient. In striking down the husband-notification requirement the Court sets up a framework for evaluating abortion regulations in the social context of women facing issues of reproductive choice. The Court failed to strike down the information, waiting period, parental consent, and reporting requirements on their face, but the Court's standard at least allows future courts to hold that in practice such regulations are undue burdens. The reporting requirement does not further maternal health. Fearing harassment, many doctors will stop performing abortions if their names appear on public reports. However, none of these requirements would survive under the strict-scrutiny standard of review. The trimester framework should be maintained. No other approach better protects a woman's fundamental right while accommodating legitimate state interests. The Court's cases do not create a list of personal liberties: they are a principled account of how these rights are grounded in a general right of privacy.

CONCURRENCE AND DISSENT: (Rehnquist, C.J.) *Roe* was wrongly decided, has led to a confusing body of law, and should be overturned. The Court's decision, replacing *Roe*'s strict scrutiny standard and trimester framework with a new, unworkable undue burden test, cannot be justified by stare decisis. Authentic principles of stare decisis do not require erroneous decisions to be maintained. The Court's integrity is enhanced when it repudiates wrong decisions. Americans have grown accustomed to *Roe*, but that should not prevent the Court from correcting a wrong decision. The Fourteenth Amendment's concept of liberty does not incorporate any all-encompassing right of privacy. Unlike marriage, procreation, and contraception, abortion terminates potential life and must be analyzed differently. Historic traditions of the American people, critical to an understanding of fundamental rights, do not support a right to abortion. A woman's interest in having an abortion is liberty protected by due process, but

states may regulate abortion in ways rationally related to a legitimate state interest. All provisions of the Pennsylvania law do so and are constitutional. The husband-notification requirement is reasonably related to promoting state interests in protecting the husband's interests, potential life, and the integrity of marriage.

CONCURRENCE AND DISSENT: (Scalia, J.) Applying the rational basis test, the Pennsylvania statute in its entirety should be upheld. The Court's description of the place of *Roe* in the social history of the United States is unrecognizable. Not only did *Roe* not resolve the deeply divisive issue of abortion, it did more than anything else to nourish it by elevating it to the national level where it is infinitely more difficult to resolve. *Roe* fanned into life an issue that has inflamed our national politics in general and has obscured with its smoke the selection of Justices to this Court in particular, ever since.

ANALYSIS

The Court also affirmed *Roe*'s holding that after viability the state may regulate, or even proscribe, abortion, except where it is necessary to preserve the life or health of the mother. This is only the second time in modern Supreme Court jurisprudence that an opinion has been jointly authored. Justice Kennedy's portion of the opinion addresses the importance of public faith in and acceptance of the Court's work by opening with the statement: "Liberty finds no refuge in a jurisprudence of doubt." Justice O'Connor expounds on the essential nature of a woman's right to an abortion, while Justice Souter performs the stare decisis analysis, concluding that there is no reason to reverse the essential holding of *Roe*. It appears that the instant case marks the first time the Court has downgraded a fundamental right to a protected liberty and by so doing removed from the usual strict scrutiny standard of review.

Quicknotes

FUNDAMENTAL RIGHT A basic and essential right; freedoms expressed in the Bill of Rights and implied freedoms not expressly stated in the Constitution.

STARE DECISIS Doctrine whereby courts follow legal precedent unless there is good cause for departure.

STRICT SCRUTINY Method by which courts determine the constitutionality of a law, when a law affects a fundamental right. Under the test, the legislature must have a compelling interest to enact law and measures prescribed by the law must be the least restrictive means possible to accomplish goal.

Continued on next page.

SUBSTANTIVE DUE PROCESS A constitutional safeguard limiting the power of the state, irrespective of how fair its procedures may be; substantive limits placed on the power of the state.

UNDUE BURDEN Unlawfully oppressive or troublesome.

VIABILITY The point at which a newborn child is capable of existing outside the womb.

Gonzales v. Carhart

Attorney General (D) v. Abortion doctor (P)

550 U.S. 124 (2007).

NATURE OF CASE: Certiorari review of constitutionality of the federal Partial-Birth Abortion Ban Act.

FACT SUMMARY: Congress passed a statute that criminalized doctors' performance of partial-birth abortions.

RULE OF LAW
The Partial-Birth Abortion Ban Act does not place a substantial obstacle to late-term, but pre-viability, abortions.

FACTS: In 2003, Congress enacted the Partial-Birth Abortion Ban Act (the "Act"), which criminalized doctors' performance of partial-birth abortions. The Act explicitly and precisely defined "partial-birth abortion," in part, as an abortion following the "deliver[y] [of] a living fetus." [Carhart (P), a doctor who performed partial-birth abortions, filed suit for injunctive relief to prohibit the Act from being applied against him. The trial court granted the injunction, and the intermediate appellate court affirmed.] The Government (D) sought further review in the Supreme Court.

ISSUE: Does the Partial-Birth Abortion Ban Act place a substantial obstacle to late-term, but pre-viability, abortions?

HOLDING AND DECISION: (Kennedy, J.) No. The Partial-Birth Abortion Ban Act (the "Act") does not place a substantial obstacle to late-term, but pre-viability, abortions. The Act can be construed as not prohibiting the standard form of partial-birth abortion invalidated in *Stenberg v. Carhart*, 530 U.S. 914 (2000), and the Act therefore is not facially invalid on that basis. Further, instead of placing a substantial obstacle to a partial-birth abortion, the Act simply respects human life—an objective that lies within the legislative power. The Act advances that objective by ensuring that women will be fully informed about the methods of abortion to which they consent. Moreover, Congress can legitimately legislate even in the face of the medical uncertainty on whether such a prohibition on one form of abortion subjects women "to significant health risks." Such uncertainty does not support a facial challenge to the Act. The proper way to attack the Act would be through an as-applied challenge that would permit review of a more precise factual scenario. [Reversed.]

CONCURRENCE: (Thomas, J.) The Court correctly applies existing law, but the Constitution provides no basis at all for the Court's abortion jurisprudence.

DISSENT: (Ginsburg, J.) This decision mocks *Casey*, 505 U.S. 833 (1992), and *Stenberg*, and it flies in the face of medical approval of abortion procedures. The Act does subject women to significant health risks by forcing them to choose less safe methods of abortion, and, in the process, the statute does not save even one fetus because the Act merely criminalizes a method of abortion, not abortion itself. As the Court suggests, the real basis for today's decision is "moral concerns" for what the majority sees as emotionally fragile women. This rationale circumvents the concerns for stare decisis that have supported our prior decisions in this area. Today's decision is actually only a veiled attempt to undermine, in a piecemeal fashion, a woman's established right to an abortion.

ANALYSIS

The right to an abortion announced in *Roe v. Wade*, 410 U.S. 113 (1973), remains intact after *Gonzales v. Carhart*. That right is now more difficult to exercise, though, and, as Justice Ginsburg suggests in dissent, the federal statute's omission of safeguards for women's health is at best problematic under the Court's prior abortion decisions.

Quicknotes

DUE PROCESS The constitutional mandate requiring the courts to protect and enforce individuals' rights and liberties consistent with prevailing principles of fairness and justice and prohibiting the federal and state governments from such activities that deprive its citizens of life, liberty, or property interest.

INJUNCTION A court order requiring a person to do, or prohibiting that person from doing, a specific act.

INJUNCTIVE RELIEF A court order issued as a remedy, requiring a person to do, or prohibiting that person from doing, a specific act.

STARE DECISIS Doctrine whereby courts follow legal precedent unless there is good cause for departure.

Lawrence v. Texas

Sodomy convict (D) v. State (P)

539 U.S. 558 (2003).

NATURE OF CASE: Certiorari review of state statute prohibiting consensual sodomy.

FACT SUMMARY: When Lawrence (D) and his male partner, both adults, were prosecuted and convicted for consensual sodomy in their own private dwelling, they argued the unconstitutionality of the statute.

> ## 🏛 RULE OF LAW
> Legislation that makes consensual sodomy between adults in their own dwelling criminal violates due process.

FACTS: Two Houston, Texas, police officers were dispatched to a private residence in response to a reported weapons disturbance. They entered an apartment where Lawrence (D) resided. The right of the police to enter was not an issue. The officers observed Lawrence (D) and another man engaging in sodomy. Both men were arrested, charged, and convicted before a justice of the peace of the statutory crime of "deviate sexual intercourse, namely anal sex, with a member of the same sex." Each defendant entered a plea of nolo contendere and was fined $200. Both men were adults at the time of the alleged offense. Their conduct was in private and consensual. Lawrence (D) and his partner appealed to the Supreme Court, arguing the Texas statute to be unconstitutional.

ISSUE: Does legislation that makes consensual sodomy between adults in their own dwelling criminal violate due process?

HOLDING AND DECISION: (Kennedy, J.) Yes. Legislation that makes consensual sodomy between adults in their own dwelling criminal violates due process. Liberty protects the person from unwarranted government intrusions into a dwelling or other private places. In our tradition, the state is not omnipresent in the home. Furthermore, freedom extends beyond spatial bounds. Liberty presumes an "autonomy of self" that includes freedom of thought, belief, expression, "and certain intimate conduct." This case involves liberty of the person both in its spatial and more transcendent dimensions. The penalties and purposes of the Texas statute in the instant case have far-reaching consequences, touching upon the most private human conduct, sexual behavior, and in the most private of places, the home. The statute seeks to control a personal relationship that, whether or not entitled to formal recognition in the law, is within the liberty of persons to choose without being punished as criminals. This Court acknowledges that adults may choose to enter into private relationships in the confines of their own homes and their own private lives and still retain their dignity as free persons. When sexuality finds

expression in intimate conduct with another person, the conduct can be but one element in a personal bond that is more enduring. The liberty protected by the Constitution allows homosexual persons the right to make this choice. Here, two adults who, with full and mutual consent from each other, engaged in sexual practices common to a homosexual lifestyle. They are entitled to respect in their private lives. The state cannot demean their existence or control their destiny by making their private sexual conduct a crime. Reversed.

CONCURRENCE: (O'Connor, J.) Rather than relying on the substantive component of the Fourteenth Amendment's Due Process Clause, as the Court does, unconstitutionality exists based on the Fourteenth Amendment's Equal Protection Clause.

DISSENT: (Scalia, J.) Homosexual sodomy is not a right "deeply rooted in our Nation's history and tradition." Constitutional entitlements do not spring into existence because some states choose to lessen or eliminate sanctions on criminal behavior. Today's opinion is the product of a Court that has largely signed on to the so-called homosexual agenda.

DISSENT: (Thomas, J.) The instant Texas statute is "uncommonly silly" and the Texas Legislature should repeal it; however, no general constitutional right of privacy was violated in this situation.

▶ ANALYSIS

In *Lawrence*, the Supreme Court noted that of the 13 states with laws prohibiting sodomy, only four have enforced their legislation. In those states in which sodomy was still proscribed, whether for same-sex or heterosexual conduct, there was a pattern of nonenforcement with respect to consenting adults acting in private. Even Texas admitted in 1994 that as of that date it had not prosecuted anyone under those circumstances.

Quicknotes

DUE PROCESS CLAUSE Clauses found in the Fifth and Fourteenth Amendments to the United States Constitution providing that no person shall be deprived of "life, liberty, or property, without due process of law."

EQUAL PROTECTION CLAUSE A constitutional guarantee that no person should be denied the same protection of the laws enjoyed by other persons in like circumstances.

Washington v. Glucksberg

State (D) v. Doctors (P)

521 U.S. 702 (1997).

NATURE OF CASE: Certiorari review of constitutionality of state law prohibiting assisted suicide.

FACT SUMMARY: A group of Washington physicians (P) and a nonprofit organization (P) that counseled people considering physician-assisted suicide filed suit seeking a declaration that the state's assisted-suicide ban was facially unconstitutional.

🏛 RULE OF LAW
The right to assistance in committing suicide is not a fundamental liberty interest protected by the Due Process Clause.

FACTS: A Washington law stated that "a person is guilty of promoting a suicide attempt when he knowingly causes or aids another person to attempt suicide." Breaking the law was a felony punishable by up to five years' imprisonment and up to a $10,000 fine. Washington also had a Natural Death Act which stated that withholding or withdrawal of life-sustaining treatment at a patient's discretion did not constitute a suicide. Physicians (P), who are practicing in Washington, and Compassion in Dying (P), a nonprofit organization that counseled people considering physician-assisted suicide, filed suit seeking a declaration that the ban on assisted suicide was unconstitutional. The physicians (P), who treated many terminally ill, suffering patients, declared that they would have assisted some of these patients in ending their lives were it not for Washington's law. The district court found the statute invalid, and the court of appeals ultimately affirmed. The appellate court held that the Constitution encompasses a due process liberty interest in controlling the time and manner of one's death, and that the state's assisted-suicide ban was unconstitutional as applied to terminally ill competent adults who wish to hasten their deaths with medication prescribed by their physicians. The Supreme Court granted certiorari.

ISSUE: Is the right to assistance in committing suicide a fundamental liberty interest protected by the Due Process Clause?

HOLDING AND DECISION: (Rehnquist, C.J.) No. The right to assistance in committing suicide is not a fundamental liberty interest protected by the Due Process Clause. In almost every state and every western democracy, it is a crime to assist a suicide. These laws reflect a longstanding commitment to the protection and preservation of human life. In 1991, Washington voters rejected a ballot measure that would have permitted a form of physician-assisted suicide. The Court must exercise extreme prudence in expanding the Due Process Clause to include new fundamental rights and liberties. In *Cruzan v. Director, Missouri Dept. of Health*, 497 U.S. 261 (1990), the Court suggested that the Due Process Clause protects the right to refuse unwanted lifesaving medical treatment. The physicians' (P) reliance on *Cruzan* is misplaced. At common law, forced medication was a battery; however, the decision to commit suicide has never been afforded similar legal protection. Washington (D) also has a fundamental interest in protecting the integrity of the medical profession, and the American Medical Association has concluded that physician-assisted suicide is fundamentally incompatible with the physician's role as a healer. Finally, the state has an interest in protecting vulnerable groups from abuse, neglect, and mistakes. There is a very real risk of subtle coercion and undue influence in end-of-life situations that legalized physician-assisted suicide would likely exacerbate. Therefore, the statute does not violate the Fourteenth Amendment either on its face or as applied. Reversed.

CONCURRENCE: (O'Connor, J.) While the majority correctly holds that there is no generalized "right" to commit suicide, the question of whether a mentally competent person experiencing great suffering has a constitutional right to control the circumstances of his or her imminent death should not be precluded by this decision.

CONCURRENCE: (Stevens, J.) The Court's holding that Washington's statute is not invalid on its face does not foreclose the possibility that some applications of the statute might well be invalid. While the Court correctly held that *Cruzan* does not decide the issue here, *Cruzan* did give recognition to an individual's interest in making decisions about how to confront an imminent death. Furthermore, the state's interest in supporting a general rule banning the practice of physician-assisted suicide does not have the same force in all cases.

CONCURRENCE: (Souter, J.) While Washington (D) has persuasively demonstrated that its ban on physician-assisted suicide should not be found facially unconstitutional, this does not preclude the possibility that the individual interests at stake here will at some point or in some cases be held "fundamental." While that day is yet to come, the Court has presently correctly deferred to Washington's institutional legislative competence.

CONCURRENCE: (Breyer, J.) The Court has misstated the claimed liberty interest. A more accurate formulation would use words like a "right to die with

Continued on next page.

dignity" and would be closely linked with a right to avoid severe physical pain connected with death. Nevertheless, given the facts at hand, the Court need not decide now whether or not such a right is "fundamental."

▶ *ANALYSIS*

The four concurring justices all left the door wide open for the Court to revisit this decision given a more fact-specific case. While they all strongly suggested that an individual under certain, limited circumstances may have a constitutionally protected right to assisted suicide, they were cautious in taking that leap given the specific question at issue here. While several states, including Washington and California, have voted down statutes permitting physician-assisted suicide, it is likely that one will eventually pass, and the Court will again be presented with these issues.

■■■

Quicknotes

BATTERY Unlawful contact with the body of another person.

DUE PROCESS CLAUSE Clauses found in the Fifth and Fourteenth Amendments to the United States Constitution providing that no person shall be deprived of "life, liberty, or property, without due process of law."

LIBERTY INTEREST A right conferred by the Due Process Clauses of the state and federal constitutions.

■■■

Kelo v. City of New London

Homeowner (P) v. City (D)

545 U.S. 469 (2005).

NATURE OF CASE: Certiorari review of constitutionality of taking in underlying case involving defendant city in condemnation suit.

FACT SUMMARY: New London, Connecticut (D) condemned the private residences of Kelo (P) and others in order to use their property as part of a planned economic development.

🏛 RULE OF LAW
Governmental economic development constitutes a "public use" under the Fifth Amendment's eminent domain.

FACTS: New London, Connecticut (D) revitalized the New London Development Corp. (NLDC) to propose plans for economic development after decades of decline. Pfizer, a pharmaceutical company, also announced plans to build a $300 million facility next to Fort Trumball in the New London (D) area. The NLDC operated as a private entity but its plans intended to benefit the city's growth. New London (D) authorized NLDC to purchase or condemn property in its name for the purpose of its approved development plan. Kelo (P) owned property in the Fort Trumball development area and refused to sell. New London (D) initiated condemnation proceedings although Kelo's (P) property was not blighted or otherwise deteriorating. Kelo (P) filed suit in state court against New London (D) claiming that the condemnation violated the taking clause's "public use" restriction. The Connecticut Supreme Court held for the defendant city and Kelo (P) appealed to the United States Supreme Court.

ISSUE: Does governmental economic development constitute a "public use" under the Fifth Amendment's eminent domain?

HOLDING AND DECISION: (Stevens, J.) Yes. Governmental economic development constitutes a "public use" under the Fifth Amendment's eminent domain. The government cannot transfer private property from one private entity to another even if the first is adequately compensated. The government can, however, take private property from one private entity with just compensation for "public use." This particular case does not fit in either scenario. New London (D) cannot offer a pretextual "public use" if the true benefit is to a definable class of private individuals, but no such class can be identified here. It is true that the planned development will not be completely open to the public and the stores will not act as common carriers to the public, but such a literal definition of "public use" is not required. The precedent in *Berman*, 348 U.S.

26 (1954), and *Midkiff*, 467 U.S. 229 (1984), supports a broad interpretation of "public use." Kelo (P) requests a bright-line rule for "public use" that would not include economic development. It is longstanding tradition of government to promote economic development and that development may be better served by using a private entity rather than government agencies. A bright-line rule cannot issue because legislatures need flexibility when determining appropriate action for the economic development of its cities. States are free to further restrict "public use" requirements beyond those of the federal government and many have already done so. Affirmed.

CONCURRENCE: (Kennedy, J.) A party may make a claim of pretextual "public use" taking that actually benefits a private entity. A presumption exists that the government acted reasonably in its taking, but courts should review all claims to the contrary by looking closely at the facts of the case. A city may take property with the public only incidentally benefiting. Here, no facts existed to show that Pfizer alone would benefit from New London (D) condemning Kelo's (P) property.

DISSENT: (O'Connor, J.) The Court's decision eliminates "for public use" from the takings clause because it allows for incidental public benefit from ordinary private use of property. The government simply cannot condemn private property when the condemnation is to benefit another private person or entity. The Court's reliance on *Berman* and *Midkiff* is misplaced because those cases actually underscore the public use versus private benefit. Both cases involved takings that directly benefited the public. Those properties were blighted and causing harm to the public in their current use. When private property is being used in its ordinary, non-harmful fashion, it cannot be taken to benefit another private user. It is nearly impossible to isolate the true motives behind a governmental taking, so the government can now condemn with near impunity. The government can also always seek to improve a property's use if the private owner is not making the most productive or attractive use of it. The facts of today's case do not justify the holding.

DISSENT: (Thomas, J.) The Court adopts the overly broad "public use" definitions of *Berman* and *Midkiff* without reasoned analysis. A legislature's determination of what constitutes "public use" is not entitled to such blind deference. The original intent of the Public Use Clause was to provide full legal rights to the public for the use of any condemned property. The Court should return to the

Continued on next page.

original intent. Further, the property most likely to be taken under this new definition will be that of poor communities lacking political power and likely using their property at less than its most productive use. These communities should be protected rather than exploited.

▶ *ANALYSIS*

This case caused a firestorm of fury throughout the United States. Multiple states quickly passed legislation tightening the state eminent domain laws to restrict the ability of governmental entities to take private property for anything less than blatantly public purposes. A small but vocal group of citizens began a petition to condemn Judge Breyer's private vacation residence so that the property may be put to a "better" use for the public.

■▬■

Quicknotes

CONDEMNATION The taking of private property for public use as long as just compensation is paid therefor.

EMINENT DOMAIN The governmental power to take private property for public use so long as just compensation is paid therefor.

PUBLIC USE Basis for governmental taking of property pursuant to its power of eminent domain so that property taken may be utilized for the benefit of the public at large.

■▬■

Pennsylvania Coal Co. v. Mahon

Coal mining company (D) v. Landowner (P)

260 U.S. 393 (1922).

NATURE OF CASE: Certiorari review of state statute.

FACT SUMMARY: A Pennsylvania statute forbade the mining of coal in such fashion as to cause the subsidence of any structure used as a human habitation.

🏛 RULE OF LAW
A state, that through legislation destroys previously existing contractual and property rights between private parties which results in the severe diminution of property value, must give compensation to the affected party.

FACTS: In 1878, the Pennsylvania Coal Co. (the "coal company") (D) conveyed some land but reserved in the deed the right to remove all coal under the land. The grantee agreed to assume any resulting damage. Mahon (P), who later acquired the land, was bound by the deed. Mahon (P), wanting to prevent further mining under the land, claimed that a 1922 state law changed the coal company's (D) rights. The law forbade the mining of coal in such manner as to cause the subsistence of any structure used as a human habitation with certain exceptions. Mahon's (P) injunction was denied, the trial court maintaining that the law would be unconstitutional if applied to the present case. On appeal, the state supreme court reversed, holding that the statute was a legitimate exercise of the police power.

ISSUE: Must a state, that through legislation destroys previously existing contractual and property rights between private parties which results in the severe diminution of property value, give compensation to the affected party?

HOLDING AND DECISION: (Holmes, J.) Yes. A state, that through legislation destroys previously existing contractual and property rights between private parties which results in the severe diminution of property value, must give compensation to the affected party. While private property may be regulated to a certain degree, a taking under the Fifth Amendment will be found if the regulation results in a severe diminution of value. At a certain magnitude, there must be an exercise of eminent domain and compensation to sustain the regulatory act. While considerable deference is to be given the legislature's judgment, each case will turn upon its particular facts. Where damage is inflicted on a single private house, even if similar damage is inflicted on others in different places, there is no public interest. On the other hand, the damage to the coal company's (D) contractual and property rights is considerable. The act cannot be sustained where, as an exercise of the police power, it affects reserved rights. To make coal mining commercially unprofitable is, in effect, to destroy it. The rights of the public in a street purchased by eminent domain are those it has paid for. A strong public desire to improve the public condition is not enough to justify achieving it by a shorter cut than the constitutional way of paying for the charge. This is a question of degree and cannot be disposed of by general propositions. So long as private individuals or communities take the risk of contracting for or purchasing only surface rights, they must bear the loss. Reversed.

DISSENT: (Brandeis, J.) Every restriction on the use of property is an abridgment by the state of rights in property without making compensation. Here, the restriction was only against a noxious use of property that remains in the coal company's (D) possession. The coal company (D), once it discontinues its noxious use, is free to enjoy its property as before. A restriction does not cease to be public simply because some individuals may be benefited. The means chosen here may be the only way to prevent the subsistence of land. Because values are relative, the value of the coal kept in place by the restriction should be compared with the value of other parts of the land. The state should not have to follow a theory of reciprocal advantage to justify exercising its police power for the public good. The reciprocal advantage given by the law to the coal company (D) is that of doing business in a civilized community.

▶ ANALYSIS

Eventually, the same analysis of the "taking" issue was used in *United States v. Causby*, 328 U.S. 265 (1946). There, a group of chicken farmers who owned land adjacent to a military airport claimed that, as a result of the noise of planes flying over their property, their chickens were literally frightened to death and egg production fell off. Rejecting the government's argument that any damage was merely consequential of the public's right of freedom of transit, Justice Douglas, writing for the majority, stated, "It is the owner's loss, not the taker's gain, which is the measure of the value of the property taken. . . . The owner's right to possess and exploit the land—that is, to say, his beneficial ownership of it—would be destroyed. . . . It would not be a case of incidental damages arising from a legalized nuisance." In dissent, Justice Black warned "the effect of the Court's decision is to limit, by the imposition of relatively absolute constitutional barriers, possible future

Continued on next page.

adjustments through legislation and regulation that might become necessary with the growth of air transportation, and [because] the Constitution does not contain such barriers."

■≡■

Quicknotes

EMINENT DOMAIN The governmental power to take private property for public use so long as just compensation is paid therefor.

TAKING A governmental action that substantially deprives an owner of the use and enjoyment of his property, requiring compensation.

■≡■

Home Building & Loan Assn. v. Blaisdell

Mortgagee (D) v. Mortgagor (P)

290 U.S. 398 (1934).

NATURE OF CASE: Certiorari review of state statute in underlying foreclosure action.

FACT SUMMARY: During the "Great Depression," Minnesota authorized county courts to extend the redemption period from foreclosure sales.

🏛 RULE OF LAW
A state may affect the obligations between two contracting parties so long as: (1) an emergency exists; (2) the legislation is addressed to a legitimate end; (3) the relief afforded and justified by the emergency could only be of a character appropriate to that emergency; (4) the conditions upon which relief is granted do not appear to be unreasonable; and (5) the legislation is temporary in operation.

FACTS: In 1933, Minnesota enacted the Minnesota Mortgage Moratorium Law (the "Act") authorizing country courts to extend the period of redemption from foreclosure sales "for such additional time as the court may deem just and equitable (but not extending beyond May 1, 1935)." The Blaisdells (P) applied for a judicial extension, and the court granted the extension but also ordered the Blaisdells (P) to pay Home Building and Loan Association (Home) (D), the mortgagee of their home, $40 a month through the extended period. Home (D) appealed on the ground that the Minnesota Act violated Article I, § 10, of the United States Constitution ("No State shall . . . pass any . . . law impairing the obligation of Contracts"). The state supreme court upheld the Act's constitutionality.

ISSUE: May a state change the existing contractual obligations between two private parties?

HOLDING AND DECISION: (Hughes, C.J.) Yes. A state may affect the obligations between two contracting parties so long as: (1) an emergency exists; (2) the legislation is addressed to a legitimate end; (3) the relief afforded and justified by the emergency could only be of a character appropriate to that emergency; (4) the conditions upon which relief is granted do not appear to be unreasonable; and (5) the legislation is temporary in operation. The reservation of the reasonable exercise of the state's protective power is read into all contracts. The prohibition embodied in the Contract Clause is not an absolute one. The state continues to possess authority to safeguard the vital interests of its people. The protection of contracts presupposes a government that views contractual obligations as worthwhile. A rational compromise must be found between public need and private rights, especially when an emergency is found to exist upon judicial review. Provisions of the Constitution must yield to interpretations that respond to current problems not envisioned by the original Framers. The Contract Clause should not be used to frustrate the states in advancing their fundamental interests. Here, the Act was an appropriate response because: (1) a true emergency in Minnesota existed; (2) the legislation was for the protection of a basic interest of society rather than the advantage of a few individuals; (3) the relief afforded was geared to the emergency (mass foreclosures); (4) the mortgagee's interests are not impaired; and (5) the legislation does not outlast the emergency, being temporary in duration. Affirmed.

DISSENT: (Sutherland, J.) "The phrase 'obligation of a contract' in the constitutional sense imports a legal duty to perform the specified obligation of that contract, not to substitute and perform, against the will of one of the parties, a different, albeit equally valuable, obligation."

▮ ANALYSIS

Despite the sweeping language of the instant opinion, the Court struck down state acts impairing contractual obligations in the following instances: exemption of payments on life insurance policies from garnishment (no time limitation, no limitation of amount to necessities); repeal of law protecting purchasers at state-conducted tax sales from attempts by the state to invalidate the transaction because of irregularities (purchaser had right to rely on earlier law so as to make land marketable); change of procedures for enforcement of payment of benefit assessments pledged as security for Municipal Improvement District bonds. Nonetheless, the *Blaisdell* decision marked the death knell of the Contract Clause's viability as a means to assail the validity of state laws.

Quicknotes

CONTRACTS CLAUSE Article I, Section 10 of the Constitution which prohibits states from passing laws impairing contractual obligations.

FORECLOSURE The termination of a property interest due to non-payment of a debt and the sale of that property to satisfy the debt.

REDEMPTION The regaining of possession of property by payment of a debt or fulfillment of other conditions.

Quick Reference Rules of Law

Railway Express Agency v. New York

Trucking company (D) v. City (P)

336 U.S. 106 (1949).

NATURE OF CASE: Certiorari review of constitutionality of state advertising statute.

FACT SUMMARY: New York City (P) had a regulation that prohibited advertising on vehicles but allowed advertising on business vehicles so long as the vehicles are engaged in their owner's usual work and are not used mainly for advertising. Railway Express Agency (D) was convicted of violating this regulation.

> 🏛 **RULE OF LAW**
> The Equal Protection Clause does not require that a statute eradicate all evils of the same type or none at all.

FACTS: A New York City (P) regulation prohibited advertising on vehicles. The statute did not prohibit, however, advertising on business vehicles so long as the vehicles are engaged in their owner's usual work and are not used merely or mainly for advertising. Railway Express Agency (D) is engaged in a nationwide express business. It operated 1,900 trucks in New York City (P). It sold space on the exterior of its trucks for advertising. Such advertising was generally unconnected with its business.

ISSUE: Does the Equal Protection Clause require that a statute eradicate all evils of the same type or none at all?

HOLDING AND DECISION: (Douglas, J.) No. The Equal Protection Clause does not require that a statute eradicate all evils of the same type or none at all. The court of special sessions concluded that advertising on vehicles using the streets of New York City (P) constituted a distraction to vehicle drivers and pedestrians, therefore affecting the public's safety in the use of the streets. The local authorities may well have concluded that those who advertise their own products on their trucks do not present the same traffic problem in view of the nature and extent of their advertising. The court cannot say that such a judgment is not an allowable one. The classification has a relation to the purpose for which it is made and does not contain the kind of discrimination against which the Equal Protection Clause protects. The fact that New York City (P) does not eliminate all distractions from its streets is immaterial. It is no requirement of equal protection that all evils of the same genus be eradicated or none at all. Conviction affirmed.

CONCURRENCE: (Jackson, J.) Laws must not discriminate between people except upon some reasonable differentiation fairly related to the object of regulation. There is a real difference between doing in self-interest and doing for hire so that it is one thing to tolerate an action done in self-interest and another thing to permit the same action to be done for hire.

▌ **ANALYSIS**

Traditionally, the Equal Protection Clause supported only minimal judicial intervention. During the late sixties, however, it became the favorite and most far-reaching tool for judicial protection of fundamental rights not specified in the Constitution. For many years, the impact of the Equal Protection Clause was a very limited one. During the decades of extensive court intervention with state economic legislation, substantive due process, not equal protection, provided the means to determine a statute's constitutionality. Also, as the concurring opinion points out, equal protection demanded only a "reasonable differentiation fairly related to the object of regulation." As demonstrated by this case, the rational classification requirement could be satisfied fairly easily, as the courts were extremely deferential to legislative judgment and easily convinced that the means used might relate rationally to a plausible end.

■=■

Quicknotes

EQUAL PROTECTION A constitutional guarantee that no person shall be denied the same protection of the laws enjoyed by other persons in like circumstances.

RATIONAL BASIS REVIEW A test employed by the court to determine the validity of a statute in equal protection actions, whereby the court determines whether the challenged statute is rationally related to the achievement of a legitimate state interest.

■=■

U.S. Railroad Retirement Bd. v. Fritz

Federal agency (D) v. Restored railroad employees (P)

449 U.S. 166 (1980).

NATURE OF CASE: Certiorari review of constitutionality of Railroad Retirement Act of 1974.

FACT SUMMARY: Fritz (P) and other active and retired railroad workers alleged that the portions of the Railroad Retirement Act of 1974, which denied them retirement benefits, violated equal protection standards.

RULE OF LAW
Social and economic legislation enacted by Congress will be upheld under the Equal Protection Clause if it is rationally related to a permissible government objective.

FACTS: Congress enacted the Railroad Retirement Act of 1974 (the "1974 Act") to place that industry's retirement system on a sound financial basis. Under the former system, a person who worked for both railroad and nonrailroad employers received both railroad retirement benefits and Social Security retirement benefits. Under the 1974 Act, railroad employees who had qualified for both sets of benefits as of the effective date of the legislation, but who had not yet actually retired, were entitled to receive benefits under both retirement schemes if they had either performed some railroad service during 1974 or as of December 31, 1974 had been employed by the railroad industry for 12 of the preceding 30 calendar months or had completed 25 years of railroad service as of December 31, 1974. Fritz (P) claimed that the distinctions used to determine eligibility for both sets of benefits violated equal protection standards. The lower court agreed, and the Board (D) appealed.

ISSUE: Will social and economic legislation enacted by Congress be upheld under equal protection provisions if it is rationally related to a permissible government objective?

HOLDING AND DECISION: (Rehnquist, J.) Yes. Social and economic legislation enacted by Congress will be upheld under the Equal Protection Clause if it is rationally related to a permissible government objective. In the field of economic and social welfare, a legislative classification complies with equal protection standards if it has a reasonable basis. A classification is not unconstitutional merely because it results in some inequality. Here, because Congress could have eliminated dual benefits for all classes of employees, it was permissible for Congress to draw lines between groups of employees for the purpose of phasing out those benefits. The test used to determine benefits is not a patently arbitrary method of accomplishing the congressional objective. Reversed.

CONCURRENCE: (Stevens, J.) To be valid, there must be a correlation between the statutory classification and either the actual purpose of the statute or a legitimate legislation objective. The congressional purpose of eliminating dual benefits is legitimate, and the timing of the employee's railroad service is a reasonable basis for the statutory classification.

DISSENT: (Brennan, J.) A legislative classification may be upheld only if it bears a rational relationship to a legitimate state purpose. Congress has stated that a principal purpose of the Act was to preserve the vested earned benefits of retirees who had already qualified for them. Because the statutory classification here deprives some retirees of vested dual benefits, it is not rationally related to Congress's stated purpose and therefore violates equal protection standards.

ANALYSIS

The Supreme Court has used a reasonableness standard when reviewing legislative and administrative classifications contained in socioeconomic legislation. To be reasonable, a law or regulation must have a legitimate public purpose based upon some conception of the public good. However, the Court has traditionally given great deference to congressional determinations of the nature of public good.

Quicknotes

EQUAL PROTECTION A constitutional guarantee that no person shall be denied the same protection of the laws enjoyed by other persons in like circumstances.

RATIONAL BASIS REVIEW A test employed by the court to determine the validity of a statute in equal protection actions, whereby the court determines whether the challenged statute is rationally related to the achievement of a legitimate state interest.

Brown v. Board of Education (Brown I)

Students (P) v. School board (D)

347 U.S. 483 (1954).

NATURE OF CASE: Certiorari review of the "separate but equal" doctrine and its constitutionality.

FACT SUMMARY: Black children were denied admission to public schools attended by white children.

🏛 RULE OF LAW
The segregation of children in public schools solely on the basis of race, even though the physical facilities are equal, deprives the children of the minority group of equal protection of the law.

FACTS: Black children had been denied admission to public schools attended by white children under laws requiring or permitting segregation according to race. It was found that the black children's schools and the white children's schools had been or were being equalized with respect to buildings, curricula, qualifications, and salaries of teachers.

ISSUE: Does segregation of children in public schools solely on the basis of race, even though the physical facilities are equal, deprive the children of the minority group of equal protection of the law?

HOLDING AND DECISION: (Warren, C.J.) Yes. The segregation of children in public schools solely on the basis of race, even though the physical facilities are equal, deprives the children of the minority group of equal protection of the law. The "separate but equal" doctrine has no application in the field of education. The segregation of children in public schools based solely on their race violates the Equal Protection Clause. First, intangible as well as tangible factors may be considered. Hence, the fact that the facilities and other tangible factors in the schools have been equalized is not controlling. Segregation of white and black children in public schools has a detrimental effect on the black children because the policy of separating the races is usually interpreted as denoting the inferiority of the black children. A sense of inferiority affects children's motivation to learn. Segregation tends to deprive black children of some of the benefits they would receive in an integrated school. Any language in found in *Plessy v. Ferguson*, 163 U.S. 537 (1896), that is contrary to this is hereby rejected. The "separate but equal" doctrine has no place in the field of education. Separate facilities are inherently unequal. Such facilities deprive black children of their right to equal protection of the laws. Remanded for further argument.

▶ ANALYSIS

In *Plessy v. Ferguson*, the Court sustained a Louisiana statute requiring "equal, but separate accommodations" for black and white railway passengers. The separate but equal doctrine was born and under it a long line of statutes providing separate but equal facilities were upheld. Justice Harlan was the only dissenter in *Plessy*. He stated, "The arbitrary separation of citizens, on the basis of race, while they are on a public highway ... cannot be justified upon any legal grounds. The thin disguise of equal accommodations for passengers in railway cars will not mislead anyone, nor atone for the wrong done this day." After the 1954 decision in *Brown v. Board of Education*, the Court found segregation unconstitutional in other public facilities as well. Despite the emphasis on the school context in *Brown*, the later cases resulted in per curiam orders simply citing *Brown*. Facilities that were desegregated included beaches, buses, golf courses, and parks.

Quicknotes

EQUAL PROTECTION A constitutional guarantee that no person shall be denied the same protection of the laws enjoyed by other persons in like circumstances.

PER CURIAM Announcement of a brief decision without a written opinion.

SEGREGATION The use of separate institutions and facilities for persons of different races.

SEPARATE BUT EQUAL DOCTRINE Doctrine pursuant to the holding in *Plessy v. Ferguson* that "separate but equal" facilities for persons of different races do not violate equal protection.

Loving v. Virginia

Interracial couple (D) v. State (P)

388 U.S. 1 (1967).

NATURE OF CASE: Constitutional review of state law barring interracial marriage.

FACT SUMMARY: Loving (D), a white man, and Jeter (D), a black woman, both Virginia residents, were married in the District of Columbia. When they returned to Virginia, they were indicted for violating the state's ban on interracial marriage.

🏛 RULE OF LAW
A state law restricting the freedom to marry solely because of racial classification violates the Equal Protection Clause.

FACTS: In June 1958, Loving (D), a white man, and Jeter (D), a black woman, both Virginia residents, were married in the District of Columbia, pursuant to its laws. Shortly after their marriage, the Lovings (D) returned to Virginia and were indicted for violating the state's law barring interracial marriage. They pleaded guilty and were sentenced to one year in jail. The trial judge suspended the sentence for 25 years on the condition that the Lovings (D) leave the state and not return for 25 years. In 1963, they filed a motion to have the judgment vacated and set aside.

ISSUE: Does a state law restricting the freedom to marry solely because of racial classifications violate the Equal Protection Clause?

HOLDING AND DECISION: (Warren, C.J.) Yes. A state law restricting the freedom to marry solely because of racial classification violates the Equal Protection Clause. At the very least, the Equal Protection Clause demands that racial classifications, especially suspect in criminal statutes, be subjected to the most rigid scrutiny. If they are ever to be upheld, they must be shown to be necessary to the accomplishment of some legitimate state objective. Here, there is no question that Virginia's miscegenation statutes rest solely upon distinctions drawn according to race. The statutes proscribe generally accepted conduct if engaged in by members of different races. The fact that the statute prohibits only interracial marriages involving white persons indicates that its aim is to maintain white supremacy. There is patently no legitimate overriding purpose independent of invidious discrimination that justifies the classification. A statute restricting marriage solely because of race violates the Equal Protection Clause. These statutes also deprive the Lovings (D) of liberty without due process. Since marriage is a basic human civil right, to deny this freedom on so insupportable a basis as racial classifications deprives all the state's citizens of liberty without due process of the law. Reversed.

▶ ANALYSIS

In *McLaughlin v. Florida*, 379 U.S. 184 (1964), a state law banning habitual nighttime cohabitation between whites and blacks not married to each other was held to violate the Equal Protection Clause, since other nonmarried couples were not subject to prosecution for the same acts. Ordinances establishing ghettos in which blacks must reside were found to violate the Clause (*Buchanan v. Warley*, 245 U.S. 60 [1917]), as was judicial enforcement of covenants restricting ownership land to whites (*Shelley v. Kraemer*, 334 U.S. 1 [1948]); racial discrimination in the selection of jurors (*Patton v. Mississippi*, 332 U.S. 463 [1947]); hiring blacks for certain occupations; and establishing racial qualifications for public offices (*Anderson v. Martin*, 375 U.S. 399 [1964]).

Quicknotes

EQUAL PROTECTION CLAUSE A constitutional guarantee that no person should be denied the same protection of the laws enjoyed by other persons in like circumstances.

INVIDIOUS DISCRIMINATION Unequal treatment of a class of persons that is particularly malicious or hostile.

MISCEGENATION Marriage between two persons of different races.

STRICT SCRUTINY Method by which courts determine the constitutionality of a law when a law affects a fundamental right.

SUSPECT CLASSIFICATION A class of persons that have historically been subject to discriminatory treatment; statutes drawing a distinction between persons based on a suspect classification, i.e., race, nationality or alienage, are subject to a strict scrutiny standard of review.

Washington v. Davis

Federal agency (D) v. Civil service applicants (P)

426 U.S. 229 (1976).

NATURE OF CASE: Certiorari review of constitutionality of testing requirement.

FACT SUMMARY: A qualifying test for positions as police officers in the District of Columbia was failed by a disproportionately high number of black applicants (P).

🏛 RULE OF LAW

A law or official governmental practice must have a "discriminatory purpose," not merely a disproportionate effect on one race, to constitute "invidious discrimination" under the Fifth Amendment's Due Process Clause or the Fourteenth Amendment's Equal Protection Clause.

FACTS: To be accepted in the District of Columbia Metropolitan Police Department, all applicants must receive a grade of at least 40 on "Test 21." This test was developed by the Civil Service Commission for use throughout the federal service to test "verbal ability, vocabulary, reading and comprehension." After failing this test, several black applicants (P) brought an action against the Commissioners of the United States Civil Service Commission (D) for a declaratory judgment that "Test 21" was unconstitutional. In this action, the black applicants (P) claimed that "Test 21" was unlawfully discriminatory against blacks and, therefore, was in violation of the Fifth Amendment's Due Process Clause. After the test was invalidated by the court of appeals, the Commissioners (D) appealed to this court.

ISSUE: Does a law or official governmental practice constitute "invidious discrimination" merely because it affects a greater proportion of one race than another?

HOLDING AND DECISION: (White, J.) No. A law or official governmental practice must have a "discriminatory purpose," not merely a disproportionate effect on one race, in order to constitute "invidious discrimination" under the Fifth Amendment's Due Process Clause or the Fourteenth Amendment's Equal Protection Clause. Of course, a disproportionate impact may be relevant as "evidence" of a "discriminatory purpose." However, such impact "is not the sole touchstone of invidious racial discrimination forbidden by the Constitution," and, standing alone, "it does not trigger the rule that racial classifications are to be subjected to the strictest scrutiny." Here, "Test 21" is racially "neutral" on its face (i.e., it is designed to disqualify anyone who cannot meet the requirements of the police training program). As such, it is valid even though it has a disproportionate effect on blacks. Reversed.

CONCURRENCE: (Stevens, J.) The line between discriminatory purpose and discriminatory impact is not nearly as bright, and perhaps not quite as critical, as the reader of the Court's opinion might assume. A constitutional issue is not presented every time some disproportionate impact is shown, but when the disproportion is especially great, it doesn't matter whether the standard is phrased in terms of purpose or effect. In the case at bar, there is no "purposeful discrimination," since "Test 21" serves "the neutral and legitimate purpose of requiring all applicants to meet a uniform minimum standard of literacy."

▶ ANALYSIS

Generally classifications based upon race are considered "suspect" and, therefore, subjected to "strict scrutiny" under the Equal Protection Clause or the Due Process Clause (i.e., such classifications must be justified by a "compelling state interest"). However, as this case illustrates, such "strict scrutiny" is only applied when there is "purposeful discrimination." As such, the court (as here) can avoid applying "strict scrutiny" by finding that any discriminatory impact is merely incidental. Note that here the Court also avoided applying the strict standard in Title VII of the Civil Rights Act of 1964 (by saying that only the constitutional issue was raised). Under Title VII, whenever hiring and promotion practices disqualify disproportionate numbers of blacks, they must be justified by more than a rational basis (i.e., must be validated in terms of job performance) even if no discriminatory purpose is shown.

━■━■

Quicknotes

DECLARATORY JUDGMENT A judgment of the court establishing the rights of the parties.

DISCRIMINATORY PURPOSE Intent to discriminate; established an Equal Protection violation.

INVIDIOUS DISCRIMINATION Unequal treatment of a class of persons that is particularly malicious or hostile.

━■━■

Regents of Univ. of California v. Bakke

University (D) v. Applicant (P)

438 U.S. 265 (1978).

NATURE OF CASE: Certiorari review of constitutionality of admission standards.

FACT SUMMARY: Bakke (P) was denied admission to the University of California, Davis (D) Medical School because it employed a racial quota to aid minorities.

RULE OF LAW

Race may not be made the sole criterion for an admissions decision.

FACTS: Bakke (P) applied for admission to the University of California, Davis (U.C., Davis) (D) Medical School. The School (D) admitted 100 students per year. However, the Regents (D) had adopted a policy of setting aside a minimum number of seats for minority applicants to increase the number of minority members in the medical profession. Members of minorities were screened by a separate admissions panel and were subject to lesser standards in the admissions. Bakke (P), a white male, was denied admission to the medical school even though his overall test scores and grade point were significantly higher than many of those admitted under the minorities program. Bakke (P) filed suit to compel his admission to the School (D). Bakke (P) alleged that the special admissions program violated the Equal Protection Clause and § 601 of Title VI of the C.R.A. of 1964. The court found that Bakke (P) had been discriminated against and ordered his admission, finding that the School (D) had not carried its burden of proof to establish that he would not have been admitted even without the program. The School (D) appealed, alleging that benign discrimination was not violative of the Fourteenth Amendment.

ISSUE: May race be made the sole criterion for an admissions decision?

HOLDING AND DECISION: (Powell, J.) No. Race may not be made the sole criterion for an admissions decision. Before reaching the constitutional issue, we must first determine whether the program is invalid under Title VI since this would obviate the necessity of determining constitutional issues. We do not need to pass upon the issue of standing under Title VI, since this was neither briefed nor argued by the parties. Section 601 states that no person shall, on the ground of race, color or national origin, be excluded from participation in any program or benefit receiving federal financial assistance. Based on its legislative history, we find that Title VI proscribes only those racial classifications which would violate the Equal Protection Clause of the Fourteenth Amendment. When racial classifications are involved, strict judicial scrutiny is required even where the class being subjected to the discrimination is white males. The Fourteenth Amendment, regardless of its original roots, is now applied to eliminate discrimination against any group. We decline to restrict its reach to encompass only minorities. Discrimination is never benign. White males may be the minority in certain areas and allegedly benign discrimination may actually have more invidious purposes. While racial classifications have been approved as remedial devices where a court has found prior racial discrimination, U.C., Davis (D) has no history of discrimination. To justify the use of a suspect classification such as race, a state must establish that it has a constitutionally permissible purpose or interest which is substantial and the classification is necessary to accomplish it. The Regents (D) allege that the classification is necessary to increase the number of minority doctors, counter the effect of societal discrimination, increase the number of physicians willing to practice in minority areas, and obtain the benefit of a racially diverse student body. U.C., Davis (D) has no history of racial discrimination and it may not employ racial quotas merely to assume that its student body will have a set percentage of students from each of the races. Racial classifications to eliminate societal discrimination have never been sanctioned. The School (D) is in the business of educating, not formulating social and legislative policy. Since there is no showing that minority applicants will practice in disadvantaged areas or are in anyway required to do so, the School (D) cannot justify its admission policy on this basis. While an ethnically diverse student body is a legitimate and important purpose, it is only one of the elements in the range of factors that must be considered by a school in attaining a goal of a heterogeneous student body. A school may not base its admissions policies solely on the criterion of race. Racial quotas are violative of the Equal Protection Clause. Race may be considered, but only as one of the factors involved in the admissions decision. Race may be deemed a "plus" so long as all other relevant factors are considered. Affirmed.

CONCURRENCE AND DISSENT: (Brennan, J.) The central import of the opinion herein is that race may be taken into account when it does not demean or insult any racial group, but is used to remedy past disadvantages suffered by the minority or group. Based on our Nation's past history of discrimination, affirmative action programs are necessary to make up for past acts of societal discrimination. Title VI could not have been intended to

Continued on next page.

reach such programs. This is borne out by the fact that many affirmative action programs are required as a condition to federal funding. Therefore, we find that classifications need not be color-blind where race is used to eliminate the effects of past discrimination so long as it is not the sole criterion used, i.e., racial quotas. The government must establish that no less intrusive method for accomplishing its purpose is available. U.C., Davis (D) had a sound basis for determining that minorities were seriously underrepresented and had been subjected to prior acts of societal and government discrimination. This condition would be perpetuated absent some affirmative action program. Moreover, judicial decrees in California had established discriminatory official acts which had the effect of exacerbating the situation. We feel that the U.C., Davis (D) program was remedial. The admissions program did not stigmatize any race, minority or majority. The number of minority applicants admitted was less than their proportion of the population in California. No quota within these minorities was established and the best qualified of minority applicants were admitted. In light of the circumstances and objectives herein, race was a reasonable criterion. We would, therefore, reverse the finding that the program was unconstitutional.

SEPARATE OPINION: (Marshall, J.) "It must be remembered that, during most of the past 200 years, the Constitution as interpreted by this Court did not prohibit the most ingenious and pervasive forms of discrimination against the Negro." The Thirteenth and Fourteenth Amendments were designed to eliminate discrimination against minorities. They should not be applied to benign discrimination programs.

SEPARATE OPINION: (Blackmun, J.) The Equal Protection Clause cannot be used as a shield to perpetuate the supremacy of the majority. I hope some day that affirmative action programs will become unnecessary, but we are not at that point yet. "In order to get beyond racism, we must first take account of race. There is no other way."

CONCURRENCE AND DISSENT: (Stevens, J.) This is not a class action and the scope of the opinion is far beyond that which is necessary to conclude the controversy between Bakke (P) and U.C., Davis (D). The basis of the plain language of § 601 permits affirmation. Race cannot be used under it and U.C., Davis's (D) admissions policy clearly violates this prohibition.

▶ **ANALYSIS**

Bakke, based on the failure of the Court to achieve any consensus, stands merely for the proposition that racial quotas cannot be used where there is no court finding of discrimination. The loose standards enunciated herein should allow a school to establish what amounts to a racial quota merely by giving inordinate weight to race in its

admissions decision; that is, of course, if any schools will want to bother now that they are under no legal obligation to do so.

Quicknotes

AFFIRMATIVE ACTION PROGRAM A program designed to create benign discrimination for the purpose of remedying existing discrimination by favoring one group over another.

EQUAL PROTECTION A constitutional guarantee that no person shall be denied the same protection of the laws enjoyed by other persons in like circumstances.

FOURTEENTH AMENDMENT Declares that no state shall make or enforce any law which shall abridge the privileges and immunities of citizens of the United States.

THIRTEENTH AMENDMENT The constitutional provision which abolished slavery in the United States.

Adarand Constructors, Inc. v. Pena

Contractor (P) v. Federal government (D)

515 U.S. 200 (1995).

NATURE OF CASE: Certiorari review of constitutionality of federal program.

FACT SUMMARY: A federal program favoring minority-owned businesses was challenged by Adarand Constructors (P), a white contractor who lost a job to a Hispanic-owned company, as violative of equal protection.

🏛 RULE OF LAW
Federal programs that set racial classifications for awarding contracts or jobs will be subject to strict judicial scrutiny.

FACTS: A general contractor to a project involving the federal government solicited bids for the subcontracts. For the guardrail portion of this highway project, Adarand Constructors (P), a white contractor, submitted the low bid. The general contractor, however, signed a competing Hispanic-owned company because of a congressionally created program that awarded contractors bonus monies for hiring minority-owned businesses. Adarand (P) sued in district court, contending that the program violated equal protection. The district court evaluated the program under a relaxed standard resembling intermediate scrutiny, held the program valid, and dismissed. The Tenth Circuit affirmed, and the Supreme Court granted review.

ISSUE: Will federal programs that set racial classifications for awarding contracts or jobs be subject to strict judicial scrutiny?

HOLDING AND DECISION: (O'Connor, J.) Yes. Federal programs that set racial classifications for awarding contracts or jobs will be subject to strict judicial scrutiny. Three general propositions exist with respect to governmental racial classifications. The first is skepticism: all such classifications are inherently suspect. The second is consistency: the standard of review does not vary depending on race. The third proposition is congruence: that which applies to the states must apply to the national government as well. From this, the proposition naturally follows that any person of any race has the right to demand that any governmental actor explain, through the standard of strict scrutiny, why he is being treated differently than a person of another race. Consequently, any racial classification scheme enacted by Congress must pass strict scrutiny, which is to say, must be narrowly tailored to serve a compelling governmental interest. This was not the standard used by the courts below. Vacated and remanded.

CONCURRENCE: (Scalia, J.) Government can never have a compelling interest in discriminating on the basis of race to "make up" for past discrimination. We are just one race in the eyes of government.

CONCURRENCE: (Thomas, J.) There is a moral and constitutional equivalence between all racial distinctions, "benign" or otherwise, that justifies subjecting them to strict scrutiny analysis.

DISSENT: (Stevens, J.) There is no moral or constitutional equivalence between a policy designed to perpetuate racial subjugation and one designed to eradicate it.

DISSENT: (Ginsburg, J.) The difficulty of this case should not obscure the Court's recognition of the persistence of racial inequality and the acknowledgment of Congress's authority to act affirmatively, not only to end discrimination, but also to counteract discrimination's lingering effects. In light of the attention the political branches are currently giving to affirmative action, there is no compelling cause for the intervention the Court has made in this case.

▶ ANALYSIS

Subjecting affirmative action policies to a rigorous examination will inevitably jeopardize a whole host of programs designed to convey special federal benefits to members of minority groups. However, Justice O'Connor stopped short of the Scalia-Thomas approach that would simply bar all racial preferences as unconstitutional. Instead, she invites the executive and legislative branches to take unspecified steps to address "the unhappy persistence of both the practice and the lingering effects of racial discrimination."

Quicknotes

AFFIRMATIVE ACTION A form of benign discrimination designed to remedy existing discrimination by favoring one group over another.

INJUNCTIVE RELIEF A count order issued as a remedy, requiring a person to do, or prohibiting that person from doing, a specific act.

STARE DECISIS Doctrine whereby courts follow legal precedent unless there is good cause for departure.

STRICT SCRUTINY Method by which courts determine the constitutionality of a law when a law affects a fundamental right. Under the test, the legislature must have a compelling interest to enact law and measures prescribed by the law must be the least restrictive means possible to accomplish goal.

Grutter v. Bollinger

Law school applicant (P) v. Law school (D)

539 U.S. 306 (2003).

NATURE OF CASE: Certiorari review of constitutionality of admissions policy.

FACT SUMMARY: When Grutter (P), a white applicant for admission to the University of Michigan Law School (D), was rejected, she argued the law school's (D) use of race as a factor in admissions decisions resulted in discrimination against her on the basis of race in violation of the Fourteenth Amendment.

🏛 RULE OF LAW
The Equal Protection Clause does not prohibit a school's narrowly tailored use of race in admissions decisions to further a compelling interest in obtaining educational benefits flowing from a diverse student body.

FACTS: The University of Michigan Law School (D), as part of its admission policy, expressly seeks to admit a group of students who, among other things, will reflect "diversity." The policy reaffirms the Law School's (D) commitment to "racial and ethnic diversity" with special reference to the inclusion of students who have been historically discriminated against, such as African-Americans, Hispanics, and Native Americans. Each year the Law School (D) admits a class of 350 from over 3,500 applications. Grutter (P), a white Michigan resident, applied to the Law School (D) with a 3.8 grade point average and 161 LSAT score. When her application was rejected, she sued the Law School (D) in federal district court, alleging the latter (D) had discriminated against her on the basis of race in violation of the Fourteenth Amendment. The district court agreed, concluding that the Law School's (D) use of race as a factor in admissions decisions was unlawful. The federal court of appeals reversed, and Grutter (P) appealed to the Supreme Court.

ISSUE: Does the Equal Protection Clause prohibit a school's narrowly tailored use of race in admissions decisions to further a compelling interest in obtaining educational benefits flowing from a diverse student body?

HOLDING AND DECISION: (O'Connor, J.) No. The Equal Protection Clause does not prohibit a school's narrowly tailored use of race in admissions decisions to further a compelling interest in obtaining educational benefits flowing from a diverse student body. Here, the Law School's (D) admission policy aspires to achieve that diversity which has the potential to enrich everyone's education and thus make a law school class stronger than the sum of its parts. By enrolling a "critical mass" of underrepresented minority students, the Law School (D) seeks to ensure their

ability to make unique contributions to the character of the law school. The policy does not define diversity solely in terms of racial and ethnic status. Racial classifications imposed by government must be strictly analyzed; such classifications are constitutional only if they are narrowly tailored, as here, to further compelling governmental interests. Not every decision influenced by race is equally objectionable. In keeping with the Court's tradition in giving a degree of deference to a university's academic decisions, the Law School's (D) "educational judgment" that such diversity is essential to its educational mission is one to which the Court defers. This Court has long recognized that, given the important purpose of public education and the expansive freedoms of speech and thought associated with the university environment, universities occupy a special niche in our constitutional tradition. The Court's conclusion of the Law School's (D) "compelling interest" in a diverse student body is informed by the view that attaining a diverse student body is at the heart of the Law School's (D) proper institutional mission. Furthermore, in order to cultivate national leaders with legitimacy in the eyes of the citizenry, it is necessary that the path to leadership be visibly open to talented and qualified individuals of every race and ethnicity. Affirmed.

CONCURRENCE: (Ginsburg, J.) It is well documented that conscious and unconscious race bias, even rank discrimination based on race, remain alive in our land, impeding realization of our highest values and ideals. One may hope, but not firmly forecast, that over the next generation's span, progress toward nondiscrimination and genuinely equal opportunity will make it safe to sunset affirmative action.

CONCURRENCE AND DISSENT: (Scalia, J.) Litigation can be expected on behalf of minority groups intentionally shortchanged in the institution's composition of its generic minority "critical mass." The Constitution proscribes government discrimination on the basis of race, and state-provided education is no exception.

CONCURRENCE AND DISSENT: (Thomas, J.) Blacks can achieve in every avenue of American life without the meddling of university administrators. The Constitution does not tolerate institutional devotion to the status quo in admissions policies when such devotion ripens into racial discrimination.

DISSENT: (Rehnquist, C.J.) The Law School's (D) means are not narrowly tailored to the interest it asserts. While the Law School (D) claims that it must take steps to

Continued on next page.

achieve a "critical mass" of underrepresented minority students, its actual program bears no relation to this asserted goal, but rather there is a direct correlation between the applicants and the admittees of a given race. This is precisely the type of racial balancing the Court calls "patently unconstitutional."

ANALYSIS

In *Grutter*, the Supreme Court noted it was true that the Court's language in some of its cases since *Bakke*, 438 U.S. 265 (1978), might be read to suggest that remedying past discrimination is the permissible justification only for race-based governmental action. Nevertheless, said the Court, it had never held that the only governmental use of race that can survive strict scrutiny is remedying past discrimination.

Quicknotes

AFFIRMATIVE ACTION A form of benign discrimination designed to remedy existing discrimination by favoring one group over another.

EQUAL PROTECTION CLAUSE A constitutional guarantee that no person should be denied the same protection of the laws enjoyed by other persons in like circumstances.

FOURTEENTH AMENDMENT Declares that no state shall make or enforce any law which shall abridge the privileges and immunities of citizens of the United States.

Gratz v. Bollinger

College applicants (P) v. University (D)

539 U.S. 244 (2003).

NATURE OF CASE: Certiorari review of constitutionality of admissions policy.

FACT SUMMARY: Gratz (P) and other "qualified" white students denied admission as undergraduates to the University of Michigan (D) sued the University (D), arguing the admission policy of automatically distributing one-fifth of the points needed to guarantee admission to every single "underrepresented minority" solely because of race constituted prohibited racial discrimination.

🏛 RULE OF LAW

A university admissions policy that automatically distributes one-fifth of the points needed to guarantee admission to every single "underrepresented minority" solely because of race is not narrowly tailored to achieve the interest in educational diversity so as to avoid violation of the Equal Protection Clause of the Fourteenth Amendment.

FACTS: Gratz (P) and other white students, who were denied admission as undergraduates to the University of Michigan (D), although they were deemed "qualified" by the college admissions committee, brought suit against the University (D), arguing that its applicant selection method violated the Equal Protection Clause of the Fourteenth Amendment on the grounds that the University (D) automatically distributes one-fifth of the points needed to guarantee admission to every single "underrepresented minority" solely because of race. [The procedural posture of the case is not set forth in the textbook excerpt.]

ISSUE: Is a university admissions policy that automatically distributes one-fifth of the points needed to guarantee admission to every single "underrepresented minority" solely because of race narrowly tailored to achieve the interest in educational diversity so as to avoid violation of the Equal Protection Clause of the Fourteenth Amendment?

HOLDING AND DECISION: (Rehnquist, C.J.) No. A university admissions policy that automatically distributes one-fifth of the points needed to guarantee admission to every single "underrepresented minority" solely because of race is not narrowly tailored to achieve the interest in educational diversity so as to avoid violation of the Equal Protection Clause of the Fourteenth Amendment. This Court emphasizes the importance of considering each particular applicant as an individual, assessing all of the qualities that an individual possesses, and in turn, evaluating that individual's ability to contribute to the unique setting of higher education. In this

regard, the Court does not contemplate that any single characteristic automatically ensures a specific and identifiable contribution to a university's diversity. Here, the University's (D) admission policy does not provide such individualized consideration; to the contrary, it automatically distributes 20 points to "underrepresented minority" groups, the only consideration being whether the applicant is a member of one of these minority groups. Even if an applicant's extraordinary artistic talent rivaled that of Monet or Picasso, the applicant would receive, at most, five points under the University's (D) admissions system. Clearly, such a system does not offer applicants an individualized selection process. Nor does the fact that the implementation of a program capable of providing individualized consideration might present administrative challenges render constitutional an otherwise problematic system. The admissions policy violates the Equal Protection Clause of the Fourteenth Amendment.

CONCURRENCE: (O'Connor, J.) The selection index, by setting up automatic, predetermined point allocations for the soft variables, ensures that the diversity contributions of applicants cannot be individually assessed. This is in sharp contrast to the law school's admission plan, which enables admissions officers to make nuanced judgments as to the contributions each applicant is likely to make.

CONCURRENCE: (Thomas, J.) A state's use of racial discrimination in higher education admissions is categorically prohibited by the Equal Protection Clause.

DISSENT: (Souter, J.) On its face, the assignment of specific points does not set race apart from all other weighted considerations. Since college admission is not left entirely to inarticulate intuition, it is hard to see what is inappropriate in assigning some stated value to a relevant characteristic, whether it be reasoning ability, writing style, running speed, or minority race.

DISSENT: (Ginsburg, J.) The stain of generations of racial oppression is still visible in our society, and the determination to hasten its removal remains vital. Here, there has been no demonstration that the University (D) unduly constricts admissions opportunities for students who do not receive special consideration based on race.

▌ ANALYSIS

As made clear by the Supreme Court in its *Gratz*, and also *Grutter*, 539 U.S. 306 (2003), decisions, achieving diversity

Continued on next page.

in higher education, whether it be at college level or graduate school, remains a compelling state interest sufficient to justify some degree of racial preferences without violating the Equal Protection Clause of the Fourteenth Amendment.

■■■

Quicknotes

EQUAL PROTECTION CLAUSE A constitutional guarantee that no person should be denied the same protection of the laws enjoyed by other persons in like circumstances.

■■■

Parents Involved in Community Schools v. Seattle School District

Parents of unadmitted students (P) v. Public school district (D)

551 U.S. 701 (2007).

NATURE OF CASE: Certiorari review of constitutionality of school-assignment plans.

FACT SUMMARY: Two metropolitan school districts sought to assign students to schools to achieve racial balance.

🏛 RULE OF LAW
Racial balance between local high-school districts is not a compelling government interest under the Equal Protection Clause.

FACTS: The Seattle School District (Seattle) (D) implemented a student assignment plan designed to achieve numerically defined racial balance between Seattle's (D) ten public high schools. Seattle (D), however, had never been found to run racially segregated schools. The Jefferson County Public Schools in Louisville, Kentucky (Louisville) was under a desegregation order from 1975 to 2000; the order was dissolved in 2001 when a federal court ruled that Louisville (D) had reached unitary status by largely eliminating the district's earlier racial segregation. After the decree was dissolved, Louisville (D) voluntarily adopted a student assignment plan that required specific minimum and maximum enrollment percentages for black students. Parents (P) of students who were denied admission in each school district sued their respective district, alleging, in part, violations of the Equal Protection Clause. After the intermediate appellate courts in both cases upheld the assignment plans, the parents (P) petitioned the Supreme Court for further review.

ISSUE: Is racial balance between local high-school districts a compelling government interest under the Equal Protection Clause?

HOLDING AND DECISION: (Roberts, C.J.) No. Racial balance between local high-school districts is not a compelling government interest under the Equal Protection Clause. Because both school districts (D) have apportioned government benefits on the basis of race, the applicable standard of review in these cases is strict scrutiny: Seattle (D) and Louisville (D) must show that their race-based discrimination (1) advances a compelling government interest through (2) means that are narrowly tailored to achieve the intended purpose. The asserted interests in both Seattle (D) and Louisville (D) reduce to nothing more than the goal of numerical racial balance between each district's (D) schools. This Court has consistently found such a purpose illegitimate. *Grutter v. Bollinger*, 539 U.S. 306 (2003), does not control here because *Grutter* involved the specific interests of higher education; it is also

instructive, though, that *Grutter* upheld the law-school admission policy there because racial diversity was only one of a mix of admissions criteria. Here, on the other hand, pure numerical racial balance, by itself, is the government interest, and that interest has never been recognized as valid. The plans at issue here also fail because the school districts (D) have failed to show that they seriously considered other means besides explicit racial classifications. Reversed.

CONCURRENCE: (Thomas, J.) Racial imbalance and racial segregation are not synonymous; it is possible to have racial imbalance through no conscious decision to segregate. Further, forced racial mixing of students may or may not provide educational benefits in general or higher achievement for black students in particular. The color-blind Constitution, then, requires that these student assignment plans be struck down.

CONCURRENCE: (Kennedy, J.) Contrary to the Chief Justice's plurality opinion, race can be considered as one among several factors in examining school enrollments. General, indirect solutions to problems of racial composition of schools are much better than the crude plans in these cases as ways to address those problems. The United States has special obligations to ensure equal opportunity for all children, and government should be permitted to consider race in its attempts to fulfill that mission. As the plurality correctly notes, though, government may not classify students based solely on race without first making a showing that such a step is necessary.

DISSENT: (Stevens, J.) In his demand of strict equality under the Constitution, the Chief Justice forgets that, before *Brown*, 347 U.S. 483 (1954), only black students were told where they could and could not go to school. Today's plurality decision rewrites the history of our landmark school-desegregation decision.

DISSENT: (Breyer, J.) These voluntary plans bear striking resemblances to plans that this Court has long required, permitted, and encouraged local school districts to formulate and use. Every branch of government has acknowledged that government may voluntarily use race-conscious plans to address race-based problems even when such plans are not constitutionally obligatory. The plurality overlooks the fact that no case has ever decided that all racial classifications should receive precisely the same scrutiny. Actually, our decisions have applied different standards to assess racial classifications depending on whether the government's purpose was to exclude persons

Continued on next page.

from, or to include persons in, government programs. The plurality's interpretation of strict scrutiny, however, would automatically invalidate all race-conscious government action. The school districts' (D) interest here serves remedial, educational, and democratic purposes; such a multiplicity of concerns means that *Grutter*'s rationale controls here and requires upholding these assignment plans. Even under the strictest scrutiny, though, the plans here pass muster under the Equal Protection Clause because they are more narrowly tailored than the plan approved in *Grutter*. Accordingly, these plans are consistent with equal protection of the laws.

▶ ANALYSIS

Chief Justice Roberts's plurality opinion in Parents Involved focuses on the firm percentages used by Seattle (D) and Louisville (D) in making student-assignment decisions. Despite Justice Breyer's objections in dissent, it is difficult to see how such an overtly numerical approach differs from the quota-based systems that the Court consistently has struck down under the Equal Protection Clause. See, e.g., *Regents of the University of California v. Bakke*, 438 U.S. 265, 307 (1978), "If [the University's] purpose is to assure within its student body some specified percentage of a particular group merely because of its race or ethnic origin, such a preferential purpose must be rejected not as insubstantial but as facially invalid."

■■■■

Quicknotes

EQUAL PROTECTION CLAUSE A constitutional provision that each person be guaranteed the same protection of the laws enjoyed by other persons in like circumstances.

STRICT SCRUTINY Method by which courts determine the constitutionality of a law when a law affects a fundamental right. Under the test, the legislature must have had a compelling interest to enact the law and measures prescribed by the law must be the least restrictive means possible to accomplish its goal.

■■■■

Shaw v. Reno (Shaw I)

Voters (P) v. State (D)

509 U.S. 630 (1993).

NATURE OF CASE: Certiorari review of constitutionality of a congressional redistricting plan.

FACT SUMMARY: Shaw (P) alleged that a North Carolina reapportionment plan that included one majority-black district with boundary lines of dramatically irregular shape constituted unconstitutional racial gerrymandering.

> **RULE OF LAW**
> An allegation that a reapportionment scheme is so irrational on its face that it can be understood only as an effort to segregate voters based on race without sufficient justification states a cognizable claim under the Fourteenth Amendment.

FACTS: North Carolina, after becoming entitled to a twelfth seat in the U.S. House of Representatives as a result of the 1990 census, enacted a reapportionment plan that included one majority-black district with boundary lines of dramatically irregular shape. Shaw (P), on behalf of a number of voters, sued, alleging the creation of the irregular district was unconstitutional racial gerrymandering under the Fourteenth Amendment. The district court dismissed the action for failure to state a cognizable claim. Shaw (P) appealed to the Supreme Court, which granted certiorari.

ISSUE: Does an allegation that a reapportionment scheme is so irrational on its face that it can be understood only as an effort to segregate voters based on race without sufficient justification state a cognizable claim under the Fourteenth Amendment?

HOLDING AND DECISION: (O'Connor, J.) Yes. An allegation that a reapportionment scheme is so irrational on its face that it can be understood only as an effort to segregate voters based on race without sufficient justification states a cognizable claim under the Fourteenth Amendment. The Fourteenth Amendment requires that legislation that is unexplainable on grounds other than race is narrowly tailored to further a compelling governmental interest, even if facially race-neutral. An example of such unexplainable legislation would be a reapportionment plan so highly irregular on its face that it rationally cannot be understood as anything other than an effort to segregate voters on the basis of race. Such a plan perpetuates impermissible racial stereotypes by reinforcing the perception that members of the same racial group, regardless of age or economic status, share the same political ideology. Shaw's (P) complaint alleged that the North Carolina plan was such a plan and thus stated a cognizable claim. Reversed and remanded.

DISSENT: (White, J.) Shaw (P) failed to state a claim because no cognizable injury was alleged. There is neither an outright deprivation of the right to vote nor a demonstration that the challenged action had the intent and effect of unduly diminishing a group's influence on the political process.

DISSENT: (Blackmun, J.) It is ironic that today's case in which the majority chooses to abandon settled law and for the first time to recognize this "analytically distinct" constitutional claim, is a challenge by white voters to the plan under which North Carolina has sent black representatives to Congress for the first time since Reconstruction.

DISSENT: (Stevens, J.) The Equal Protection Clause prohibits states from creating bizarre district boundaries such as the one at issue for the sole purpose of making it more difficult for members of a minority group to win an election. However, it does not prohibit gerrymandering when the majority acts to facilitate the election of a member of a group that lacks power because it remains underrepresented in the state legislature.

DISSENT: (Souter, J.) Until today, the Court has analyzed equal protection claims involving race in electoral districting differently from equal protection claims involving other forms of governmental conduct. Unlike other contexts in which we have addressed the State's conscious use of race, electoral districting calls for decisions that nearly always require some consideration of race for legitimate reasons where there is a racially mixed population. There is no justification for treating the narrow category of bizarrely shaped district claims differently from other districting claims.

▶ ANALYSIS

Though the holding of *Shaw* is limited, the Court spoke extensively in dicta about what constituted sufficient justification for race-based districting. If on remand a plan were found to be in fact racial gerrymandering, the plan must then be found narrowly tailored to further a compelling governmental interest. This high level of scrutiny is imposed because the Court believes racial classifications with respect to voting rights "carry particular dangers" such as "Balkanizing" citizens into competing racial factions, thus moving the country away from the goal of a

Continued on next page.

political system in which race is irrelevant. In *Shaw*, the challenged district was unusually long and narrow and ran along an interstate. One pundit suggested that if a driver on the interstate opened his car doors, he would risk running over every voter in the district.

■—■

Quicknotes

FOURTEENTH AMENDMENT Declares that no state shall make or enforce any law which shall abridge the privileges and immunities of citizens of the United States.

GERRYMANDER The designation of voting districts in a geographic area to provide unfair advantage to one political party over another.

REAPPORTIONMENT PLAN The alteration of a voting district's boundaries or composition to reflect the population of that district.

■—■

Craig v. Boren

Males 18 to 20 years of age (P) v. State (D)

429 U.S. 190 (1976).

NATURE OF CASE: Certiorari review of constitutionality of state statute.

FACT SUMMARY: Craig (P) appealed after a federal district court upheld two sections of an Oklahoma statute prohibiting the sale of "nonintoxicating" 3.2 percent beer to males under the age of 21 and to females under the age of 18 on the ground that such a gender-based differential did not constitute a denial to males 18–20 years of age equal protection of the laws.

RULE OF LAW
Laws that establish classifications by gender must serve important governmental objectives and must be substantially related to achievement of those objectives to be constitutionally in line with the Equal Protection Clause.

FACTS: Craig (P) brought suit to have two sections of an Oklahoma statute, which prohibits the sale of "nonintoxicating" 3.2 percent beer to males under the age of 21 and to females under the age of 18, declared unconstitutional. Craig (P) contended that such a gender-based differential constituted a denial to males 18 to 20 years of age of the equal protection of the laws in violation of the Fourteenth Amendment. Boren (D), representing the state of Oklahoma, argued that this law was enacted as a traffic safety measure and that the protection of public health and safety was an important function of state and local governments. Boren (D) introduced statistical data demonstrating that 18–20-year-old male arrests for "driving under the influence" and "drunkenness" substantially exceeded female arrests for the same age period. The district court upheld the ordinance on the ground that it served the important governmental objective of traffic safety. Craig (P) appealed.

ISSUE: Are laws that establish classifications by gender constitutional if they do not serve important governmental objectives and are not substantially related to achievement of those objectives?

HOLDING AND DECISION: (Brennan, J.) No. Laws that establish classifications by gender must serve important governmental objectives and must be substantially related to achievement of those objectives to be constitutionally in line with the Equal Protection Clause. It appears that the objective underlying the statute in controversy is the enhancement of traffic safety. Clearly, the protection of public health and safety represents an important function of state and local governments. However, the statistics presented by Boren (D) in this court's

view cannot support the conclusion that the gender-based distinction closely serves to achieve the objective. The most relevant of the statistical surveys presented as evidence by Boren (D) in support of the statute, arrests of 18–20-year-olds for alcohol related driving offenses, establish two percent more males than females are arrested for that offense. Such a disparity can hardly form the basis for employment of a gender line as a classifying device. Certainly, if maleness is to serve as a proxy for drinking and driving, a correlation of two percent must be considered unduly tenuous. Indeed, prior cases have consistently rejected the use of sex as a decision-making factor. Therefore, since the gender-based differential does not serve an important governmental objective, the Oklahoma statute constitutes a denial of the equal protection of the laws to males ages 18 to 20 and is unconstitutional. Reversed.

CONCURRENCE: (Powell, J.) The state legislature, by the classification it has chosen, has not adopted through the enactment of the statute a means that bears a fair and substantial relation to the objective of traffic safety.

CONCURRENCE: (Stevens, J.) It is difficult to believe that the statute in question was actually intended to cope with the problem of traffic safety, since it has only a minimal effect on access to a not-very-intoxicating beverage and does not prohibit its consumption.

DISSENT: (Rehnquist, J.) The Court's disposition of this case is objectionable on two grounds. First is its conclusion that men challenging a gender-based statute that treats them less favorably than women may invoke a more stringent standard of judicial review than pertains to most other types of classifications. Second is the Court's enunciation of this standard, without citation to any source, as being that "classifications by gender must serve important governmental objectives and must be substantially related to achievement of those objectives." The Equal Protection Clause contains no such language, and none of our previous cases adopt that standard.

ANALYSIS

Cases concerning whether males and females should be considered as reaching a majority age equally has met with some stiff opposition. In *Stanton v. Stanton*, 564 P.2d 303 (1977), a Utah justice observed: "Regardless of what a judge may think about equality, his thinking cannot change the facts of life. To judicially hold that males and

Continued on next page.

females attain their maturity at the same age is to be blind to the biological facts of life."

■━■

Quicknotes

EQUAL PROTECTION CLAUSE A constitutional guarantee that no person should be denied the same protection of the laws enjoyed by other persons in like circumstances.

FOURTEENTH AMENDMENT Declares that no state shall make or enforce any law which shall abridge the privileges and immunities of citizens of the United States.

■━■

United States v. Virginia

Federal government (P) v. State (D)

518 U.S. 515 (1996).

NATURE OF CASE: Certiorari review of constitutionality of a college's male-only admission policy.

FACT SUMMARY: Virginia Military Institute (D), a state-sponsored university, had a policy of excluding women from admission or attendance.

 RULE OF LAW
Public schools may not exclude women.

FACTS: Since 1839, Virginia Military Institute (VMI) (D), a Virginia (D) public institution, had been a male-only college that sought to train "citizen-soldiers." In 1990, the Attorney General (P) sued VMI (D) and Virginia (D), claiming that the admission policy violated the Equal Protection Clause. Virginia (D) eventually proposed a remedial plan under which a parallel program would be developed for women. The Virginia Women's Institute for Leadership (VWIL) would be created at Mary Baldwin College. The trial court and an appellate court upheld this remedial plan, but the Attorney General (P) appealed and the Supreme Court granted a writ of certiorari.

ISSUE: May public schools exclude women?

HOLDING AND DECISION: (Ginsburg, J.) No. Public schools may not exclude women. States must show that a sex-based government action serves important governmental objectives and that the discriminatory means employed are substantially related to the achievement of those objectives. There must an exceedingly persuasive justification for the action. This heightened review standard prevents classifications that perpetuate the legal, social, and economic inferiority of women. While single-sex education may provide benefits to some students, Virginia (D) has not shown that it pursued this option as a means to providing a diversity of educational opportunities. On the other hand, the historical record shows that Virginia (D) has systematically prevented women from obtaining higher education until relatively recently. The fact that women have been successfully integrated into the armed forces and service academies demonstrates that VMI's (D) stature will not be downgraded by admitting women. The proposed VWIL does not qualify as VMI's (D) equal in terms of faculty, facilities, course offerings, and its reputation. Accordingly, since Virginia (D) is unable to provide substantial equal opportunities for women who desire to attend VMI (D), the male-only admission policy is unconstitutional. Remanded.

CONCURRENCE: (Rehnquist, C.J.) The majority decision is correct but there is no basis for stating that states must demonstrate an exceedingly persuasive justification to support sex-based classifications.

DISSENT: (Scalia, J.) The majority sweeps away an institution that has thrived for 150 years and the precedents of this Court to embark on a course of proscribing its own elite opinions on society. Virginia (D) has an important interest in providing education, and single-sex instruction is an approach substantially related to this goal.

▶ *ANALYSIS*

Justice Scalia's dissent carries a tone of disgust for the majority opinion. As he did in *Romer v. Evans*, 517 U.S. 620 (1996), Scalia states the majority seeks to satisfy some unidentified group of anti-majoritarian elites. This attitude is unusual for a member of the Supreme Court since dissents are usually restricted to attacks on the majority's legal reasoning.

■■■

Quicknotes

CERTIORARI A discretionary writ issued by a superior court to an inferior court in order to review the lower court's decisions; the Supreme Court's writ ordering such review.

■■■

Romer v. Evans

[Parties not identified.]

517 U.S. 620 (1996).

NATURE OF CASE: Certiorari review of constitutionality of an amendment to a state constitution.

FACT SUMMARY: A Colorado (D) constitutional amendment, Amendment 2, which struck down local antidiscrimination laws based on sexual orientation, was challenged for being violative of the Equal Protection Clause.

🏛 RULE OF LAW
Colorado's Amendment 2 violates the Equal Protection Clause because it singles out a class of citizens—homosexuals—for disfavored legal status.

FACTS: In 1992, Colorado (D) amended its state constitution by a statewide referendum. Amendment 2, as it was designated, provided that the state and local branches of government were forbidden from enacting any laws or regulations that would protect homosexuals from discrimination. Amendment 2 was challenged in court as unconstitutional for violating the Equal Protection Clause. Colorado (D) responded that Amendment 2 simply denied homosexuals any special rights given to protected classes, such as minorities. The trial court enjoined enactment of Amendment 2, the Colorado Supreme Court affirmed, and the United States Supreme Court granted certiorari to decide the issue.

ISSUE: Does Colorado's Amendment 2 violate the Equal Protection Clause because it singles out a class of citizens—homosexuals—for disfavored legal status?

HOLDING AND DECISION: (Kennedy, J.) Yes. Colorado's Amendment 2 violates the Equal Protection Clause because it singles out a class of citizens—homosexuals—for disfavored legal status. The Colorado Supreme Court's construction of Amendment 2 found that its objective was to repeal existing antidiscrimination ordinances. Thus, Amendment 2 is far-reaching in that it places homosexuals in a solitary class, withdrawing legal protection against discrimination and forbidding reinstatement of these policies except by constitutional amendment. Thus, it imposes a special disability on homosexuals who can now change the law only by amending the state constitution, no matter how local the harm. Generally, legislative classifications are constitutional if they bear a rational relation to a legitimate end. However, Amendment 2 identifies persons by a single trait and denies them protection across the board. Therefore, it violates the principle that the government remains open on impartial terms to all who seek its assistance. Finally, equal protection means that the desire to harm a politically unpopular group is not a legitimate government interest. Amendment 2 is extraordinary and explainable only by animus toward homosexuals. Accordingly, Amendment 2 violates the Equal Protection Clause and is unconstitutional. Affirmed.

DISSENT: (Scalia, J.) Amendment 2 only prohibits the special treatment of homosexuals in that they may not obtain preferential treatment without amending the state constitution. Surely, Colorado has the right to be hostile toward homosexuals just as they may have animosity toward murderers or polygamists. In fact, laws against polygamy are the best analogy and have been ignored by the majority. Also, since homosexuals are segregated in certain communities, they possess political power much greater than their numbers. Amendment 2 seeks to counter this disproportionate political power. The majority has taken the side of the elites in this culture law.

▌ ANALYSIS

Justice Scalia's dissenting opinion is astonishing for its not-at-all disguised animosity toward homosexuals, who will no doubt be surprised to find that they are politically powerful. The dissent is also remarkable for its tone of disgust toward the majority. At the heart of the majority decision is the recognition that homosexuality is more of a status (like sex, race, or ethnicity) than a conduct or lifestyle.

■▬■

Quicknotes

EQUAL PROTECTION A constitutional guarantee that no person shall be denied the same protection of the laws enjoyed by other persons in like circumstances.

■▬■

Cleburne v. Cleburne Living Center, Inc.

Municipality (D) v. Zoning permit applicant (P)

473 U.S. 432 (1985).

NATURE OF CASE: Certiorari review of constitutionality of municipal special use permit ordinance.

FACT SUMMARY: Cleburne Living Center, Inc. (P) contended that laws impacting the mentally retarded should be given heightened constitutional scrutiny.

🏛 RULE OF LAW
Laws impacting the mentally retarded are not to be given heightened constitutional scrutiny.

FACTS: The city of Cleburne, Texas, (D) had zoned multiple-residence dwellings as R-3. Most R-3 structures required no permit; however, any proposed home for the mentally retarded did. The Cleburne Living Center, Inc. (P) applied for such a permit. Responding to objections from nearby residents, the city council refused the application. The Center (P) challenged the ordinance as a denial of equal protection. The Fifth Circuit, applying a heightened level of scrutiny toward the mentally retarded, voided the ordinance. The Supreme Court granted review.

ISSUE: Are laws impacting the mentally retarded to be given heightened constitutional scrutiny?

HOLDING AND DECISION: (White, J.) No. Laws impacting the mentally retarded are not to be given heightened scrutiny. This Court has defined certain characteristics to be so irrelevant to a person's potential contribution to society that, when combined with their political minority status, the conclusion follows that they are entitled to special protection under the Equal Protection Clause. Examples include race, alienage, and religious belief. Mental retardation does not fit this profile. The retarded person's status does relate to his ability to contribute to society. Second, there is ample evidence that lawmakers are responsive to retarded people's plights, showing that they are not politically powerless. Finally, if a large and amorphous class such as the mentally retarded were to be given special Fourteenth Amendment protection, it is hard to see where the process would stop. For these reasons, the Court concludes that the mentally retarded are not entitled to heightened scrutiny. [The Court went on to hold that, even under low-level scrutiny, the ordinance failed to pass constitutional scrutiny.] Affirmed.

CONCURRENCE: (Stevens, J.) The Court's equal protection analysis is better seen as a continuum than specific levels of scrutiny.

CONCURRENCE AND DISSENT: (Marshall, J.) The ordinance in question would no doubt survive the Court's classic "rational basis" test. What the Court has done is fashion a heightened level of scrutiny without so stating.

▶ ANALYSIS

The Court's Equal Protection Clause analysis continues to evolve. As of the time of this case, three levels of scrutiny existed: rational basis, heightened, and strict. In years past, strict scrutiny automatically led to invalidation, rational basis to approval. As this case shows, this is no longer true.

Quicknotes

EQUAL PROTECTION A constitutional guarantee that no person shall be denied the same protection of the laws enjoyed by other persons in like circumstances.

HEIGHTENED SCRUTINY A purposefully vague judicial description of all levels of scrutiny more exacting than minimal scrutiny.

QUASI-SUSPECT CLASS A specific class of persons subjected to unequal treatment but deserving less than strict scrutiny.

Harper v. Virginia State Board of Elections

Residents (P) v. State (D)

383 U.S. 663 (1966).

NATURE OF CASE: Certiorari review of the constitutionality of Virginia's poll tax.

FACT SUMMARY: Harper (P) and other Virginia residents brought this suit to have Virginia's (D) poll tax declared unconstitutional.

🏛 RULE OF LAW
The right to vote is a fundamental and basic right, and where such rights are asserted under the Equal Protection Clause, classifications that might restrain those rights must be closely scrutinized and carefully confined.

FACTS: Harper (P) and other Virginia residents brought these suits to have Virginia's (D) poll tax declared unconstitutional. The three-judge district court, feeling bound by the court's decision in *Breedlove v. Suttles*, 302 U.S. 277 (1937), dismissed the complaint. Harper (P) appealed. The law at issue conditions the right to vote in state elections upon the payment of a poll tax.

ISSUE: Is the right to vote a fundamental and basic right, and where such rights are asserted under the Equal Protection Clause, must the classifications that might restrain those rights be closely scrutinized and carefully confined?

HOLDING AND DECISION: (Douglas, J.) Yes. The right to vote is a fundamental and basic right, and where such rights are asserted under the Equal Protection Clause, classifications that might restrain those rights must be closely scrutinized and carefully confined. A state violates the Equal Protection Clause whenever it makes the affluence of the voter or the payment of a fee an electoral standard. The right to vote is a basic and fundamental one, especially since it preserves other rights. Any alleged infringement on the right to vote, such as a poll tax, must be carefully scrutinized. A state's interest, when it comes to voting, is limited to the power to fix qualifications. Wealth, like race or creed or color, is irrelevant to one's ability to participate intelligently in the electoral process. Further lines drawn on the basis of wealth or property, like those of race, are traditionally disfavored. The requirement of the payment of a fee as a condition of obtaining a ballot causes invidious discrimination. *Breedlove* sanctioned this use of the poll tax, and to that extent it is overruled. Reversed.

DISSENT: (Black, J.) So long as a distinction drawn is not irrational, unreasonable, or invidious, it must be upheld. There are certainly rational reasons for Virginia's poll tax, such as the state's desire to collect revenue and its belief that voters who pay poll tax will be interested in furthering the state's welfare. Hence, the tax must be upheld. If it is to be struck down, it should be done by the legislature rather than the courts.

DISSENT: (Harlan, J.) The Equal Protection Clause does not impose upon this country an ideology of unrestrained equalitarianism.

▶ ANALYSIS

If, as the dissenters in *Harper* argue, the poll tax classification is not wholly "irrational," the case represents a greater intervention than the courts undertook under old equal protection. There is some question as to whether this greater scrutiny was because the "fundamental rights" of voting are affected or because "lines drawn on the basis of wealth" are traditionally disfavored. In *McDonald v. Board of Election Commissioners*, 394 U.S. 802 (1969), the Court sees wealth as an independent ground (apart from impact on fundamental rights) for strict scrutiny. There is a series of cases preceding and following *Harper* (among them *Reynolds v. Sims*, 377 U.S. 533 [1964]) that supports the invoking of strict scrutiny when voting rights are affected.

Quicknotes

EQUAL PROTECTION CLAUSE A constitutional guarantee that no person should be denied the same protection of the laws enjoyed by other persons in like circumstances.

FUNDAMENTAL RIGHT A liberty that is either expressly or impliedly provided for in the United States Constitution, the deprivation or burdening of which is subject to a heightened standard of review.

POLL TAX A specific amount taxed to persons of a certain class living in a designated area.

Kramer v. Union Free School District No. 15

Ineligible voter (P) v. School district (D)

395 U.S. 621 (1969).

NATURE OF CASE: Certiorari review of constitutionality of voter eligibility requirements.

FACT SUMMARY: Kramer (P) claimed that Union's (D) School District voter eligibility requirements denied him equal protection of the laws.

🏛 RULE OF LAW
Legal classifications must be tailored so that exclusion of a certain class of persons is necessary to achieve an articulated state goal.

FACTS: The New York Education Code provided that in certain school districts residents may vote in a school district election only if they or their spouse own or lease taxable real property within the district, or are parents or have custody of children enrolled in local public schools. Kramer (P), an unmarried man who neither owned nor leased taxable real property, argued that the voter eligibility requirements denied him equal protection. Union (D) argued that the state has a legitimate interest in limiting the right to vote in school district elections and may reasonably conclude that parents are those primarily interested in school affairs. A three-judge federal district court dismissed Kramer's (P) complaint, and he appealed.

ISSUE: Must legal classifications be tailored so that exclusion of a certain class of persons is necessary to achieve an articulated state goal?

HOLDING AND DECISION: (Warren, C.J.) Yes. Legal classifications must be tailored so that exclusion of a certain class of person is necessary to achieve an articulated state goal. As statutes distributing voting rights are at the foundation of representative society, any unjustified discrimination in who may vote undermines the legitimacy of representative government. Thus a statute that allows some to vote while prohibiting others must promote a compelling state interest to be valid. Assuming for purposes of argument that New York can limit the right to vote in school district elections to persons primarily interested in school affairs, that statute does not accomplish that goal. The statute excludes persons who have a distinct and direct interest in school affairs while it includes those whose interest is remote and indirect. Here, Kramer (P), who lives with his parents and pays state and federal taxes, cannot vote, while an unemployed man who pays no taxes, but who rents an apartment in the district, can vote. Reversed.

DISSENT: (Stewart, J.) The statute does not impinge on constitutionally protected rights, "for the Constitution of the United States does not confer the right of suffrage

upon anyone." Accordingly, the "compelling state interest" test should not have been applied. The classification appeared to have been rationally related to a permissible legislative end and should have been upheld.

▶ ANALYSIS

It appears that the Court will not be quick to sustain "interest" voting tests but will tend to uphold competency voting tests such as requirements based on age and sanity. It is not a denial of equal protection for the state to deny ex-convicts the right to vote. An interest classification that has been upheld involved allowing only landowners in a water storage district to vote. The district had a very limited purpose, *Salyer Land Co. v. Tulare Lake Basin Water Storage District*, 410 U.S. 719 (1973).

Quicknotes

EQUAL PROTECTION CLAUSE A constitutional guarantee that no person should be denied the same protection of the laws enjoyed by other persons in like circumstances.

Reynolds v. Sims

[Parties not identified.]

377 U.S. 533 (1964).

NATURE OF CASE: Certiorari review of constitutionality of one existing and two proposed plans for apportionment.

FACT SUMMARY: The federal district court held that the existing and two proposed plans for apportionment of seats in the Alabama legislature violated the Equal Protection Clause.

🏛 RULE OF LAW

The Equal Protection Clause guarantees the opportunity for equal protection by all voters in the election of state legislators and requires that the seats in both houses of a bicameral state legislature be apportioned on a population basis.

FACTS: The federal district court for the Middle District of Alabama held that the existing and two legislatively proposed plans for the apportionment of seats in the two houses of the Alabama legislature violated the Equal Protection Clause. The court ordered into effect a temporary reapportionment plan comprised of part of the proposed plans.

ISSUE: Does the Equal Protection Clause require that seats in both houses of a bicameral state legislature be apportioned on a population basis?

HOLDING AND DECISION: (Warren, C.J.) Yes. The Equal Protection Clause guarantees the opportunity for equal protection by all voters in the election of state legislators and requires that the seats in both houses of a bicameral state legislature be apportioned on a population basis. Concededly, the basic aim of legislative apportionment is the achieving of fair and effective representation for all citizens. The Equal Protection Clause guarantees the opportunity for equal participation by all voters in the election of state legislators. Overweighting and overvaluation of the votes of persons living in one area has the effect of dilution and undervaluation of those living in another area. Diluting the weight of votes because of place of residence impairs basic constitutional rights under the Fourteenth Amendment, just as much as invidious discrimination based upon race. It is argued that the apportionment issue is a political one that the court should leave alone. However, a denial of constitutionally protected rights demands judicial protection. The weight of a citizen's vote cannot be made to depend on where he lives. The Equal Protection Clause requires that the seats in both houses of a bicameral state legislature must be apportioned on a population basis. Analogy to the federal system will not sustain a system not based on population. The federal system grew out of compromise and concession needed to band together states that formerly were independent. Political subdivisions of states (cities, counties) never were independent entities. The decision does not mean that the two bodies in a state legislature cannot consist of different constituencies, have different length terms, represent geographical districts of different sizes or be of different sizes. It does mean that in apportionment's overriding objective—whatever the method used—must be substantial equality of population among the various districts. Neither history, nor economics, nor other group interests, will justify disparity from population-based representation. One factor that could justify some deviation from such representation is political subdivisions. Decennial reapportionment would meet the requirement for reasonable currency. It will be for the federal courts to devise the particular remedies to be utilized in such cases. Affirmed.

DISSENT: (Harlan, J.) State legislative apportionments are wholly free of constitutional limitations save those imposed by the Republican Form of Government Clause (Article IV, § 4). This decision places basic aspects of state political systems under the overlordship of the federal judiciary, a move that is ill-advised and constitutionally impermissible.

DISSENT: (Stewart, J.) The Equal Protection Clause demands but two basic attributes of any state legislative apportionment plan. The plan must be a rational one, and it must not permit the systematic frustration of the will of a majority of the voters. Beyond this, there is nothing in the federal Constitution to prevent a state from choosing any electoral legislative plan it thinks best suited to the interests, temper, and customs of its people.

▶ ANALYSIS

For many years, the Court refused jurisdiction of cases challenging the fairness of the representation in state legislatures, on the ground that the issue involved was a "political question." The Court abandoned this position in *Baker v. Carr*, 369 U.S. 186 (1962), and ever since has held that the federal courts have the jurisdiction to determine the fairness and validity of state legislative apportionment plans. The result has been that a traditionally political question has become justiciable, and the courts have exerted what was traditionally deemed a legislative power in determining what is, and what is not, a fair plan of legislative apportionment.

Continued on next page.

Quicknotes

APPORTIONMENT The division of property costs in proportion to the parties' respective interests therein.

BICAMERALISM The necessity of approval by a majority of both houses of Congress in ratifying legislation or approving other legislative action.

EQUAL PROTECTION CLAUSE A constitutional guarantee that no person should be denied the same protection of the laws enjoyed by other persons in like circumstances.

INVIDIOUS DISCRIMINATION Unequal treatment of a class of persons that is particularly malicious or hostile.

POLITICAL QUESTION An issue more appropriately left to the determination of another governmental branch and which the court declines to hear.

REAPPORTIONMENT PLAN The alteration of a voting district's boundaries or composition to reflect the population of that district.

■■■

Davis v. Bandemer

State (D) v. Democrats (P)

478 U.S. 109 (1986).

NATURE OF CASE: Certiorari review of constitutionality of Indiana's 1981 state apportionment.

FACT SUMMARY: Democrats (P) challenged a state reapportionment plan that did not include exactly proportional representation.

🏛 RULE OF LAW
When determining unconstitutional vote dilution, the challenging party must show a discriminatory vote dilution to make out a prima facie case.

FACTS: In 1981, the Republican-controlled state legislature of Indiana reapportioned the state. The districts were of roughly equal population. The plan was apparently drafted without much debate due to the limited amount of information available to voting politicians. In the next election, Democrats (P) won majority popular votes but received less than half of the seats in the house and senate. The Democrats (P) then filed suit. The district court found that both discriminatory intent and actual discrimination had been proven. The decision was appealed.

ISSUE: When determining unconstitutional vote dilution, must the challenging party show a discriminatory vote dilution to make out a prima facie case?

HOLDING AND DECISION: (White, J.) Yes. When determining unconstitutional vote dilution, the challenging party must show a discriminatory vote dilution to make out a prima facie case. The Constitution mandates one-person, one-vote. However, there is no requirement that all districts in a voting region have mathematically equivalent proportional representations of the various voting populations. Here, a single election was used as evidence of an equal protection voting violation. But it would be next to impossible to conclude that actual discrimination had occurred after a single election. Since there is no requirement districts contain populations exactly proportional to the total population, the election result will most likely vary from the total popular vote. Furthermore, it would be a difficult task to ascertain how to apportion districts to even achieve exactly proportional representation of all population groups. Reversed.

CONCURRENCE: (O'Connor, J.) Political gerrymandering poses a nonjusticiable political question. Because the most easily measured indicia of political power relate solely to winning and losing elections, there is a grave risk that the plurality's various attempts to qualify and condition the group the Court has created will gradually pale in importance. What is likely to remain is a loose form of proportionality, under which some deviations from proportionality are permissible, but any significant, persistent deviations from proportionality are suspect.

DISSENT: (Powell, J.) An analysis should be used that focuses upon whether voting districts have been deliberately distorted and are arbitrary. The shape of districts is very telling when searching for an improper purpose in reapportionment. Other relevant considerations include legislative goals and procedures, evidence concerning population disparities, and statistics showing vote dilution.

▌ANALYSIS

Commentators have suggested that the Court opened a can of worms when it agreed that there was even a justiciable issue on the question of whether political parties deserved protection from discriminatory reapportionment. Traditionally, the focus was on protecting racial minorities. This case added yet another factor to complicate the reapportionment picture.

■=■

Quicknotes

PRIMA FACIE CASE An action where the plaintiff introduces sufficient evidence to submit the issue to the judge or jury for determination.

PROPORTIONAL REPRESENTATION An election method designed to permit the proportional representation of minority group interests.

REAPPORTIONMENT PLAN The alteration of a voting district's boundaries or composition to reflect the population of that district.

■=■

M.L.B. v. S.L.J.

Parent (P) v. [Party not identified (D)]

519 U.S. 102 (1996).

NATURE OF CASE: Certiorari review of appeal from decree terminating parental rights and state requirements regarding appellate procedure.

FACT SUMMARY: A Mississippi court dismissed M.L.B.'s (P) appeal of the termination of her parental rights to her two minor children when she was unable to pay the required record preparation fees.

🏛 RULE OF LAW
A state may not condition appeals from trial court decrees terminating parental rights on the affected parent's ability to pay record preparation fees.

FACTS: A Mississippi court ordered M.L.B.'s (P) parental rights to her two minor children terminated. M.L.B. (P) sought to appeal the termination decree, but the state required that she pay in advance over $2,000 in record-preparation fees. Because M.L.B. (P) did not have the money to pay the fees, her appeal was dismissed. The Supreme Court granted certiorari to determine whether the Due Process and Equal Protection Clauses of the Fourteenth Amendment permitted such appeals to be conditioned on the ability to pay certain fees.

ISSUE: May a state condition appeals from trial court decrees terminating parental rights on the affected parent's ability to pay record preparation fees?

HOLDING AND DECISION: (Ginsburg, J.) No. A state may not condition appeals from trial court decrees terminating parental rights on the affected parent's ability to pay record preparation fees. Fee requirements are generally examined only for their rationality. While the Court has not prohibited state controls on every type of civil action, it has consistently distinguished those involving intrusions on family relationships. However, the stakes for M.L.B. (P), i.e., the forced dissolution of her parental rights, are far greater than any monetary loss. Mississippi's interest, on the other hand, in offsetting the costs on its court system, is purely financial. Decrees forever terminating parental rights fit in the category of cases in which a state may not "bolt the door to equal justice." Reversed.

CONCURRENCE: (Kennedy, J.) Decisions concerning the rights and privileges inherent in family and personal relations [*Boddie v. Connecticut*, 401 U.S. 371 (1971), and *Lassiter v. Department of Social Services of Durham City*, 452 U.S. 18 (1981)] are on point—cases resting exclusively upon the Due Process Clause. Here, due process is a sufficient basis for the Court's holding.

DISSENT: (Thomas, J.) The majority's new-found constitutional right to free transcripts in civil appeals cannot be effectively restricted to this case. M.L.B. (P) requested relief under both the Due Process and Equal Protection Clauses, yet the majority does not specify the source of relief it has granted. Mississippi's transcript rule reasonably obliges all potential appellants to bear the cost of availing themselves of a service that the state is not constitutionally required to provide. The Equal Protection Clause is not a panacea for all perceived social and economic inequities.

▶ ANALYSIS

While the majority's rationale in granting M.L.B. (P) relief may have been vaguely articulated, as the dissent has alleged, it would seem that the issues at stake here go beyond simple textual analysis. It is not merely M.L.B.'s (P) rights that must be considered, but the impact that the termination of those rights will have on her two minor children. It will likely not be as great of a problem (as the dissent suggests) to limit the application of this holding to similarly situated parents.

Quicknotes

DUE PROCESS CLAUSE Clauses, found in the Fifth and Fourteenth Amendments to the United States Constitution, providing that no person shall be deprived of "life, liberty, or property, without due process of law."

EQUAL PROTECTION CLAUSE A constitutional guarantee that no person should be denied the same protection of the laws enjoyed by other persons in like circumstances.

San Antonio Independent School Dist. v. Rodriguez

School district (D) v. Students (P)

411 U.S. 1 (1973).

NATURE OF CASE: Certiorari review of constitutionality of state educational funding plan.

FACT SUMMARY: The Texas state educational system was partially funded through the use of local property taxes resulting in lower per-pupil expenditure in the poorer school districts. This system was challenged as a denial of equal protection to those students who resided in the poorer districts.

> ## RULE OF LAW
> Education is not a fundamental right, and students who live in school districts with a lower property tax base do not constitute a suspect classification, so a school financing system is not subject to a strict standard of judicial review on an equal protection challenge to the financing system.

FACTS: Public elementary schools in Texas were funded by a combination of state and district contributions. Each district supplemented the state contribution to education by a property tax on property within the district. This system resulted in significant disparities in per-pupil expenditures among the various districts that resulted from the differences in taxable property values in the district: the richer districts spent up to $594 per pupil, and the poorer districts spent $356. Rodriguez (P) was the parent of a child in a district with low per-pupil expenditure and brought a class action suit on behalf of all children similarly situated. Rodriguez (P) alleged that the state's reliance on property tax to finance education favored the more affluent districts and therefore violated the Equal Protection Clause because of the disparities in expenditures. Rodriguez (P) further alleged that this discrimination on the basis of wealth is a suspect classification and that education is a fundamental right, requiring a strict standard of judicial review.

ISSUE: Is education a fundamental right, and do students who live in school districts with a lower property tax base constitute a suspect classification, so a school financing system is subject to a strict standard of judicial review on an equal protection challenge to the financing system?

HOLDING AND DECISION: (Powell, J.) No. Education is not a fundamental right, and students who live in school districts with a lower property tax base do not constitute a suspect classification, so a school financing system is not subject to a strict standard of judicial review on an equal protection challenge to the financing system. The strict scrutiny standard is not appropriate in this case because it involves neither a suspect classification nor a

fundamental right, and the state system does not violate the Equal Protection Clause because it bears a rational relationship to a legitimate state interest. The system does not disadvantage a suspect class because there is no definable class of "poor" people that are discriminated against. The poorest families are not necessarily residents of the poorest property tax districts. The system does not result in an absolute deprivation of a desired benefit because all students in Texas get an adequate education despite the differences in per-pupil expenditures. Education is not a fundamental right. The fundamental nature of a right is established only if that right is explicitly or implicitly guaranteed by the Constitution. Rodriguez (P) argues that education is guaranteed because it is a necessary prerequisite to the exercise of other constitutionally protected rights, such as the right to free speech. This "nexus" theory is unacceptable because it is unlimited in scope. Even if it were assumed that education is constitutionally protected because it is a prerequisite to other rights, there is no evidence that the level of education given to the students in the poorer district falls short of the minimum education that would be required. Additionally, this is an inappropriate case for the use of a strict judicial scrutiny test because it is an attack on state expenditure of taxes, a field in which the court, because of its lack of expertise, has traditionally deferred to state legislative judgments. It also involves considerations of educational policy, another area in which the court should not interfere because of its lack of experience. The Texas system is, then, not a violation of the Equal Protection Clause because it does bear a rational relationship to a legitimate state purpose. Although the system may be imperfect and result in some inequalities, the financing system is not so irrational as to constitute invidious discrimination. Such a financing system is common practice among the states, and suggested alternatives to this system are untested. Reversed.

CONCURRENCE: (Stewart, J.) All laws have some measure of discriminatory treatment. The Equal Protection Clause is used only to test the validity of classifications created by state laws, and, unless a fundamental right or suspect classification is involved, the Clause is violated only by classifications that are wholly arbitrary or capricious.

DISSENT: (White, J.) In this case, the means chosen to further a permissible state goal, local control of education, are not rationally related to that goal. The state must establish a financing system that provides a rational basis for encouraging local control and not the current system,

Continued on next page.

which gives unequal treatment to groups that are determined on the basis of criteria wholly unrelated to that goal.

DISSENT: (Marshall, J.) Rather than dividing all cases into either strict scrutiny or rational basis test, the court should adopt a sliding scale approach to testing violations of the Equal Protection Clause based on the constitutional and societal importance of the affected interest and the invidiousness of the basis on which the state has drawn the classification. The fundamental nature of a right is not entirely derived from the face of the Constitution, but the proper question is the extent to which constitutionally protected rights are dependent on interests not verbalized in the Constitution. As the connection between the two increases, the unarticulated interests become more fundamental and the level of judicial scrutiny increases. On this basis, education is a fundamental right because of the close relationship between education and other constitutionally protected rights such as freedom of speech and the right to vote. Past cases have shown that the court will carefully scrutinize discriminations based on wealth. Here, a careful scrutiny of the asserted state interest in local control of education shows that this interest is offered merely as an excuse for interdistrict inequality. Therefore, the financing system is a violation of the Equal Protection Clause.

▶ *ANALYSIS*

Under the holding of this case, no right or interest is considered fundamental, requiring strict judicial review under the Equal Protection Clause, unless that right is explicitly or implicitly guaranteed by the Constitution. Education is not a fundamental interest because it is not so protected, and the Court also holds that wealth is not a suspect classification. Since the strict standard is not required, the classification will be upheld if it has a rational relationship to a legitimate state interest and is not invidiously discriminatory, a test that is very easy for the state to meet. This case clearly indicates that the current court will not extend the fundamental right and suspect classification analysis beyond the traditionally well-established categories, such as classification based on race.

■═■

Quicknotes

EQUAL PROTECTION CLAUSE A constitutional guarantee that no person should be denied the same protection of the laws enjoyed by other persons in like circumstances.

FUNDAMENTAL RIGHT A liberty that is either expressly or impliedly provided for in the United States Constitution, the deprivation or burdening of which is subject to a heightened standard of review.

INVIDIOUS DISCRIMINATION Unequal treatment of a class of persons that is particularly malicious or hostile.

RATIONAL BASIS TEST A test employed by the court to determine the validity of a statute in equal protection

actions, whereby the court determines whether the challenged statute is rationally related to the achievement of a legitimate state interest.

STRICT SCRUTINY Method by which courts determine the constitutionality of a law when a law affects a fundamental right. Under the test, the legislature must have a compelling interest to enact law and measures prescribed by the law must be the least restrictive means possible to accomplish goal.

SUSPECT CLASSIFICATION A class of persons that have historically been subject to discriminatory treatment; statutes drawing a distinction between persons based on a suspect classification, i.e., race, nationality or alienage, are subject to a strict scrutiny standard of review.

■═■

Congress's Civil Rights Enforcement Powers

Quick Reference Rules of Law

Civil Rights Cases

Citizens (P) v. Federal government (D)

109 U.S. 3 (1883).

NATURE OF CASE: Certiorari review of the constitutionality of § 1 of the Civil Rights Act of 1875.

FACT SUMMARY: Private citizens of five states who had suffered either criminal indictments or civil penalty actions for violating § 1 of the Civil Rights Act of 1875 challenged its constitutionality.

🏛 RULE OF LAW
The Fourteenth Amendment does not reach private acts of discrimination but encompasses only state action that is discriminatory.

FACTS: In § 1 of the Civil Rights Act of 1875, Congress provided that all persons were entitled to full and equal enjoyment of accommodations provided by public inns, public conveyances on land or water, theaters, and other places of public amusement, regardless of race. The statute went on to provide that violation of its provisions was a misdemeanor and also declared that aggrieved persons could recover $500 "for every such offense." Five individuals, private citizens, who had excluded blacks from such facilities, challenged the constitutionality of the law and their indictments or fines.

ISSUE: Can the Fourteenth Amendment reach private acts of discrimination?

HOLDING AND DECISION: (Bradley, J.) No. The Fourteenth Amendment does not reach private acts of discrimination but encompasses only state action that is discriminatory. Since the Fourteenth Amendment is concerned with prohibiting certain types of state laws and actions, it cannot reach private acts of discrimination such as occurred in these cases. Thus, it gives Congress no power to enact laws reaching private acts of discrimination, as this law attempts to do. While the Thirteenth Amendment does reach private as well as state actions, it gives Congress power to deal only with problems of involuntary servitude and not mere racial discrimination. Thus, the challenged law is unconstitutional.

DISSENT: (Harlan, J.) The Thirteenth Amendment was designed to destroy any and all burdens and disabilities constituting badges of slavery and servitude, such as racial discrimination, and not just the institution of slavery. Furthermore, the Fourteenth Amendment affirmatively establishes the citizenship of all persons born or naturalized in the United States and is thus not limited to prohibiting certain state actions. Even if it were, railroads, inns, and public places of amusement can be seen as agents of the state whose actions are reachable anyway.

▶ ANALYSIS

Although the Court would probably reach the opposite result were this case decided today, it continues to hold to the position that the Fourteenth Amendment can reach only state action and not private discrimination. The difference is that the Court has changed its concept of state action to include private actions attributable to the state through agency theories, etc.

■■■

Quicknotes

DISCRIMINATION Unequal treatment of a class of persons.

FOURTEENTH AMENDMENT, 42 U.S.C. § 1983 Defamation by state officials in connection with a discharge implies a violation of a liberty interest protected by the due process requirements of the U.S. Constitution.

STATE ACTION Actions brought pursuant to the Fourteenth Amendment claiming that the government violated the plaintiff's civil rights.

■■■

Shelley v. Kraemer

Purchaser (D) v. Property owner (P)

334 U.S. 1 (1948).

NATURE OF CASE: Certiorari review of constitutionality of enforcing a racially related restrictive covenant in the sale of real property.

FACT SUMMARY: Kraemer (P) sought to void a sale of real property to Shelley (D) from a Mr. Fitzgerald, relying on a racially restrictive covenant.

> 🏛 **RULE OF LAW**
> Judicial enforcement of a private racially restrictive covenant is considered state action for Fourteenth Amendment purposes.

FACTS: In 1911, 30 out of a total of 39 owners of area property signed an agreement, which was subsequently recorded, providing in part that the property could not be used or occupied by anyone of "the Negro or Mongolian race" for a period of 50 years. This covenant was to be valid whether it was included in future conveyances or not and was to attach to the land as a condition precedent to the sale of the property. Shelley (D), a black man, purchased a parcel of land subject to the restrictive covenant from a Mr. Fitzgerald. Kraemer (P), an owner of other property subject to the terms of the restrictive covenant, brought suit in the circuit court of St. Louis to enjoin Shelley (D) from taking possession of the property. The trial court held for Shelley (D) and the Supreme Court granted certiorari.

ISSUE: Does the Equal Protection Clause of the Fourteenth Amendment prevent judicial enforcement by state courts of restrictive covenants based on race or color?

HOLDING AND DECISION: (Vinson, C.J.) Yes. Judicial enforcement of a private racially restrictive covenant is considered state action for Fourteenth Amendment purposes. Because the restrictive covenants did not involve any action by the state legislature or City Council, the restrictive covenant itself did not violate any rights protected by the Fourteenth Amendment, since it was strictly a private covenant. But the judicial enforcement of the covenant did qualify as state action. From the time of the adoption of the Fourteenth Amendment until the present, the court has consistently ruled that the action of the states to which the amendment has reference includes action of state courts and state judicial officers. In this case because there was a willing buyer and seller, Shelley (D) would have been able to enforce the restrictive covenants only with the active intervention of the state courts. The court rejected Kraemer's (P) argument that since the state courts would enforce restrictive covenants excluding white persons from ownership of property there was no denial of equal protection. The court stated that equal protection of the law is not achieved through indiscriminate imposition of inequalities. As to Kraemer's (P) contention that he was being denied equal protection of the laws because his restrictive covenant was not being enforced, the court stated that the Constitution does not confer the right to demand action by the state that would result in the denial of equal protection of the laws to other individuals. Therefore, in granting judicial enforcement of the restrictive agreement, the state has denied Shelley (D) equal protection of the laws and the action of the state courts cannot stand. The court noted that the enjoyment of property rights, free from discrimination by the states, was among the objectives sought to be effectuated by the framers of the Fourteenth Amendment. Reversed.

▶ ANALYSIS

The Court in its post-*Shelley v. Kraemer* decisions has given this decision a fairly narrow reading. A broad reading of this case requires that whenever a state court enforces a private racial restrictive covenant that such action constitutes state action which is forbidden by the Fourteenth Amendment. In cases where the ruling in this case could have been found to be applicable, the Court has used a different rationale. Some of the Court's statements suggest that more state involvement than evenhanded enforcement of private biases was necessary to find unconstitutional state action. Justice Black, in a dissenting opinion, stated that the decision in this case only is applicable in cases involving property rights.

■■■

Quicknotes

EQUAL PROTECTION A constitutional guarantee that no person shall be denied the same protection of the laws enjoyed by other persons in like circumstances.

FOURTEENTH AMENDMENT, 42 U.S.C. § 1983 Defamation by state officials in connection with a discharge implies a violation of a liberty interest protected by the due process requirements of the U.S. Constitution.

RESTRICTIVE COVENANT A promise contained in a deed to limit the uses to which the property will be made.

STATE ACTION Actions brought pursuant to the Fourteenth Amendment claiming that the government violated the plaintiff's civil rights.

■■■

Jackson v. Metropolitan Edison Co.

Customer (P) v. Utility company (D)

419 U.S. 345 (1974).

NATURE OF CASE: Certiorari review of alleged state action in violation of constitutional rights.

FACT SUMMARY: Jackson (P) claimed that Metropolitan Edison Co.'s (D) (a privately owned utility company) action in terminating service to her for nonpayment without notice, a hearing, or an opportunity to pay, constituted state action and violated due process.

🏛 RULE OF LAW
The mere fact that a business is subject to state regulation does not necessarily transform its actions into those of the state for the purposes of the Fourteenth Amendment.

FACTS: [Metropolitan Edison Co. (Metropolitan) (D) is a privately owned utility which holds a certificate of public convenience issued by the state public utilities commission, empowering it to deliver electricity. It has filed a general tariff with the commission, a provision of which states Metropolitan's (D) right to terminate electricity to a user for nonpayment. Metropolitan (D) terminated Jackson's (P) electric service for nonpayment. She claims that this constituted state action and because it was done without notice, a hearing, or opportunity to pay, such action deprived her of her property (her alleged right to reasonably continuous electrical service) without due process.]

ISSUE: Does the fact that a business is subject to state regulation necessarily transform its actions into those of the state for the purposes of the Fourteenth Amendment?

HOLDING AND DECISION: (Rehnquist, J.) No. The mere fact that a business is subject to state regulation does not necessarily transform its actions into those of the state for the purposes of the Fourteenth Amendment. Evidence showing a heavily regulated private utility, enjoying at least a partial monopoly in the providing of electrical service, which elected to terminate service to a customer in a manner found by the state public utilities commission to be permissible under state law, does not demonstrate a sufficiently close nexus between the state and the utility's action to make that action state action. Nor does the fact that it enjoys a monopoly make its action state action. It's true that Metropolitan's (D) services affect the public interest. However, the actions of all businesses which affect the public interest cannot be called state action. Metropolitan (D) is not performing a public function since state law imposes no obligation on the state to furnish utility service. Finally, the state public utilities commission's approval of Metropolitan's (D) tariff merely constituted a finding by the commission that Metropolitan's (D) termination procedure was permissible under state law. It did not convert Metropolitan's (D) actions into state actions. Hence, the evidence did not demonstrate a sufficiently close nexus between the state and Metropolitan's (D) action so that Metropolitan's (D) termination of services may be treated as state action. Affirmed.

DISSENT: (Marshall, J.) The Court's previous state-action cases have relied on factors that are clearly present in this case: a state-sanctioned monopoly, an extensive pattern of cooperation between the "private" entity and the state, and a service uniquely public in nature. The holding in this case would tend to repudiate these factors. State authorization and approval of "private" conduct support a finding of state action. The majority's analysis would seem to apply as well to a company that refused service to blacks, welfare recipients, or any other group. I cannot believe this Court would hold that the state's involvement with Metropolitan (D) was not sufficient to require that it not discriminate. However, nothing in the majority's analysis suggests otherwise.

▶ ANALYSIS

In *Moose Lodge v. Irvis*, 407 U.S. 163 (1972), the lodge refused service to a black guest of a lodge member. The guest claimed that although the lodge was a private club, its action was unconstitutional because it held a state liquor license. The Court held that the state was not sufficiently implicated in the lodge's discriminatory policies to make its action state action. The dissent argued that the "state was putting the weight of its liquor license, concededly a valued and important adjunct to a private club, behind racial discrimination."

■=■

Quicknotes

MONOPOLY A privilege or right conferred upon an individual or entity granting it the exclusive power to manufacture, sell and distribute a particular service or commodity; a market condition in which one or a few companies control the sale of a product or service thereby restraining competition in respect to that article or service.

PRIVATE FIGURE/CITIZEN An individual that does not hold a public office or that is not a member of the armed forces.

PUBLIC UTILITY A private business that provides a service to the public which is of need.

STATE ACTION Activity where the state is involved sufficiently enough to permit protection under due process.

■=■

United States v. Guest

Federal government (P) v. Conspirators (D)

383 U.S. 745 (1966).

NATURE OF CASE: Certiorari review of dismissal of civil rights law indictment.

FACT SUMMARY: Guest (D) and others were charged with violating various civil rights of Georgia blacks.

🏛 RULE OF LAW
Congress may constitutionally legislate to protect federal civil rights from private abridgment.

FACTS: Guest (D) and others were indicted under 18 U.S.C. § 241 with conspiring to deprive black citizens of Georgia of the free exercise and enjoyment of "several specified rights secured by the Constitution and laws of the United States." Two counts of the indictment specifically charged them with: (1) preventing blacks from using public facilities maintained by the State of Georgia (protected by the Fourteenth Amendment); and (2) preventing blacks from using public highways and roads in interstate commerce (protected by the "right to travel"). From a dismissal of the indictments, the United States (P) appealed.

ISSUE: May Congress constitutionally legislate to protect federal civil rights from private abridgment?

HOLDING AND DECISION: (Stewart, J.) Yes. Congress may constitutionally legislate to protect federal civil rights from private abridgment. The Enabling Clause of the Fourteenth Amendment permits Congress to reach private action (e.g., conspiracy) that abridges Fourteenth Amendment rights so long as some active state involvement in such action is also present, but the right to travel is a right so fundamental to the concept of federal union that Congress has an inherent power to reach private action that abridges it independently. It is true that Fourteenth Amendment rights are broad and not fully delineated, but this does not justify preventing Congress from protecting those rights that are established on some kind of vagueness theory as the federal court below has done. The indictment below adequately sets out violations of federal civil rights that Congress is empowered to protect. The dismissal of the indictments below must be reversed and the case remanded.

CONCURRENCE: (Clark, J.) The Enabling Clause of the Fourteenth Amendment permits Congress to ban wholly private action that abridges Fourteenth Amendment rights, regardless of the existence or nonexistence of state involvement.

CONCURRENCE AND DISSENT: (Brennan, J.) State action is not necessary for Congress to proscribe private conduct that abridges any "right secured by the Constitution." The Court above found that the possibility of state involvement with the alleged conspiracy to deny blacks access to Georgia public facilities was enough to sustain the indictment. Proof of such state action, difficult as it will be to provide, will undermine the ultimate prosecution of the case improperly. The Enabling Clause of the Fourteenth Amendment allows Congress to make any laws that it reasonably believes necessary to the enforcement of that Amendment. Clearly, preventing private conspiracies that deny equal use of public facilities to blacks is within the scope of that clause.

▶ ANALYSIS

This case demonstrates the continuous expansion of the Enabling Clause of the Fourteenth Amendment to permit Congress to reach wholly private acts of discrimination with its laws. In 1945, in *Screws v. United States*, 325 U.S. 91 (1945), the Court upheld federal legislation that punished state officials who acted "under color of state law." In 1966, in *United States v. Price*, 383 U.S. 787 (1966), the Court upheld federal legislation that punished private individuals who acted jointly with state officials to abridge the civil rights of others. In *Guest*, a majority of the Court (six Justices: Brennan, Warren, Douglas, Clark, Black, and Fortas) approved the power of Congress to punish wholly private action that serves to abridge civil rights of others. Note that the conduct that the Fourteenth Amendment's Enabling Clause allows Congress to proscribe is not necessarily unconstitutional itself (i.e., no state action), but merely is such as might result in deprivation of some constitutional right.

■=■

Quicknotes

ABRIDGMENT A diminishing or curtailing of rights.

ENABLING CLAUSE OF FOURTEENTH AMENDMENT A constitutional provision giving the power to implement and enforce the law.

FEDERAL CIVIL RIGHTS Rights protected by the federal Constitution.

■=■

Jones v. Alfred H. Mayer Co.

Buyer (P) v. Real estate company (D)

392 U.S. 409 (1968).

NATURE OF CASE: Certiorari review of private action of refusal of property owners to sell to blacks.

FACT SUMMARY: Jones (P) brought suit in federal district court against the Alfred H. Mayer Co. (D) alleging that Mayer (D) refused to sell a home to him for the sole reason that Jones (P) was black.

RULE OF LAW
Congress, pursuant to the authority vested in it by the Thirteenth Amendment, which clothes "Congress with power to pass all laws necessary and proper for abolishing all badges and incidents of slavery," may validly bar all racial discrimination, private as well as public, in the sale or rental of property.

FACTS: Relying upon 42 U.S.C. § 1982 (all citizens have the same right to inherit, purchase, lease, hold, and convey real and personal property as is enjoyed by white citizens), Jones (P) brought suit in federal district court against the Alfred H. Mayer Co. (Mayer) (D) alleging that Mayer (D) refused to sell a home to him for the sole reason that Jones (P) was black.

ISSUE: May Congress, pursuant to the authority vested in it by the Thirteenth Amendment, which clothes "Congress with power to pass all laws necessary and proper for abolishing all badges and incidents of slavery," validly bar all racial discrimination, private as well as public, in the sale or rental of property?

HOLDING AND DECISION: (Stewart, J.) Yes. Congress, pursuant to the authority vested in it by the Thirteenth Amendment, which clothes "Congress with power to pass all laws necessary and proper for abolishing all badges and incidents of slavery," may validly bar all racial discrimination, private as well as public, in the sale or rental of property. Section 1982 is only a limited attempt to deal with discrimination in a select area of real estate transactions, even though, on its face, § 1982 appears to prohibit all discrimination against blacks in the sale or rental of property. If § 1982, originally enacted as § 1 of the Civil Rights Act of 1866, had been intended to grant nothing more than an immunity from governmental interference, then much of § 2 of the 1866 Act, which provides for criminal penalties where a person has acted "under color" of any law, would have been meaningless. The broad language of § 1982 was intentional. In 1866, Congress had before it considerable evidence showing private mistreatment of blacks. The focus of Congress, then, was on private groups (e.g., the Ku Klux Klan) operating outside the law. At the very least, the Thirteenth Amendment

includes the freedom to buy whatever a white man can buy, and the right to live wherever a white man can live. Reversed.

DISSENT: (Harlan, J.) The term "right" in § 1982 operates only against state-sanctioned discrimination. There is a difference between depriving a man of a right and interfering with the enjoyment of that right in a particular case. The enforcement provisions of the 1866 Act talk of "law, statute, ordinance, regulation, or custom." As for legislative history, residential racial segregation was the norm in 1866. The Court has always held that the Fourteenth Amendment reaches only "state action."

ANALYSIS

In *Sullivan v. Little Hunting Park, Inc.*, 396 U.S. 229 (1969), the Court invalidated a refusal by a homeowner's association to permit a member to assign his recreation share to a black. Once again, Harlan in dissent questioned whether the Court should expand a century-old statute to encompass today's real estate transactions. After these two cases, it is questionable whether the Court will place any limits on its reading of the Thirteenth Amendment when reviewing legislation aimed at private discrimination.

Quicknotes

42 U.S.C. § 1982 "All citizens of the United States shall have the same right in every state at territory, as is enjoyed by white citizens thereof to inherit, purchase, lease, sell, hold, and convey real and personal property."

THIRTEENTH AMENDMENT The constitutional provision that abolished slavery in the United States.

Katzenbach v. Morgan

Voters (P) v. State (D)

384 U.S. 641 (1966).

NATURE OF CASE: Certiorari review of constitutionality of federal statute.

FACT SUMMARY: As part of the Voting Rights Act, Congress inserted a provision that prohibited restrictions on the right to register to vote and the applicant's inability to read and write English where the applicant had at least a sixth-grade education in a Puerto Rican school, where instruction was primarily in Spanish. New York had a statutory requirement of an ability to read and write English as a prerequisite to voter registration.

> 🏛 **RULE OF LAW**
> A federal statute enacted pursuant to the Enabling Clause of the Fourteenth Amendment supersedes any state constitutional or statutory provision that is in conflict with the federal law.

FACTS: New York had a statute that required all persons seeking to register to vote be able to read and write the English language. In the Voting Rights Act of 1965, Congress inserted a provision that prohibited a requirement of ability to read and write English where the person seeking to vote had completed at least a sixth-grade education in Puerto Rico, where the language of instruction is primarily Spanish. This suit was instituted by a group of registered voters in New York who challenged that the provision of the federal statute insofar as it would prohibit enforcement of the New York requirement. At issue were the several hundred thousand Puerto Rican immigrants in New York who were prevented from voting by the New York statute, but who would be qualified under the federal law. The Attorney General of New York filed a brief in which he argued that the federal legislation would supersede the state law only if the state law were found to violate the provisions of the Fourteenth Amendment, without reference to the federal statute. Also advanced was the argument that the federal statute violated the Equal Protection Clause of the Fourteenth Amendment, since it discriminated between non-English-speaking persons from Puerto Rico and non-English-speaking persons from other countries.

ISSUE: Does a federal statute enacted pursuant to the Enabling Clause of the Fourteenth Amendment supersede any state constitutional or statutory provision that is in conflict with the federal law?

HOLDING AND DECISION: (Brennan, J.) Yes. A federal statute enacted pursuant to the Enabling Clause of the Fourteenth Amendment supersedes any state constitutional or statutory provision that is in conflict with the federal law. There is no need to determine if the New York

English literacy law is violative of the Fourteenth Amendment Equal Protection Clause in order to validate the federal law respecting voter qualifications. If Congress were limited to restricting only those state laws that violated the Amendment, there would be no need for the federal law, since the state law could be invalidated in the courts. Rather, the test must be whether the federal legislation is appropriate to enforcement of the Equal Protection Clause. Section 5 of the Fourteenth Amendment is to be read to grant the same powers as the Necessary and Proper Clause of Article I, § 8. Therefore, the federal statute must be examined to see if it is "plainly adapted to that end" and whether it is not prohibited by but is consistent with "the letter and spirit of the Constitution." It was well within congressional authority to say that the need to vote by the Puerto Rican community warranted intrusion upon any state interests served by the English literacy test. The federal law was "plainly adapted" to furthering the aims of the Fourteenth Amendment. There is a perceivable basis for Congress to determine that this legislation was a proper way to resolve an inequity resulting from Congress's evaluation that an invidious discrimination existed. As to the contention that the federal law itself violates the Equal Protection Clause, the law does not restrict anyone's voting rights, but rather extends the franchise to a previously ineligible group. This was a reform measure and Congress need not correct an entire evil with one law but may "take one step at a time, addressing itself" to that problem that seems most pressing. We hold, therefore, that the federal law was a proper exercise of the powers granted Congress by the Fourteenth Amendment and that the Supremacy Clause prevents enforcement of the New York statute insofar as it is inconsistent with the federal law. Reversed.

DISSENT: (Harlan, J.) The majority has confused the question of legislative enforcement power with the area of proper judicial review. The question here is whether the state law is so arbitrary or irrational as to violate the Equal Protection Clause. And that is a judicial, not legislative, determination. The majority has validated a legislative determination by Congress that a state law is violative of the Constitution. There is no record of any evidence secured by Congress to support this determination. The judiciary is the ultimate arbiter of constitutionality, not Congress.

▍**ANALYSIS**

As has occurred before, there was a footnote to the decision that caused as much controversy as the decision itself. In this footnote, the Court stated that Congress

Continued on next page.

could enact legislation giving force to the Fourteenth Amendment that expanded the rights provided in the Amendment, but could not dilute or restrict the Amendment by legislation. In other words, Congress can make determinations of constitutionality so long as they expand rights but cannot make those determinations if they restrict rights. However, there is serious debate as to whether allowing Congress to take an independent role in interpreting the Constitution can be justified under any circumstances, in view of *Marbury v. Madison*, 5 U.S. (1 Cranch) 137 (1803). Once allowed in this area, can any restraint be thereafter imposed? Congress has traditionally tried to stay within judicially circumscribed bounds of constitutionality. But, if it has an "independent role" in this area, the restraints are removed. An example is shown in the Omnibus Crime Control Act, where Congress made legislative inroads to judicially granted rights as expressed in the *Miranda* decision, 384 U.S. 436 (1966). The Court can always rule on these inroads, but is it not better that Congress is not encouraged to embark on them in the first case?

■═■

Quicknotes

SUPREMACY CLAUSE Article VI, § 2 of the Constitution, which provides that federal action must prevail over inconsistent state action.

■═■

City of Boerne v. Flores

City (D) v. Archbishop (P)

521 U.S. 507 (1997).

NATURE OF CASE: Certiorari review of the constitutionality of the Religious Freedom Restoration Act of 1993.

FACT SUMMARY: After the City of Boerne (D) denied Archbishop Flores (P) a building permit to expand a church, he contended that the permit denial violated the Religious Freedom Restoration Act.

🏛 RULE OF LAW
The Religious Freedom Restoration Act unconstitutionally exceeds Congress's enforcement power under the Due Process Clause of the Fourteenth Amendment.

FACTS: The Religious Freedom Restoration Act (RFRA) prohibited the government from substantially burdening a person's exercise of religion, even if the burden is the result of a generally applicable law, unless the government has a compelling interest and is using the least restrictive means. Boerne (D) enacted a city ordinance requiring city pre-approval for any construction on any of the city's historic landmarks. Archbishop Flores (P) sought a building permit to expand his church, a historic landmark. Boerne (D) denied the permit and Flores (P) sued, invoking the RFRA. The district court determined that the RFRA exceeded congressional power, but the Fifth Circuit reversed, holding the Act constitutional. Boerne (D) appealed.

ISSUE: Does the RFRA unconstitutionally exceed Congress's enforcement power under the Due Process Clause of the Fourteenth Amendment?

HOLDING AND DECISION: (Kennedy, J.) Yes. The RFRA unconstitutionally exceeds Congress's enforcement power under the Due Process Clause of the Fourteenth Amendment. Here, Congress, with the RFRA, attempts to replace, with the compelling interest test, this Court's decision asserting that the compelling interest test is inappropriate in cases involving general prohibitions with free exercise challenges. See *Employment Div., Oregon Dept. of Human Resources v. Smith*, 494 U.S. 872 (1990). Such an action violates the long tradition of separation of powers established by the Constitution. The judiciary is to determine the constitutionality of laws and the powers of the legislature are defined and limited. While Congress can enact remedial, preventive legislation that deters violations, the RFRA is not a preventive law. Instead, the RFRA redefines the scope of the Free Exercise Clause and nothing in our history extends to Congress the ability to take such action. The RFRA is so out of proportion to a supposed remedial or preventive object that it cannot be regarded as a response to unconstitutional behavior. Reversed.

▶ ANALYSIS

The Religious Freedom Restoration Act was one of the four federal laws overturned by the Supreme Court during its 1997 term. Although the Court has endorsed judicial restraint in recent years, it has not hesitated to quash improper intrusions on its authority to set unconstitutional standards. The Court, however, chose not to revisit the religious freedom issue in its *Boerne* decision, leaving intact the ruling in *Smith* that inspired Congress to pass the RFRA. In *Smith*, the Court approved Oregon's use of its ban on peyote to prohibit the drug's use in Native American religious rituals. The RFRA was intended to guarantee religious observance a higher degree of statutory protection than the *Smith* Court thought necessary.

Quicknotes

DUE PROCESS CLAUSE Clauses found in the Fifth and Fourteenth Amendments to the United States Constitution providing that no person shall be deprived of "life, liberty, or property, without due process of law."

FOURTEENTH AMENDMENT Declares that no state shall make or enforce any law which shall abridge the privileges and immunities of citizens of the United States.

FREE EXERCISE CLAUSE The guarantee of the First Amendment to the United States Constitution prohibiting Congress from enacting laws regarding the establishment of religion or prohibiting the free exercise thereof.

United States v. Morrison

Federal government (P) v. Students (D)

529 U.S. 598 (2000).

NATURE OF CASE: Certiorari review of the constitutionality of the federal Violence Against Women Act.

FACT SUMMARY: Brzonkala (P) brought suit against two football-playing male students (D) and Virginia Polytechnic University under the Violence Against Women Act.

RULE OF LAW
Section 13891 of the Violence Against Women Act may not be upheld as an exercise of Congress's remedial power under § 5 of the Fourteenth Amendment.

FACTS: Brzonkala (P), a student at Virginia Polytechnic Institute, complained that football-playing students Morrison (D) and Crawford (D) assaulted and repeatedly raped her. Virginia Tech's Judicial Committee found insufficient evidence to punish Crawford (D), but found Morrison (D) guilty of sexual assault and sentenced him to immediate suspension for two semesters. The school's vice president set this aside as excessive punishment. Brzonkala (P) then dropped out of the university and brought suit against the school and the male students (D) under the Violence Against Women Act, 42 U.S.C. § 13981, providing a federal cause of action of a crime of violence motivated by gender.

ISSUE: May § 13891 of the Violence Against Women Act be upheld as an exercise of Congress's remedial power under § 5 of the Fourteenth Amendment?

HOLDING AND DECISION: (Rehnquist, C.J.) No. Section 13891 of the Violence Against Women Act may not be upheld as an exercise of Congress's remedial power under § 5 of the Fourteenth Amendment. This case required the Court to address the Constitutionality of 42 U.S.C. § 13981, which provides a federal civil remedy for victims of gender-motivated violence. Since every law enacted by Congress must be based upon a power enumerated in the Constitution, and the Court concludes that the Commerce Clause does not provide Congress with the authority to enact § 13981, the Court addresses Brzonkala's (P) alternative argument that § 5 of the Fourteenth Amendment authorized the statutory cause of action under Congress's remedial power. This argument is based on the assertion that there is pervasive bias in various state justice systems against victims of gender-motivated violence and is supported by a voluminous congressional record. Case law had established that state-sponsored gender discrimination violates equal protection unless it serves important governmental objectives and the discriminatory means employed are substantially related to the achievement of such objectives. While sex discrimination is one of the objects of the Fourteenth Amendment, the Amendment only prohibits state action. In two cases, *United States v. Harris* (106 U.S. 629 [1882]) and the *Civil Rights Cases* (109 U.S. 3 [1883]), the Court interpreted the Fourteenth Amendment's provisions and concluded that laws enacted to punish private persons were beyond the scope of Congress's § 5 power. Brzonkala (P) also argued that here there has been gender-disparate treatment by state officials, whereas in those cases there was no indication of state action. Section 13891 is unlike any of the § 5 remedies that this Court has previously upheld since it has no consequence on any public official involved in investigating or prosecuting Brzonkala's (P) assault. Congress's power under § 5 does not extend to the enactment of § 13891. Affirmed.

DISSENT: (Breyer, J.) The Court's reasoning rejecting Congress's source of authority under § 5 of the Fourteenth Amendment is questionable. This Court has held that Congress may enact remedial legislation that prohibits conduct that is not itself unconstitutional.

ANALYSIS

The primary issue here is that the federal government is seeking to regulate areas traditionally regulated exclusively by the states. The majority concludes that the regulation and punishment of intrastate violence that is not directed to the instrumentalities of interstate commerce is the exclusive jurisdiction of local government. What the dissent argues here is that Congress in this case has amassed substantial findings to demonstrate that such intrastate violence does have an effect on the instrumentalities of commerce.

Quicknotes

COMMERCE CLAUSE Article 1, section 8, clause 3 of the United States Constitution, granting Congress the power to regulate commerce with foreign countries and between the states.

EQUAL PROTECTION A constitutional guarantee that no person shall be denied the same protection of the laws enjoyed by other persons in like circumstances.

Continued on next page.

FOURTEENTH AMENDMENT No state shall deny to any person within its jurisdiction the equal protection of the laws.

REMEDIAL ACTION Actions taken pursuant to the Fourteenth and Fifteenth Amendments to provide remedies for violations of those amendments.

■━■

CHAPTER 1

Freedom of Speech—Categories of Speech— Degrees of Protected Expression

Quick Reference Rules of Law

Schenck v. United States

Publisher (D) v. Federal government (P)

249 U.S. 47 (1919).

NATURE OF CASE: Certiorari review of federal statute restricting speech.

FACT SUMMARY: During a time of war, Schenck (D) mailed circulars to draftees that were calculated to cause insubordination in the armed services and to obstruct the U.S. recruiting and enlistment program in violation of military laws.

🏛 RULE OF LAW
The test to determine the constitutionality of a statute restricting free speech is whether, under the circumstances, the speech is of such a nature as to create a clear and present danger that it will bring about the substantive evils that Congress has a right to prevent.

FACTS: During a time of war, Schenck (D) mailed circulars to draftees. The circulars stated that the Conscription Act was unconstitutional and likened conscription to conviction. They intimated that conscription was a monstrous wrong against humanity in the interest of Wall Street's chosen few and described nonconscription arguments as coming from cunning politicians and a mercenary capitalist press. They urged: "Do not submit to intimidation," but advised only peaceful actions such as a petition to repeal the Conscription Act. Schenck (D) did not deny that the jury could find that the circulars could have no purpose except to influence draftees to obstruct the carrying out of the draft.

ISSUE: Is the test to determine the constitutionality of a statute restricting free speech whether, under the circumstances, the speech is of such a nature as to create a clear and present danger that it will bring about the substantive evils that Congress has a right to prevent?

HOLDING AND DECISION: (Holmes, J.) Yes. The test to determine the constitutionality of a statute restricting free speech is whether, under the circumstances, the speech is of such a nature as to create a clear and present danger that it will bring about the substantive evils that Congress has a right to prevent. The character of every act depends on the circumstance in which it is done. The most stringent protection of free speech would not protect a person's falsely shouting fire in a theatre and causing a panic. It is a question of proximity and degrees. During a war, things that could be said during peaceful times may be such a hindrance to the war effort that they will not be permitted. Schenck's (D) convictions are affirmed.

▶ ANALYSIS

The Court's first significant encounter with the problem of articulating the scope of constitutionally protected speech came in a series of cases involving agitation against the draft and war during World War I (*Schenck, Frohwerk*, 249 U.S. 204 [1919], *Debs*, 249 U.S. 211 [1919]). *Schenck* announces the "clear and present danger" test, the test for determining the validity of legislation regulating speech. In *Schenck*, Holmes rejected perfect immunity for speech. But he also rejected a far more restrictive, far more widely supported, alternative test: that "any tendency in speech to produce bad acts, no matter how remote, would suffice to validate a repressive statute."

Quicknotes

CLEAR AND PRESENT DANGER TEST Doctrine that restraints on freedom of speech are permissible if the speech incites persons to engage in unlawful conduct.

CONSPIRACY Concerted action by two or more persons to accomplish some unlawful purpose.

FREEDOM OF SPEECH The right to express oneself without governmental restrictions on the content of that expression.

Abrams v. United States

Russian immigrants (D) v. Federal government (P)

250 U.S. 616 (1919).

NATURE OF CASE: Certiorari review of speech restriction.

FACT SUMMARY: Russian immigrants (D) issued fliers that advocated a general strike in ammunition factories to prevent ammunition from being used against Russian revolutionaries.

🏛 RULE OF LAW
The United States may constitutionally restrict speech that has the intended effect of hindering the United States in a war effort by means of riots and sedition.

FACTS: During World War I, in 1918, the United States sent forces to Russia following the overthrow of the Czarist government as part of a strategic operation against Germany on the eastern front. Russian immigrants (D) to the United States circulated literature advocating a general strike in ammunition plants to hinder the U.S. effort, as they perceived it, to crush the revolutionary struggle in Russia. The Russians (D) were charged under the Espionage Act for inciting actions that hindered the U.S. war effort. Abrams (D) and others appealed.

ISSUE: May the United States constitutionally restrict speech that has the intended effect of hindering the United States in a war effort by means of riots and sedition?

HOLDING AND DECISION: (Clarke, J.) Yes. The United States may constitutionally restrict speech that has the intended effect of hindering the United States in a war effort by means of riots and sedition. Individuals may be held accountable for the intended consequences of their actions. While speech is protected by the Constitution, it is not without limits. When speech is intended to incite riots and rebellion in such a critical time as that of war, it cannot be given the protection normally accorded to speech in the United States. Here, the Russian immigrants (D) hoped to generate a sympathetic revolution in the United States for the purpose of defeating military plans in Europe. Such a goal was so contrary to the concerns of the United States during time of war that it could not be permitted to proceed. Affirmed.

DISSENT: (Holmes, J.) This decision deeply undermines the liberties that the First Amendment was drafted to protect. Expression of dissenting opinions is the very foundation of freedom. It is only the present danger of immediate evil or intent to bring it about that warrants Congress's setting a limit to expression of opinion. These convictions on the basis of two leaflets should not be sustained.

▶ ANALYSIS

Holmes' famous dissent sounds as though it requires greater immediacy of threat than his opinion, a few months earlier, in *Schenck v. United States*, 249 U.S. 47 (1919), which articulated the clear and present danger test. Commentators have found support for this interpretation in other writings by Holmes. It appears that he realized the need to leave some element in place to protect speech, even while permitting some level of protection against dangerous speech.

Quicknotes

ESPIONAGE ACT Federal law prohibiting espionage.

FIRST AMENDMENT Prohibits Congress from enacting any law respecting an establishment of religion, prohibiting the free exercise of religion, abridging freedom of speech or the press, the right of peaceful assembly and the right to petition for a redress of grievances.

FREEDOM OF SPEECH The right to express oneself without governmental restrictions on the content of that expression.

SEDITION Unlawful action advocating the overthrow of the government.

Masses Publishing Co. v. Patten

Publishing company (P) v. Postmaster (D)

244 Fed. 535 (S.D.N.Y. 1917).

NATURE OF CASE: Action for preliminary injunction to require postmaster to accept magazine.

FACT SUMMARY: Patten (D) refused Masses Publishing Company's (P) magazine access through mails for violating the 1917 Espionage Act.

RULE OF LAW
An opinion critical of a draft statute, no matter how seditious in nature, cannot be deemed to be advocacy of the violation of that statute unless there is a direct urging of such violation.

FACTS: Masses Publishing Co. (Masses) (P) published a monthly magazine called "The Masses," which contained cartoons and text of a politically revolutionary nature. During the First World War, Masses (P) ran political material in the magazine violently attacking the draft and the war and expressing sympathy for conscientious objectors. In July of 1917, under directions from the Postmaster General, Patten (D), Postmaster of New York, told Masses (P) that their August issue would be denied use of the mails. Patten (D) stated that the magazine violated the Espionage Act of 1917 by: (1) making false statements with the intent to interfere with the operation of the military forces of the United States; (2) arousing discontent among potential draftees and thereby promoting insubordination among troops already in the war; and (3) counseling resistance and disobedience to the law. Masses (P) brought this suit for a preliminary injunction against Patten's (D) refusal to accept the magazine in the mails.

ISSUE: Can an opinion critical of a draft statute, no matter how seditious in nature, be deemed to be advocacy of the violation of that statute unless there is a direct urging of such violation?

HOLDING AND DECISION: (Hand, J.) No. An opinion critical of a draft statute, no matter how seditious in nature, cannot be deemed to be advocacy of the violation of that statute unless there is a direct urging of such violation. Unless there is some direct advocacy by a person for others to resist a particular law, then that person may not be held responsible for attempting to cause a violation of the law. Here, the publications of Masses (P) may have created national dissension and thereby assisted, indirectly, the cause of the enemy. But the statute in question provides that such publications be willfully false and made with the intent to interfere with military operations. The publications were mere opinions and not publications of facts. Thus, they fall within the scope of the right to criticize, normally the privilege of individuals in countries dependent on free expression of opinions as an ultimate source of authority. The statute was intended to prevent the spreading of false rumors embarrassing to the military, not the dissemination of inflammatory public opinion. It is also contended by Patten (D) that to allow Masses (P) to arouse discontent among the public as to the conduct of the war and draft causes insubordination among wartime troops. But to interpret the word "causes" too broadly would be to suppress all hostile criticism of the war except those officially sanctioned opinions. There are recognized limits to criticisms of existing laws or policies of war. One may not counsel or advise others to violate the law as it stands. The present statute is limited to punishing direct advocacy of resistance to recruiting and enlistment, within which neither the cartoons nor text of Masses' (P) publications fall.

ANALYSIS

The present test, later supplanted with the "clear and present danger" test, as to what type of conduct constitutes advocacy of resistance to law, focuses on the speaker and the value of the speech. This decision weighs the value of content of freely spoken opinions against its impact on the orderly conduct of governmental policy. The burden is on the government as accuser to show that such speech or publication is so detrimental to the orderly process of government that freedom of speech should bow to governmental will. The *Masses* case takes a liberal view of First Amendment rights and allows the free expression of opinion that falls short of direct advocacy of resistance to governmental authority. Judge Hand's decision in this case was overturned by the court of appeals on the ground that a person would be held accountable for the natural consequences of his words. If his words strongly imply that a particular law should be violated, that person will not be immune from prosecution merely because he omitted a direct appeal for violations. Judge Hand later wrote to a friend that his opinion in this case had apparently received little or no professional approval.

Continued on next page.

Quicknotes

FIRST AMENDMENT Prohibits Congress from enacting any law respecting an establishment of religion, prohibiting the free exercise of religion, abridging freedom of speech or the press, the right of peaceful assembly and the right to petition for a redress of grievances.

INJUNCTION A remedy imposed by the court ordering a party to cease the conduct of a specific activity.

■≡■

Gitlow v. New York

Publisher (D) v. State (P)

268 U.S. 652 (1925).

NATURE OF CASE: Certiorari review of speech restriction.

FACT SUMMARY: Gitlow (D) printed and circulated literature advocating a Communist revolt against the U.S. government.

🏛 RULE OF LAW
Under its police powers, a state may validly forbid any speech or publication that has a tendency to produce action dangerous to public security, even where such speech or publication presents no clear and present danger to the security of the public.

FACTS: Gitlow (D) was a member of the Left Wing Section of the Socialist Party in New York (P), and he was responsible for printing the official organ of the Left Wing called the "Revolutionary Age." In this paper, Gitlow (D) printed articles advocating the accomplishment of the Communist revolution through militant revolutionary socialism. Gitlow (D) further advocated a class struggle mobilization of the proletariat through mass industrial revolts and political strikes to conquer and destroy the U.S. Government and replace it with a dictatorship of the proletariat. Although there was no evidence that these writings resulted in any such action, Gitlow (D) was arrested, tried, and convicted for advocating the overthrow of the government by force under a New York (P) criminal anarchy act. At trial, Gitlow's (D) counsel urged that since there was no resulting action flowing from the publication of the Gitlow (D) "Manifesto," the statute penalized the mere utterance of doctrine having no propensity toward incitement of concrete action.

ISSUE: Under its police powers, may a state validly forbid any speech or publication that has a tendency to produce action dangerous to public security, even where such speech or publication presents no clear and present danger to the security of the public?

HOLDING AND DECISION: (Sanford, J.) Yes. Under its police powers, a state may validly forbid both speech and publication if they have a tendency to result in action that is dangerous to public security, even though such utterances present no "clear and present danger." The New York (P) criminal anarchy act did not punish the utterance of abstract doctrine, having no quality of incitement to action. It prohibits advocacy to overthrow organized government by unlawful means. These words imply advocacy of action. Clearly, Gitlow's (D) "Manifesto," which spoke in terms of "mass action" of the proletariat for the "Communist reconstruction of socie-

ty—the struggle for these," is language of direct incitement. The means suggested imply force and violence and are inherently unlawful in a constitutional form of government based on law and order. Although freedom of speech and press are protected by the First and Fourteenth Amendments, it is fundamental that this freedom is not absolute. The police power extends to a state the right to punish those who abuse this freedom by advocating action inimical to the public welfare, tending to corrupt public morals, incite to crime, or to threaten the public security. The state need not wait for such dangers to arise. It may punish utterances likely to bring about such substantive evils. The "clear and present danger" test announced in *Schenck*, 249 U.S. 47 (1919), does not apply here since the legislature has previously determined the danger of the substantive evils which may arise from specified utterances. As long as the statute is constitutional and the use of the language sought to be penalized comes within the prohibition, the statute will be upheld. And it is not necessary that the defendant advocates some definite or immediate act of force or violence. It is sufficient if they were expressed in general terms. Affirmed.

DISSENT: (Holmes, J.) The "clear and present danger" test applies, and there was no clear and present danger here. The followers of Gitlow (D) were too few to present one. Every idea is an incitement. The only meaning of free speech is to allow everyone to have their say.

▶ ANALYSIS

The *Gitlow* case is an example of what has been termed the "bad tendency" test. This test punishes utterances whose meaning lies somewhere between "clear and present danger" and mere advocacy of abstract ideas. The key question here is whether the language "tends" to produce action resulting in a danger to public security. The holding of the Court in this case, while recognizing Gitlow's (D) constitutional rights of free speech and press, bypassed these rights by saying that the New York (P) statute did not unduly restrict such freedom. However, in light of the modern test of "clear and present danger," it seems that the "bad tendency" test is all but dead. The "clear and present danger" test requires language that results in imminent lawless action. Tendency is not enough. It is important to note that the "bad tendency" test has not been used by the Court since *Gitlow*.

■ ▬ ■

Continued on next page.

Quicknotes

CLEAR AND PRESENT DANGER TEST Doctrine that restraints on freedom of speech are permissible if the speech incites persons to engage in unlawful conduct.

FIRST AMENDMENT Prohibits Congress from enacting any law respecting an establishment of religion, prohibiting the free exercise of religion, abridging freedom of speech or the press, the right of peaceful assembly and the right to petition for a redress of grievances.

FREEDOM OF SPEECH The right to express oneself without governmental restrictions on the content of that expression.

POLICE POWER The power of a government to impose restrictions on private persons, as long as those restrictions are reasonably related to the promotion of the public welfare, health, safety, and morals.

Whitney v. California

Communist party member (D) v. State (P)

274 U.S. 357 (1927).

NATURE OF CASE: Certiorari review of speech restriction.

FACT SUMMARY: Whitney (D), organizer and member of the Communist Labor Party of California, was convicted of aiding in that organization's violation of the Criminal Syndicalism Act.

📜 RULE OF LAW

A state may, in the exercise of its police power, punish abuses of freedom of speech where such utterances are inimical to the public welfare as tending to incite crime, disturb the peace, or endanger organized government through threats of violent overthrow.

FACTS: In 1919, Whitney (D) attended a convention of the Socialist Party. When the convention split into factions, Whitney (D) went with the radicals and helped form the Communist Labor Party (CLP). Later that year, Whitney (D) attended another convention to organize a new California unit of CLP. There, Whitney (D) supported a resolution that endorsed political action and urged workers to vote for CLP member-candidates at all elections. This resolution was defeated and a more extreme program of action was adopted, over Whitney's (D) protests. At trial, upon indictment for violation of the California Criminal Syndicalism Act, which held it unlawful to organize a group that advocated unlawful acts of violence as a means of effecting change in industrial ownership and in political change, Whitney (D) contended that she never intended the CLP to become a terrorist organization. Whitney (D) further contended that since she had no intent to aid the CLP in a policy of violent political reform, her mere presence at the convention was not a crime. Whitney (D) contends that the Act thus deprived her of her liberty without due process and freedom of speech, assembly, and association.

ISSUE: May a state, in the exercise of its police power, punish abuses of freedom of speech where such utterances are inimical to the public welfare as tending to incite crime, disturb the peace, or endanger organized government through threats of violent overthrow?

HOLDING AND DECISION: (Sanford, J.) Yes. A state may, in the exercise of its police power, punish abuses of freedom of speech where such utterances are inimical to the public welfare as tending to incite crime, disturb the peace, or endanger organized government through threats of violent overthrow. Freedom of speech, secured by the Constitution, does not confer an absolute right to speak, without responsibility. A state may in the exercise of its

police power, punish abuses of freedom of speech where such utterances are inimical to the public welfare as tending to incite crime, disturb the peace, or endanger organized government through violent overthrow. Here, the Syndicalism Act of California declared that to become a knowing member of or to assist in an organization that advocates crimes involving danger to the public peace and security of the state was punishable in the exercise of the state's police powers. The essence of the offense was the combining with others to accomplish desired ends through advocacy and use of criminal means. This is in the nature of criminal conspiracy and involves an even greater danger to public security than individual acts. Miss Whitney's (D) contention the California Criminal Syndicalism Act as applied to her in this case is unconstitutional is foreclosed to the court, since it is an effort to review a trial verdict. Affirmed.

CONCURRENCE: (Brandeis, J.) Whitney (D) is here punished for a step in the preparation of incitement that only threatens the public remotely. The Syndicalism Act of California aims at punishing those who propose to preach, not put into action, criminal syndicalism. The right of freedom of speech, assembly, and association, protected by the Due Process Clause of the Fourteenth Amendment and binding on the states, is restricted if it threatens political, moral, or economic injury to the state. However, such restriction does not exist unless speech would produce a clear and imminent danger of some substantive evil to the state. The Court has not yet fixed standards in determining when a danger shall be clear. But no danger flowing from speech can be deemed clear and present unless the threatened evil is so imminent that it may strike before opportunity for discussion on it. There must be, however, probability of serious injury to the state. As to review by this Court of an allegation of unconstitutionality of a criminal syndicalism act, whenever fundamental rights of free speech and assembly are alleged to have been invaded, the defendant must be allowed to present the issue of whether a clear and present danger was made imminent by his actions. Here, mere advocacy of revolution by mass action at some future date was within the Fourteenth Amendment protection. But our power of review was lacking since there was evidence of a criminal conspiracy and such precludes review by this court of errors at a criminal trial absent a showing that constitutional rights were deprived.

Continued on next page.

▶ *ANALYSIS*

The *Whitney* case is important for having added to the *Schenck* test, 249 U.S. 47 (1919), of "clear and present danger" the further requirement that the danger must be "imminent." The Brandeis opinion in the *Whitney* case should be viewed as a dissenting opinion. His addition of "imminent" flies directly in the face of the majority opinion, that punished "mere advocacy" of threatened action against the state. The "mere advocacy" test has not survived. Today, through the Smith Act that continues to punish criminal syndicalism, "mere advocacy" is not punishable. The urging of action for forcible overthrow is necessary before punishment will be imposed. Thus, the "urging of action" is the modern test of "clear and present imminent danger" espoused by Brandeis in *Whitney*.

■■■■

Quicknotes

FREEDOM OF ASSOCIATION The right to peaceably assemble.

■■■■

Dennis v. United States

Communist party leaders (D) v. Federal government (P)

341 U.S. 494 (1951).

NATURE OF CASE: Certiorari review of convictions of conspiracy to overthrow the government by force or violence.

FACT SUMMARY: Dennis (D) and other Communist Party leaders were convicted for violation of the Smith Act, which is directed at conspiracy to teach or advocate the overthrow of the government by force or violence.

🏛 RULE OF LAW
Where an offense is specified by a statute in nonspeech or nonpress terms, a conviction relying upon speech or press as evidence of violation may be sustained only when the speech of publication created a clear and present danger of attempting or accomplishing the prohibited crime.

FACTS: The Smith Act made it unlawful to advocate or teach the overthrow of the government by force or violence, or to organize people to teaching and advocating. It also prohibited a conspiracy to do any of the above. Dennis (D) and other Communist Party leaders were convicted of conspiracy to overthrow the government by force or violence. The evidence showed that the Communist Party was a highly disciplined organization, adept at infiltration into strategic positions, with the use of aliases and double-meaning language. The Communist Party was rigidly controlled and tolerated no dissension. Communist Party literature and statements advocated a successful overthrow of the government by force and violence.

ISSUE: Where an offense is specified by a statute in nonspeech or nonpress terms, may a conviction relying upon speech or press as evidence of violation be sustained only when the speech of publication created a clear and present danger of attempting or accomplishing the prohibited crime?

HOLDING AND DECISION: (Vinson, C.J.) Yes. Where an offense is specified by a statute in nonspeech or nonpress terms, a conviction relying upon speech or press as evidence of violation may be sustained only when the speech of publication created a clear and present danger of attempting or accomplishing the prohibited crime. In determining the constitutionality of a statute which restricts First Amendment rights, the test is: where the offense is specified in nonspeech on nonpress terms, a conviction relying upon speech or press as evidence of violation may be sustained only when the speech or publication created a clear and present danger of attempting or accomplishing the prohibited crime. Here, the Smith Act seeks to protect the government from overthrow by force or violence. This is certainly a substantial enough interest for the government to limit speech. Now it must be determined whether a clear and present danger existed. Success or probability of success of an attempt to overthrow the government is not a criterion of whether that attempt constitutes a clear and present danger. The question is whether the gravity of the evil, discounted by its improbability, justifies such an invasion of free speech as is necessary to avoid the danger. Here, the formation by Dennis (D) and the others of such a highly organized conspiracy with rigidly disciplined members subject to call when the leaders felt the time had come, coupled with the inflammable nature of world conditions, similar uprisings in other countries, and our relations with Communist countries, convinces us that a clear and present danger existed here. Convictions affirmed.

CONCURRENCE: (Frankfurter, J.) The validity of the statute depends on a balancing of competing interests, such as the nature of the speech and the nature of the advocacy. This balancing should be done by the legislatures, not by the courts. The courts can overturn a statute, including statutes dealing with First Amendment rights, only if there is no reasonable basis for it.

CONCURRENCE: (Jackson, J.) A statute making it a criminal offense to conspire for the purpose of teaching and advocating the overthrow of the government by force or violence may be applied without infringing free speech rights even where there is no clear and present danger.

DISSENT: (Black, J.) First Amendment rights should have a preferred position in a free society. Laws restricting those rights should not be sustained by the courts on the grounds of mere reasonableness.

DISSENT: (Douglas, J.) A restriction of First Amendment rights can be sustained only where there is plain and objective proof of danger that the evil advocated is imminent. This was not shown here, where it is inconceivable that Dennis (D) and other Communists advocating the violent overthrow of the government have any chance of success.

▶ ANALYSIS

After *Dennis*, the government brought Smith Act cases against a number of Communists who were lower echelon figures, rather than leaders. In *Yates v. U.S.*, 354 U.S. 298

Continued on next page.

(1957), the Court reversed the convictions of 14 defendants. It distinguished and explained *Dennis* on the ground that it had involved group indoctrination toward future violent action, under circumstances that reasonably justified the apprehension that violence would result. In *Scales v. U.S.*, 367 U.S. 203 (1961), the Court sustained the membership clause of the Smith Act, making it clear that to be convicted under that clause one must have had knowledge of an organization's illegal advocacy and must have joined the group with the specific intent of furthering its illegal aims.

■■■

Quicknotes

CONSPIRACY Concerted action by two or more persons to accomplish some unlawful purpose.

■■■

Brandenburg v. Ohio

Ku Klux Klan leader (D) v. State (P)

395 U.S. 444 (1969).

NATURE OF CASE: Certiorari review of constitutionality of state statute.

FACT SUMMARY: Brandenburg (D) was convicted under a state statute that proscribes advocacy of the duty, necessity, or propriety of crime, sabotage, violence, or unlawful methods of terrorism as a means of accomplishing reform.

🏛 RULE OF LAW
The constitutional guarantees of freedom of speech and freedom of press do not permit a state to forbid or proscribe advocacy of the use of force or of law violation except where such advocacy is directed to inciting or producing imminent lawless action and is likely to produce or incite such action.

FACTS: Brandenburg (D), a Ku Klux Klan leader, was convicted under Ohio's (P) criminal syndicalism statute. The statute prohibited advocacy of the duty, necessity, or propriety of crime, sabotage, violence, or unlawful methods of terrorism as a means of accomplishing reform, and the assembling with any group formed to teach or advocate the doctrine of criminal syndicalism. The case against Brandenburg (D) rested on some films. One film showed 12 hooded figures, some carrying firearms, gathered around a wooden cross, which they burned. Scattered words could be heard that were derogatory to Jews and African-Americans. Brandenburg (D) made a speech and stated, "We are not a revengent group, but if our President, our Congress, and our Supreme Court, continues to suppress the White, Caucasian race, it's possible that there might have to be some revengence taken."

ISSUE: Do the constitutional guarantees of freedom of speech and freedom of press permit a state to forbid or proscribe advocacy of the use of force or of law violation where such advocacy is not directed to inciting or producing imminent lawless action and is not likely to produce or incite such action?

HOLDING AND DECISION: (Per curiam) No. The constitutional guarantees of free speech and free press do not permit a state to forbid or proscribe advocacy of the use of force or of law violation except where such advocacy is directed to inciting or producing imminent lawless action and is likely to incite or produce such action. The mere abstract teaching of the moral propriety or even moral necessity for a resort to force and violence is not the same as preparing a group for violent action and steering it to such action. A statute that fails to draw this distinction impermissibly intrudes upon the freedoms

guaranteed by the First and Fourteenth Amendments. It sweeps within its condemnation speech that the Constitution has immunized from governmental control. The Ohio statute purports to punish mere advocacy and to forbid assembly with others merely to advocate the described type of action. Hence, it cannot be sustained. Brandenburg's (D) conviction is reversed.

CONCURRENCE: (Black, J.) The "clear and present danger" doctrine should have no place in the interpretation of the First Amendment.

CONCURRENCE: (Douglas, J.) The line between what is permissible and not subject to control and what may be made impermissible and subject to regulation is the line between ideas and overt acts. Apart from rare exceptions, speech is immune from prosecution.

▎ ANALYSIS

This case demonstrates that imminence of danger is an essential requirement to the validity of any statute curbing freedom of speech. This requirement was reiterated in *Bond v. Floyd*, 385 U.S. 116 (1966), in which the Court reversed a state legislature's resolution excluding Bond from membership. The exclusion was based on the ground that Bond could not take the oath to support the state and U.S. Constitutions after his endorsement of a SNCC statement and his remarks criticizing the draft and the Vietnam War. The Court found no incitement to violation of law in Bond's remarks.

Quicknotes

FREEDOM OF SPEECH The right to express oneself without governmental restrictions on the content of that expression.

FREEDOM OF THE PRESS The right to publish and publicly disseminate one's views.

Chaplinsky v. New Hampshire

Jehovah's Witness (D) v. State (P)

315 U.S. 568 (1942).

NATURE OF CASE: Appeal of a conviction for violation of statute forbidding utterance of words derisive or annoying to another.

FACT SUMMARY: Chaplinsky (D), a Jehovah's Witness, first denounced all other religions as "rackets" and then called a Marshall a "fascist" and "racketeer."

> 🏛 **RULE OF LAW**
> A government may proscribe language tending to incite violence.

FACTS: Chaplinsky (D), a Jehovah's Witness, had been calling other religions "rackets." An unfriendly crowd began to assemble. A Marshall warned Chaplinsky (D) that the crowd was getting ugly, whereupon Chaplinsky (D) called the Marshall a "racketeer" and a "fascist." Chaplinsky (D) was convicted under an ordinance prohibiting the utterance of words tending to harass, annoy, or deride another. Chaplinsky (D) appealed.

ISSUE: May a government proscribe language tending to incite violence?

HOLDING AND DECISION: (Murphy, J.) Yes. A government may proscribe language tending to incite violence. It is established that words constituting a clear and present danger to the public health may be banned. So-called "fighting words" do constitute such a danger. The ordinance in question basically is a prohibition of fighting words, and therefore the ordinance is valid. Affirmed.

▌ *ANALYSIS*

This case presents one of the first enunciations of the concept of "protected" and "unprotected" speech, among them libel, obscenity, and "fighting words." The scope of the former two categories has been the subject of much subsequent analysis.

∎══∎

Quicknotes

FIGHTING WORDS Unprotected speech under the First Amendment, which is likely to instigate a violent reaction.

∎══∎

Feiner v. New York

Public speaker (D) v. State (P)

340 U.S. 315 (1951).

NATURE OF CASE: Certiorari review of conviction for speech offense.

FACT SUMMARY: Feiner (D) gave an open-air speech before a racially mixed audience. The crowd that gathered forced pedestrians into the street. Feiner (D) urged blacks to rise up in arms against whites and fight for equal rights. He refused to stop when asked to do so by a police officer and was arrested.

🏛 RULE OF LAW
When clear and present danger of riot, disorder, interference with traffic on the streets, or other immediate threat to public safety, peace, or order appears, the state has the power to punish or prevent such disorder.

FACTS: Feiner (D) addressed an open-air meeting. A racially mixed crowd of about 80 people gathered. The crowd forced pedestrians walking by into the street. In response to a complaint about the meeting, two police officers arrived. They heard Feiner (D) urge blacks to take up arms and fight against whites for equal rights. The remarks stirred up the crowd a little, and one person commented on the police's inability to control the crowd. Another threatened violence if the police did not act. The officers finally "stepped in to prevent it all resulting in a fight." They asked Feiner (D) to stop speaking twice. He ignored them, and they arrested him.

ISSUE: When clear and present danger of riot, disorder, interference with traffic on the streets, or other immediate threat to public safety, peace, or order appears, does the state have the power to punish or prevent such disorder?

HOLDING AND DECISION: (Vinson, C.J.) Yes. When clear and present danger of riot, disorder, interference with traffic on the streets, or other immediate threat to public safety, peace, or order appears, the state has the power to punish or prevent such disorder. Here, the crowd's behavior and Feiner's (D) refusal to obey the police requests presented a sufficient danger to warrant his arrest and to persuade the Court that Feiner's (D) conviction for violation of public peace, order and authority does not exceed the bounds of proper state police action. Feiner (D) was neither arrested nor convicted for the making or the content of his speech. Rather, it was the reaction it engendered. The community's interest in maintaining peace and order on its streets must be protected. Hence, Feiner's (D) conviction is affirmed.

DISSENT: (Black, J.) This decision is a long step toward totalitarian authority. Disagreement, mutterings, and objections from a crowd do not indicate imminent threat of a riot, nor does one threat to assault the speaker. Even assuming that a critical situation existed, it was the police's duty to protect Feiner's (D) right to speak, which they made no effort to do. Finally, a person making a lawful address is not required to be silent merely because an officer so directs. Here, Feiner (D) received no explanation as to why he was being directed to stop speaking. This decision means that the police have the discretion to silence minority views in any city as soon as the customary hostility to such views develops.

▶ ANALYSIS

As *Feiner* demonstrates, free speech is not an absolute right. The conflicting interest of community order must also be considered. *Feiner* points out the question of whether the boundaries of protected speech depend on the content of the speech and the speaker's words or on the environment, the crowd reaction or potential crowd reaction. This question arose again in *Gregory v. Chicago,* 394 U.S. 111 (1969), which reversed convictions of disorderly conduct. There, participants in a "peaceful and orderly procession" to press their claims for desegregation were arrested when, after the number of bystanders increased, and some became unruly, they were asked to disperse and did not. The majority asserted that this was a simple case as the marchers' peaceful conduct was a protected activity within the First Amendment. The concurring opinion saw *Gregory* as involving some complexities, since, as the judge noted, both the demonstrators and the officers had tried to restrain the hecklers but were unable to do so. He concluded that "this record is a crying example of a need for some narrowly drawn law," rather than the sweeping disorderly conduct law.

Quicknotes

CLEAR AND PRESENT DANGER A threat that is proximate and impending.

FIRST AMENDMENT Prohibits Congress from enacting any law respecting an establishment of religion, prohibiting the free exercise of religion, abridging freedom of speech or the press, the right of peaceful assembly and the right to petition for a redress of grievances.

FREEDOM OF SPEECH The right to express oneself without governmental restrictions on the content of that expression.

Cohen v. California

Defendant (D) v. State (P)

403 U.S. 15 (1971).

NATURE OF CASE: Certiorari review of state statute restricting speech.

FACT SUMMARY: Cohen (D) wore a jacket with the words "Fuck the Draft" on it in a courthouse corridor and was arrested and convicted under a disturbing the peace statute.

🏛 RULE OF LAW
A state cannot bar the use of offensive words either because such words are inherently likely to cause a violent reaction or because the state wishes to eliminate such words to protect the public morality.

FACTS: Cohen (D) was arrested in a courthouse because he was wearing a jacket bearing the words, "Fuck the Draft." Cohen (D) did not engage in any act of violence or any other unlawful act. There was also no evidence that anyone who saw the jacket became violently aroused or even protested the jacket. Cohen (D) testified that he wore the jacket to inform people of his feelings against the Vietnam War and the draft. He was convicted under a statute prohibiting "maliciously and willfully disturbing the peace or quiet . . . by offensive conduct." The state court held that "offensive conduct" meant conduct that had a tendency to provoke others to disturb the peace.

ISSUE: Can a state constitutionally prevent the use of certain words on the ground that the use of such words is offensive conduct?

HOLDING AND DECISION: (Harlan, J.) No. A state cannot constitutionally prohibit the use of offensive words either because such words are inherently likely to cause a violent reaction or because the state wishes to eliminate such words to protect the public morality. Here, Cohen (D) could not be punished for criticizing the draft, so the statute could be upheld, if at all, only as a regulation of the manner, not the substantive content, of his speech. Cohen's (D) speech does not come within any of the exceptions to the general rule that the form and content of speech cannot be regulated: (1) this is not a prohibition designed to protect courthouse decorum because the statute is not so limited; (2) this is not an obscenity case because Cohen's (D) words were not erotic; (3) this is not a case of fighting words which are punishable as inherently likely to provoke a violent reaction because here the words were not directed as a personal insult to any person; and (4) this is not a captive audience problem since a viewer could merely avert his eyes, there is no evidence of objection by those who saw the jacket, and the statute is not so limited. The state tries to justify the conviction because the words are inherently likely to cause a violent reaction, but this argument cannot be upheld because these are not fighting words and there is no evidence that words that are merely offensive would cause such a response. Next, the state justifies the conviction on the ground that the state is guardian of the public morality. This argument is unacceptable because "offensive" is an unlimited concept and forbidding the use of such words would also cause the risk of suppressing the accompanying ideas. Therefore, there is no valid state interest that supports the regulation of offensive words in public. Reversed.

DISSENT: (Blackmun, J.) Cohen's (D) conviction can be upheld both because his speech was fighting words and also because his act was conduct and not speech. Additionally, the state court subsequently restricted the statute in question to the fighting words context, so the case should be remanded and reconsidered under this construction.

▶ ANALYSIS

This case reasserts the *Chaplinsky*, 315 U.S. 568 (1942), holding that fighting words are not protected by the First Amendment. Fighting words, then, are only those words that are likely to cause an immediate breach of the peace by another person, and are not just offensive words. More importantly, this case holds that a state has no valid interest in preventing the use of offensive words when there is no competing privacy interest. Here, the public in general has no right to protection from hearing either offensive words or offensive ideas.

Quicknotes

DECORUM Observance of commonly accepted standards of propriety.

FIGHTING WORDS Unprotected speech that inflicts injury by its very utterance and provokes violence from the audience.

Beauharnais v. Illinois

Publisher (D) v. State (P)

343 U.S. 250 (1956).

NATURE OF CASE: Appeal from a criminal conviction.

FACT SUMMARY: Beauharnais (D) was convicted under an Illinois (P) statute making it a crime to publish any material criticizing members of a group in a way that subjects them to ridicule or invited civil unrest.

🏛 **RULE OF LAW**
A statute that makes it a crime to libel the members of any class or group is not repugnant to the Constitution.

FACTS: An Illinois (P) law made it a crime to publish or exhibit any lithograph, movie, play or sketch that attributed depravity, criminality, or other conduct lacking in virtue to a racial or religious group in such a way as to expose the members of that group to derision or cause a breach of the peace. Beauharnais (D), president of the White Circle League, arranged for the distribution of lithographs that urged whites to prevent further encroachment by blacks and that described the alleged criminality, violence, and drug use rampant among blacks. Beauharnais (D) was charged with violating the State (P) statute, but argued that the enactment deprived him of freedom of speech and press and was unconstitutionally vague. Beauharnais (D) was found guilty and his conviction was affirmed by the Illinois Supreme Court, which identified the challenged statute as "a form of criminal libel law." The United States Supreme Court then agreed to review the conviction.

ISSUE: Is a statute that makes it a crime to libel the members of any class or group repugnant to the Constitution?

HOLDING AND DECISION: (Frankfurter, J.) No. A statute that makes it a crime to libel the members of any class or group is not repugnant to the Constitution. Originally, libel was a common law crime to which even truth was not a defense. In Illinois (P), as in most states, truth is now a defense to a criminal libel charge only if publication was made "with good motives and for justifiable ends." Since Beauharnais's (D) offers of proof made no effort to establish motive or justification, the trial court properly concluded the lithographs were libelous as a matter of law, and permitted the jury to decide only the issue of publication. Profane or cruelly pejorative expressions may be punished by a state without interfering with anyone's constitutionally guaranteed privileges. Historically, violence and bloodshed have accompanied racial disputes in Illinois (P). Whether or not the contested statute is the best way of dealing with the problem, it is a reasonable exercise of the legislature's power to preserve the peace and protect the public. The statute is drawn with sufficient narrowness and clarity, and punishes only utterances which are indisputably libelous. Therefore, the law is constitutional and Beauharnais's (D) conviction must be affirmed.

DISSENT: (Black, J.) This "group libel law" exemplifies an invidious form of censorship. Traditional criminal libel laws apply only to attacks upon individuals, not groups. In racial controversies, angry accusations are so prevalent virtually anyone could end up violating a statute such as enacted by Illinois (P). This law precludes free public discussion, and thus stifles cherished First Amendment rights. It is argued judicial discretion could prevent Illinois (P) from abusing the statute, but the rights secured to all citizens by the Constitution should not be dispensed at the whim of an arbitrary and sometimes capricious tribunal.

▶ *ANALYSIS*

Common law criminal libel statutes were apparently designed to discourage feuding individuals from launching personal attacks upon one another in public. Such laws were not applied to punish allegedly libelous assaults upon groups. Nevertheless, some contemporary commentators argue group libel laws would be an effective and desirable method of preventing scurrilous public campaigns of hatred against particular races or religious groups. Although such laws would tend to stifle protected First Amendment rights, it may be possible to imagine situations similar to that cited by the *Beauharnais* majority in which such restraint would be justified by a need to protect against threats to the public peace and tranquility.

Quicknotes

FIRST AMENDMENT Prohibits Congress from enacting any law respecting an establishment of religion, prohibiting the free exercise of religion, abridging freedom of speech or the press, the right of peaceful assembly and the right to petition for a redress of grievances.

LIBEL A false or malicious publication subjecting a person to scorn, hatred or ridicule, or injuring him or her in relation to his or her occupation or business.

Collin v. Smith

Head of political group (P) v. Municipal official (D)

578 F.2d 1197 (7th Cir. 1978).

NATURE OF CASE: Appeal in action challenging local ordinances on First Amendment grounds. [The procedural posture of the case is not presented in the casebook extract.]

FACT SUMMARY: The National Socialist Party of America (NSPA) (P), a neo-Nazi group, wished to demonstrate in Skokie, Illinois (D), which included a large Jewish population, including thousands of survivors of the Nazi Holocaust. After Skokie (D) enacted three ordinances aimed at prohibiting such demonstrations, the NSPA (P) and its leader, Collin (P), challenged the ordinances in federal district court, claiming the ordinances violated the First Amendment.

RULE OF LAW
Content legislation that does not fall within any exceptions to the rule against governmental content control violates the First Amendment, notwithstanding the speech the legislation is intended to control is generally deemed offensive and hateful.

FACTS: The National Socialist Party of America (NSPA) (P), a neo-Nazi group, wished to demonstrate in Skokie, Illinois (D), which included a large Jewish population, including thousands of survivors of the Nazi Holocaust. The demonstration was to last about a half hour, and would involve 30 to 50 demonstrators wearing uniforms including swastikas and carrying a party banner with a swastika and placards with statements thereon such as "White Free Speech," "Free Speech for the White Man," and "Free Speech for White America." Skokie (D) enacted three ordinances to prohibit such demonstrations. The first ordinance established a comprehensive permit system for all parades or public assemblies. The second ordinance prohibited the dissemination of any materials within Skokie (D) which promoted and incited hatred against persons by reason of their race, national origin, or religion. The third ordinance prohibited public demonstrations by members of political parties while wearing "military-style" uniforms. The NSPA (P) and its leader, Collin (P), challenged the ordinances in federal district court, claiming the ordinances violated the First Amendment. The court of appeals granted review. [The procedural posture of the case is not presented in the casebook extract.]

ISSUE: Does content legislation that does not fall within any exceptions to the rule against governmental content control violate the First Amendment, notwithstanding the speech the legislation is intended to control is generally deemed offensive and hateful?

HOLDING AND DECISION: (Pell, J.) Yes. Content legislation that does not fall within any exceptions to the rule against governmental content control violates the First Amendment, notwithstanding the speech the legislation is intended to control is generally deemed offensive and hateful. While content legislation is not per se invalid, it is the most direct threat to the vitality of First Amendment rights. Here, the ordinances do not fall within the generally recognized exceptions to the rule against content control. The NSPA's (P) speech cannot be considered obscenity, which requires erotic content, and there is no indication that the demonstration will incite violence, or be violent in nature. Therefore, the speech cannot be considered incitement to riot, or "fighting words." Skokie's (D) arguments in support of the ordinances are also unavailing. Skokie (D) asserts that the NSPA's (P) speech has no social content and consists of false statements of fact. To the extent the speech asserts anything it is the Nazi ideology, which cannot be treated as a mere false "fact." Under the First Amendment, there is no such thing as a false idea. However pernicious an opinion may seem, its correction does not depend on the conscience of judges and juries but on the competition of other ideas. Another argument pressed by Skokie (D) is that the ordinances are valid because they are aimed at eliminating the tendency to induce violence. Given that it is conceded that no violence from NSPA (P), or those incited by its speech is anticipated, this argument finds no support. Skokie's (D) third argument is that it has a policy of fair housing, which the dissemination of racially defamatory material could undercut. This argument is rejected. Merely because the effective exercise of First Amendment rights may undercut a given government's policy on some issue is, indeed, one of the purposes of those rights. Skokie's (D) last argument in support of the ordinances is that the Nazi march, involving as it does the display of uniforms and swastikas, will create a substantive evil that it has a right to prohibit: the infliction of psychic trauma on resident holocaust survivors and other Jewish residents. Such speech may not be criminalized, even if it could form the basis of a tort (i.e., intentional infliction of severe emotional distress). Although it is undeniable that the proposed demonstration would seriously disturb, emotionally and mentally, at least some, and probably many of Skokie's (D) residents, the speech at issue may not be protected by an exception to the First Amendment because such speech is indistinguishable in principle from speech that invites dispute; a state many not "make criminal the peaceful expression of unpopular

Continued on next page.

views." Regardless of the court's personal views of NSPA's (P) ideology—which is that it is repugnant—its members' civil rights under the First Amendment must be upheld so that these rights remain vital for all; First Amendment rights must protect not only those society deems acceptable, but also those whose ideas it quite justifiably rejects and despises. [The procedural outcome of the case is not presented in the casebook extract.]

▶ *ANALYSIS*

The United States Supreme Court declined to grant certiorari in this case. Justice Blackmun, dissenting, believed this case afforded the Court an opportunity to consider whether, in the context of the unique facts presented, there is no limit whatsoever to the exercise of free speech. He indicated when citizens assert, not casually but with deep conviction, that a proposed demonstration is scheduled at a place and in a manner that is taunting and overwhelmingly offensive to the citizens of that place, that assertion, uncomfortable though it may be for judges, deserves to be examined, and upon close scrutiny, such speech just might fall into the same category as one's "right" to cry "fire" in a crowded theater, given "the character of every act depends upon the circumstances in which it is done." However, as was pointed out by Judge Wood in *Collin*, since in this case there was ample warning of the proposed demonstration, this situation was not equivalent to the sudden and unfounded cry of "fire" in a crowded and unsuspecting theater to which it was sometimes analogized. As Judge Wood observed, "[r]ecognition of the full scope of freedom of speech does not compel anyone to listen, or if listening to believe."

Quicknotes

FIRST AMENDMENT Prohibits Congress from enacting any law respecting an establishment of religion, prohibiting the free exercise of religion, abridging freedom of speech or the press, the right of peaceful assembly and the right to petition for a redress of grievances.

FREEDOM OF SPEECH The right to express oneself without governmental restrictions on the content of that expression.

R.A.V. v. City of St. Paul

Teenager (D) v. Municipality (P)

505 U.S. 377 (1992).

NATURE OF CASE: Certiorari review of constitutionality of "hate crime" ordinance.

FACT SUMMARY: When R.A.V. (D) was charged with allegedly burning a cross inside the fenced yard of a black family, the City of St. Paul (P) charged R.A.V. (D) under the Bias-Motivated Crime Ordinance.

RULE OF LAW
Where content discrimination in an ordinance is not reasonably necessary to achieve a city's compelling interests, the ordinance cannot survive First Amendment scrutiny.

FACTS: R.A.V. (D) and several other teenagers allegedly assembled a crudely made cross and burned it inside the fenced yard of a black family. This conduct could have been punished under any of a number of laws, but the City of St. Paul (P) chose to charge R.A.V. (D) under the Bias-Motivated Crime Ordinance, which made criminally punishable conduct known as "hate crimes." R.A.V. (D) moved to dismiss on the ground that the ordinance was substantially overbroad and impermissibly content based and therefore facially invalid under the First Amendment. The trial court granted this motion, but the Minnesota Supreme Court reversed because the modifying phrase "arouses anger, alarm or resentment in others" limited the reach of the ordinance to conduct that amounted to "fighting words," and therefore the ordinance reached only expression "that the First Amendment does not protect." The court also concluded that the ordinance was not impermissibly content based because it was a narrowly tailored means toward accomplishing the compelling governmental interest of protecting the community against bias-motivated threats to public safety and order.

ISSUE: Where content discrimination in an ordinance is not reasonably necessary to achieve a city's compelling interests, can the ordinance survive First Amendment scrutiny?

HOLDING AND DECISION: (Scalia, J.) No. Where content discrimination in an ordinance is not reasonably necessary to achieve a city's compelling interests, the ordinance cannot survive First Amendment scrutiny. Assuming that all of the expression reached by the ordinance is proscribable under the fighting words doctrine, the ordinance is nonetheless facially unconstitutional in that it prohibits otherwise permitted speech solely on the basis of the subjects the speech addresses. Some areas of speech can, consistent with the First Amendment, be regulated because of their constitutionally proscribable content, namely, obscenity, defamation, and fighting words. Although the Minnesota Supreme Court construed the modifying phrase in the ordinance to reach only those symbols or displays that amount to fighting words, the remaining, unmodified terms make clear that the ordinance applies only to fighting words that insult, or provoke violence, on the basis of race, color, creed, religion, or gender. The First Amendment does not permit St. Paul (P) to impose special prohibitions on those speakers who express views on disfavored subjects. Burning a cross in someone's front yard is reprehensible, but St. Paul (P) has sufficient means at its disposal to prevent such behavior without adding the First Amendment to the fire. Reversed.

CONCURRENCE: (White, J.) The judgment of the Minnesota Supreme Court should be reversed. However, this case could easily be decided under First Amendment law by holding that the ordinance is fatally overbroad because it criminalizes not only unprotected expression but expression protected by the First Amendment. The Court's new "under-breadth" creation serves no desirable function.

CONCURRENCE: (Blackmun, J.) The result of the majority opinion is correct because this particular ordinance reaches beyond fighting words to speech protected by the First Amendment. However, by its decision today, the majority appears to relax the level of scrutiny applicable to content-based laws, thus weakening the traditional protections of speech.

CONCURRENCE: (Stevens, J.) The majority establishes a near-absolute ban on content-based regulation. Content-based distinctions are an inevitable and indispensable aspect of First Amendment law. On the basis of content, the First Amendment does not protect the right to fix prices, breach contracts, make false warranties, place bets, threaten, or coerce. "Unprotected" or "proscribable" categories are based on content. Courts must consider the content and context of regulated speech and the scope of restrictions. This ordinance regulates low-value speech, fighting words, and only expressive conduct, not written or spoken words. The context is confrontational and potentially violent situations. Cross-burning is not a political statement; it is the first step in an act of assault that can be no more protected than holding a gun to someone's head. The scope of the restriction is the narrow. R.A.V. (D) is free to burn a cross or express racial supremacy, so long as the burning is not so threatening and so directed at an individual as to by its very execution inflict injury. That the

Continued on next page.

ordinance singles out threats based on race, color, creed, religion, or gender is justifiable because these threats cause more harm to society and individuals than others. While not invalid as a content-based speech regulation, the ordinance is, however, overbroad.

▶ *ANALYSIS*

The text of the St. Paul Bias-Motivated Crime Ordinance provides that: "Whoever places on public or private property a symbol, object, appellation, characterization or graffiti, including, but not limited to, a burning cross or Nazi swastika, which one knows or has reasonable grounds to know arouses anger, alarm or resentment in others on the basis of race, color, creed, religion or gender commits disorderly conduct and shall be guilty of a misdemeanor." The flaw in the wording of the ordinance was that it required the person who committed the hateful act to discern the reaction of the victim to the perpetrator's conduct. It is likely that hate crime ordinances that are worded to punish conduct intended by the perpetrator to frighten, anger, etc., on the basis of race, religion, etc., would be upheld. Even if no hate crime ordinance could be upheld, the hateful conduct could still be punished under criminal trespass, arson, battery, homicide statutes, etc.

■■■

Quicknotes

CONTENT-BASED Refers to statutes that regulate speech based on its content.

CONTENT-NEUTRAL Refers to statutes that regulate speech regardless of its content.

FIGHTING WORDS Any words that have the tendency to incite an immediate, violent reaction in the listener or hearer.

OVERBREADTH Refers to a statute that proscribes lawful as well as unlawful conduct.

■■■

Virginia v. Black

State (P) v. Person convicted under cross-burning statute (D)

538 U.S. 343 (2003).

NATURE OF CASE: Certiorari review of constitutionality of state cross-burning statute.

FACT SUMMARY: When Black (D) was prosecuted and convicted under Virginia's (P) cross-burning statute, he argued its unconstitutionality because of a provision treating any cross burning as prima facie evidence of intent to intimidate.

🏛 RULE OF LAW
A provision in a state's cross-burning statute treating any cross burning as prima facie evidence of intent to intimidate is unconstitutional.

FACTS: Black (D) was prosecuted and convicted by a jury under Virginia's (P) cross-burning statute, which bans cross burning with intent to intimidate a person or group of persons. The statute contains a provision that any burning of a cross constitutes prima facie evidence of intent to intimidate a person or group of persons. The Supreme Court of Virginia reversed the conviction, and the United States Supreme Court granted certiorari to review the statute's constitutionality.

ISSUE: Is a provision in a state's cross-burning statute treating any cross burning as prima facie evidence of intent to intimidate unconstitutional?

HOLDING AND DECISION: (O'Connor, J.) Yes. A provision in a state's cross-burning statute treating any cross burning as prima facie evidence of intent to intimidate is unconstitutional. To this day, regardless of whether the message is a political one or whether the message is also meant to intimidate, the burning of a cross is a symbol of hate. While cross burning sometimes carries no intimidating message, at other times the intimidating message is the only message conveyed. This Court has long held that the government may regulate certain categories of expression consistent with the Constitution and that indeed intimidation in the constitutionally proscribable sense of the word is a type of true threat. The First Amendment, accordingly, permits Virginia (P) to outlaw cross burnings done with the intent to intimidate because burning a cross is a particularly virulent form of intimidation. Furthermore, instead of prohibiting all intimidating messages, Virginia (P) may choose to regulate this subset of intimidating messages in light of cross burnings' long and pernicious history as a signal of impending violence. However, this particular cross-burning statute is unconstitutionally overbroad due to its provision stating that any burning of a cross is prima facie evidence of an intent to intimidate a person or group of persons. The prima facie provision strips away the very

reason why a state may ban cross burning with the intent to intimidate because this provision permits a jury to convict in every cross-burning case in which defendants exercise their constitutional right not to put on a defense. It is apparent that the provision as so interpreted "would create an unacceptable risk of the suppression of ideas." Anger or hatred is not sufficient to ban all cross burnings in the absence of actual intimidation or threat. The First Amendment does not permit shortcuts. The prima facie evidence provision in this case is unconstitutional on its face. Reversed.

CONCURRENCE: (Stevens, J.) Cross burning with "an intent to intimidate" unquestionably qualifies as the kind of threat that is unprotected by the First Amendment.

CONCURRENCE AND DISSENT: (Scalia, J.) While agreeing with the Court that a state may, without infringing the First Amendment, prohibit cross burning carried out with the intent to intimidate, there is no justification for the plurality's apparent decision to invalidate the prima facie evidence provision on its face.

CONCURRENCE AND DISSENT: (Souter, J.) While agreeing that the statute makes a content-based distinction within the category of punishable intimidating or threatening expression, I disagree that any exception should save the statute from unconstitutionality. No content-based statute should survive without a high probability that no official suppression of ideas is being encouraged.

DISSENT: (Thomas, J.) The majority errs in imputing an expressive component to the activity in question. In our culture, cross burning has almost invariably meant lawlessness and understandably instills in its victims a well-grounded fear of physical violence. Those who hate cannot terrorize and intimidate to make their point. The statute here addressed only conduct; there is no need for First Amendment analysis.

▶ ANALYSIS

As articulated by the plurality in the *Black* decision, the prima facie evidence provision in the Virginia cross-burning statute ignored all of the contextual factors that would be necessary in order for a court or jury to decide whether a particular cross burning was in fact intended to intimidate. On the other hand, some legal commentators express the viewpoint such as that conveyed in Justice Thomas's

Continued on next page.

dissent, that a cross burning always and necessarily represents intimidation.

====

Quicknotes

FIRST AMENDMENT   Prohibits Congress from enacting any law respecting an establishment of religion, prohibiting the free exercise of religion, abridging freedom of speech or the press, the right of peaceful assembly and the right to petition for a redress of grievances.

PRIMA FACIE EVIDENCE   Evidence presented by a party that is sufficient, in the absence of contradictory evidence, to support the fact or issue for which it is offered.

====

New York Times Co. v. Sullivan

Newspaper publisher (D) v. Public official (P)

376 U.S. 254 (1964).

NATURE OF CASE: Certiorari review of defamation judgment.

FACT SUMMARY: New York Times (D) published an editorial advertisement in which false statements were made which concerned Sullivan (P).

🏛 RULE OF LAW
Defamatory falsehoods regarding public officials have limited protection by constitutional guarantees of freedom of speech and press.

FACTS: Sullivan (P) was a commissioner in the city of Montgomery, Alabama, charged with supervision of the Police Department. During a series of civil rights demonstrations in that city in 1960, the New York Times (D) published an editorial advertisement entitled, "Heed Their Rising Voices," in which several charges of terrorism were leveled at the Police Department. The falsity of some of these statements was uncontroverted. The advertisement charged that nine students at a local college had been expelled for leading a march on the state capitol when, in fact, the reason had been an illegal lunch counter sit-in. The advertisement charged that the police had padlocked the dining hall of the college to starve the demonstrators into submission when, in fact, no padlocking had occurred. Other false statements also were made. Sullivan (P) brought a defamation action against New York Times (D) for these statements and recovered $500,000. Under Alabama law, a publication is libel per se (no special damages need be proved—general damages are presumed), whenever a defamatory falsehood is shown to have injured its subject in his public office or impute misconduct to him in his office. New York Times (D) appealed the Alabama judgment, challenging this rule.

ISSUE: Do defamatory falsehoods regarding public officials have limited protection by constitutional guarantees of freedom of speech and press?

HOLDING AND DECISION: (Brennan, J.) Yes. Defamatory falsehoods regarding public officials have limited protection by constitutional guarantees of freedom of speech and press. The First Amendment requires that a public official may not recover damages for defamatory falsehoods relating to his official conduct unless he proves that the statement involved was made with "actual malice—that is, with knowledge that it was false or with reckless disregard of whether it was false or not." First Amendment protections do not turn upon the truth, popularity, or social utility of ideas and beliefs which are involved. Rather, they are based upon the theory that

erroneous statements are inevitable in free debate and must be protected if such freedom is to survive. Only where malice is involved do such protections cease. Here, the Alabama rule falls short of this standard and the evidence at trial was insufficient to determine its existence. Reversed and remanded.

CONCURRENCE: (Black, J.) All statements about public officials should be constitutionally protected—even malicious ones.

▶ ANALYSIS

New York Times is the landmark case in constitutional defamation law. The subsequent cases have expanded this concept even further. In *Rosenblatt v. Baer*, 383 U.S. 75 (1966), the Court defined "public official" as anyone having substantial responsibility for conduct of government affairs. In *Curtis Publishing v. Butts*, 388 U.S. 130 (1967), New York Times was extended to "public figures" as well as officials. In *Gertz*, 418 U.S. 323 (1974), however, the Court retreated a bit by stating that, "As long as they do not impose liability without fault, the states may define for themselves the appropriate standard of liability for a publisher . . . of defamatory falsehood injurious to a private individual." Note that the Court has also taken steps to toughen the *New York Times'* recklessness standard. In *St. Amant v. Thompson*, 390 U.S. 727 (1968), the Court ruled that recklessness was not to be measured by the reasonable man standard, but rather by the subjective standard of whether or not the defendant in the case subjectively entertained serious doubts about the truth of his statements.

■■■

Quicknotes

ACTUAL MALICE The issuance of a publication or utterance with knowledge of its falsity or with reckless disregard as to its truth.

DEFAMATION An intentional false publication, communicated publicly in either oral or written form, subjecting a person to scorn, hatred or ridicule, or injuring him or her in relation to his or her occupation or business.

FIRST AMENDMENT Prohibits Congress from enacting any law respecting an establishment of religion, prohibiting the free exercise of religion, abridging freedom of speech or the press, the right of peaceful assembly and the right to petition for a redress of grievances.

Continued on next page.

PUBLIC FIGURE A person, who has achieved or assumed a special prominence in society either willingly or by virtue of his or her social status.

REASONABLE PERSON STANDARD The standard of care exercised by a hypothetical person who possesses the intelligence, education, knowledge, attention, and judgment required by society of its members when governing behavior; the standard applies to a person's judgment when determining breach of a duty under the theory of negligence.

RECKLESSNESS The conscious disregard of substantial and justifiable risk.

Gertz v. Robert Welch, Inc.

Attorney (P) v. Publisher (D)

418 U.S. 323 (1974).

NATURE OF CASE: Action for defamation.

FACT SUMMARY: Gertz (P) sued Welch (D), a publisher of a John Birch Society newsletter, when Welch (D) published an article calling Gertz (P) a long-time Communist who helped frame a Chicago policeman's conviction for murder, all of which was untrue.

🏛 **RULE OF LAW**
In an action for defamation, a private individual must show the publisher to be at fault and may recover no more than actual damages when liability is not based on a showing of knowledge of falsity or reckless disregard for the truth.

FACTS: Welch (D) published *American Opinion*, a monthly newsletter of the John Birch Society. An article appeared in that publication purporting to illustrate that the conviction of Nuccio, a Chicago policeman, for the murder of Nelson, a young man, was a communist frameup led by Gertz (P). It was said further that Gertz (P) had a criminal record, was an official of the Marxist League, a Leninist, and an officer of the National Lawyers Guild, which was falsely described as a communist organization in the forefront of the attack on Chicago police during the 1968 Democratic Convention. The only element of truth was that 15 years earlier Gertz (P) had been a National Lawyers Guild officer. Actually, he was a reputable lawyer whose only connection with the Nuccio case was to represent the Nelson family in civil litigation against Nuccio. Gertz (P) attended the coroner's inquest into Nelson's death and filed an action for damages, but did not discuss the matter with the press or play any part in the criminal proceedings. At trial, the evidence showed that *American Opinion*'s managing editor knew nothing of the defamatory content but had belief in the reputation and accuracy of the author. The jury found the matter libelous per se and not privileged, and awarded a $50,000 judgment, but the judge applied the *New York Times* standard, [*New York Times Co. v. Sullivan*, 376 U.S. 254 (1964)], as pertaining to any discussion of a public issue without regard to the status of the person defamed. Judgment n.o.v. was entered for Welch (D). The court of appeals affirmed, and Gertz (P) appealed.

ISSUE: In an action for defamation, must a private individual show the publisher to be at fault and recover no more than actual damages when liability is not based on a showing of knowledge of falsity or reckless disregard for the truth?

HOLDING AND DECISION: (Powell, J.) Yes. In an action for defamation, a private individual must show

the publisher to be at fault and may recover no more than actual damages when liability is not based on a showing of knowledge of falsity or reckless disregard for the truth. The *New York Times* standard applies to public figures and public officials, but the state interest in compensating injury to reputation of private individuals requires that a different rule should apply to them. A public figure or official has greater access to the media to counteract false statements than private individuals normally enjoy. Being more vulnerable to injury, the private individual deserves greater protection and recovery. As long as the states do not impose liability without fault, the states themselves may define the appropriate standard of liability for a publisher of defamatory matter injurious to a private person. And the states may not permit the recovery of presumed or punitive damages, at least when liability is not based on a showing of knowledge of falsity or reckless disregard for the truth. Here, Gertz (P) was not publicly involved. The public figure question should look to the nature and extent of an individual's participation in the controversy giving rise to the action. Reversed as the jury was allowed to impose liability without fault and presume damages without proof of damages.

DISSENT: (Brennan, J.) "We strike the proper accommodation between avoidance of media self-censorship and protection of individual reputations only when we require states to apply the *Times*' 'knowing-or-reckless falsity' standard in civil libel actions concerning media reports of the involvement of private individuals in events of public or general interest."

DISSENT: (White, J.) Federalizing major aspects of libel law is a radical change and a severe invasion of the prerogatives of the states not shown to be necessitated by present circumstances or required by the First Amendment. Neither *New York Times* nor the First Amendment should deprive this private citizen of his historic recourse to redress damaging falsehoods. The risk of falsehood here is shifted to the victim. While a statement may be wholly false, wrong and unjustified, a defamation case will be dismissed if the victim cannot prove negligence or other fault.

▶ **ANALYSIS**

The majority advances the view that it is necessary to restrict victims of defamation who do not prove knowledge of falsity or reckless disregard for the truth to compensation for actual injury alone. Actual injury is not limited to

Continued on next page.

out-of-pocket loss. Actual harm includes impairment of reputation and standing in the community, personal humiliation, and mental anguish and suffering. While the court noted the fact that juries in the past were tempted to award excess damages, there was no proof trial judges have failed to keep judgments within reasonable bounds.

■==■

Quicknotes

DEFAMATION An intentional false publication, communicated publicly in either oral or written form, subjecting a person to scorn, hatred or ridicule, or injuring him in relation to his occupation or business.

JUDGMENT NOTWITHSTANDING THE VERDICT A judgment entered by the trial judge reversing a jury verdict if the jury's determination has no basis in law or fact.

PUNITIVE DAMAGES Damages exceeding the actual injury suffered for the purposes of punishment of the defendant, deterrence of the wrongful behavior or comfort to the plaintiff.

■==■

Bartnicki v. Vopper

Cell phone user (P) v. Radio commentator (D)

532 U.S. 514 (2001).

NATURE OF CASE: Appeal from decision that provisions of federal anti-wiretapping laws that prohibit disclosure of illegally intercepted communications violate the First Amendment when applied to disclosures relating to matters of public concern.

FACT SUMMARY: The cell phone conversation between two union representatives, Bartnicki (P) and Kane (P) was illegally intercepted and recorded during a period of collective-bargaining negotiations in which the union representatives were involved. Vopper (D), a radio commentator, played a tape of the intercepted conversation on his radio show in connection with news reports about the settlement. Bartnicki (P) and Kane (P) filed suit for damages, alleging, among other things, that Vopper (D) and others had repeatedly published the conversation even though they knew or had reason to know that it had been illegally intercepted. Vopper (D) claimed that the disclosures were protected by the First Amendment.

🏛 RULE OF LAW
Provisions of anti-wiretapping laws that prohibit disclosure of illegally intercepted communications violate the First Amendment when applied to disclosures of information that has been legally obtained from the intercepting party and that relates to matters of public concern.

FACTS: An unidentified person intercepted and recorded a cell phone conversation between Bartnicki (P), the chief negotiator for a local teacher's union, and Kane (P), the union president. In the conversation, Bartnicki (P) threatened violence (at least as a matter of speaking) if the union's demands were not met. After the parties accepted a proposal favorable to the teachers, Vopper (D), a radio commentator, played a tape of the intercepted conversation on his show in connection with news reports about the settlement. Vopper (D), however, had nothing to do with the interception and did not know who the responsible party was. Also, the tapes themselves had been obtained legally. Bartnicki (P) and Kane (P) filed a damages suit under federal wiretapping laws, which, under § 2511(1)(a) prohibited intercepting cell phone calls, and under § 2511(1)(c) prohibited disclosure of the contents of any illegally intercepted material. The Supreme Court granted review on appeal.

ISSUE: Do provisions of anti-wiretapping laws that prohibit disclosure of illegally intercepted communications violate the First Amendment when applied to disclosures of information that has been legally obtained from the intercepting party and that relates to matters of public concern?

HOLDING AND DECISION: (Stevens, J.) Yes. Provisions of anti-wiretapping laws that prohibit disclosure of illegally intercepted communications violate the First Amendment when applied to disclosures of information that has been legally obtained from the intercepting party and that relates to matters of public concern. First, the Court accepts Vopper's (D) assertion that he played no part in the illegal interception, that his access to the information was obtained lawfully, and that the conversations dealt with a matter of public concern. Generally, state action that punishes the publication of truthful information is usually unconstitutional. The issue here is whether a publisher of information who has obtained the information in a lawful manner from someone who has obtained it unlawfully may be punished for the ensuing publication. The government's first asserted interest served by the statute—removing an incentive for parties to intercept private conversations—does not justify applying the statute to an otherwise innocent disclosure of public information. The normal method of deterring unlawful conduct is to punish the person engaging in it. It would be remarkable to hold that speech by a law-abiding possessor of information can be suppressed in order to deter conduct by a non-law-abiding third party. The Government's second interest—minimizing the harm to persons whose conversations have been illegally intercepted—is considerably stronger. Privacy of communication is an important interest. However, in this suit, privacy concerns give way when balanced against the interest in publishing matters of public importance. One of the costs associated with participation in public affairs is an attendant loss of privacy. It is clear that a stranger's illegal conduct does not suffice to remove the First Amendment shield from speech about a matter of public concern. Affirmed.

CONCURRENCE: (Breyer, J.) The Court's holding is limited to the particular facts of this case and does not extend beyond these present circumstances. These facts are that (1) the broadcasters acted lawfully up to the time of final disclosure; and (2) the information involved a matter of unusual public concern—a threat of potential physical harm to others.

DISSENT: (Rehnquist, C.J.) In an attempt to prevent egregious violations of privacy, the federal and state governments have enacted laws prohibiting the intentional interception and knowing disclosure of electronic communications. The majority holds that all of these statutes violate the First Amendment insofar as the illegally inter-

Continued on next page.

cepted conversation touches upon a matter of "public concern," a concept the majority does not even attempt to define. But the majority's decision diminishes, rather than enhances, the purposes of the First Amendment, and chills the speech of the millions of Americans who rely upon electronic technology to communicate. The statutes are content neutral, applying only to illegally obtained information. It is hard to imagine a more narrowly tailored prohibition of the disclosure of illegally intercepted communications, and, therefore, it goes contrary to precedent to review these laws under strict scrutiny. These laws should be upheld under intermediate scrutiny because they further the substantial government interest in protecting privacy; the Constitution should not be used to protect the involuntary disclosure of private conversations.

▶ ANALYSIS

The issue in this case was one of first impression and enabled the Court to expand its jurisprudence in this area. Before this case, the Court had held that the First Amendment prevents liability for public disclosure of private facts if the information was lawfully obtained from public records, unless there was a state interest of the "highest order" justifying liability. The result in this case can be explained by the majority's emphasis on the relatively "public" nature of the communication involved, which consequently did not rise to the "highest order" that a purely private communication would have risen to.

Quicknotes

COLLECTIVE BARGAINING Negotiations between an employer and employee that are mediated by a specified third party.

FIRST AMENDMENT Prohibits Congress from enacting any law respecting an establishment of religion, prohibiting the free exercise of religion, abridging freedom of speech or the press, the right of peaceful assembly and the right to petition for a redress of grievances.

Hustler Magazine v. Falwell

Magazine publisher (D) v. Minister (P)

485 U.S. 46 (1988).

NATURE OF CASE: Review of a diversity action alleging invasion of privacy, libel, and intentional infliction of emotional distress.

FACT SUMMARY: Jury ruled in favor of Falwell (P) on intentional infliction of emotional distress claim.

RULE OF LAW

Recovery for the tort of intentional infliction of emotional distress must meet the *New York Times* standard.

FACTS: Hustler Magazine (D) published a parody of a Campari Liqueur ad featuring Jerry Falwell (P), a nationally known minister. The parody was a play on a Campari ad campaign that featured interviews with celebrities about their "first time" partaking of Campari Liqueur. The "first time" nature of the ad campaign had strong sexual undertones. The caption on the Hustler Magazine (D) fictional ad read: "Jerry Falwell talks about his first time." The ad went on to detail a fictional interview with Jerry Falwell (P) in which he states that his "first time" was during a drunken incestuous rendezvous with his mother in an outhouse. In small print on the bottom of the page, the ad contained the disclaimer "ad parody—not to be taken seriously." The magazine's (D) table of contents also listed the ad as "Fiction; Ad and Personality Parody." Following publication of this ad, Falwell (P) brought this diversity action alleging invasion of privacy, libel and intentional infliction of emotional distress.

ISSUE: May public figures and public officials recover for the tort of intentional infliction of emotional distress by reason of publications such as the one at issue here?

HOLDING AND DECISION: (Rehnquist, C.J.) Yes, but only if the public figure or public official can demonstrate that the publication contains a false statement of fact that was made with "actual malice." The *New York Times* standard, 376 U.S. 254 (1964), as applied in this area reflects a First Amendment limitation upon a state's authority to protect its citizens from intentional infliction of emotional distress. Reversed.

▶ ANALYSIS

The *Hustler Magazine* decision upholds the right and prerogative of the American citizenry to criticize public figures and measures.

Quicknotes

ACTUAL MALICE The issuance of a publication with knowledge of its falsity or with reckless disregard as to its truth.

DEFAMATION An intentional false publication, communicated publicly in either oral or written form, subjecting a person to scorn, hatred or ridicule, or injuring him in relation to his occupation or business.

Snyder v. Phelps

Parent of slain soldier (P) v. Funeral picketer (D)

131 S. Ct. 1207 (2011).

NATURE OF CASE: Appeal by defendants from conviction in action asserting tort claims based on the defendants' speech, which the defendants claim is protected by the First Amendment as public speech. [The complete procedural posture of the case is not presented in the casebook extract.]

FACT SUMMARY: Members of the Westboro Baptist Church (Westboro) (D) contended that they could not be held liable in tort for picketing a soldier's funeral because any tort liability would be based on their speech, which, they contended, was public speech and protected by the First Amendment.

🏛 RULE OF LAW
Speech that can fairly be characterized as public speech is shielded by the First Amendment from tort liability, notwithstanding the speech is found by a jury to be "outrageous," where the speaker is on public land and conforms to local time and place restrictions.

FACTS: For over 20 years, the congregation of the Westboro Baptist Church (Westboro) (D) picketed military funerals to communicate its belief God hates the United States for its tolerance of homosexuality, particularly in the military. Westboro's (D) picketing also condemned the Catholic Church for scandals involving its clergy. Members of Westboro (D) picketed the funeral of Matthew Snyder, a soldier killed in the line of duty. The picketing took place on public land approximately 1,000 feet from the church where the funeral was held, in accordance with guidance from local law enforcement officers. The picketers peacefully displayed their signs, which stated, e.g., "Thank God for Dead Soldiers," "Fags Doom Nations," "America is Doomed," "Priests Rape Boys," and "You're Going to Hell." They did so for about 30 minutes before the funeral began. Matthew Snyder's father (Snyder) (P), who saw the tops of the signs, brought suit against Westboro (D), alleging state tort claims of intentional infliction of emotional distress, civil conspiracy, and intrusion upon seclusion. A jury, finding that Westboro's (D) conduct was "outrageous," held Westboro (D) liable for $2.9 million in compensatory damages, and for $8 million in punitive damages. The district court reduced the punitive damages award, but left the verdict otherwise intact. The Supreme Court granted certiorari. [The complete procedural posture of the case is not presented in the casebook extract.]

ISSUE: Is speech that can fairly be characterized as public speech shielded by the First Amendment from tort

liability, notwithstanding the speech is found by a jury to be "outrageous," where the speaker is on public land and conforms to local time and place restrictions?

HOLDING AND DECISION: (Roberts, C.J.) Yes. Speech that can fairly be characterized as public speech is shielded by the First Amendment from tort liability, notwithstanding the speech is found by a jury to be "outrageous," where the speaker is on public land and conforms to local time and place restrictions. Whether the First Amendment prohibits holding Westboro (D) liable for its speech in this case turns largely on whether that speech is of public or private concern, as determined by all the circumstances of the case, including its content, form, and context. Speech on public issues occupies the highest rung of the hierarchy of First Amendment values and is entitled to special protection. Although the boundaries of what constitutes speech on matters of public concern are not well defined, speech is of public concern when it can be fairly considered as relating to any matter of political, social, or other concern to the community, or when it is a subject of general interest and of value and concern to the public. Here, the "content" of Westboro's (D) signs plainly relates to public, rather than private, matters. The placards highlighted issues of public import—the political and moral conduct of the United States and its citizens, the fate of the Nation, homosexuality in the military, and scandals involving the Catholic clergy—and Westboro (D) conveyed its views on those issues in a manner designed to reach as broad a public audience as possible. The "context" of the speech—its connection with Matthew Snyder's funeral—cannot by itself transform the nature of Westboro's (D) speech, as the signs reflected Westboro's (D) condemnation of much in modern society, and the funeral setting does not change that conclusion. Moreover, the picketing was conducted on a public space, adjacent to a public street, which is the archetype of a public forum. While protected public speech is not beyond reasonable, content-neutral time, place and manner restrictions, Westboro's (D) conduct here complied with such restrictions. Any distress occasioned by Westboro's (D) picketing turned on the content and viewpoint of the message conveyed, rather than any interference with the funeral itself. Such speech cannot be restricted simply because it is upsetting or arouses contempt; it is a bedrock principle of First Amendment law that the government may not prohibit the expression of an idea simply because society finds the idea itself offensive or disagreeable. The special protection afforded to what Westboro (D) said, in the whole context

Continued on next page.

of how and where it chose to say it, cannot be overcome by a jury finding that the picketing was "outrageous" for purposes of applying the state law tort of intentional infliction of emotional distress, especially given that "outrageousness" is a highly malleable standard with an inherent subjectiveness about it that would pose too great a danger the jury would punish Westboro (D) for its views on matters of public concern. Such a risk is unacceptable, since in public debate we must tolerate insulting, and even outrageous, speech so sufficient breathing room can be afforded to the freedoms protected by the First Amendment. For all these reasons, Westboro (D) must be shielded in this case from tort liability for its speech, and the jury verdict imposing tort liability on Westboro (D) for intentional infliction of emotional distress must be set aside. [The procedural outcome of the case is not presented in the casebook extract.]

CONCURRENCE: (Breyer, J.) A state can sometimes regulate picketing on matters of public concern, depending on all the circumstances. Here, the majority is correct in holding that in light of those circumstances, Westboro's (D) means of communicating was lawful and in compliance with all police directions. Therefore, under such circumstances, to allow the application of state tort law against Westboro (D) would punish Westboro (D) for seeking to communicate its views on matters of public concern without proportionately advancing the state's interest in protecting its citizens against severe emotional harm.

DISSENT: (Alito, J.) The First Amendment does not protect the vicious speech made by Westboro (D) at Matthew Snyder's funeral that inflicted severe and lasting emotional injury. The profound national commitment to free and open debate permits Westboro (D) to express itself in countless other ways, but it does not protect Westboro's (D) right to brutalize Snyder (P). Westboro (D) may not intentionally inflict severe emotional injury on private persons at a time of intense emotional sensitivity by launching vicious verbal attacks that make no contribution to public debate. The Court has recognized the First Amendment does not protect words that by their very utterance inflict injury and are of inconsequential social value. Notwithstanding that Westboro (D) could have delivered its message in countless other venues, it chose to conduct its brutal attack in a manner that would garner the most public attention—by inflicting the greatest amount of emotional injury and media attention. The attack on Matthew Snyder was personal, as it attacked him because he was a Catholic and a member of the military. Because Matthew and his father are not public figures, the attack on them was not one of public concern. The Court now compounds Snyder's (P) injury; it is not necessary to allow the brutalization of innocent victims in order to have a society in which public issues can be openly and vigorously debated.

ANALYSIS

In the majority opinion, Chief Justice Roberts indicates Maryland now has a law restricting funeral picketing, but reasons because that law was not in effect at the time of Westboro's (D) picketing, the Court has no occasion to consider whether that law is a reasonable time, place, or manner restriction under the standards announced by the Court. Justice Alito, in his dissent, remarks it is doubtful that the wounds inflicted by vicious verbal assaults at funerals will be prevented or at least mitigated in the future by new laws, such as Maryland's, that restrict picketing within a specified distance of a funeral. Justice Alito concludes the enactment of these laws is no substitute for the protection provided by the established intentional infliction of emotional distress (IIED) tort, since, according to the majority, Westboro's (D) speech in this case would have complied with the new Maryland law regulating funeral picketing, and since there is absolutely nothing to suggest Congress and the state legislatures, in enacting these laws, intended them to displace the protection provided by the well-established IIED tort.

Quicknotes

CONTENT BASED Refers to statutes that regulate speech based on its content.

FIRST AMENDMENT Prohibits Congress from enacting any law respecting an establishment of religion, prohibiting the free exercise of religion, abridging freedom of speech or the press, the right of peaceful assembly and the right to petition for a redress of grievances.

United States v. Alvarez

Federal government (P) v. Convicted violator of the Stolen Valor Act (D)

132 S. Ct. 2537 (2012).

NATURE OF CASE: Appeal from reversal of conviction for violation of the Stolen Valor Act, 18 U.S.C. §§ 704 (b), (c).

FACT SUMMARY: Alvarez (D), who was convicted of violating the Stolen Valor Act (the "Act"), 18 U.S.C. §§ 704 (b), (c), based on his having made false statements about his having served in the military and receiving the Congressional Medal of Honor, contended the Act unconstitutionally criminalized his speech in violation of the First Amendment.

🏛 RULE OF LAW

A statute that criminalizes the making of false statements regarding military decorations or medals, including the Congressional Medal of Honor, violates the First Amendment as a content-based suppression of pure speech.

FACTS: The Stolen Valor Act (the "Act"), 18 U.S.C. §§ 704 (b), (c), made it a crime to falsely claim receipt of military decorations or medals and provided an enhanced penalty if the Congressional Medal of Honor was involved. Alvarez (D), a member of a water district board, falsely stated at a meeting of the board that he had served in the marines, had been wounded in combat, and had received the Congressional Medal of Honor. Alvarez (D) pleaded guilty to a charge of falsely claiming he had received the Medal of Honor, in violation of the Act, but reserved his right to appeal his claim the Act was unconstitutional as a content-based suppression of pure speech. The court of appeals, agreeing with Alvarez (D), reversed, and the Supreme Court granted certiorari.

ISSUE: Does a statute that criminalizes the making of false statements regarding military decorations or medals, including the Congressional Medal of Honor, violate the First Amendment as a content-based suppression of pure speech?

HOLDING AND DECISION: (Kennedy, J.) Yes. A statute that criminalizes the making of false statements regarding military decorations or medals, including the Congressional Medal of Honor, violates the First Amendment as a content-based suppression of pure speech. Content-based restrictions on speech have been permitted only for a few historic categories of speech, including incitement, obscenity, defamation, speech integral to criminal conduct, so-called "fighting words," child pornography, fraud, true threats, and speech presenting some grave and imminent threat the government has the power to prevent. The making of false statements is not among

these. The Government (P) argues precedent supports its claim that false statements have no value and hence no First Amendment protection. However, the Government (P) relies on cases discussing defamation, fraud, or some other legally cognizable harm associated with a false statement. These prior decisions have not confronted a measure, like the Stolen Valor Act, that targets falsity and nothing more. The Act seeks to control and suppress all false statements on this one subject in almost limitless times and settings without regard to whether the lie was made for the purpose of material gain. Permitting the Government (P) to decree this speech to be a criminal offense would endorse government authority to compile a list of subjects about which false statements are punishable. That governmental power has no clear limiting principle, and even the mere threat of such power chills free speech, thought and discourse. Moreover, the governmental interests served by the Act, while not insignificant, do not survive exacting scrutiny. While military medals serve the purposes of expressing public gratitude for acts of heroism and sacrifice, and fostering morale and esprit de corps among military members, the Government (P) has failed to show, and cannot show, why counterspeech, such as the outrage and contempt directed at Alvarez (D) for his lies, would not suffice to achieve its interest. In fact, such counterspeech might reawaken and reinforce the public's respect for the Medal and its recipients. Ultimately, the remedy for speech that is false is speech that is true, and governmental suppression of speech can make the exposure of falsity more difficult, not less so. Even if most find Alvarez's (D) statements contemptible, his right to make those statements is protected by the First Amendment. Affirmed.

CONCURRENCE: (Breyer, J.) Because the Stolen Valor Act works disproportionate constitutional harm, it fails intermediate scrutiny, and thus violates the First Amendment. In determining whether a statute violates the First Amendment, the Court has often found it appropriate to examine the fit between statutory ends and means, taking into account the seriousness of the speech-related harm the provision will likely cause, the nature and importance of the provision's countervailing objectives, the extent to which the statute will tend to achieve those objectives, and whether there are other, less restrictive alternatives. "Intermediate scrutiny" describes this approach. Since false factual statements are less likely than true factual statements to make a valuable contribution to

Continued on next page.

the marketplace of ideas, and the government often has good reason to prohibit such false speech, but its regulation can threaten speech-related harm, such an approach should be applied here. Although the Court has frequently said or implied false factual statements enjoy little First Amendment protection, those statements cannot be read to mean "no protection at all." False factual statements serve useful human objectives in many contexts. Moreover, the threat of criminal prosecution for making a false statement can inhibit the speaker from making true statements, thereby chilling a kind of speech that lies at the First Amendment's heart. Further, the pervasiveness of false factual statements provides a weapon to a government broadly empowered to prosecute falsity without more. Those who are unpopular may fear government will use that weapon selectively against them. Here, the Act ranges broadly, and that breadth means it creates a significant risk of First Amendment harm. The Act nonetheless has substantial justification. It seeks to protect the interests of those who have sacrificed their health and life for their country by seeking to preserve intact the country's recognition of that sacrifice in the form of military honors. Permitting those who have not earned those honors to claim otherwise dilutes the value of these awards. Accordingly, it must be determined whether the Government's (P) objectives may be achieved in a less constitutionally burdensome way. Although the First Amendment risks flowing from the Act's breadth of coverage could be diminished or eliminated by a more finely tailored statute, the Act as currently drafted works disproportionate harm.

DISSENT: (Alito, J.) Free speech does not protect false factual statements that inflict real harm and serve no legitimate interest. The Act is limited in five significant respects. First, the Act applies to only a narrow category of false representations about objective facts that can almost always be proved or disproved with near certainty. Second, the Act concerns facts that are squarely within the speaker's personal knowledge. Third, a conviction under the Act requires proof beyond a reasonable doubt the speaker actually knew that the representation was false. Fourth, the Act applies only to statements that could reasonably be interpreted as communicating actual facts; it does not reach dramatic performances, satire, parody, hyperbole, or the like. Fifth, the Act is strictly viewpoint neutral. Further, the Act is aimed at conduct that inflicts actual harm, much of which is tangible, since many of those who lie about having received military awards do so to obtain financial or other material awards, such as lucrative contracts or government benefits. While the harm to deserving medal recipients and their families is less tangible, it is nevertheless substantial. Contrary to the plurality's assertion, this harm cannot be remedied by counterspeech, since a database of all actual award recipients would, as a result of practical constraints, be incomplete. Nor would this harm be remedied by a more finely tuned statute that insists on showing actual harm, since much of the damage

inflicted by those who lie about having received military honors is inflicted on real award recipients and the system of military awards, without any linkage to any financial or other tangible reward. The Court has repeatedly recognized that, generally, false factual statements have no intrinsic First Amendment value, and has held that many kinds of such statements are not entitled to First Amendment protection, e.g., fraud, defamation, perjury, etc. While protection to lies has been afforded in those instances where there is a risk truthful speech will be suppressed—e.g., lies about philosophy, religion, history, and other matters of public concern—the Act poses no risk valuable speech will be suppressed. The speech punished by the Act is verifiably false and lacks any intrinsic value. Such speech also fails to serve any purpose that the First Amendment might protect.

▶ ANALYSIS

The decision in this case was rendered by a fragmented plurality, rather than by a majority, and this reflects the fact this case did not categorically resolve the question of how the First Amendment should treat factual lies. Justice Kennedy applied a strict scrutiny approach to what he characterized as a content-based restriction. Justice Breyer applied a balancing approach under intermediate scrutiny without even mentioning the content-based nature of the Act. And Justice Alito, who also barely alluded to the content-based nature of the Act, focused on the fact the statute was limited to knowingly false statements of facts that are directly within the personal knowledge of the speaker. This doctrinal incoherence seems to suggest that, at least for now, and possibly going forward, there may not be a categorical answer to the key issue presented by *Alvarez*. Instead, it seems that how certain factual lies will be treated under the First Amendment will vary, on a case-by-case basis, depending on the content of the lies, the context in which they are made, and the type of injury they cause.

Quicknotes

BALANCING TEST A court's balancing of an individual's constitutional rights against the state's right to protect its citizens.

CONTENT BASED Refers to statutes that regulate speech based on its content.

FIRST AMENDMENT Prohibits Congress from enacting any law respecting an establishment of religion, prohibiting the free exercise of religion, abridging freedom of speech or the press, the right of peaceful assembly and the right to petition for a redress of grievances.

Roth v. United States; Alberts v. California

Publisher (D) v. Federal government (P)

354 U.S. 476 (1957).

NATURE OF CASE: Constitutional review of obscenity statutes.

FACT SUMMARY: Two defendants were convicted under obscenity statutes for selling obscene material. Roth (D) was convicted under a federal statute, Alberts (D) under a state statute.

RULE OF LAW
Obscenity is not a constitutionally protected expression and if the material, taken as a whole, has a dominant theme that appeals to prurient interest as judged by contemporary community standards, it may be proscribed.

FACTS: Roth (D) was a publisher and seller of books, magazines, and photographs. He was convicted under a federal statute for mailing obscene circulars and advertising and an obscene book. Alberts (D) was convicted under a California (P) statute that prohibited the keeping for sale of obscene and indecent books or the writing, composing, and publishing of an obscene advertisement therefor.

ISSUE: Is obscenity a constitutionally protected expression?

HOLDING AND DECISION: (Brennan, J.) No. Obscenity is not a constitutionally protected expression and if the material, taken as a whole, has a dominant theme that appeals to prurient interest as judged by contemporary community standards, it may be proscribed. The apparently unconditional phrasing of the First Amendment has been held by this Court not to protect every utterance. However, all ideas having even the slightest degree of socially redeeming value are fully protected unless they encroach upon the limited areas of more important interests. Obscenity has been held to carry no socially redeeming value and is, therefore, outside the protection of the First Amendment. A properly drawn and enforced statute outlawing obscenity will withstand the test of constitutionality. The portrayal of sex is not obscenity per se, as is evidenced by the large range of classic presentations in art, literature, and scientific works. Any attempt to proscribe obscenity must clearly define that which is prohibited. A work must be judged in its entirety, not by selected portions since many valuable and socially important materials could thereby be suppressed. The test should be, whether to the average person, applying contemporary community standards, the dominant theme of the material, taken as a whole, appeals to prurient interest. The words of this standard are sufficiently clear to give notice as to what is, or is not, permissible conduct. Both defendants were convicted under statutes applying the stated standard and both convictions are affirmed.

DISSENT: (Douglas, J.) The First Amendment is expressed in absolute terms and any law that purports to regulate material that can only produce thoughts is a clearly impermissible encroachment on these absolute guarantees. While the state and federal governments can regulate conduct, they should not be allowed to regulate the thought that precedes the conduct.

ANALYSIS

The purported standard of the *Roth* case soon became a thorn in the side of the Court. As Justice Harlan had predicted, the Court was reduced to a case-by-case review of obscenity convictions. In each case, the Court was forced to make a factual analysis of the material to determine if it was obscene. This despite the fact the same determination had already been made in every lower court. The one clarification of the *Roth* standard came in *Jacobellis v. Ohio,* 378 U.S. 184 (1964). In that case, a split Court stated the "community standard" was a national standard since a national constitution was being applied. The other noteworthy concept to come from that case was from Justice Stewart. He stated that the Court was attempting to deal with "hard core" pornography. While he admitted he could not define that term, he stated he knew it when he saw it, and the motion picture involved in that case was not it.

Quicknotes

OBSCENITY Actions that corrupt the public morals through their indecency.

PRURIENT Refers to the shameful and morbid interest in nudity or sex.

Miller v. California

Bookseller (D) v. State (P)

413 U.S. 15 (1973).

NATURE OF CASE: Certiorari review of criminal prosecution for knowingly distributing obscene matter.

FACT SUMMARY: Miller (D) sent out advertising brochures for adult books to unwilling recipients.

🏛 RULE OF LAW
Material is obscene and not protected by the First Amendment if: (1) the average person, applying contemporary community standards, would find that the work, taken as a whole, appeals to the prurient interest; (2) the work depicts in a patently offensive way sexual conduct specifically defined by the applicable state law; and (3) the work, taken as a whole, lacks serious literary, artistic, political, or scientific value.

FACTS: Miller (D) conducted a mass mailing campaign to advertise the sale of adult books. The advertising brochures were themselves found obscene. These brochures were sent to unwilling recipients who had not requested the material. Miller (D) was convicted of violating a statute that forbade knowingly distributing obscene matter.

ISSUE: Is material obscene and not protected by the First Amendment if: (1) the average person, applying contemporary community standards, would find that the work, taken as a whole, appeals to the prurient interest; (2) the work depicts in a patently offensive way sexual conduct specifically defined by the applicable state law; and (3) the work, taken as a whole, lacks serious literary, artistic, political, or scientific value?

HOLDING AND DECISION: (Burger, C.J.) Yes. Material is obscene and not protected by the First Amendment if: (1) the average person, applying contemporary community standards, would find that the work, taken as a whole, appeals to the prurient interest; (2) the work depicts in a patently offensive way sexual conduct specifically defined by the applicable state law; and (3) the work, taken as a whole, lacks serious literary, artistic, political or scientific value. If material meets this definition of obscenity, then the state can prohibit its distribution if the mode of distribution entails the risk of offending unwilling recipients or exposing the material to juveniles. The burden of proof of the *Memoirs* test, 383 U.S. 413 (1966), that the material be utterly without redeeming value, is virtually impossible for the prosecution to meet and must be abandoned. There is no fixed national standard of "prurient interest" or "patently offensive" and these first two parts of the test are questions of fact to be resolved by the jury by

applying contemporary community standards. Vacated and remanded.

DISSENT: (Douglas, J.) The test put forth by the majority offers no guidelines for defining obscenity. "Offensive" is so vague as to completely destroy the protection of the First Amendment.

DISSENT: (Brennan, J.) The statute in question is unconstitutionally overbroad and therefore invalid on its face.

▶ ANALYSIS

The *Miller* test of obscenity is the most current test. If the three requirements are met, then the material in question is considered obscene and outside the protection of the First Amendment. *Miller* is a turnaround from *Memoirs*, 383 U.S. 413 (1966), for many reasons: the *Memoirs* standard was too difficult to prove: the lower courts had no clear-cut guidelines because *Memoirs* was a plurality opinion; the Court decided to use local community standards to allow greater jury power; and the Court was beginning to feel institutional pressures, since every obscenity question was a constitutional question. Therefore, *Miller* was an attempt by the Court to decentralize decisionmaking.

Quicknotes

BURDEN OF PROOF The duty of a party to introduce evidence to support a fact that is in dispute in an action.

OBSCENITY Conduct tending to corrupt the public morals by its indecency or lewdness.

OVERBROAD Refers to a statute that proscribes lawful as well as unlawful conduct.

PRURIENT Refers to the shameful and morbid interest in nudity or sex.

Paris Adult Theatre I v. Slaton

Movie theatres (D) v. State (P)

413 U.S. 49 (1973).

NATURE OF CASE: Certiorari review of state statute prohibiting showing of sexually explicit films.

FACT SUMMARY: Two adult films were shown at theatres (D) that advertised the nature of the films and required proof that all patrons were over 21.

🏛 RULE OF LAW
A state can forbid the dissemination of obscene material to consenting adults in order to preserve the quality of the community and to prevent the possibility of resulting antisocial behavior.

FACTS: Two movie theatres (D) in Atlanta showed "adult" films exclusively. The State of Georgia (P) sought to enjoin the showing of sexually explicit movies in these theatres under an obscenity statute. It was determined that the exterior advertising was not obscene or offensive, but that there were signs at the entrance stating that patrons must be 21 years of age and able to prove it. There was a further warning that those who would be offended by nudity should not enter. However, the films in question included, in addition to nudity, various simulated sex acts.

ISSUE: Can a state forbid the dissemination of obscene material to consenting adults in order to preserve the quality of the community and to prevent the possibility of resulting antisocial behavior?

HOLDING AND DECISION: (Burger, C.J.) Yes. A state can forbid the dissemination of obscene material to consenting adults in order to preserve the quality of the community and to prevent the possibility of resulting antisocial behavior. A state has a valid interest in preventing exposure of obscene material to consenting adults. Even if exposure to juveniles and unwilling observers is prevented, the state has a further interest in preserving the quality of life, the community environment, and possible threats to public safety, which will allow the regulation of obscenity. Even if there is no conclusive scientific proof that exposure to obscenity adversely affects either an individual or society, it is for the legislature, not the courts, to resolve these empirical uncertainties. A legislature can determine that a connection between obscenity and antisocial behavior exists, even in the absence of conclusive proof. Here, even though only consenting adults are involved, the state can make a judgment that public exhibition of obscenity has a tendency to injure the community and can, therefore, enjoin the distribution of obscenity. Vacated and remanded.

DISSENT: (Brennan, J.) Prior obscenity standards have proved unworkable because they fail to give adequate notice of the definition of obscenity, producing a chilling effect on constitutionally protected speech. Because of the vague nature of these standards, every case is marginal, producing a vast number of constitutional questions that creates institutional stress in the judicial system. States do have a valid interest in protecting children and unconsenting adults from exposure to allegedly obscene material, but other possible state interests, as discussed in the majority opinion, are vague, speculative, and cannot be proven. Therefore, in the absence of threat of exposure to juveniles or unconsenting adults, material cannot be suppressed, but the state can regulate the manner of distribution.

▶ ANALYSIS

The Court, in three companion cases to the principal case, also upheld obscenity convictions on seizures involving the importation of films from a foreign country, the interstate transportation of obscene materials for private use, and the sale of an obscene book that contained no pictures. In 1974, however, the Court overturned an obscenity conviction for the showing of "Carnal Knowledge," a film with an MPAA rating of "R." While asserting that the finding of obscenity was essentially a question of fact for the jury, the Court warned that the jury did not have an unbridled discretion in this area. In another case, the Court also stated that the community standard to be applied was local, not national. Justice Brennan dissented, arguing that requiring a national distributor to comply with numerous local standards was totally unreasonable.

━━━

Quicknotes

CHILLING EFFECT Resulting in the inhibition or restriction of an activity.

OBSCENITY Actions that corrupt the public morals through their indecency.

━━━

American Booksellers Assn. v. Hudnut

Book publishers association (P) v. Municipality (D)

771 F.2d 323 (7th Cir. 1985), *aff'd mem.*, 475 U.S. 1001 (1986).

NATURE OF CASE: Appeal from decision invalidating municipal ordinance.

FACT SUMMARY: Hudnut (D) appealed from a decision finding an Indianapolis municipal statute defining pornography in violation of the First Amendment since it discriminated on the basis of the content of speech.

🏛 RULE OF LAW
Ordinances that discriminate on the basis of the content of speech are unconstitutional in violation of the First Amendment.

FACTS: Indianapolis enacted a municipal statute defining pornography as a practice that discriminates against women and that could be redressed through the administrative and judicial methods used for other discrimination. More specifically, the statute defines pornography as the graphic sexually explicit subordination of women, whether in pictures or in words, and listed a number of examples that would qualify as pornography. The American Booksellers Association, Inc. (P) brought suit, contending that the ordinance was unconstitutional in that it discriminated on the basis of the content of speech. The district court agreed, and from this decision, Hudnut (D) appealed.

ISSUE: Are ordinances that discriminate on the basis of the content of speech unconstitutional in violation of the First Amendment?

HOLDING AND DECISION: (Easterbrook, J.) Yes. Ordinances that discriminate on the basis of the content of speech are unconstitutional in violation of the First Amendment. There is no question that the ordinance in question in the present case operates in this manner. The City (D) has determined what it considers the appropriate way in which to portray women. Speech that portrays women in positions of equality is allowed, and that which portrays women in positions of subservience is not, regardless of literary or artistic value. This is simply thought control, which cannot be tolerated. Even accepting the premises of the legislation, that pornographic materials, as defined, tend to perpetuate the subordination of women, this ordinance cannot stand. The fact that such speech would tend to perpetuate subordination illustrates its power as speech, and the cornerstone of our society is that our citizens have the absolute right to propagate opinions that our government finds wrongful, or even hateful. Speech is protected regardless of how insidious. This definition of pornography is unconstitutional. Affirmed.

▶ ANALYSIS

This decision was affirmed upon appeal to the Supreme Court. Three justices of the Court would have set the case for oral arguments. The Court makes it quite clear that regulations on the content of speech, unless proper time, place, and manner restrictions are delineated, will not withstand constitutional challenge.

■■■■

Quicknotes

CONTENT-BASED Refers to statutes that regulate speech based on its content.

■■■■

Erznoznik v. Jacksonville

Drive-in movie theater manager (P) v. Municipality (D)

422 U.S. 205 (1975).

NATURE OF CASE: Appeal from judgment upholding, as not violative of the First Amendment, an ordinance prohibiting drive-in movie theaters with screens visible from a public street from showing films containing nudity. [The complete procedural posture of the case is not presented in the casebook extract.]

FACT SUMMARY: Erznoznik (P) challenged, as violating the First Amendment, Jacksonville's (D) ordinance prohibiting drive-in movie theaters with screens visible from the street from showing films containing nudity.

RULE OF LAW
An ordinance that prohibits drive-in movie theaters with screens visible from public streets from showing nonobscene films containing nudity is facially invalid under the First Amendment.

FACTS: Erznoznik (P) challenged, as violating the First Amendment, Jacksonville's (D) ordinance prohibiting drive-in movie theaters with screens visible from a public street from showing films containing nudity. Exhibiting nudity was defined to include exhibiting the human male or female bare buttocks, human female bare breasts, or human bare pubic areas. Jacksonville (D) conceded the ordinance applied to nonobscene movies. Jacksonville's (D) primary argument was it had the right to protect its citizens against unwilling exposure to materials that might be offensive. The ordinance was judicially upheld. The Supreme Court granted certiorari. [The procedural posture of the case is not presented in the casebook extract.]

ISSUE: Is an ordinance that prohibits drive-in movie theaters with screens visible from public streets from showing nonobscene films containing nudity facially invalid under the First Amendment?

HOLDING AND DECISION: (Powell, J.) Yes. An ordinance that prohibits drive-in movie theaters with screens visible from public streets from showing nonobscene films containing nudity is facially invalid under the First Amendment. Although a state or municipality may protect individual privacy by enacting reasonable time, place and manner regulations applicable to all speech irrespective of content, the First Amendment strictly limits its power when it acts as censor, undertaking selectively to shield the public from some kinds of speech on the ground they are more offensive than others. However, such censorship has been upheld only if the speech invades the privacy of the home, or the viewer cannot readily avoid exposure to it. In our pluralistic society, absent these narrow circum-

stances, the burden falls on the viewer to avoid exposure to the speech the viewer finds offensive. Applying these principles here, the Jacksonville (D) ordinance discriminates among movies solely on the basis of content, and it deters drive-ins from showing movies containing any nudity, no matter how innocent or educational. Viewers who happen to be on public streets and places can readily avert their eyes, because drive-in theater screens are not so obtrusive as to make viewers a captive audience. Thus, such censorship of the content of otherwise protected speech cannot be justified on the basis of the limited privacy interest of persons on the public streets. The ordinance also cannot be justified as an exercise of the city's police power for the protection of children against viewing the films. Even assuming such is its purpose, the restriction is broader than permissible since it is not directed against obscene, sexually explicit nudity or otherwise limited. Nor can the ordinance be justified as a traffic regulation. If this were its purpose, it would be invalid as a strikingly underinclusive legislative classification since it singles out movies containing nudity from all other movies that might distract a passing motorist. For these reasons, the ordinance is facially invalid under the First Amendment; where First Amendment freedoms are at stake the precision of drafting and clarity of purpose are essential, and those elements are absent from the Jacksonville (D) ordinance. Reversed. [The complete procedural outcome of the case is not presented in the casebook extract.]

DISSENT: (Burger, C.J.) The majority's approach is rigidly simplistic and fails to account for the diverse interests at issue here. It is unrealistic to say, as does the majority, that a passerby can avert his or her eyes when confronted with the outsize screen of a drive-in movie theater. The purpose of these screens is to attract and hold the attention of all observers, and thus, it is not unreasonable for legislators to believe that public nudity shown on these screens might distract drivers who pass by, thus causing traffic accidents. Moreover, those individuals who desire to view the films that would be banned by the ordinance may do so in indoor theaters or in drive-in movie theaters, which are shielded from public view. The ordinance does not restrict any "message," and any First Amendment interests involved are trivial, at best. It is narrowly drawn to regulate only certain unique public exhibitions of nudity, and it does not operate to suppress expression of ideas.

Continued on next page.

▶ *ANALYSIS*

The Court's holding a total ban on the display of nudity violates the First Amendment was upheld in *Schad v. Mount Ephraim,* 452 U.S. 61 (1981), which held that live entertainment may not be prohibited merely because it displays the nude human figure. Accordingly, the Court in *Schad* struck down a zoning ordinance that banned all live entertainment in a commercial zone in an attempt to outlaw nude dancing.

■══■

Quicknotes

FIRST AMENDMENT Prohibits Congress from enacting any law respecting an establishment of religion, prohibiting the free exercise of religion, abridging freedom of speech or the press, the right of peaceful assembly and the right to petition for a redress of grievances.

■══■

Young v. American Mini Theatres, Inc.

City (D) v. Theatre owner (P)

427 U.S. 50 (1976).

NATURE OF CASE: Review of order enjoining zoning law enforcement.

FACT SUMMARY: After Detroit enacted a zoning ordinance prohibiting the operation of "adult" theatres within 1,000 feet of any two other "regulated use" establishments, which were those showing specified sexual acts and specified anatomical areas, American Mini Theatres, Inc. (P), owner of two offending theatres, sought an injunction against enforcement of the ordinance on free speech grounds.

RULE OF LAW
A zoning ordinance may validly place reasonable limits on locations where establishments displaying sexual conduct or sexual organs may be operated within a municipality without offending the First Amendment.

FACTS: A Detroit ordinance set forth a zoning requirement that any "regulated use" establishment must be located at least 1,000 feet away from any two other such establishments. "Regulated use" establishments were those which showed sexual conduct specified by the ordinance or anatomical areas also specified in the ordinance. American Mini Theatres, Inc. (American) (P) owned two theatres which violated the ordinance by being within 1,000 feet of two other "regulated use" establishments, and American (P) sought to enjoin the municipality from enforcing the law against them on the ground that such enforcement constituted a violation of American's (P) First Amendment right to free speech. The Supreme Court granted certiorari to review the court of appeal's grant of the injunction.

ISSUE: May a zoning ordinance validly place reasonable limits on locations where establishments displaying sexual conduct or sexual organs may be operated within a municipality without offending the First Amendment?

HOLDING AND DECISION: (Stevens, J.) Yes. American (P) urged that the ordinance in question failed to provide adequate procedures for waiver of the 1,000-foot requirement and thus the ordinance is too vague. American (P), however, falls within the law and is not entitled to a waiver under any construction of it. The interest of the government in exhibiting material on the borderline of pornography and artistic expression is less vital than that in disseminating political ideas, and the vagueness regarding the hypothetical applicability of the ordinance to the letter will not suffice to overturn it. The ordinance is furthermore not a prior restraint on protected expression. The 1,000-foot restriction does not prevent the operation of American's (P) theatres, but merely controls the locations of them. A zoning ordinance may validly place reasonable limits on locations where establishments displaying sexual conduct or organs may be operated within a municipality without offending the First Amendment. American (P) was not entitled to the injunction granted by the court of appeals. Reversed.

CONCURRENCE: (Powell, J.) This case is one of permissible land-use regulation and involves the First Amendment only incidentally. There is no restriction on the availability of adult movies. The ordinance is addressed only to the places at which this type of expression may be presented. This restriction does not interfere with content.

DISSENT: (Stewart, J.) The Court today permits a city to use a system of prior restraints and criminal sanctions to enforce a content-based restriction on the geographic location of theatres exhibiting sexually oriented films.

ANALYSIS

It seems that the Court is affording expressions of sexual content less First Amendment protection than other forms of expression, even in the absence of a finding of obscenity. As a content-based discrimination, this ordinance was subject to the constitutional argument presented here, but bolstered by the municipality's zoning power, it was nevertheless upheld.

Quicknotes

FIRST AMENDMENT Prohibits Congress from enacting any law respecting an establishment of religion, prohibiting the free exercise of religion, abridging freedom of speech or the press, the right of peaceful assembly and the right to petition for a redress of grievances.

PRIOR RESTRAINT A restriction imposed on speech prior to its communication.

ZONING ORDINANCE A statute that divides land into defined areas and which regulates the form and use of buildings and structures within those areas.

Renton v. Playtime Theatres, Inc.

Municipality (D) v. Adult movie theaters (P)

475 U.S. 41 (1986).

NATURE OF CASE: Appeal from reversal of summary judgment in an obscenity action.

FACT SUMMARY: Renton (D) enacted an ordinance geographically limiting adult motion picture theaters.

🏛 RULE OF LAW
A municipality may enact zoning regulations limiting the area where adult motion picture theaters may operate.

FACTS: The City of Renton (D), concerned about the effect of adult movie houses on the surrounding areas, enacted a zoning ordinance proscribing the operation of such an establishment within 1,000 feet of certain public and private facilities and within a mile of a school. This effectively removed 95 percent of the City (D) from such enterprises. Playtime Theaters (P) brought an action, claiming the ordinance violated the free speech provisions of the First and Fourteenth Amendments. The district court granted summary judgment in favor of Renton (D), but the Ninth Circuit reversed. Renton (D) appealed.

ISSUE: May a municipality enact zoning regulations limiting the area where adult motion picture theaters may operate?

HOLDING AND DECISION: (Rehnquist, J.) Yes. A municipality may enact zoning regulations limiting the area where adult motion pictures theaters may operate. "Content-neutral" restrictions on speech are permissible so long as they serve a substantial interest and do not unreasonably limit alternative avenues of communication. Here, the regulations are content-neutral, as the purpose of the ordinance was to prevent the blight associated with adult theaters, not the content of the films. This is a substantial interest. Affirmed.

DISSENT: (Brennan, J.) The regulations are not content neutral, and the ordinance must be looked at much more critically.

▶ ANALYSIS

The Court often finds itself fashioning standards of review for an issue. Historically, the Court has employed either a rubber-stamp rationality test or a very-difficult-to-meet strict scrutiny standard. The standard enunciated here seems to fall in between the two.

Quicknotes

CONTENT BASED Refers to statutes that regulate speech based on its content.

CONTENT NEUTRAL Refers to statutes that regulate speech regardless of its content.

■=■

City of Los Angeles v. Alameda Books, Inc.

Municipality (D) v. Bookstore (P)

535 U.S. 425 (2002).

NATURE OF CASE: Appeal from a summary judgment which held unconstitutional an adult-establishment ordinance on freedom of speech grounds.

FACT SUMMARY: The owners of adult entertainment businesses sought to enjoin enforcement of an ordinance that prohibited more than one adult entertainment business in the same building on First Amendment grounds.

> ## 🏛 RULE OF LAW
> A municipal ordinance that prohibits more than one adult entertainment business in the same building does not violate the First Amendment.

FACTS: A provision of the Los Angeles Municipal Code prohibits establishment or maintenance of more than one adult entertainment business in the same building or structure. Two adult establishments, one of which was Alameda Books (P), each of whom operated an adult bookstore and an adult video arcade in the same building, sued Los Angeles (D) in federal district court, seeking injunctive and declaratory relief against enforcement of the code provision, arguing the provision was unconstitutional as violating the First Amendment. The district court agreed and granted summary judgment to Alameda Books (P). The federal court of appeals affirmed, and Los Angeles (D) appealed.

ISSUE: Does a municipal ordinance that prohibits more than one adult entertainment business in the same building violate the First Amendment?

HOLDING AND DECISION: (O'Connor, J.) No. A municipal ordinance that prohibits more than one adult entertainment business in the same building does not violate the First Amendment. It is rational for a city to determine that reducing the concentration of adult operations in a neighborhood, whether within separate establishments or in one large establishment, will reduce crime rates. The record reflects that Los Angeles (D) conducted a comprehensive study of adult establishments and concluded that concentrations of adult businesses are in fact associated with higher rates of prostitution, robbery, assaults, and thefts in surrounding communities. There was evidence that the intent of the city council, when enacting the instant prohibition, was not only to disperse distinct adult establishments housed in separate buildings, but also to disperse distinct adult businesses operated and housed in a single structure. The ordinance does not ban adult businesses, but merely requires that they be distanced from one another. The ordinance is not content-based and is aimed not at the content

of the establishments but rather at the secondary effects of such businesses on the surrounding community. A municipality may rely on any evidence that is reasonably believed to be relevant for demonstrating a connection between speech and a substantial independent government interest. At this stage of the proceedings, Los Angeles (D) has done so. Our deference to the evidence presented by Los Angeles (D) is the product of a careful balance between competing interests. Here, there is less reason to be concerned that municipalities will use these ordinances to discriminate against unpopular speech. Reversed.

CONCURRENCE: (Kennedy, J.) The law does not require a city to ignore the consequences of adult entertainment businesses if it uses its zoning power in a reasonable way to ameliorate them without suppressing speech.

DISSENT: (Souter, J.) The government's freedom of experimentation cannot displace its burden under the intermediate scrutiny standard to show that the restriction of speech is no greater than essential to realizing an important objective.

▶ ANALYSIS

As the *Alameda* decision makes clear, a zoning measure can be consistent with the First Amendment if it is likely to cause a significant decrease in secondary effects and a trivial decrease in the quality of speech. A dispersal ordinance causes deleterious businesses to separate rather than to close, so negative externalities are diminished but speech is not.

▬▬■

Quicknotes

FIRST AMENDMENT Prohibits Congress from enacting any law respecting an establishment of religion, prohibiting the free exercise of religion, abridging freedom of speech or the press, the right of peaceful assembly and the right to petition for a redress of grievances.

FREEDOM OF SPEECH The right to express oneself without governmental restrictions on the content of that expression.

SUMMARY JUDGMENT Judgment rendered by a court in response to a motion by one of the parties, claiming that the lack of a question of material fact in respect to an issue warrants disposition of the issue without consideration by the jury.

▬▬■

New York v. Ferber

State (P) v. Distributor (D)

458 U.S. 747 (1982).

NATURE OF CASE: Appeal from conviction under statute prohibiting persons from distributing child pornography.

FACT SUMMARY: Ferber (D) contended that a New York statute prohibiting persons from knowingly promoting sexual performances by children under the age of 16 by distributing material that depicts such performances was unconstitutional in that it encroached upon protected First Amendment interests.

> ## RULE OF LAW
> Child pornography does not constitute speech protected under the First Amendment.

FACTS: New York Criminal Code § 263.15 prohibits persons from knowingly promoting sexual performances by children under the age of 16 by distributing material that depicts such performances. A sexual performance is defined as any performance or part thereof that includes sexual conduct by a child less than 16 years of age. Criminal Code § 263.10 bans only the knowing dissemination of obscene material. Ferber (D), the proprietor of a Manhattan bookstore specializing in sexually oriented products, was indicted on two counts of violating § 263.10 and two counts of violating § 263.15 after selling two films to an undercover police officer. The films were devoted almost exclusively to depicting young boys masturbating. After a jury trial, Ferber (D) was acquitted of the two counts of promoting an obscene sexual performance, but found guilty of two counts under § 263.15, which did not require proof that the films were obscene. After the New York Court of Appeals reversed the conviction, the State (P) brought this appeal.

ISSUE: Does child pornography constitute speech not protected under the First Amendment?

HOLDING AND DECISION: (White, J.) Yes. Child pornography does not constitute speech protected under the First Amendment. The states are entitled to great leeway in the regulation of pornographic depictions of children. A state's interest in safeguarding the physical and psychological well-being of a minor is compelling. The use of children as subjects of pornographic materials is harmful to the physiological, emotional, and mental health of the child. The distribution of photographs and films depicting sexual activity by juveniles is intrinsically related to the sexual abuse of children in at least two ways. First, the materials produced are a permanent record of the children's participation and the harm to the child is exacerbated by their circulation. Second, the distribution network for child pornography must be closed if the production of material that requires the sexual exploitation of children is to be effectively controlled. The value of permitting live performances and photographic reproductions of children engaged in lewd sexual conduct is exceedingly modest, if not de minimis. Reversed.

CONCURRENCE: (O'Connor, J.) It is quite possible that New York's statute is overbroad because it bans depictions that do not actually threaten the harms identified by the Court. It is not necessary to address these possibilities further, however, because this potential overbreadth is not sufficiently substantial to warrant facial invalidation of New York's statute.

CONCURRENCE: (Brennan, J.) The application of § 263.15 or any similar statute to depictions of children that in themselves do have serious literary, artistic, scientific, or medical value, would violate the First Amendment.

▶ ANALYSIS

This decision separated the test for child pornography from the general standard for determining obscenity under the well-known *Miller* standard, 413 U.S. 15 (1973). The *Miller* standard was adjusted in three respects: a trier of fact need not find that the material appeals to the prurient interest of the average person; it is not required that sexual conduct portrayed is done so in a patently offensive manner; and the material at issue need not be considered as a whole.

■■■

Quicknotes

FREEDOM OF SPEECH The right to express oneself without governmental restrictions on the content of that expression.

OBSCENITY Conduct tending to corrupt the public morals by its indecency or lewdness.

OVERBREADTH That quality or characteristic of a statute, regulation, or order which reaches beyond the problem it was meant to solve causing it to sweep within it activity it cannot legitimately reach.

PRURIENT INTEREST Abnormal or obsessive interest in sex.

■■■

FCC v. Pacifica Foundation

Federal agency (P) v. Broadcasting company (D)

438 U.S. 726 (1978).

NATURE OF CASE: Certiorari review of speech restriction.

FACT SUMMARY: The Federal Communications Commission (P) disciplined Pacifica Foundation (D) for broadcasting "indecent language" over the radio airwaves.

🏛 RULE OF LAW
Government may validly regulate speech that is indecent but not obscene.

FACTS: Pacifica Foundation (D) broadcasted a monologue performed by comedian George Carlin over its radio station. The monologue sought to express Carlin's view of the public perception of "obscene" language and included the use of certain words which were considered "indecent" by a listener of the station. This listener filed a complaint with the Federal Communications Commission (FCC) (P), contending he was harmed by being exposed to Carlin's monologue. The FCC (P) found the words "indecent" and issued an order that would be considered when the station's license came up for renewal. The court of appeals overturned the order as in violation of the First Amendment freedom of speech. It held that because the FCC (P) specifically found the speech not to be obscene, it had no power to regulate it. The Supreme Court granted certiorari.

ISSUE: May government regulate speech that is indecent but not obscene?

HOLDING AND DECISION: (Stevens, J.) Yes. Government may regulate speech that is indecent yet not obscene. Government may regulate the content of speech where such speech, in context, is vulgar, offensive, and shocking. Patently offensive speech is not entitled to complete constitutional protection. It may be limited under time and place restrictions. As a result, the order was properly issued. Reversed.

CONCURRENCE AND DISSENT: (Powell, J.) Limiting speech to appropriate times and places reduces its indecency while still affording access to willing listeners. But this is a problem where the broadcast media is involved, because during most of broadcast hours, the broadcaster cannot reach willing adults without reaching children as well. A second problem is that the broadcasts come directly into one's home. But I do not share the theory that the Justices of this Court are "free generally to decide on the basis of its content which speech protected by the First Amendment is most 'valuable' and hence deserving of protection." The result in this case turns not on the "value" of Carlin's monologue, but on the unique charac-

teristics of the broadcast media and the potential harm to children and unwilling adults.

DISSENT: (Brennan, J.) The statutory term "indecent" under which the FCC (P) order was issued must be construed only to apply to obscene language. Because this language was held not to be obscene, the order was improper.

▶ ANALYSIS

Justice Stevens, in this plurality decision, was careful to point out that if there had been any basis for concluding that the FCC (P) characterization of Carlin's monologue rested upon its political content, First Amendment protection might be required. If it is the speaker's opinion being expressed gives offense, constitutional protection is mandated. In this case the objection was not to Carlin's expressing his opinion, but to the manner in which it was expressed.

Quicknotes

FREEDOM OF SPEECH The right to express oneself without governmental restrictions on the content of that expression.

Sable Communications, Inc. v. FCC

Communications company (P) v. Federal government (D)

492 U.S. 115 (1989).

NATURE OF CASE: Appeal by federal government from district court's holding of the unconstitutionality of Section 223(b) of the Federal Communications Act insofar as it banned indecent telephone messages.

FACT SUMMARY: Sable Communications, Inc. (P) offered "dial-a-porn" prerecorded telephone messages through the Pacific Bell telephone system. The district court held unconstitutional legislation that placed an outright ban on indecent interstate commercial telephone messages, but upheld the legislation insofar as it criminally prohibited telephone messages that were obscene.

> **RULE OF LAW**
> The Federal Communications Act's outright criminal ban on indecent interstate commercial telephone messages constitutes a First Amendment violation.

FACTS: Sable Communications, Inc. (P) began offering sexually oriented prerecorded telephone messages ("dial-a-porn") through the Pacific Bell telephone network through special phone lines requiring access codes and scrambling so that only subscribers could obtain the messages. Those who called the adult message number were charged a special fee. Section 223(b) of the Communications Act of 1934 (the "Act"), as amended in 1988, imposed an outright criminal ban on indecent as well as obscene interstate commercial telephone messages. The district court upheld the Act's prohibition on obscene telephone messages, but enjoined enforcement of the statute insofar as it applied to indecent messages. The Supreme Court granted certiorari.

ISSUE: Does the Federal Communications Act's outright criminal ban on indecent interstate commercial telephone messages constitute a First Amendment violation?

HOLDING AND DECISION: (White, J.) Yes. The Federal Communications Act's outright criminal ban on indecent interstate commercial telephone messages constitutes a First Amendment violation. Sexual expression that is indecent but not obscene is protected by the First Amendment and may be sold to adults. However the Government (D) has a compelling interest in protecting minors from such expression. The private telephone communications here at issue are substantially different from public radio broadcasts. In contrast to public displays, unsolicited mailings, and other means of expression the recipient has no meaningful opportunity to avoid, the dial-in medium requires the listener to take affirmative steps to receive the

communication. There is no "captive audience" here; callers will generally not be unwilling listeners. Placing a telephone call is not the same thing as turning on a radio and being taken by surprise by an indecent message. The Government (D) nevertheless argues a complete ban is the only means of preventing children from gaining access to indecent messages. This argument is unpersuasive because there is evidence that the access codes, scrambling, and other technologies in place to keep such messages out of the reach of minors will be extremely effective. Accordingly, the statute is not sufficiently narrowly drawn, since its denial of adult access to indecent telephone messages is far broader than it needs to be to limit access to minors. Affirmed.

CONCURRENCE: (Scalia, J.) The majority correctly holds that the statute has the invalid effect of limiting the content of adult telephone conversations to that which is suitable for children to hear, and that the denial of adult access to telephone messages that are indecent but not obscene far exceeds that which is necessary to limit the access of minors to such messages. However, the question of how few children being able to access such messages renders the risk unacceptable depends on what "indecency" includes. Since "indecency" encompasses pornography that "obscenity" excludes, the more narrowly "obscenity" is understood, the more pornographic "indecency" becomes, and the more reasonable it becomes to insist on limiting access to minors. Moreover, although the First Amendment prevents Congress from banning indecent speech in this manner, this does not mean public utilities are required to carry such speech.

CONCURRENCE AND DISSENT: (Brennan, J.) Even the criminalization of the distribution of obscene materials to consenting adults should be unconstitutional, and forbidding the transmission of all obscene telephone messages is unduly heavy handed because the statute curtails freedom of speech far more broadly than warranted by the Government's (D) interest in preventing harm to minors.

> ## ANALYSIS
>
> The Court noted that credit cards, access codes, and scrambling rules were a satisfactory solution to the problem of keeping indecent dial-a-porn messages out of reach of minors. The Court's reasoning in this case could be extended to the distribution of indecent, sexually

Continued on next page.

explicit materials on the internet, where access to a particular web site could be limited to minors through the use of technology, such as blocking and filtering software. In fact, in *Ashcroft v. American Civil Liberties Union,* 542 U.S. 656 (2004), the Court ruled the Child Pornography Act (COPA) was unconstitutional because such software was a plausible, less restrictive alternative to the statute.

■=■

Quicknotes

FREEDOM OF SPEECH The right to express oneself without governmental restrictions on the content of that expression.

OBSCENITY Indecency, lewdness or offensive behavior in appearance or expression.

■=■

Reno v. American Civil Liberties Union

Attorney General of the United States (D) v. Civil liberties advocacy group (P)

521 U.S. 844 (1997).

NATURE OF CASE: Certiorari review of constitutionality of the Communications Decency Act of 1996.

FACT SUMMARY: The American Civil Liberties Union (P) challenged the constitutionality of provisions of the Communications Decency Act of 1996 that purported to protect minors from harmful transmissions over the Internet.

RULE OF LAW
Content-based government regulations on speech are unconstitutional unless the government can demonstrate that it has a compelling interest for the regulation and that the regulation is the least restrictive means of achieving that interest.

FACTS: The Communications Decency Act of 1996 (CDA) contained provisions designed to protect minors from "indecent" and "patently offensive" communication on the Internet. The "indecent transmission" provision prohibited the knowing transmission of obscene or indecent messages to any recipient less than 18 years of age. The "patently offensive display" provision prohibited the knowing sending or displaying of patently offensive messages to a person less than 18 years of age. The American Civil Liberties Union (ACLU) (P) filed an action alleging that the CDA abridged freedom of speech protected by the First Amendment. The district court found in its favor and enjoined the enforcement of the "indecent" communications provisions, but expressly preserved the government's right to investigate and prosecute the obscenity or child pornography activities prohibited by the provision. The court also issued an unqualified injunction against the enforcement of the "patently offensive displays" provision because it contained no separate reference to obscenity or child pornography.

ISSUE: Are content-based government regulations on speech unconstitutional unless the government can demonstrate that it has a compelling interest for the regulation and that the regulation is the least restrictive means of achieving that interest?

HOLDING AND DECISION: (Stevens, J.) Yes. Content-based government regulations on speech are unconstitutional unless the government can demonstrate that it has a compelling interest for the regulation and that the regulation is the least restrictive means of achieving that interest. Although the congressional goal of protecting children from harmful materials is a legitimate and important one, the CDA provisions at issue here are so broad and

imprecise that they cannot be upheld. The Internet is a unique medium in that it provides a relatively unlimited, low-cost capacity for communication of all kinds including traditional print and news services, audio, video, still images, and interactive real-time dialogue. It unquestionably deserves the highest level of First Amendment protection. The breadth of the CDA's coverage is wholly unprecedented and would undoubtedly impact adult as well as minor access to such materials. It does not limit its restrictions to commercial speech or entities, but encompasses anyone posting messages on a computer, regardless of time of day, website, or any other factor. The district court heard evidence that in the near future a reasonably effective and less restrictive method by which parents can prevent their children from accessing sexually explicit material will become widely available. The current provisions cannot stand as they are more likely to interfere with the free exchange of ideas than to encourage it. Affirmed.

CONCURRENCE AND DISSENT: (O'Connor, J.) The CDA is little more than an attempt by Congress to create "adult zones" on the Internet. Such zoning laws are valid if: (1) they do not unduly restrict adult access to materials, and (2) the materials are such that minors have no right to read or view. The CDA "display" provision and some applications of the "indecency transmission" provision fail to adhere to the first of these requirements, and should therefore be invalidated only to those extents.

ANALYSIS

Issues surrounding speech, pornography, and access to the Internet will undoubtedly be revisited often in the next several years. The issues are extremely complex because the technology is so novel, and are further complicated by the fact that the Internet extends worldwide. The Court was appropriately cautious in striking down the provisions and leaving the issue in the hands of parents until further developments evolve.

Quicknotes

CONTENT-BASED Refers to statutes that regulate speech based on its content.

FIRST AMENDMENT Prohibits Congress from enacting any law respecting an establishment of religion, prohibiting

Continued on next page.

the free exercise of religion, abridging freedom of speech or the press, the right of peaceful assembly and the right to petition for a redress of grievances.

OBSCENITY   Conduct tending to corrupt the public morals by its indecency or lewdness.

■═■

United States v. Stevens

Federal government (P) v. Purveyor of animal cruelty videos (D)

130 S. Ct. 1577 (2010).

NATURE OF CASE: Appeal in action involving the indictment under 18 U.S.C. § 48 for creating, selling and possessing depictions of animal cruelty. [The procedural posture of the case is not presented in the casebook extract.]

FACT SUMMARY: Stevens (D), who was indicted under 18 U.S.C. § 48 for creating, selling and possessing depictions of animal cruelty—specifically, for selling dogfighting videos—contended the statute was facially invalid under the First Amendment.

🏛 RULE OF LAW
A statute that criminalizes the commercial creation, sale, or possession of certain depictions of animal cruelty in which a living animal is intentionally maimed, mutilated, tortured, wounded, or killed is overbroad and facially invalid under the First Amendment as a content-based regulation of protected speech.

FACTS: Congress enacted 18 U.S.C. § 48 to criminalize the commercial creation, sale, or possession of certain depictions of animal cruelty. The statute addressed only portrayals of harmful acts, not the underlying conduct. It applied to any visual or auditory depiction "in which a living animal is intentionally maimed, mutilated, tortured, wounded, or killed," if that conduct violates federal or state law where "the creation, sale, or possession takes place." Another clause exempted depictions with "serious religious, political, scientific, educational, journalistic, historical, or artistic value." The legislative background of § 48 focused primarily on "crush videos," which feature the torture and killing of helpless animals and are said to appeal to persons with a specific sexual fetish. Stevens (D) was indicted under § 48 for selling videos depicting dogfighting, which is illegal in all states and the District of Columbia. He moved to dismiss, arguing § 48 is facially invalid under the First Amendment. The Supreme Court granted certiorari. [The procedural posture of the case is not presented in the casebook extract.]

ISSUE: Is a statute that criminalizes the commercial creation, sale, or possession of certain depictions of animal cruelty in which a living animal is intentionally maimed, mutilated, tortured, wounded, or killed overbroad and facially invalid under the First Amendment as a content-based regulation of protected speech?

HOLDING AND DECISION: (Roberts, C.J.) Yes. A statute that criminalizes the commercial creation, sale, or possession of certain depictions of animal cruelty in which

a living animal is intentionally maimed, mutilated, tortured, wounded, or killed is overbroad and facially invalid under the First Amendment as a content-based regulation of protected speech. Depictions of animal cruelty are not, as a class, categorically unprotected by the First Amendment. Since its enactment, the First Amendment has permitted restrictions on a few historic categories of speech that have never been thought to raise any constitutional problem. Depictions of animal cruelty should not be added to that list. While the prohibition of animal cruelty has a long history in American law, there is no evidence of a similar tradition prohibiting depictions of such cruelty. The Government's (P) proposed test would broadly balance the value of the speech against its societal costs to determine whether the First Amendment even applies, but the First Amendment's free speech guarantee does not extend only to categories of speech that survive an ad hoc balancing of relative social costs and benefits. The Amendment itself reflects a judgment by the American people that the benefits of its restrictions on the Government (P) outweigh the costs. Limiting § 48's reach to crush videos and depictions of animal fighting or other extreme cruelty, as the Government (P) suggests, requires an unrealistically broad reading of the statute's exceptions clause. Nor does the Government (P) seriously contest that the presumptively impermissible applications of § 48 far outnumber any permissible ones. The Court therefore does not decide whether a statute limited to crush videos or other depictions of extreme animal cruelty would be constitutional. Section 48 is not so limited but is instead substantially overbroad, and therefore invalid under the First Amendment. [The procedural outcome of the case is not presented in the casebook extract.]

DISSENT: (Alito, J.) The First Amendment does not protect criminal conduct engaged in for expressive purposes. One of the principal reasons § 48 was enacted was to combat crush videos. Congress concluded that the only effective way of stopping the underlying criminal conduct was to prohibit the commercial exploitation of the videos of that conduct. Crush videos present a highly unusual free speech issue because they are so closely linked with violent criminal conduct: the videos record the commission of violent criminal acts, and it appears these crimes are committed for the sole purpose of creating the videos. Given these realities, the First Amendment does not require Congress to step aside and allow the underlying crimes to continue. The Court's reasoning underlying its precedents

Continued on next page.

regarding child pornography applies here. As with child pornography, the conduct depicted in crush videos is criminal in every jurisdiction in the country. That conduct, which is what is shown in the crush videos, cannot be prevented without targeting the sale of the videos. Finally, the harm caused by the underlying criminal conduct vastly outweighs any minimal value the depictions might conceivably be thought to possess.

▶ ANALYSIS

After the Court's decision in this case, Congress enacted a much narrower version of § 48 that was focused on just crush videos, thus eliminating the kind of overbreadth challenges accepted by the Court here. As Justice Alito pointed out in his dissent, Congress's efforts in this area seem to have been vindicated. By 2007, sponsors of § 48 declared the crush video industry dead, and even overseas websites shut down in the statute's wake. Moreover, right after the Third Circuit's decision in this case, which facially invalidated the statute, crush videos were already back online. Thus, criminalizing the display of crush videos seems to have greatly reduced, or even eliminated, the underlying animal torture.

■■■

Quicknotes

CONTENT BASED Refers to statutes that regulate speech based on its content.

FREEDOM OF SPEECH The right to express oneself without governmental restrictions on the content of that expression.

■■■

Ashcroft v. Free Speech Coalition

Attorney General (D) v. Trade organization (P)

535 U.S. 234 (2002).

NATURE OF CASE: Appeal from holding a federal statute unconstitutional on First Amendment grounds.

FACT SUMMARY: The Free Speech Coalition (P) argued that the federal Child Pornography Prevention Act violated the First Amendment by defining prohibited child pornography to include sexually explicit images that appear to depict minors but were produced without using any real children, such as by using computer imaging.

🏛 RULE OF LAW
The Child Pornography Prevention Act of 1996, which proscribes speech that is neither obscene nor child pornography, abridges freedom of speech and is unconstitutional.

FACTS: In 1996, Congress enacted the Child Pornography Prevention Act (CPPA) which extended the federal prohibition against child pornography to sexually explicit images that appear to depict minors but were produced without using any real children. The statute prohibits, in specific circumstances, possessing or distributing these images that may be created by using adults who look like minors or by using computer imaging. The new technology makes it possible to create realistic images of children who do not exist. The Free Speech Coalition (P), a trade organization for the adult-entertainment industry, and others, brought suit in federal district court challenging the constitutionality of the CPPA and the grounds that the "appears to be" and "conveys the impression" provisions of the statute are overbroad and vague, chilling them from producing works protected by the First Amendment. The district court disagreed, granting summary judgment for the Government (D). The federal court of appeals reversed, and the Government (D) appealed.

ISSUE: Does the Child Pornography Prevention Act (CPPA) of 1996, which proscribes speech that is neither obscene nor child pornography, abridge freedom of speech, and is it therefore unconstitutional?

HOLDING AND DECISION: (Kennedy, J.) Yes. The Child Pornography Prevention Act (CPPA) of 1996, which proscribes speech that is neither obscene nor child pornography, abridges freedom of speech and is unconstitutional. By prohibiting child pornography that does not depict an actual child, the CPPA goes beyond this Court's decisions, which distinguish child pornography from other sexually explicit speech because of the government's interest in protecting the children exploited by the production process. Pictures of young children engaged in certain acts

might be obscene where similar depictions of adults, or perhaps even older adolescents, would not. The CPPA, however, is not directed at speech that is obscene but seeks to reach beyond obscenity and makes no attempt to conform to obscenity standards. For instance, the CPPA would reach visual depictions, such as movies, even if they have redeeming social value. The statute's prohibition of "any visual depiction" does not depend at all on how the image is produced. The statute captures a range of depictions, sometimes called "virtual child pornography," including computer-generated images, as well as images produced by more traditional means. The literal terms of the CPPA, therefore, would embrace a Renaissance painting depicting a scene from classical mythology, a picture that "appears to be" of a minor engaging in sexually explicit conduct, and a Hollywood movie, filmed without child actors, if a jury believes an actor "appears to be" a minor engaging in actual or simulated sexual intercourse. These images do not involve, let alone harm, any children in the production process. Yet, under the CPPA, *any* depiction of sexually explicit activity, no matter how it is presented, is proscribed; the CPPA, for example, applies to a picture in a psychology manual, as well as a movie depicting the horrors of sexual abuse. The prohibitions of the CPPA are overbroad and unconstitutional. Affirmed.

CONCURRENCE: (Thomas, J.) In the event technology evolves to the point where it becomes impossible to enforce actual child pornography laws because the government cannot prove that certain pornography images are of real children, the government should not be foreclosed from enacting a regulation of virtual child pornography that contains an appropriate affirmative defense or some other narrowly drawn restriction.

DISSENT: (O'Connor, J.) Although the CPPA's ban on youthful-adult pornography appears to violate the First Amendment, the ban on virtual child pornography does not. Invalidating a statute due to overbreadth is an extreme remedy and should be employed sparingly and only as a last resort.

DISSENT: (Rehnquist, C.J.) This Court does not normally strike down a statute on First Amendment grounds when a limiting instruction could be placed on the challenged statute. Here, the CPPA could be limited so as not to reach any material that was not already unprotected before the CPPA.

Continued on next page.

▶ *ANALYSIS*

In the *Free Speech Coalition* decision, the Supreme Court noted that, under the CPPA, even if a film contained no sexually explicit scenes involving minors, it could be treated as child pornography if the title and trailers conveyed the impression that the scenes would be found in the movie. Hence, the determination of child pornography turned "on how the speech is presented, not on what is depicted."

Quicknotes

FIRST AMENDMENT Prohibits Congress from enacting any law respecting an establishment of religion, prohibiting the free exercise of religion, abridging freedom of speech or the press, the right of peaceful assembly and the right to petition for a redress of grievances.

Brown v. Entertainment Merchants Assn.

State official (D) v. Video game association (P)

131 S. Ct. 2729 (2011).

NATURE OF CASE: Appeal in action to determine whether California's (D) prohibition of the sale or rental to minors of violent video games violated the First Amendment. [The procedural posture of the case is not presented in the casebook extract.]

FACT SUMMARY: A video game association (P) brought suit challenging as violative of the First Amendment California's (D) statute prohibiting the sale or rental to minors of violent video games.

🏛 RULE OF LAW
A statute that purports to prohibit the rental or sale to minors of violent video games violates the First Amendment as being both underinclusive and over-inclusive.

FACTS: California (D) enacted a statute that prohibited the sale or rental to minors of violent video games. The statute covered games "in which the range of options available to a player includes killing, maiming, dismembering, or sexually assaulting an image of a human being, if those acts are depicted" in a manner that "appeals to a deviant or morbid interest of minors," that is "patently offensive to prevailing standards in the community as to what is suitable for minors," and that "causes the game, as a whole, to lack serious literary, artistic, political, or scientific value for minors." A video game association (P) brought suit challenging the statute as violative of the First Amendment. The Supreme Court granted certiorari. [The procedural posture of the case is not presented in the casebook extract.]

ISSUE: Does a statute that purports to prohibit the rental or sale to minors of violent video games violate the First Amendment as being both underinclusive and over-inclusive?

HOLDING AND DECISION: (Scalia, J.) Yes. A statute that purports to prohibit the rental or sale to minors of violent video games violates the First Amendment as being both underinclusive and overinclusive. Video games qualify for First Amendment protection. Like protected books, plays, and movies, they communicate ideas through familiar literary devices and features distinctive to the medium, and the basic principles of freedom of speech do not vary with a new and different communication medium. A legislature cannot create new categories of unprotected speech simply by weighing the value of a particular category against its social costs and then punishing it if it fails the test. California's (D) statute does not adjust the boundaries of an existing category of unprotect-

ed speech to ensure that a definition designed for adults is not uncritically applied to children. Instead, California (D) wishes to create a wholly new category of content-based regulation that is permissible only for speech directed at children. That is unprecedented and mistaken. While a state may protect children from harm, its power to do so does not include a free-floating power to restrict the ideas to which children are exposed. This country has no tradition of specially restricting children's access to depictions of violence; in fact, numerous well-known children's stories and fairytales contain depictions of violence, as do books read in school through high school. Because the Act imposes a restriction on the content of protected speech, it is invalid unless California (D) can demonstrate that it passes strict scrutiny, i.e., it is justified by a compelling government interest and is narrowly drawn to serve that interest. California (D) cannot meet that standard. Psychological studies purporting to show a connection between exposure to violent video games and harmful effects on children do not prove such exposure causes minors to act aggressively. Any demonstrated effects are both small and indistinguishable from effects produced by other media. Since California (D) has declined to restrict those other media, e.g., Saturday morning cartoons, or violent comic books, its video-game regulation is wildly underinclusive, raising serious doubts about whether California (D) is pursuing the interest it invokes or is instead disfavoring a particular speaker or viewpoint. California (D) also cannot show the statute's restrictions meet the alleged substantial need of parents who wish to restrict their children's access to violent videos. The video-game industry's voluntary rating system already accomplishes that to a large extent. Moreover, as a means of assisting parents, the statute is greatly overinclusive, since not all of the children who are prohibited from purchasing violent video games have parents who disapprove of their doing so. Accordingly, because the statute is both underinclusive and overinclusive, it cannot satisfy strict scrutiny. This does not mean that the California legislature's concerns are not meritorious. Instead, it means the regulation the legislature has enacted is not justified by a compelling state interest. Even where the legislature's goal is the laudable goal of protecting children, the constitutional limits on governmental action apply. [The procedural outcome of the case is not presented in the casebook extract.]

CONCURRENCE: (Alito, J.) The statute at issue, although well intentioned, does not define "violent video

Continued on next page.

games" with the precision the Constitution demands, so it violates the First Amendment by failing to provide fair notice. That analysis should be the end of the question in this case. The majority's approach in reaching that conclusion, however, is flawed because it does not proceed with caution in the face of new technology, but merely assumes that new technology is just like old technology. The majority too readily dismisses the possibility that the effect of playing video games on minors is very different from the effects of other forms of entertainment previously encountered. Some of the games contain an astounding amount of violence and antisocial content. Given that this content may be enhanced by new technologies, e.g., high-definition, 3-D, violent video games may in the near future enable troubled teens to experience in an extraordinarily personal and vivid way what it would be like to carry our unspeakable acts of violence. There are reasons to suspect that the experience of playing violent video games might be very different from reading a book, listening to the radio, or watching a movie or a television show—even if those contain elements of violence. The Court here should not have expressed its views as to whether a properly drawn statute would or would not survive constitutional scrutiny.

DISSENT: (Thomas, J.) The majority's decision does not comport with the original understanding of the First Amendment. That understanding did not encompass rights of adults to speak to minors or of minors to access speech absent approval from parents or guardians. Therefore, the statute at issue is not facially unconstitutional. This comports with evidence showing that the Founders believed parents had absolute authority over their minor children and expected parents to use that authority to direct the proper development of their children. Thus, the Framers could not possibly have understood the freedom of speech to include an unqualified right to speak to minors.

DISSENT: (Breyer, J.) The statute at issue only imposes a modest restriction on expression, as it only prevents a child or adolescent from buying a violent video game without a parent's assistance, and no one is prevented from playing the game. The statute also significantly furthers the state's compelling interest, which is supported by studies and expert opinions that conclude the video games at issue are particularly likely to harm children. Here, the Court, as it has done in the past, should have deferred to the legislature and these legislative facts, especially given they involve technical matters that are beyond the Court's competence.

▶ *ANALYSIS*

With this decision, the Court affirmed its holding in *United States v. Stevens*, 130 S. Ct. 1577 (2010), where it held that new categories of unprotected speech may not be added to the list by a legislature that concludes certain speech is too harmful to be tolerated. In *Stevens*, the Court emphatically rejected the government's argument that lack of a

historical warrant did not matter, and that it could create new categories of unprotected speech by applying a "simple balancing test" that weighs the value of a particular category of speech against its social costs and then punishes that category of speech if it fails the test. In both *Stevens* and this case, the majority emphasized that, based on longstanding tradition and history, obscenity is not protected speech, but non-obscene speech is protected. The Court indicated that because speech about violence is not obscene, it is protected. However, it is arguable that such a rigid, history-based approach will never permit First Amendment law to reflect changing community attitudes about non-obscene speech. Accordingly, Justice Breyer in his dissent asks "what sense does it make to forbid selling to a 13-year-old boy a magazine with an image of a nude woman, while protecting a sale to that 13-year-old of an interactive video game in which he actively, but virtually, binds and gags the woman, then tortures and kills her? What kind of First Amendment would permit the government to protect children by restricting sales of that extremely violent video game only when the woman— bound, gagged, tortured, and killed—is also topless?" The answer, according to the majority, is that regardless of the result, precedent must be adhered to, with no room for new categories of unprotected speech.

━■━

Quicknotes

FIRST AMENDMENT Prohibits Congress from enacting any law respecting an establishment of religion, prohibiting the free exercise of religion, abridging freedom of speech or the press, the right of peaceful assembly and the right to petition for a redress of grievances.

FREEDOM OF SPEECH The right to express oneself without governmental restrictions on the content of that expression.

━■━

Virginia Pharmacy Board v. Virginia Citizens Consumer Council

State board (D) v. Residents (P)

425 U.S. 748 (1976).

NATURE OF CASE: Certiorari review of constitutionality of commercial speech restriction.

FACT SUMMARY: The Virginia Pharmacy Board (D) was charged with enforcing a state law that made it illegal for a pharmacist to advertise the prices of his prescription drugs.

🏛 RULE OF LAW
The First Amendment guarantee of freedom of speech extends to the recipients as well as the sources of the speech; and, as such, the consumer's interest in the free flow of advertising information brings such "commercial speech" within the protection of the First Amendment.

FACTS: Virginia law provides that licensed pharmacists are guilty of "unprofessional conduct" if they advertise "in any manner whatsoever, any amount, price, fee, premium, discount, rebate or credit terms . . . for any drugs which may be dispensed only by prescription." Consumer Council (P) is comprised of Virginia residents who require prescription drugs. Citing statistics that show that drugs vary in price strikingly from outlet to outlet (e.g., from $2.59 to $6.00 for one drug), they filed this action to have the advertising ban declared an unconstitutional infringement on their First Amendment right to free speech. From a judgment for the Council (P), the Virginia Pharmacy Board (D) appealed contending that "commercial speech" such as this is not protected by the First Amendment.

ISSUE: Does the First Amendment protect "commercial speech" as manifested in price advertising by professional groups?

HOLDING AND DECISION: (Blackmun, J.) Yes. The First Amendment guarantee of freedom of speech extends to the recipients as well as the sources of the speech; and, as such, the consumer's interest in the free flow of advertising information brings such "commercial speech" within the protection of the First Amendment. The traditional rule that "commercial speech" is not protected has been gradually eroded by the court and today, it is set to rest. Advertising, however tasteless, is information nevertheless and entitled to constitutional deference thereby. To be sure, the holding today does not prevent reasonable regulation as to "time, place, and manner" or prevent illegal or misleading speech. It only recognizes the legitimacy of commercial speech for First Amendment purposes. Affirmed.

DISSENT: (Rehnquist, J.) The Court's decision today is troublesome for two reasons. First, it extends standing to sue to a group not asserting their right to receive information but rather the right of third parties to publish it. Second, by raising commercial speech to the level of First Amendment protection, the Court has usurped the constitutionally mandated power of state legislatures to regulate public health, etc.

▶ ANALYSIS

Justice Burger's concurrence to the contrary notwithstanding, this case has brought many observers to the conclusion that advertising bans on professionals are no longer constitutional. Indeed, the American Bar Association and several state bar associations have begun to promulgate standards for advertising by attorneys that will protect the public from the perceived evils of a competitive bar. *Virginia Citizens Consumer Council* claims to overrule the 1951 case of *Breard v. Alexandria*, 341 U.S. 622 (1951). Note, however, that the ban on door-to-door sales upheld therein would appear to be precisely the kind of "time, place, and manner restriction" that the Court in *Virginia Citizens Consumer Council* expressly sanctioned.

Quicknotes

COMMERCIAL SPEECH Any speech that proposes a commercial transaction, or promotes products or services.

TIME, PLACE, MANNER RESTRICTION Refers to certain types of regulations on speech that are permissible since they only restrict the time, place, and manner in which the speech is to occur.

Central Hudson Gas v. Public Service Commn.

Gas company (P) v. Federal agency (D)

447 U.S. 557 (1980).

NATURE OF CASE: Certiorari review of the constitutionality of a federal regulation.

FACT SUMMARY: Central Hudson Gas (P) claimed the First Amendment prohibited the New York Public Service Commission's (D) regulation completely banning promotional advertising by an electrical utility.

🏛 RULE OF LAW
Where there is a substantial governmental interest, a restriction on commercial speech protected by the First Amendment is constitutional if it directly advances that interest and is not more extensive than is necessary to serve that interest.

FACTS: The Public Service Commission (PSC) (D) banned all promotional advertising by an electrical utility as contrary to the national policy of conserving energy. Central Hudson Gas (P) challenged the regulation on First Amendment grounds.

ISSUE: Can the government place a restriction on commercial speech protected by the First Amendment if it directly advances a substantial governmental interest and is not broader than is necessary to serve that interest?

HOLDING AND DECISION: (Powell, J.) Yes. Where there is a substantial governmental interest, a restriction on commercial speech protected by the First Amendment is constitutional if it directly advances that interest and is not more extensive than is necessary to serve that interest. Commercial speech that concerns lawful activity and is not misleading is protected under the First Amendment, although at a lesser level than other speech. However, this protection prevents governmental restrictions on covered commercial speech unless they advance a substantial governmental interest and are not more extensive than is necessary to serve that interest. These principles produce a four-step analysis which, when applied to this case, indicates that the regulation at issue is unconstitutional. It satisfies all the requirements except the last. It is so broad that it suppresses speech about electrical devices or services that would cause no increase in total energy usage and thus be unrelated to the energy conservation interest of the state. Reversed.

CONCURRENCE: (Blackmun, J.) The intermediate level of scrutiny advanced by the four-part analysis the Court sets up in this decision is appropriate for a restraint on commercial speech designed to protect consumers from misleading or coercive speech, or a regulation related to time, place, or manner of commercial speech. It is not, however, properly applied when a state seeks to suppress information about a product in order to manipulate a private economic decision that the state cannot or has not regulated or outlawed directly. No differences between commercial and other protected speech justify suppression of commercial speech in order to influence public conduct through manipulation of the availability of information.

CONCURRENCE: (Stevens, J.) This is not a "commercial speech" case, for the ban at issue would prohibit speech outside the limited boundaries of commercial speech. For example, it would seem to prohibit an electric company's advocacy of the use of electric heat for environmental reasons, as opposed to wood-burning stoves. Thus, it is not necessary to decide if the four-part analysis the Court adopts adequately protects commercial speech. This is a "regular" speech case. If the perceived harm associated with greater electrical usage is not sufficiently serious to justify direct regulation, surely it does not constitute the kind of clear and present danger that can justify the suppression of speech.

DISSENT: (Rehnquist, J.) The speech of a state-created monopoly, which is the subject of a comprehensive regulatory scheme, is not entitled to protection under the First Amendment. Furthermore, the Court errs in failing to recognize that the state law at issue in this case is most accurately viewed as an economic regulation and that the speech involved (if it falls within the First Amendment at all) occupies a significantly more subordinate position in the hierarchy of First Amendment values than the Court gives it today. Finally, in reaching its judgment, the Court improperly substitutes its own judgment for that of the state in deciding how a proper ban on promotional advertising should be drafted. On that point, in adopting a "no more extensive than necessary" analysis as the last part of its four-part test, the Court has embraced a test that will unduly impair a state legislature's ability to adopt legislation reasonably designed to promote interests that have always been rightly thought to be of great importance to the state.

▶ ANALYSIS

Historically, the Court had always held that commercial speech was not within the protections of the First Amendment. In the mid-1970s, however, a new trend began in which the Court recognized that the First Amendment did encompass certain commercial speech and offered it protection, although of a more limited sort than other speech. In recent years, though, there is evidence that the

Continued on next page.

enthusiasm among the Justices for including commercial speech within the First Amendment is waning.

■=■

Quicknotes

COMMERCIAL SPEECH Any speech that proposes a commercial transaction, or promotes products or services.

■=■

44 Liquormart, Inc. v. Rhode Island

Liquor distributor (P) v. State (D)

517 U.S. 484 (1996).

NATURE OF CASE: Certiorari review of a state law prohibiting alcohol advertising.

FACT SUMMARY: Rhode Island (D) banned the advertising of retail prices of alcoholic beverages.

RULE OF LAW

Complete bans on truthful commercial advertising are unconstitutional.

FACTS: In 1956, Rhode Island (D) enacted a prohibition against advertising the retail price of any alcoholic beverage offered for sale in the state. The law also proscribed the news media from publishing this information. Rhode Island (D) claimed that the law was enacted to reduce market-wide consumption of alcohol. The law was challenged as an unconstitutional abridgement of free speech. The district court concluded that the ban was unconstitutional because liquor price advertising had no impact on levels of alcohol consumption in Rhode Island (D), and thus the ban did not directly advance the State's (D) interest. The court of appeals reversed. The Supreme Court granted certiorari to decide the issue.

ISSUE: Are complete bans on truthful commercial advertising unconstitutional?

HOLDING AND DECISION: (Stevens, J.) Yes. Complete bans on truthful commercial advertising are unconstitutional. Traditionally, commercial messages have provided consumers with information about the availability of goods and services. The common law prohibited fraudulent and misleading advertising. However, prior cases have recognized that regulation of commercial advertising is not protected to the same degree as core First Amendment speech. In *Central Hudson v. Public Service Commission of N.Y.*, 447 U.S. 557 (1980), this Court held that regulation of commercial speech had to be related to a significant state interest and that more limited alternatives are not available. When a state entirely prohibits the dissemination of truthful advertising for reasons unrelated to protecting consumers, strict scrutiny of the law is applicable. In the present case, Rhode Island (D) could reduce alcohol consumption by other methods, such as taxes, rather than through speech regulation. Thus, there is no reasonable relationship between the regulation and state objective. Accordingly, Rhode Island's (D) law is unconstitutional. Reversed.

CONCURRENCE: (Scalia, J.) Although the test enunciated in *Central Hudson* may not be correct, both parties argued accepting its validity, so it should stand until there is a suitable replacement.

CONCURRENCE: (Thomas, J.) The government's manipulation of consumers' choices by keeping them ignorant is per se illegitimate. Thus, the balancing test of *Central Hudson* is not appropriate. Accurate commercial speech is entitled to full protection.

CONCURRENCE: (O'Connor, J.) Because Rhode Island's (D) regulation fails even the less stringent standard set out in *Central Hudson*, nothing here requires adoption of a new analysis for the evaluation of commercial speech regulation.

ANALYSIS

The Court also overruled the case of *Posados de Puerto Rico Associates v. Tourism Co. of P.R.*, 478 U.S. 328 (1986), in which the Court held that a ban on casino advertising was valid since the state could choose to entirely ban casinos themselves. The decision correctly points out that banning speech may be more intrusive than banning conduct and that the speech ban is not necessarily a lesser included state power. The Court also rejected any "vice" exception that *Posados* may have implied.

Quicknotes

BALANCING TEST Court's balancing of an individual's constitutional rights against the state's right to protect its citizens.

COMMERCIAL SPEECH Any speech that proposes a commercial transaction, or promotes products or services.

STRICT SCRUTINY Method by which courts determine the constitutionality of a law when a law affects a fundamental right. Under the test, the legislature must have a compelling interest to enact law and measures prescribed by the law must be the least restrictive means possible to accomplish goal.

CHAPTER 12

Freedom of Speech—Modes of Regulation and Standards of Review

Quick Reference Rules of Law

United States v. O'Brien

Federal government (P) v. Demonstrator (D)

391 U.S. 367 (1968).

NATURE OF CASE: Certiorari review of speech restriction with nonspeech aspect of conduct.

FACT SUMMARY: O'Brien (D) was convicted of a violation of a federal statute after he publicly burned his draft card during a demonstration against the compulsory draft and the war in Vietnam.

🏛 RULE OF LAW
When both speech and nonspeech elements are combined in the same conduct, sufficiently important governmental interest in regulating the nonspeech element can justify incidental limitations of First Amendment freedoms.

FACTS: During a public demonstration directed against the compulsory draft and the war in Vietnam, O'Brien (D) and several others burned their Selective Service Registration Certificates. His act was witnessed by several FBI agents who arrested him. The arrest was for violating a federal statute prohibiting the knowing destruction or knowing mutilation of a Selective Service Certificate. The act also prohibited any changes, alterations, or forgeries of the Certificates. O'Brien (D) was convicted and appealed, contending a violation of his First Amendment right to free speech.

ISSUE: May the government incidentally limit First Amendment rights where it seeks to regulate the nonspeech aspect of conduct composed of both speech and nonspeech elements, where that regulation is supported by a sufficiently important governmental interest?

HOLDING AND DECISION: (Warren, C.J.) Yes. When both speech and nonspeech elements are combined in the same conduct, sufficiently important governmental interest in regulating the nonspeech element can justify incidental limitations of First Amendment freedoms. The Court considered two aspects of O'Brien's (D) appeal. First, it considered that the statute was unconstitutional in its application to him, and secondly, that the statute was unconstitutional as enacted. Where conduct is composed of speech and nonspeech elements, the speaker can invoke his freedom of speech rights to defend against unwarranted governmental interference. What must be determined is whether the attempted regulation of the nonspeech element also impermissibly inhibits the speech aspect. An incidental restriction on speech can be justified where the government can show a substantial interest in furthering a constitutional power that is not directed at the suppression of speech. In order to facilitate the implementation of the power to raise and support armies, Congress has enacted a system

for classifying individuals as to eligibility for military service. The Selective Service cards provide an efficient and reasonable method for identifying those persons previously deemed fit for military service should a national emergency arise. The court found the requirement that the card be in the possession of the holder to be a valid requirement. The court also found an independent justification for both the possession requirement and the prohibition against mutilation or destruction. While admitting some overlap, the possession requirement was intended for a smooth functioning of the draft system, while the prohibition against mutilation was a sabotage prevention measure. A person could destroy another's card while retaining his own intact. The statute was intended as a necessary and proper method to carry out a vital governmental interest. No reasonable alternative is apparent and the narrow construction of the statute indicates it was not intended to suppress communication. As to the contention the statute was unconstitutional on its face, the court found congressional intent to be the smooth functioning of the draft system, not the suppression of anti-war sentiment. Reversed.

▶ ANALYSIS

Many articles written about this decision have been critical of the court's superficial analysis of the interests involved on both sides of this case. The commentators felt that O'Brien's (D) contention that the draft card was not a vital document was dismissed out of hand. They also felt there should have been a more probing analysis of the operation of the Selective Service System and an examination of the actual, not supposed, importance of the draft card in that system. The strongest criticism of this case has been that the Court justified the suppression of expression, not on the basis of a compelling interest but on a bureaucratic system designed for convenience. There was no analysis of alternative systems. Finally, some observers saw in this decision a desire to counterbalance the long string of cases decided by the Warren Court upholding individual rights in the face of much stronger governmental interests.

■■■■

Quicknotes

CONSCRIPTION Compulsory service in the military; the state of being drafted.

FIRST AMENDMENT Prohibits Congress from enacting any law respecting an establishment of religion, prohibiting

Continued on next page.

the free exercise of religion, abridging freedom of speech
or the press, the right of peaceful assembly and the right
to petition for a redress of grievances.

SYMBOLIC SPEECH An activity that expresses an idea
without the use of words.

Texas v. Johnson

State (P) v. Flag owner (D)

491 U.S. 397 (1989).

NATURE OF CASE: Certiorari review of constitutionality of state statute criminalizing flag-burning.

FACT SUMMARY: Johnson (D), who burned a U.S. flag as a means of political protest, was convicted under Texas (P) law of desecrating a venerated object.

🏛 RULE OF LAW
Burning a U.S. flag as a means of political protest may not be criminalized.

FACTS: Johnson (D) joined a protest at the site of the 1984 Republican National Convention. Except for some minor vandalism in which Johnson (D) took no part, the protest was peaceful. At one point Johnson burned a U.S. flag. He was convicted under a state law criminalizing the desecration of a venerated object. The state court of criminal appeals reversed, holding Johnson's (D) actions protected under the First Amendment. The Supreme Court granted review.

ISSUE: May burning the U.S. flag as a means of political protest be criminalized?

HOLDING AND DECISION: (Brennan, J.) No. Burning a U.S. flag as a means of political protest may not be criminalized. While the First Amendment literally protects only "speech," it has long been the rule that conduct that is meant to express an idea also raises First Amendment concerns. Johnson's (D) behavior undoubtedly was so meant, and Texas (P) conceded this. This being so, the prosecution of Johnson (D) could be upheld only if Texas (P) could show an interest therein unrelated to the suppression of ideas. Two have been offered, keeping the peace and preserving the flag as a symbol of national unity. Here, no breach of the peace occurred, and this Court is unwilling to presume that symbolic conduct not directed at any person or group in particular constitutes such a danger to public tranquility that a state may proscribe such conduct. As to the latter justification, it is a core principle of the First Amendment that government may not prohibit expression of an idea because it finds the idea disagreeable. While the Court does not doubt that government is free to promote respect for the flag as a symbol of national unity, it may not compel how a flag, or any symbol, is used. All this being so, the conclusion must be that the law under which Johnson (D) was prosecuted constitutes an abridgment of expressive conduct for which no justification separate from such abridgment can be found, and the statute violates the First Amendment. Affirmed.

DISSENT: (Rehnquist, C.J.) The flag does not represent any idea or point of view. It is a unique symbol of our national heritage and deserves special protection. Beyond that, the acts of Johnson (D) did have a tendency to incite a breach of the peace. It is more likely to antagonize others than to communicate an idea.

DISSENT: (Stevens, J.) Due to the unique value of the flag as a symbol, government's interest in preserving that value is significant and legitimate.

▌ANALYSIS

This was one of the most controversial decisions of the Supreme Court in decades. Almost immediately, calls for a constitutional amendment to overturn the decision were made. Within the year of its decision, Congress had passed a statute, rather than an amendment, in a response that was hoped would pass First Amendment scrutiny. The amendment movement faltered because never in history has the Bill of Rights been amended.

Quicknotes

FIRST AMENDMENT Prohibits Congress from enacting any law respecting an establishment of religion, prohibiting the free exercise of religion, abridging freedom of speech or the press, the right of peaceful assembly and the right to petition for a redress of grievances.

SYMBOLIC CONDUCT Conduct that is expressive of a person's thoughts or opinions.

SYMBOLIC SPEECH An activity that expresses an idea without the use of words.

Holder v. Humanitarian Law Project

Federal government (D) v. Activists (P)

561 U.S. ___, 130 S. Ct. 2705 (2010).

NATURE OF CASE: Appeal from U.S. Court of Appeals.

FACT SUMMARY: Members of the Humanitarian Law Project (P) sought an injunction against the federal Government (D) to prevent the enforcement of 18 U.S.C. A. § 2339B(a)(1), which prohibits providing nonviolent material support for organizations that engage in terrorism.

RULE OF LAW
The federal government may prohibit providing nonviolent material support for terrorist organizations, including legal services and advice, without violating the free speech clause of the First Amendment.

FACTS: Under U.S.C.A. § 2339B(a)(1), the Secretary of State has the authority to designate any particular group as a "foreign terrorist organization." The law makes it a crime for anyone to provide "material support or resources" to even the nonviolent activities of a designated organization. Supporters of the Kurdistan Workers Party (KWP) and the Liberation Tigers of Tamil Eelam (LTTE), both of which were identified by the Secretary of State as terrorist groups, sought an injunction to prevent the U.S. Government (D) from enforcing the law. The Government (D) moved for summary judgment, arguing that the challenged provisions of the law were not unconstitutionally vague. The district court granted a partial motion for summary judgment, but held that some parts of the law were unconstitutionally vague. The U.S. Court of Appeals for the Ninth Circuit affirmed, holding that the terms "service," "training," or "other specialized knowledge" within the statute in question as applied to the plaintiffs, were unconstitutionally vague.

ISSUE: May the federal government prohibit providing nonviolent material support for terrorist organizations, including legal services and advice, without violating the free speech clause of the First Amendment?

HOLDING AND DECISION: (Roberts, C.J.) Yes. The federal government may prohibit providing nonviolent material support for terrorist organizations, including legal services and advice, without violating the free speech clause of the First Amendment. The statute may not be clear in every respect, but it is sufficiently clear with respect to the Humanitarian Law Project (P). The material support provision of the statute is not vague as applied to the specific kinds of support that the Humanitarian Law Project (P) seeks to provide to terrorist organizations, and it is not

unconstitutional. The statutory terms at issue—"training," "expert advice or assistance," "service," and "personnel"—are not similar to terms like "annoying" and "indecent" that have been struck down in the past as being too vague. Reversed.

DISSENT: (Breyer, J.) The statute is not unconstitutionally vague but the Constitution does not permit the Government (D) to prosecute the Humanitarian Law Project (P) criminally for engaging in teaching and advocacy that advances the so-called terrorist groups' lawful political objectives. The Government (D) failed to meet its burden to show that the speech prohibited by the statute served a compelling governmental interest.

ANALYSIS

This case marks the first time the Supreme Court has held that abridgment of political speech—which is ordinarily protected by the First Amendment, no matter the content—passed the strict scrutiny test. To fully understand the Court's decision, consider the legislative history of U.S. C.A. § 2339A and 2339B. Congress enacted § 2339A as part of a wide-ranging crime package, the Violent Crime Control and Law Enforcement Act of 1994, and at the time it generated little notice. Congress then amended § 2339A and supplemented it with § 2339B as part of the Antiterrorism and Effective Death Penalty Act of 1996 (AEDPA). New § 2339B reflected Congress's belief that the supply of funds, goods, or services by individuals or organizations to terrorist groups helps to mitigate the costs to the terrorist organization of running its legitimate activities, which in turn frees an equal sum that can then be spent on terrorist activities. After the terrorist attacks on 9/11, the USA PATRIOT Act was passed, and it amended both § 2339A and 2339B by increasing prison sentences and adding "expert advice or assistance" to forms of proscribed material support or resources. And finally, the Intelligence Reform and Terrorism Prevention Act of 2004 amended the definition of "material support or resources" that applies to both sections. The specific forms of support that had been used to define the term became examples of a more general definition that covers "any property, tangible or intangible, or service." Clarifying definitions of the examples "training" and "expert advice or assistance" were added, as was a clarifying explanation of the term "personnel."

Continued on next page.

Quicknotes

FIRST AMENDMENT RIGHTS Rights conferred by the First Amendment to the United States Constitution prohibiting Congress from enacting any law respecting an establishment of religion, prohibiting the free exercise of religion, abridging freedom of speech or the press, the right of peaceful assembly and the right to petition for a redress of grievances.

■═■

Members of City Council v. Taxpayers for Vincent

City council (D) v. Campaign supporters (P)

466 U.S. 789 (1984).

NATURE OF CASE: Certiorari review of constitutionality of a law prohibiting the posting of signs on public property.

FACT SUMMARY: A Los Angeles Municipal Code prohibited the posting of signs on public property, and supporters of Vincent (P), a political candidate, challenged the removal of their signs from utility poles.

🏛 RULE OF LAW
It is not an unconstitutional infringement of speech to prevent political messages from being posted on public property.

FACTS: The Los Angeles City Council (D) passed an ordinance prohibiting the posting of signs on public property. Pursuant to the ordinance, city workers removed signs attached to power poles. Some of the signs removed were political message signs for Vincent. Taxpayers for Vincent (P) filed suit, alleging an infringement of speech. The suit was dismissed. The appellate court reversed, and the City (D) appealed to the Supreme Court.

ISSUE: Is it an unconstitutional infringement of speech to prevent political messages from being posted on public property?

HOLDING AND DECISION: (Stevens, J.) No. It is not an unconstitutional infringement of speech to prevent political messages from being posted on public property. So long as the state's interest is sufficiently substantial to justify the effect of an ordinance, and the effect is no greater than necessary, the state may restrict the posting of messages on public property. A city has a justified interest in reducing visual blight. To this end, the posting of signs can be regulated within certain bounds. In this case, the City (D) removed signs from power poles to limit the visual discordance caused by haphazard posting. Since numerous other avenues existed for political speech, the ordinance was not overly restrictive. The ordinance was content-neutral and impartially administered. Reversed.

DISSENT: (Brennan, J.) The Court has undermined the First Amendment with its lenient approach toward an argument of aesthetics. The presence of so many signs in Los Angeles indicates that it may be the only avenue of communication feasibly available to many. Such a complete restriction should not be upheld.

▶ ANALYSIS

Evidently, aesthetic concerns are an important matter for government. Given the much grander matters treated in many free-speech cases, it seems unusual that aesthetics would receive such supportive treatment. However, such treatment has been used in several Supreme Court decisions, including *Metromedia, Inc. v. San Diego*, 453 U.S. 490 (1981), so evidently there is harmony on this matter.

◼■◼

Quicknotes

CONTENT-NEUTRAL Refers to statutes that regulate speech regardless of its content.

◼■◼

Clark v. Community for Creative Non-Violence

Federal agency (D) v. Organization (P)

468 U.S. 288 (1984).

NATURE OF CASE: Certiorari review of constitutionality of a state regulation limiting political demonstrations.

FACT SUMMARY: Community for Creative Non-Violence (P) contended that the application of a National Park Service regulation prohibiting camping in certain parks to its demonstration in protest of the plight of the homeless was a violation of their freedom of speech.

🏛 RULE OF LAW
Expression may be constitutionally restricted to reasonable times, places, and manners.

FACTS: Community for Creative Non-Violence (CCN) (P) received a permit from the National Park Service allowing them to set up tents in Lafayette Park (across the street from the White House) to protest the plight of the nation's homeless. The permit denied CCN (P) the right to have its members sleep in the tents. This denial was made pursuant to a National Park Service regulation prohibiting camping in Lafayette Park. CCN (P) sued, contending the application of the regulation to its demonstration violated its right to free speech. The district court upheld the regulation, and the court of appeals reversed. The Supreme Court took jurisdiction.

ISSUE: May speech be subjected to reasonable time, place, and manner restrictions?

HOLDING AND DECISION: (White, J.) Yes. Speech may be subject to reasonable time, place, and manner restrictions. Assuming that sleeping, within the context of this case, constitutes expression, it is subject to reasonable time, place, and manner restrictions. The application of the Park Service regulation had nothing to do with the content of the expression. The ban on sleeping was a restriction on the manner of expression. As a result, the application of the regulation did not violate freedom of speech. Reversed.

DISSENT: (Marshall, J.) Sleep in this context went beyond mere conduct. It was symbolic speech, and its ban served no substantial government interest. Therefore, it should not have been suppressed.

▶ ANALYSIS

The threshold question in cases of this sort is whether the action at issue can be considered speech in a constitutional context. The majority assumed that sleeping in this context was expression, but it failed to hold as such. Chief Justice Burger would deny CCN's (P) claim by find-

ing that sleeping was conduct and not entitled to First Amendment protection. Justice Marshall on the other hand would characterize sleeping as symbolic speech and worthy of protection.

■══■

Quicknotes

SYMBOLIC SPEECH An activity that expresses an idea without the use of words.

■══■

Connick v. Myers

Employer (D) v. Employee (P)

461 U.S. 138 (1983).

NATURE OF CASE: Certiorari review of speech restriction in employment context.

FACT SUMMARY: Myers (P) alleged that her employment was wrongfully terminated because she had exercised her constitutionally protected right of free speech by preparing and circulating a questionnaire soliciting the views of fellow staff members concerning office transfer policy and related matters.

🏛 RULE OF LAW

When a public employee speaks not as a citizen upon matters of public interest, but instead as an employee upon matters only of personal interest, any personnel decision taken as a result, by a public agency, should not be a matter for the courts to review.

FACTS: Myers (P), who had some opposition to her impending transfer to prosecute cases in another section of the criminal court, prepared a questionnaire soliciting the views of her fellow assistant district attorneys concerning office transfer policy, office morale, the need for a grievance committee, the level of confidence in supervisors, and whether employees felt pressured to work in political campaigns. She was told her distribution of the questionnaire was an act of insubordination and that she was terminated because of her refusal to accept the transfer. Myers (P) sued, alleging that her employment had been wrongfully terminated because she had exercised her right of free speech. The district court found that her distribution of the questionnaire was the actual reason for her termination and then held that the questionnaire involved matters of public concern and that the state had not "clearly demonstrated" that the survey "substantially interfered" with the operations of the District Attorney's office, as District Attorney Connick had claimed. The Fifth Circuit affirmed.

ISSUE: When a public employee speaks not as a citizen upon matters of public interest, but instead as an employee upon matters only of personal interest, should any personnel decision taken as a result, by a public agency, be a matter for the courts to review?

HOLDING AND DECISION: (White, J.) No. When a public employee speaks not as a citizen upon matters of public interest, but instead as an employee upon matters only of personal interest, any personnel decision taken as a result, by a public agency, should not be a matter for the courts to review. This means that when employee expression cannot be fairly considered as relating to any matter of political, social, or other concern to the commu-

nity, governmental officials should enjoy wide latitude in managing their offices, without intrusive oversight by the judiciary in the name of the First Amendment. Thus, if Myers's (P) questionnaire cannot be fairly characterized as constituting speech on a matter of public concern, it is unnecessary for this Court to scrutinize the reasons for her discharge. Whether an employee's speech addresses a matter of public concern must be determined by the content, form, and context of a given statement, as revealed by the whole record. In this case, with the exception of the question regarding being pressured to work in political campaigns, the questions Myers (P) posed to her coworkers do not fall under the rubric of matters of "public concern" but rather reflect her dissatisfaction with her transfer and an attempt to turn that displeasure into a cause célèbre. Since one of the questions she touched on in her survey does, however, touch upon a matter of public concern and contributed to her discharge, the Court must determine whether Connick (D) was justified in discharging Myers (P). The district court erred in this phase by imposing an unduly onerous burden on the state to justify her discharge, making the government bear the burden of "clearly demonstrating" that the speech in question "substantially interfered" with official responsibilities. Yet, as the *Pickering*, 391 U.S. 563 (1968), case unmistakably states, the state's burden in justifying a particular discharge varies depending upon the nature of the employee's expression. The Court must, in such cases, reach the most appropriate possible balance of the competing interests of the employee, a citizen, in commenting upon the matters of public concern and the interest of the state, as an employer, in promoting the efficiency of the public services it performs through its employees. When close working relationships are essential to the fulfilling of public responsibilities, a wide degree of deference to the employer's judgment is appropriate. It is not necessary for an employer to allow events to unfold to the extent that the disruption of the office and the destruction of working relationships is manifest before taking action. However, the Court cautions that a stronger showing may be necessary if the employee's speech more substantially involved matters of public concern. Also relevant is the manner, time, and place in which the questionnaire was distributed. Here, the questionnaire was prepared and distributed at the office, with the manner of distribution requiring not only Myers (P) but others to leave their work in order to tend to it. The fact that Myers (P) exercised her rights to speech at the office supports Connick's (D) fears that the functioning of his office was endangered, even if that potential outcome never actually came about. Finally, the context in which the dispute arose

Continued on next page.

is significant; it came upon the heels of an unwelcome transfer notice. Although Myers's (P) survey touched upon matters of public concern in a most limited sense, it is most accurately characterized as an employee grievance concerning internal office policy. Thus, the limited First Amendment interest involved here does not require that Connick (D) tolerate action that he reasonably believed would disrupt the office, undermine his authority, and destroy close working relationships. Accordingly, his discharge of Myers (P) did not offend the First Amendment. Reversed.

DISSENT: (Brennan, J.) Most of Myers's (P) questionnaire, and not just one question thereon, addressed matters of public concern because it discussed subjects that could reasonably be expected to be of interest to persons seeking to develop informed opinions about the manner in which the Orleans Parish District Attorney, an elected official charged with managing a vital government agency, discharges his responsibilities. The Court misapplied the *Pickering* test by effectively deciding, contrary to prior authority, that a public employer's mere apprehension that speech will be disruptive justifies suppression of that speech when all the objective evidence suggests that those fears are essentially unfounded.

▶ *ANALYSIS*

It was not until the 1950s and 1960s that the Court began to cast doubt on the theretofore unchallenged dogma that a public employee had no right to object to conditions placed upon the terms of employment—including those restricting his exercise of constitutional rights. While sitting on the Supreme Judicial Court of Massachusetts, Justice Holmes made the following statement expressing this position: "A policeman may have a constitutional right to talk politics, but he has no constitutional right to be a policeman." *McAuliffe v. Mayor of New Bedford*, 155 Mass. 216 (1892).

Quicknotes

FIRST AMENDMENT Prohibits Congress from enacting any law respecting an establishment of religion, prohibiting the free exercise of religion, abridging freedom of speech or the press, the right of peaceful assembly and the right to petition for a redress of grievances.

LIBEL Speech published in order to defame a living person.

TIME, PLACE, AND MANNER RESTRICTION Refers to certain types of regulations on speech that are permissible since they only restrict the time, place, and manner in which the speech is to occur.

WRONGFUL TERMINATION Unlawful termination of an individual's employment.

Near v. Minnesota

Publisher (D) v. State (P)

283 U.S. 697 (1931).

NATURE OF CASE: Certiorari review of constitutionality of state statute.

FACT SUMMARY: Minnesota (P) sought to have an injunction issued against the Saturday Press (D), which was publishing articles charging public officials with dereliction and complicity in dealing with gangsters.

🏛 RULE OF LAW
A state statute that authorizes previous restraints on publication violates the liberty of the press guaranteed by the Fourteenth Amendment if such publication relates to the malfeasance of public officials.

FACTS: A Minnesota statute authorized the abatement as a public nuisance of a "malicious, scandalous and defamatory" newspaper. The law permitted the defense of good motives and justifiable ends. The Saturday Press (D) had published a series of articles that charged that gangsters were in control of gambling, bootlegging, and racketeering in Minneapolis, and that public officials were either derelict in their duties or had illicit relations with the gangsters. Minnesota (P) sought to abate further publication of the Press (D) that is "malicious, scandalous, or defamatory." The trial court issued a permanent injunction, and the Press (D) appealed.

ISSUE: Is a state statute that authorizes abatement of a newspaper publication dealing with the corruption of public officials unconstitutional?

HOLDING AND DECISION: (Hughes, C.J.) Yes. A state statute that authorizes previous restraints on publication violates the liberty of the press guaranteed by the Fourteenth Amendment if such publication relates to the malfeasance of public officials. It is the chief purpose of the constitutional guaranty of freedom of press to prevent previous restraint on publication. Placing previous restraints on the press endangers the very nature of a free state. Only in exceptional circumstances may previous restraints be imposed. These would include where a government seeks to prevent actual obstruction to its recruiting service or the publication of the sailing dates of transports or the number and location of troops. Similarly, obscene publications, and incitements to acts of violence or the overthrow by force of orderly government, may be enjoined. However, previous restraint on a publication that seeks to expose the malfeasance of public officials is prohibited by the Fourteenth Amendment. Public officials have recourse against false accusations under the libel law. Finally, requiring newspapers to present proof of their

good intentions is merely an additional step to a complete system of censorship. So far as the Minnesota statute authorized the abatement proceedings against the Saturday Press (D), it is unconstitutional. Reversed.

DISSENT: (Butler, J.) The Minnesota statute does not operate as a "previous restraint on publication within the proper meaning of that phrase." It does not authorize administrative control in advance such as was formerly exercised by the licensers and censors but prescribes a remedy to be enforced by a suit in equity. Existing libel laws are ineffective to suppress the evils occasioned by false and malicious publications.

▶ ANALYSIS

"The issue is not whether the government may impose a particular restriction of substance in an area of public expression, such as forbidding obscenity in newspapers, but whether it may do so by a particular method, such as advance screening of newspaper copy. In other words, restrictions which could be validly imposed when enforced by subsequent punishment are, nevertheless, forbidden if attempted by prior restraint." Emerson, "The Doctrine of Prior Restraint," 20 *L. & Contemp. Prob.* 648 (1956). Traditionally, the judicial concern in prior restraint cases is on the broad discretion over free expression vested in administrative officers.

■=■

Quicknotes

FOURTEENTH AMENDMENT 42 U.S.C. § 1983 Defamation by state officials in connection with a discharge implies a violation of a liberty interest protected by the due process requirements of the U.S. Constitution.

FREEDOM OF THE PRESS The right to publish and publicly disseminate one's views.

PRIOR RESTRAINT A restriction imposed on speech imposed prior to its communication.

■=■

New York Times Co. v. United States (The Pentagon Papers Case)

News publisher (D) v. Federal government (P)

403 U.S. 713 (1971).

NATURE OF CASE: Certiorari review of injunction request regarding publication of government paper.

FACT SUMMARY: The U.S. (P) sought to enjoin the New York Times (D) and the Washington Post (D) from publishing the Pentagon papers.

🏛 **RULE OF LAW**
Any system of prior restraints of expression comes to the Court bearing a heavy presumption against its constitutional validity.

FACTS: The U.S. Government (P) sought to enjoin the New York Times (D) and the Washington Post (D) from publishing the contents of a classified study entitled, "History of U.S. Decision-Making Process on Vietnam Policy" (The Pentagon Papers). The Government (P) sought temporary restraining orders and injunctions, and these actions progressed through two district courts and two courts of appeals. The Supreme Court granted certiorari.

ISSUE: Must one seeking a prior restraint on expression meet a heavy burden of showing justification for imposition of the restraint?

HOLDING AND DECISION: (Per curiam) Yes. Any system of prior restraints of expression comes to the court bearing a heavy presumption against its constitutional validity. Here, the United States (P) carried a heavy burden of showing justification for the enforcement of such a restraint. It did not meet that burden. The denial of injunctive relief is affirmed.

CONCURRENCE: (Black, J.) The cases should have been dismissed and relief denied when they were first presented to the Court. Every moment's continuance of the injunctions against the newspapers amounts to a flagrant, indefensible violation of the First Amendment. To find that the President has "inherent power" to halt the publication of news by resort to the courts would wipe out the First Amendment.

CONCURRENCE: (Douglas, J.) The First Amendment leaves no room for government restraint on the press. Its dominant purpose was to prohibit the widespread practice of governmental suppression of embarrassing information.

CONCURRENCE: (Brennan, J.) The error that has pervaded these cases was the granting of any injunctive relief whatsoever since the entire thrust of the U.S. (P) claim was that publication of the material "could" or "might" or "may" prejudice the national interest. Only governmental allegation and proof that publication must inevitably, directly, and immediately cause the occurrence of an event kindred to imperiling the safety of a transport already at sea can support even the issuance of an interim restraining order.

CONCURRENCE: (Stewart, J.) Publication of this material will not necessary result in direct, immediate, and irreparable damage to the nation, so the relief sought must be denied.

CONCURRENCE: (White, J.) Publication will do substantial damage to public interests, but the United States (P) has not met its heavy burden. However, failure by the United States (P) to justify prior restraints does not measure its constitutional entitlement to a conviction for criminal publication. That the United States (P) mistakenly chose to proceed by injunction does not mean it could not successfully proceed in another way.

CONCURRENCE: (Marshall, J.) The issue in this case is whether this Court or Congress has the power to make law. Congress has specifically rejected passing legislation that would have clearly given the President the power he seeks here and make the New York Times' (D) current activities unlawful. When Congress has specifically declined to make conduct unlawful it is not for this Court to redecide those issues—to overrule Congress. This Court has no authority to grant the requested relief.

DISSENT: (Harlan, J.) The doctrine of prior restraints does not prevent the courts from maintaining the status quo long enough to act responsibly. The separation of powers requires that the judicial function in passing upon the activities of the executive in foreign affairs be narrowly restricted. Even if there is some room for the judiciary to override executive determinations of the probable impact of disclosure on national security, the scope of review must be very narrow. Here, the executive's conclusions were not given even the deference owing to an administrative agency, much less a coequal branch of the government.

DISSENT: (Blackmun, J.) The First Amendment is not absolute. There is a danger that publication would result in the death of soldiers, the destruction of alliances, the greatly increased difficulty of negotiation with our enemies, the prolongation of the war, and further delay in the freeing of U.S. prisoners.

▶ *ANALYSIS*

On June 13, 1971, the New York Times began publishing parts of the Pentagon Papers. On June 18, the Washington Post also began publishing parts of the papers. The Gov-

Continued on next page.

ernment brought an action to restrain publication. Between June 15 and June 28, two district courts and two courts of appeals considered the case. On June 25, the Supreme Court granted certiorari. Restraining orders were continued in effect pending decision, which was handed down on June 30. Four Justices, Brennan, Marshall, Douglas, and Black, dissented from the grants of certiorari, urging summary action and stating that they would not continue the restraint on the newspapers.

■■■

Quicknotes

PRIOR RESTRAINTS A restriction placed on communication before it is made.

■■■

CHAPTER 13

Beyond Speaking—Compelled Speech, Association, Money, and the Media

Quick Reference Rules of Law

Hurley v. Irish-American Gay, Lesbian and Bisexual Group of Boston (GLIB)

Parade sponsor (D) v. Permit applicants (P)

515 U.S. 557 (1995).

NATURE OF CASE: Review of order mandating parade permit.

FACT SUMMARY: The sponsors of a parade in Boston contended that a law compelling them to issue a permit to an organization they found repugnant violated the First Amendment.

RULE OF LAW
Private citizens organizing a parade may not be forced to include groups whose message they do not wish to convey.

FACTS: Since 1947, Boston's annual St. Patrick's Day parade had been organized by the South Boston Allied War Veterans Council (D). In 1983 the Irish-American Gay, Lesbian and Bisexual Group of Boston (the Group) (P) applied for and was refused a permit. It filed suit. The trial court held that the parade was a public accommodation subject to Massachusetts's antidiscrimination laws and ordered the Group (P) admitted. The state supreme court affirmed. The United States Supreme Court granted review.

ISSUE: May private citizens organizing a parade be forced to include groups whose message they do not wish to convey?

HOLDING AND DECISION: (Souter, J.) No. Private citizens organizing a parade may not be forced to include groups whose message they do not wish to convey. A parade is a collection of marchers who make a collective point. A parade's dependence on watchers is so extreme that a parade without spectators and media coverage is arguably not a parade at all. Consequently, a parade is without question a form of expressive conduct protected by the First Amendment. Expression in the context of a parade is more than banners and speeches; the type of participants is also part of the overall message. Free speech in the demonstration/parade context necessarily involves the right on the part of the parade organizer to not include those whose inclusion would send a message the organizer does not wish said. Here, the Veterans Council (D) was of the opinion that inclusion of the Group (P) in its parade conveyed an unwanted message. It was therefore acting within its rights not to allow the Group (P) to march. Reversed.

▶ *ANALYSIS*

A conceptually similar case, which came out differently, was *Turner Broadcasting Systems, Inc. v. F.C.C.*, 512 U.S. 622 (1994). In that case, FCC regulations mandated that cable operators include certain types of programming. This was held constitutional.

Quicknotes

FIRST AMENDMENT Prohibits Congress from enacting any law respecting an establishment of religion, prohibiting the free exercise of religion, abridging freedom of speech or the press, the right of peaceful assembly and the right to petition for a redress of grievances.

PLACE OF PUBLIC ACCOMMODATION Refers to a business providing food, lodging or entertainment to customers that either has an effect on interstate commerce or is supported by state action and in which racial discrimination is prohibited pursuant to the Civil Rights Act of 1964.

NAACP v. Alabama

Association (D) v. State (P)

357 U.S. 449 (1958).

NATURE OF CASE: Certiorari review of conviction for contempt for failure to obey state court order to produce records.

FACT SUMMARY: The National Association for the Advancement of Colored People (D), in a hearing initiated by the State of Alabama (P) to oust it from the state for failure to comply with incorporation requirements, refused to obey a state court order to produce its membership lists.

🏛 RULE OF LAW
A state must demonstrate a controlling justification for the deterrent effect on the free enjoyment of the right to associate that disclosure of membership lists is likely to have.

FACTS: [Alabama (P) brought proceedings against the National Association for the Advancement of Colored People (NAACP or the "Association") (D) to oust it from the state for failure to comply with a state statute setting forth requirements governing foreign corporations. The NAACP (D) claimed it was exempt. A state court issued an order restraining the NAACP (D) from continuing to engage in further activities or to attempt to qualify itself while the action was pending. Before the hearing began, the state moved for the production of the NAACP's (D) membership lists, alleging that the documents were necessary for adequate preparation for the hearing. The court granted the motion and issued an order to that effect. The NAACP (D) thereupon complied with the requirements of the statute but did not produce the lists. The NAACP (D) was held in civil contempt, fined, and prevented from obtaining a hearing on the merits of the ouster action until it produced the records.]

ISSUE: Must a state demonstrate a controlling justification for the deterrent effect on the free enjoyment of the right to associate that disclosure of membership lists is likely to have?

HOLDING AND DECISION: (Harlan, J.) Yes. A state must demonstrate a controlling justification for the deterrent effect on the free enjoyment of the right to associate that disclosure of membership lists is likely to have. Group association is an effective means to further advocacy of both public and private viewpoints. The fact that Alabama (P) has taken no direct steps to interfere with the Association's (D) freedom of association does not end the question because it may have engaged in more subtle intimidation. There is a vital relationship between the freedom to associate and privacy in one's associations.

Here, there is a good possibility that disclosure would expose members to economic reprisal, loss of employment, and threat of physical coercion, thus having a deterrent effect on continued membership and discouraging others from joining. It is insufficient to answer that the pressure comes from the private community and not the state as there is interplay between the two. Having found the potential for deterrence, the next inquiry is whether the state was justified in seeking the lists. The disclosure of the lists has no substantial bearing on the issue of compliance with the state statute. This case differs substantially from an earlier Supreme Court decision involving the Ku Klux Klan and its failure to produce membership lists in violation of a New York law. There, the nature of the Ku Klux Klan—its violent tendencies which the Court took notice of, and its failure to comply with any conditions, unlike in the instant situation, distinguish the two groups. Reversed.

▶ ANALYSIS

At the same time that state investigations seeking public disclosure were prevailing over countervailing claims of First Amendment freedoms in other contexts, the Court, as evidenced in *NAACP v. Alabama* above and *Shelton v. Tucker*, 364 U.S. 479 (1960), required the state to produce a relevant justification for its probe and the collateral effect of disclosure on First Amendment freedoms. *NAACP v. Alabama* thus portends a shift in the Court's focus to greater scrutiny of reasons for state inquiries that have deterrent, or "chilling" effects, on freedom of speech, association, or expression. The new approach would gain wider application in the 1960s where the state's interest in seeking information was pitted against the individual's right to privacy.

■=■

Quicknotes

CONTEMPT An act of omission that interferes with a court's proper administration of justice.

DUE PROCESS CLAUSE Clauses found in the Fifth and Fourteenth Amendments to the United States Constitution providing that no person shall be deprived of "life, liberty, or property, without due process of law."

FREEDOM OF ASSOCIATION The right to peaceably assemble.

Continued on next page.

RIGHT TO PRIVACY The violation of an individual's right to be protected against unwarranted interference in his personal affairs, falling into one of four categories: (1) appropriating the individual's likeness or name for commercial benefit; (2) intrusion into the individual's seclusion; (3) public disclosure of private facts regarding the individual; and (4) disclosure of facts placing the individual in a false light.

NAACP v. Button

Association (D) v. State (P)

371 U.S. 415 (1963).

NATURE OF CASE: Certiorari review of finding of a violation of American Bar Association Canons of Professional Ethics.

FACT SUMMARY: Virginia amended its bar regulations to ban the mass counseling and soliciting techniques of the National Association for the Advancement of Colored People.

🏛 RULE OF LAW
A state statute regulating the practice of law constitutionally may not be used to prevent minority groups from associating to seek legal redress.

FACTS: As a part of their statewide school desegregation program, National Association for the Advancement of Colored People (NAACP) lawyers held regular meetings with black parents to explain legal steps necessary to achieve such desegregation. After such meetings, forms were provided to the parents authorizing the NAACP (D) to represent them. With such authorization, NAACP (D) attorneys would then commence action. In response to this practice, Virginia added a Chapter 33 to its code of conduct for lawyers, which prohibited solicitation of legal action by agents of any organization which employs lawyers to carry out such actions. The Virginia Supreme Court of Appeals found the NAACP (D) in violation of this chapter as well as American Bar Association Canons of Professional Ethics 35 (prohibiting the control of legal services by intermediary lay agencies) and 47 (prohibiting any lawyer from assisting such an intermediary lay agency). This appeal followed.

ISSUE: May a state statute regulating the practice of law constitutionally be used to prevent minority groups from associating to seek legal redress?

HOLDING AND DECISION: (Brennan, J.) No. A state statute regulating the practice of law constitutionally may not be used to prevent minority groups from associating to seek legal redress. It is well settled that states have an inherent power to regulate the practice of law in their courts, but where solicitation and counseling activities by lawyers attain the status of political expression and association, free exercise of these rights may not be chilled by vague and overbroad bar regulations that lend themselves to selective enforcement against unpopular causes. Virginia claims that solicitation, a crime, is outside the protections of the First Amendment, but First Amendment protection of vigorous advocacy may not be so inhibited by such labeling. Association for litigation (and thereby expression) may be the most effective way to protect minority

rights. Proscribing it requires a compelling state interest which Virginia has failed to demonstrate here. Virginia claims that its interest in regulating the practice of law is sufficient. However, the purpose behind anti-solicitation rules has traditionally been to prevent improper private gain by attorneys. No such situation exists here. The ban is unconstitutional. Ruling is reversed.

DISSENT: (Harlan, J.) While the Court is correct in saying that association for litigation is a form of political expression and association, it should have balanced the state interests to reach a contrary outcome. Over and above the anti-private-gain purposes of the regulation of the bar, there is a deeper and more fundamental purpose of preventing outside interference with the attorney-client relationship. Here, even though the interests of the NAACP and the parents were identical, and the rights involved were fundamental, Virginia's attempt to so preserve the attorney-client relationship should have been upheld.

▶ ANALYSIS

This case points up the now generally recognized view that state regulation of the practice of law may not be used to interfere with any group's freedom of expression or association. This principle has been extended by the Court to cover associations less unpopular than the NAACP as well. In *Brotherhood of Railroad Trainmen v. Virginia*, 377 U.S. 1 (1964), the Court held that a labor union had a right to set up a system of referrals of members to selected attorneys as a part of its freedom of association and expression in union-related activities. In *U.M.W. v. Illinois Bar*, 389 U.S. 217 (1967), the Court similarly held that a union had the right to hire a lawyer (on salary) to represent members before a state workmen's compensation board.

■■■

Quicknotes

ATTORNEY-CLIENT RELATIONSHIP The confidential relationship established when a lawyer enters into employment with a client.

COMPELLING STATE INTEREST Defense to an alleged Equal Protection Clause violation that a state action was necessary in order to protect an interest the government is under a duty to protect.

SOLICITATION Contact initiated by an attorney for the purpose of obtaining employment.

Continued on next page.

VAGUENESS AND OVERBREADTH Characteristics of a statute that make it difficult to identify the limits of the conduct being regulated.

Boy Scouts of America v. Dale

Nonprofit organization (D) v. Member (P)

530 U.S. 640 (2000).

NATURE OF CASE: Review of the constitutionally of a private organization's membership policies.

FACT SUMMARY: Dale's (P) membership in the Boy Scouts of America (the "Boy Scouts") (D) was revoked when the Boy Scouts (D) learned that he was an avowed homosexual and gay rights activist.

🏛 RULE OF LAW
A group may constitutionally exclude an unwanted person if forced inclusion would infringe the group's freedom of expressive association by affecting in a significant way the group's ability to advocate public or private viewpoints.

FACTS: James Dale (P) is a former Eagle Scout whose adult membership in the Boy Scouts of America (the Boy Scouts) (D) was revoked when the Boy Scouts (D) learned that he was a homosexual and gay rights activist. The New Jersey Supreme Court held that the Boy Scouts (D) must admit Dale (P) and the Boy Scouts (D) appealed.

ISSUE: May a group constitutionally exclude an unwanted person if forced inclusion would infringe the group's freedom of expressive association by affecting in a significant way the group's ability to advocate public or private viewpoints?

HOLDING AND DECISION: (Rehnquist, C.J.) Yes. A group may constitutionally exclude an unwanted person if forced inclusion would infringe the group's freedom of expressive association by affecting in a significant way the group's ability to advocate public or private viewpoints. The New Jersey Supreme Court held that the state's public accommodations law requires that the Boy Scouts (D) admit Dale (P). Application of the law in this way, however, violates the Boy Scouts' (D) First Amendment right of expressive association. The statute prohibits in part discrimination on the basis of sexual orientation in places of public accommodation. The Supreme Court held that the Boy Scouts (D) was a place of public accommodation subject to the law, that the organization was not exempt from the law under any of its express exemptions, and that the Boy Scouts (D) violated the law by revoking Dale's (P) membership based on his homosexuality. The forced inclusion of an unwanted person in a group infringes the group's freedom of expressive association if that person's presence affects in a significant way the group's ability to advocate public or private viewpoints. However, the freedom of expression is not absolute. It may be overridden by regulations enacted to serve compelling state interests, unrelated to the suppression of ideas that cannot be achieved through means significantly less restrictive of associational freedoms. In determining whether a group is protected by the First Amendment's expressive associational right, it must first be determined whether the group engaged in "expressive association." Given that the Boy Scouts (D) engages in expressive activity, it must be determined whether the forced inclusion of Dale (P) as assistant scoutmaster would significantly affect the Boy Scouts' (D) ability to advocate public or private viewpoints. The Boy Scouts (D) asserts that homosexual conduct is inconsistent with the values instilled in the Scout Oath—"To keep myself physically strong, mentally awake, and morally straight." The Boy Scouts (D) asserts that it does not wish to promote homosexual conduct as a legitimate form of behavior. Thus we must determine whether Dale's (P) presence as an assistant scoutmaster would significantly burden this goal. The court must give deference both to an association's assertions regarding the nature of its expression as well as the association's view of what would impair its expression. Dale's (P) presence would force the organization to send a message that it accepts homosexual conduct as a legitimate form of behavior. Reversed.

DISSENT: (Stevens, J.) The law does not impose any serious burdens on the Boy Scouts' (D) "collective effort on behalf of its shared goals," nor does it force the Boy Scouts (D) to communicate any message that it does not wish to advocate. Thus it does not infringe any constitutional right of the Boy Scouts (D).

▶ ANALYSIS

Public accommodation laws, such as the one here, were initially promulgated in order to prevent discrimination in public places of accommodation. Such laws have gradually expanded to include many other forms of accommodation.

▬▬■

Quicknotes

FREEDOM OF ASSOCIATION The right to peaceably assemble.

PUBLIC ACCOMMODATION LAWS Laws passed pursuant to the Civil Rights Act of 1964 prohibiting discrimination in business establishments having an effect on interstate commerce.

▬▬■

Buckley v. Valeo

Congressman (P) v. Federal government (D)

424 U.S. 1 (1976).

NATURE OF CASE: Certiorari review of constitutionality of Federal Election Campaign Act.

FACT SUMMARY: Senator Buckley (P) and others challenged the Federal Election Campaign Act's contribution and expenditure limitation, reporting and disclosure requirements, and public financing of presidential elections.

🏛 **RULE OF LAW**
The strong governmental interest in preventing election corruption does not justify imposition of substantial restrictions on the effective ability of any individual to express his political beliefs and engage in political association.

FACTS: In order to curtail political corruption, Congress in the Federal Election Campaign Act of 1971, as amended in 1974, developed an intricate statutory scheme for the regulation of federal political campaigns. Among other provisions, Congress imposed a $1,000 limitation on individual contributions "to a single candidate" in § 608(b)(1), a $5,000 limitation on "contributions" to a single candidate by political committees in § 608(b)(2), a $25,000 limitation on total "contributions" by any individual in one year to political candidates in § 608(b)(3), a $1,000 ceiling on "expenditures" relative to a known candidate in § 608(e)(1), and similar ceilings on "expenditures" by the candidate and his family and on overall campaign "expenditures" § 608(a) and (c). In addition, Congress required disclosure by candidates of all "contributions" greater than $10, and by individuals of all "contributions and expenditures" aggregating over $1,000—§ 434. In a separate action, Congress provided for federal financing of presidential elections. Senator Buckley (P) and others, pursuant to a special section in the Act of 1971, brought this action to have all the above-mentioned sections declared an unconstitutional violation of their First Amendment rights of freedom of expression and association. This appeal followed.

ISSUE: Does the strong governmental interest in preventing election corruption justify imposition of substantial restrictions on the effective ability of any individual to express his political beliefs and engage in political association?

HOLDING AND DECISION: (Per curiam) No. The strong governmental interest in preventing election corruption does not justify imposition of substantial restrictions on the effective ability of any individual to express his political beliefs and engage in political associa-
tion. Although "the First Amendment protects political association as well as political expression . . . a limitation upon the amount that any one person or group may contribute to (and associate with) a candidate or a political committee entails only a marginal restriction on the contributor's ability to engage in free communication (and association)"; but, "a restriction on the amount of money a person or group can spend on political communication (as a whole) during a campaign (excessively) reduces the quantity of expression by restricting the number of issues discussed, the depth of their exploration, and the size of the audience reached." As such, the so-called "contribution" (i.e., to candidates) limitations here (§ 608(b)1-3) may be upheld as valid means for limiting political corruption by "fat cats." The so-called "expenditure" (on political expression) limitations (§ 608(a), (c), (e)), however, places too broad a restriction on the individual's ability to speak out and must therefore be voided. As for the reporting and disclosure requirements, broad as they are, they are clearly upheld by the "compelling government interest" in deterring corruption by getting important information to the voters and providing records for enforcement of the law. Finally, the challenge to the public financing of presidential elections is simply unfounded since it entails no abridgment of speech whatsoever. Affirmed in part; reversed in part.

CONCURRENCE AND DISSENT: (Burger, C. J.) I agree with the part of the Court's opinion that holds unconstitutional the limitations the Act puts on campaign expenditures. But the disclosure requirements for small contributions are unnecessarily broad intrusions into First Amendment rights since only large contributions are likely to cause the corruption the Act is supposed to remedy. The contribution limitations upheld by the Court place just as great a burden on political expression as expenditure limitations. Finally, there is no constitutional justification for the "incestuous" relationship between government and politics that the public financing law, upheld by the Court, creates.

CONCURRENCE AND DISSENT: (White, J.) Since the expenditure limitations, struck down by the Court, are neutral as to the content of speech, are not motivated by the fear of political expression and reflect the well-founded conclusion of Congress that regulation of campaign finances are essential to protect the integrity of the system, the First Amendment is not violated by them.

Continued on next page.

DISSENT: (Blackmun, J.) There is no principled constitutional distinction between limits on contributions and limits on expenditures.

DISSENT: (Marshall, J.) I dissent from the invalidation of the limits on the amount a candidate may spend from his own funds. "The perception that personal wealth wins elections may not only discourage potential candidates without person wealth [but] also undermine public confidence in the integrity of the electoral process."

DISSENT: (Burger, C.J.): Congress has "enshrined the Republican and Democratic parties in a permanently preferred position."

▶ *ANALYSIS*

In this case, the Court has identified one of the few "compelling governmental interests" that may be employed to justify congressional regulation of an area subject to strict judicial scrutiny. That interest is the interest in maintain in the integrity of the political process. Note, however, that even though the interest is held as compelling, the Court does not automatically affirm its imposition. Note that the Court's decision left the Federal Election Campaign Act rife with loopholes. Perhaps the most exploited was that which permitted individuals to "expend" (i.e., separately from any candidate or his organization) large sums to endorse a vote for a particular candidate.

■≡■

McConnell v. Federal Election Commission

Election contributor (P) v. Federal commission (D)

540 U.S. 93 (2003).

NATURE OF CASE: Certiorari review of constitutionality of Federal Election Campaign Act of 1971.

FACT SUMMARY: Several provisions of the Federal Election Campaign Act of 1971, as amended, were attacked as abridging First Amendment rights.

> ## RULE OF LAW
> The Federal Election Campaign Act, as amended, does not abridge First Amendment rights.

FACTS: The Federal Election Campaign Act of 1971 (FECA), as amended, contains a wide variety of limits on political contributions, including limits on so-called soft money contributions. Suit was brought attacking the constitutionality of many of FECA's provisions on the grounds that they abridged First Amendment rights. [The procedural posture of the case is not set forth in the textbook excerpt.]

ISSUE: Does the FECA abridge First Amendment rights?

HOLDING AND DECISION: (Stevens, J.) No. The FECA does not abridge First Amendment rights. A contribution limit or restriction involving even "significant interference" with associational rights is valid if it is being "closely drawn" to match a "sufficiently important interest." This Court's treatment of contribution restrictions reflects more than the limited burdens they impose on First Amendment freedoms. It also reflects the importance of the interests that underlie contribution limits: interests in preventing both the actual corruption threatened by large financial contributions and the eroding of public confidence in the electoral process through the appearance of corruption. When this Court reviews a congressional decision to enact contribution limits, there is no place for a strong presumption against constitutionality of the sort often thought to accompany the words "strict scrutiny." The less rigorous standard of review which this Court has applied to contribution limits shows proper deference to Congress's ability to weigh competing constitutional interests in an area in which it enjoys particular expertise. It also provides Congress with sufficient room to anticipate and respond to concerns about circumvention of regulations designed to protect the integrity of the political process. Here, FECA's restrictions have only a "marginal impact" on the ability of contributors, candidates, office-holders, and parties to engage in effective political speech; the regulations simply limit the source and individual amount of donations. Furthermore, the solicitation provisions leave open ample opportunities for soliciting federal funds on behalf of entities subject to FECA's source and amount restrictions. Restrictions on national party committees, for example, simply effect a return to schemes approved by this Court in earlier cases; the idea that large soft-money contributions to a national party can corrupt is neither novel nor implausible. Both common sense and the ample record confirm the belief of Congress that they do. So too, FECA's amendments restricting corporations' and labor unions' funding of electioneering communications do not violate First Amendment free speech since the statute is not overbroad and the government has a compelling interest in eliminating corruption in use of such funds. [Rehnquist, C.J., delivered the portion of the Court's opinion holding invalid a section of the statute prohibiting individuals 17 years old or younger from making contributions to candidates and political parties, on the grounds that "Minors enjoy the protection of the First Amendment." Breyer, J., upheld requirements that broadcasters maintain records for political advertisements.] Affirmed in part and reversed in part.

DISSENT: (Rehnquist, C.J.) The statute does not regulate only donations given to influence a particular federal election; it regulates all donations to national political committees, no matter the use to which the funds are put. The statute is overinclusive.

CONCURRENCE AND DISSENT: (Scalia, J.) This is a sad day for freedom of speech. The plurality here smiles with favor "upon a law that cuts to the heart of what the First Amendment is meant to protect." The present legislation targets for prohibition certain categories of campaign speech that are particularly harmful to incumbents. This legislation is about preventing criticism of government.

CONCURRENCE AND DISSENT: (Thomas, J.) Rather than permit the never-ending and self-justifying process of upholding this legislation, the federal government should explain why proposed speech restrictions are needed in light of actual government interests, and, in particular, why the bribery laws are not sufficient. Today's holding continues a disturbing trend: the steady decrease in the level of scrutiny applied to "restrictions on core political speech."

CONCURRENCE AND DISSENT: (Kennedy, J.) The plurality here ignores constitutional bounds and in effect interprets the anticorruption rationale to allow regulation, not just of actual or apparent quid pro quo arrangements, but of any conduct that wins goodwill

Continued on next page.

from or influences a member of Congress. This generic influence theory is at odds with standard First Amendment analysis because it is "unbounded" and susceptible to no limiting principle.

▶ *ANALYSIS*

As made clear by the Supreme Court in *McConnell*, just as troubling to a functioning democracy as classic quid pro quo corruption is the danger that officeholders will decide issues, not on the merits or the desires of their constituents, but according to the wishes of those who have made large financial contributions valued by the officeholder. Stating that the best means of prevention is to identify and to remove the temptation, the *McConnell* court accordingly rejected nearly all the First Amendment challenges to FECA.

■═■

Quicknotes

FIRST AMENDMENT Prohibits Congress from enacting any law respecting an establishment of religion, prohibiting the free exercise of religion, abridging freedom of speech or the press, the right of peaceful assembly and the right to petition for a redress of grievances.

■═■

Federal Election Commn. v. Wisconsin Right to Life

Government agency (D) v. Nonprofit advocacy group (P)

551 U.S. 449 (2007).

NATURE OF CASE: Certiorari review of constitutionality of Section 203 of the federal Bipartisan Campaign Reform Act.

FACT SUMMARY: During the Bipartisan Campaign Reform Act's blackout period, a nonprofit advocacy group wanted to run broadcast ads encouraging listeners to "call Senator Feingold" to object to the U.S. Senate's filibuster of judicial nominees.

RULE OF LAW

A broadcast ad urging listeners to "call Senator Feingold" is not the functional equivalent of express advocacy.

FACTS: Section 203 of the Bipartisan Campaign Reform Act (BCRA) criminalizes any corporate broadcast of any communication, near the time of a federal election, if the communication names a candidate for a federal elected office and it is directed toward voters. A nonprofit corporation that served as an advocacy group, Wisconsin Right to Life (WRTL) (P), ran several broadcast ads suggesting that listeners "call Senator Feingold" to complain about the U.S. Senate's filibuster of judicial nominees. WRTL (P) wanted to run similar ads near the time of the 2004 election. It therefore filed suit against the Federal Election Commission (FEC) (D), seeking a declaration that § 203 permits the broadcast of similar ads during the BCRA's blackout period near the time of the federal election.

ISSUE: Is a broadcast ad urging listeners to "call Senator Feingold" the functional equivalent of express advocacy?

HOLDING AND DECISION: (Roberts, C.J.) No. A broadcast ad urging listeners to "call Senator Feingold" is not the functional equivalent of express advocacy. In *McConnell v. Federal Election Commission*, 540 U.S. 93 (2003), this Court held that § 203 does not facially violate the First Amendment's overbreadth requirement; this case presents the as-applied question that *McConnell* reserved. *McConnell* held that § 203 can survive the strict scrutiny required for regulation of political speech if the regulated speech is express advocacy or its functional equivalent. Thus, if WRTL's (P) ads here are not express advocacy or its functional equivalent, the FEC (D) must show that prohibiting these ads near the time of a federal election is a narrowly tailored way to advance a compelling government interest. *McConnell*, however, did not articulate a standard for deciding whether an ad is the functional equivalent of express advocacy. Because such a standard should be both objective and accommodating of political

speech, we hold that an ad is the functional equivalent of express advocacy only if it cannot be reasonably interpreted as anything but an appeal to vote for or against a specific candidate. The focus of this inquiry should be on the ads themselves and seldom on the context in which the ads appear. WRTL's (P) ads clearly are not the functional equivalent of express advocacy under this standard: they are similar to an issue ad, and they do not contain the common indicia of express advocacy (such as naming a specific candidate or political party). The FEC (D) therefore must show that banning these ads is a narrowly tailored way to advance a compelling government interest. These ads are not like campaign contributions, and they therefore do not implicate the government interest of "preventing corruption and the appearance of corruption" in campaigns. Similarly, these ads do not implicate the interest in preventing the effects of aggregated wealth on the political process. As applied to WRTL's (P) ads, then, § 203 of the BCRA violates the First Amendment.

CONCURRENCE: (Alito, J.) Since § 203 is unconstitutional as applied in this case, the Court need not decide whether the statute is facially unconstitutional. The Court conceivably could be asked to reconsider *McConnell*'s holding on § 203's facial constitutionality if today's as-applied decision has the impermissible effect of chilling political speech.

CONCURRENCE: (Scalia, J.) *McConnell*'s holding on § 203 was wrong, and it should be overruled. Leaving § 203 facially intact has only had the ironic effect of concentrating even more power in the country's wealthiest persons while restricting a genuinely politically involved group such as WRTL (P).

DISSENT: (Souter, J.) The practical effect of this decision is that *McConnell*'s holding on § 203 has been overruled. What is now lost is the realistic means of limiting the effect that large corporations can have on the political process by opening their treasuries for electoral purposes. In this case, the corporation is itself largely funded by other organizations, and the context rejected by the Chief Justice clearly shows that the ads here were the functional equivalents of express advocacy. In that essential context, there is no reasonable doubt that the ads are subject to regulation under § 203 following the rationale of *McConnell*.

Continued on next page.

▶ *ANALYSIS*

Wisconsin Right to Life illustrates the special place of political speech in U.S. constitutional law. Such speech has been called the "core" of the speech guaranteed by the First Amendment. In this case, Chief Justice Roberts deferred to the fundamental importance of that speech by "giv[ing] the benefit of the doubt to speech, not censorship."

■═■

Quicknotes

FIRST AMENDMENT Prohibits Congress from enacting any law respecting an establishment of religion, prohibiting the free exercise of religion, abridging freedom of speech or the press, the right of peaceful assembly and the right to petition for a redress of grievances.

POLITICAL SPEECH Speech pertaining to the political process that is afforded the greatest amount of protection under the First Amendment.

■═■

Citizens United v. Federal Election Commission

Non-profit organization (D) v. Government agency (P)

558 U.S. 310 (2010).

NATURE OF CASE: Supreme Court review of a lower court decision denying Citizens United's motion for a preliminary injunction to stop the Federal Election Commission from enforcing provisions of the Bipartisan Campaign Reform Act of 2002, which would prevent the airing of a film criticizing a presidential candidate.

FACT SUMMARY: During the presidential campaign for the 2008 election, Citizens United (D), a conservative, non-profit organization, sought to advertise and then air a movie that was critical of then-Senator Hillary Clinton.

RULE OF LAW

The government may not suppress political speech on the basis of the speaker's corporate identity.

FACTS: In January 2008, Citizens United (D), a non-profit organization released a 90-minute documentary highly critical of then-Senator Hillary Clinton. The movie mentioned Clinton by name and featured interviews with commentators who were highly critical of the candidate. The movie was released in theatres, and Citizens United (D) attempted to increase distribution by making it available through video-on-demand. To do this, Citizens United (D) created advertisements containing short, pejorative statements about Clinton. It then wanted to promote the video-on-demand offering by running ads on broadcast and cable television. The Federal Election Commission (FEC) (P), using provisions of the Bipartisan Campaign Reform Act of 2002 (BCRA), stopped Citizens United (D) from running the film within 30 days of the 2008 Democratic primaries. Citizens United (D) tried unsuccessfully in district court to get a restraining order against the FEC's (P) action. The Supreme Court heard the appeal.

ISSUE: May the government suppress political speech on the basis of the speaker's corporate identity?

HOLDING AND DECISION: (Kennedy, J.) No. The government may not suppress political speech on the basis of the speaker's corporate identity. There is no basis for the proposition that the government may impose restrictions on certain disfavored speakers, and this First Amendment protection extends to corporations as well. In *Austin v. Michigan Chamber of Commerce*, 494 U.S. 652 (1990), the Court identified a new governmental interest in preventing the "corrosive distorting effects of immense aggregations of wealth that are accumulated with the help of the corporate form and that have little or no correlation to the public's support for the corporation's political

ideas." The Court's anti-distortion rationale thus states that the corporate form of an entity is the problem to be feared, yet media corporations, which can aggregate huge wealth as well, are exempt from the ban on corporate expenditures. Thus the anti-distortion rationale of *Austin* seems to be undercut by this exemption. Next, the Government (P) says that corporate political speech can be banned in order to prevent "corruption or its appearance." The anticorruption interest, however, is not sufficient to displace the speech in question. Furthermore, the government says that corporate expenditures can be limited because if its interest in protecting dissenting shareholders from being compelled to fund corporate political speech. The First Amendment does not allow that power, and additionally, nothing prevents shareholders from exercising their powers, which includes the possibility of removing board members, through the corporate process. *Austin* is not well reasoned, and for this reason, it must be and is now overruled. Reversed.

CONCURRENCE: (Scalia, J.) The dissent tries to show that today's decision is not supported by the original understanding of the First Amendment. It contends that the Framers were concerned about the free speech rights belonging to individuals. But the individual person's right to speak includes the right to speak in association with other individual persons. The Amendment is written in terms of "speech," not speakers.

DISSENT: (Stevens, J.) In the context of election to public office, the distinction between corporate and human speakers is significant. Corporations are not truly members of our society, despite the significant contributions that they make to it. The financial resources and legal structure of the corporate entity raise complicated questions about its proper role in the election process. Since they are not natural persons, it does not make sense to treat corporations as such when one considers the role they can play when making expenditures to support or attack a political candidate. Today's decision marks a troubling departure from this Court's previous rulings.

ANALYSIS

This five-to-four decision stands one of the most important First Amendment cases in years. Section 441b of the BCRA (commonly known as the McCain-Feingold Act) made it a felony for corporations to expressly advocate the election or defeat of a political candidate or to broadcast electioneering communications within 30 days of an election.

Continued on next page.

There was an exemption for political action committees created by a corporation, and the dissent noted this fact to rebut the argument that it was opposed to all forms of corporate speech. The dissent was troubled by the fact that a corporation, due to its structure, can marshal huge amounts of wealth and resources and thus distort the nature of the election discourse in ways that are not available to the individual advocate. The majority seemed less troubled by this fact and claimed it was simply ridding this issue of contradictions inherent in previous rulings.

■■■

Quicknotes

FIRST AMENDMENT Prohibits Congress from enacting any law respecting an establishment of religion, prohibiting the free exercise of religion, abridging freedom of speech or the press, the right of peaceful assembly and the right to petition for a redress of grievances.

■■■

Branzburg v. Hayes

News reporters (D) v. State and federal government (P)

408 U.S. 665 (1972).

NATURE OF CASE: Certiorari review of appeal from contempt citations for failure to testify before state and federal grand juries.

FACT SUMMARY: Newsmen refused to testify before state and federal grand juries, claiming that their news sources were confidential.

🏛 RULE OF LAW
The First Amendment's freedom of press does not exempt a reporter from disclosing to a grand jury information that he has received in confidence.

FACTS: Branzburg (D), who had written articles for a newspaper about drug activities he had observed, refused to testify before a state grand jury regarding his information. Pappas (D), a television newsman, even though he wrote no story, refused to testify before a state grand jury on his experiences inside Black Panther headquarters. Caldwell (D), a reporter who had interviewed several Black Panther leaders written stories about the articles, refused to testify before a federal grand jury that was investigating violations of criminal statutes dealing with threats against the President and traveling interstate to incite a riot. Branzburg (D) and Pappas (D) were held in contempt.

ISSUE: Does the First Amendment protect a newsman from revealing his sources before a grand jury which has subpoenaed him to testify, even if the information is confidential?

HOLDING AND DECISION: (White, J.) No. The First Amendment's freedom of press does not exempt a reporter from disclosing to a grand jury information that he has received in confidence. The First Amendment does not invalidate every incidental burdening of the press that may result from the enforcement of civil or criminal statutes of general applicability. Newsmen cannot invoke a testimonial privilege not enjoined by other citizens. The Constitution should not shield criminals who wish to remain anonymous from prosecution through disclosure. Forcing newsmen to testify will not impede the flow of news. The newsmen may never be called. Many political groups will still turn to the reporter because they are dependent on the media for exposure. Grand jury proceedings are secret and the police are experienced in protecting informants. More important, the public's interest in news flow does not override the public's interest in deterring crime. Here, the grand juries were not probing at will without relation to existing need; the information sought was necessary to the respective investigations. A grand jury is not restricted to seeking information from non-news-

men—it may choose the best method for its task. The contempt citations are affirmed.

CONCURRENCE: (Powell, J.) The newsman always has to resort to the courts to quash subpoenas where his testimony bears only a remote and tenuous relationship to the subject of the investigation.

DISSENT: (Stewart, J.) The press should not be treated as an investigating tool of the government. Concrete evidence exists proving that fear of an unbridled subpoena power deters sources. The Court's inquiry should be: (1) whether there is a rational connection between the government's and the deterrence of First Amendment activity; and (2) whether the effect would occur with some regularity. The government has the burden of showing: (1) that the information sought is clearly relevant to a precisely defined subject of governmental inquiry; (2) it is reasonable to think the witness in question has that information; and (3) there is no other means of obtaining that information less destructive of First Amendment freedoms.

DISSENT: (Douglas, J.) A newsman has an absolute right not to appear before a grand jury so as to have absolute privacy in uncovering information in the course of testing his hunches. Effective government depends upon a free flow of opinion and reporting.

▌ANALYSIS

Guidelines promulgated by the Attorney General for federal officials to follow when subpoenaing members of the press to testify before grand juries or at criminal trials included the following test for information: (1) whether there is "sufficient reason to believe that the information sought is essential to a successful investigation"; and (2) whether the information cannot be obtained from non-press sources. However, in "emergencies and other unusual situations, subpoenas which do not conform to the guidelines may be issued."

■═■

Quicknotes

CONTEMPT An act of omission that interferes with a court's proper administration of justice.

FREEDOM OF THE PRESS The right to publish and publicly disseminate one's views.

Continued on next page.

GRAND JURY A group summoned to investigate, inform, and accuse persons of crimes when sufficient evidence exists to do so.

SUBPOENA A court-issued mandate to compel a witness to appear at trial.

■≡■

Minneapolis Star & Tribune Co. v. Minnesota Commr. of Revenue

Newspaper publisher (P) v. State (D)

460 U.S. 575 (1983).

NATURE OF CASE: Certiorari review of constitutionality of state use tax statute.

FACT SUMMARY: The Minneapolis Star (P) contended that Minnesota had acted unconstitutionally in imposing a 4 percent use tax on the cost of ink and paper consumed in the production of any publication and then enacting an exemption that effectively resulted in only a few of the biggest newspapers having to pay any such use tax.

RULE OF LAW
In order to be constitutionally permissible, any differential taxation of the press must be necessary to the achievement of a state interest of compelling importance.

FACTS: Under the tax scheme set up by the Minnesota legislature, newspapers were exempt from the four percent sales tax. However, a four percent use tax on the costs of ink and paper consumed in the production of any publication was imposed. In addition, an exemption was provided for the first $100,000 worth of ink and paper consumed by a publication in any calendar year, which amounted to giving each publication an annual tax credit of $4,000. Only eleven papers, one of them the Tribune (P), used sufficient quantities of ink and paper to become liable for payment of use taxes beyond the amount of the tax credit in 1974. Only thirteen papers had to pay actual use taxes in 1975. In challenging the constitutionality of the use tax and seeking a refund of the use taxes it had paid, the Tribune (P) argued that there had been a violation of the guarantees of freedom of the press and equal protection found in the First and Fourteenth Amendments. The Minnesota Supreme Court upheld the tax against this constitutional challenge.

ISSUE: In order to be constitutionally permissible, must any differential taxation of the press be necessary to the achievement of a state interest of compelling importance?

HOLDING AND DECISION: (O'Connor, J.) Yes. In order to be constitutionally permissible, any differential taxation of the press must be necessary to the achievement of a state interest of compelling importance. Differential taxation of the press places such a burden on the interests protected by the First Amendment that it is not constitutionally permissible unless the state asserts a counterbalancing interest of compelling importance that cannot be achieved without differential taxation. By creating this special use tax, Minnesota singled out the press for special tax treatment. It justifies such by its need to raise revenue. Yet, that goal could be attained by taxing businesses generally, thus avoiding the censorial threat implicit in a tax that singles out the press. Minnesota offers the counterargument that the use tax actually favors the press. However, the very selection of the press for special treatment threatens the press not only with the current differential treatment, but with the possibility of subsequent differentially more burdensome treatment. Thus, this Court would hesitate to fashion a rule that automatically allowed the state to single out the press for a different method of taxation as long as the effective burden on the press was lighter than that on other businesses. Such a rule should also be avoided because the courts as institutions are poorly equipped to evaluate with precision the relative burdens of various methods of taxation. Minnesota's ink and paper tax would not survive anyway because it violates the First Amendment for another reason other than its singling out of the press. It also violates the First Amendment because it targets a small group of newspapers. Recognizing a power in the state not only to single out the press but also to tailor the tax so that it singles out a few members of the press presents such a potential for abuse that no interest suggested by Minnesota can justify the scheme. When, as in this case, a tax exemption operates to select such a narrowly defined group to bear the full burden of the tax, the tax begins to resemble more a penalty for a few of the largest newspapers than an attempt to favor struggling smaller enterprises. There having been no satisfactory justification offered for this tax on the use of ink and paper, it must be held to violate the First Amendment. Reversed.

DISSENT: (Rehnquist, J.) The $1,224,747 the Tribune (P) actually paid in use taxes over the years in question is significantly less burdensome than the $3,685,092 that it would have had to pay were the sales of its newspapers subject to the sales tax. Thus the tax scheme, which allowed newspapers to pay a use tax in return for being free of sales tax actually, benefited, not burdened, the freedom of speech and the press. If there was no burden, there was no "abridgment" of these freedoms of speech and the press. Without such an "abridgment" there is no violation of the First Amendment.

ANALYSIS

In *Washington v. United States*, 460 U.S. 536 (1983), the Court was dealing with a state tax that singled out federal contractors as a separate category. It did not evidence any reluctance in that case to assess the impact of the tax,

Continued on next page.

finding it was not impermissibly discriminatory on the United States because it imposed a tax burden no greater than what the contractors would have had to otherwise pay in state taxes were they treated the same as everyone else.

■■■

Quicknotes

DIFFERENTIAL TAXATION A marked disparity in tax rates between parties where such rates should be uniform.

■■■

The Religion Clauses: Free Exercise and Establishment

Quick Reference Rules of Law

Church of the Lukumi Babalu Aye v. City of Hialeah

Church (P) v. Municipality (D)

508 U.S. 520 (1993).

NATURE OF CASE: Certiorari review of constitutionality of an ordinance prohibiting ritual animal sacrifice.

FACT SUMMARY: A church (P), which performed the sacrificial killing of animals as required by the Santeria religion, challenged various Hialeah (D) ordinances prohibiting such killings as a violation of the Free Exercise Clause of the First Amendment.

🏛 RULE OF LAW
If a law's object is to infringe upon or restrict religious practices, it must be justified by a compelling interest and be narrowly tailored to advance that interest.

FACTS: The Church of the Lukumi Babalu Aye, Inc. (P) (Church) and its members practiced the religion of Santeria. An integral part of the religion was the sacrificial killing of animals for certain events. In 1987, the Church (P) leased land in the city of Hialeah (D) on which it planned to build various structures including a house of worship. Distressed by the Church's (P) plans, Hialeah (D) called an emergency public session during which it passed various ordinances that essentially prohibited the type of sacrifices required in Santeria. The Church (P) thereafter filed suit, arguing that the ordinances violated the Free Exercise Clause of the First Amendment by targeting its religious practices. The district court disagreed and upheld the ordinances with the court of appeals affirming. The Supreme Court granted review.

ISSUE: Must a law be justified by a compelling interest and be narrowly tailored to advance that interest if its object is to infringe upon or restrict religious practices?

HOLDING AND DECISION: (Kennedy, J.) Yes. If a law's object is to infringe upon or restrict religious practices, it must be justified by a compelling interest and be narrowly tailored to advance that interest. Neutral and generally applicable laws need not meet this higher level of scrutiny. The ordinances at issue, however, were not neutral and generally applicable. They restricted the practices because of their religious motivation. Though not evident on the face of the ordinances, their non-neutrality is clear from the expressed concerns of residents and citizens, the expressed motive of council members, and the ordinances' operation. Practically the only conduct prohibited by the ordinances is that exercised by Santeria church members. In addition, the ordinances in no way promoted the legitimate concerns of public morals, peace, or safety advanced in their support. Thus, since the ordinances were not

neutral and were not narrowly tailored to serve compelling interests, they were unconstitutional. Reversed.

CONCURRENCE: (Scalia, J.) The ordinances violate the Free Exercise Clause simply because they prohibit the free exercise of religion, regardless of the good, bad, or nonexistent motives of the lawmakers.

CONCURRENCE: (Souter, J.) "Hialeah has enacted a rare example of a law actually aimed at suppressing religious exercise." Such a law is nearly always invalid.

▶ ANALYSIS

Though a majority of the Court agree that the correct result was reached, the concurring opinions evidence the hostility of many justices to the rule announced in *Employment Div., Dept. of Human Resources of Oregon v. Smith*, 494 U.S. 872 (1992), just one year earlier, that neutral laws of general applicability are not subject to a high level of scrutiny. Thus, its continued viability is questionable as the makeup of the Court changes.

Quicknotes

COMPELLING STATE INTEREST Defense to an alleged Equal Protection Clause violation that a state action was necessary in order to protect an interest the government is under a duty to protect.

FREE EXERCISE OF RELIGION The right to practice one's religious beliefs free from governmental conduct or interference.

Sherbert v. Verner

Applicant for unemployment (P) v. Commission (D)

374 U.S. 398 (1963).

NATURE OF CASE: Certiorari review of constitutionality of state unemployment benefit program.

FACT SUMMARY: Sherbert (P) was discharged by her employer because she would not work on her religion's Sabbath.

🏛 RULE OF LAW
It is unconstitutional for a state to refuse unemployment benefits to a worker who was discharged because of her refusal to work on her religion's Sabbath.

FACTS: Sherbert (P) was discharged by her employer because she refused to work on Saturday, her religion's Sabbath. The Employment Security Commission (D) found Sherbert (P) ineligible for benefits because her refusal to work on Saturday was failure without good cause to accept available work. The state law provides that no employee shall be required to work on Sunday.

ISSUE: Is it unconstitutional for a state to refuse unemployment benefits to a worker who was discharged because of her refusal to work on her religion's Sabbath?

HOLDING AND DECISION: (Brennan, J.) Yes. It is unconstitutional for a state to refuse unemployment benefits to a worker who was discharged because of her refusal to work on her religion's Sabbath. It is an unconstitutional burden on a worker's free exercise of religion for a state to apply eligibility requirements for unemployment benefits so as to force a worker to abandon her religious principles respecting her religion's Sabbath. Sherbert (P) was forced to choose between following her religion and obtaining unemployment benefits. Such a choice puts the same kind of burden on her free exercise of religion as would a fine imposed for Saturday worship. Further, by expressly providing that no one will be compelled to work on Sunday, the state saves the Sunday worshipper from having to make such a choice. The state has shown no compelling state interest to justify this burden on Sherbert's (P) free exercise of religion. Hence, the burden is unconstitutional. This case is distinguishable from *Braunfeld v. Brown*, 366 U.S. 599 (1961). There, the state showed a strong state interest in providing one uniform day of rest for all workers. Reversed and remanded.

CONCURRENCE: (Stewart, J.) The cases dealing with the Establishment Clause have been wrongly decided, and this case is in conflict with them. They hold that the government must blind itself to differing religious traditions and beliefs. Yet, here the Court holds that because Sherbert's (P) refusal to work Saturdays is religiously mo-

tivated, she is entitled to unemployment benefits. Were she unable to work Saturdays due to indolence or lack of a babysitter, she would not be entitled to benefits. Also, this case is in conflict with *Braunfeld*. The criminal statute involved there made the burden on religious freedom much greater than here. *Braunfeld* should be overruled.

DISSENT: (Harlan, J.) The purpose of unemployment benefits was to tide people over while work was unavailable. It was not to provide relief for those who for personal reasons became unavailable for work. Secondly, this decision is in conflict with and overrules *Braunfeld*.

▶ ANALYSIS

The Court has encountered many situations unlike Sherbert's (P), in which the individual's right to freedom of religious belief and practices is subordinated to other community interests. Freedom of religion is not absolute, and does not extend to situations where its practice would jeopardize public health, safety, or morals, or the rights of third persons. Hence, laws prohibiting polygamy and bigamy have been upheld, as well as those requiring compulsory vaccination and X-rays, in spite of allegations that such laws required action in violation of the Mormon and Christian Science religions. The conscientious objector's right to avoid military service has been said to rest upon legislative grace rather than constitutional right.

■■■

Quicknotes

COMPELLING STATE INTEREST Defense to an alleged Equal Protection Clause violation that a state action was necessary in order to protect an interest the government is under a duty to protect.

ESTABLISHMENT CLAUSE The constitutional provision prohibiting the government from favoring any one religion over others, or engaging in religious activities or advocacy.

FREE EXERCISE OF RELIGION The right to practice one's religious beliefs free from governmental conduct or interference.

■■■

Employment Division, Dept. of Human Resources v. Smith

State (P) v. Applicant for unemployment compensation (D)

494 U.S. 872 (1990).

NATURE OF CASE: Certiorari review of constitutionality of an Oregon statute prohibiting the sacramental use of peyote.

FACT SUMMARY: After Smith (D) ingested peyote during a ceremony of the Native American Church, he was terminated from his job as a drug counselor.

🏛 RULE OF LAW
An individual's religious beliefs do not excuse noncompliance with an otherwise valid law prohibiting conduct that the state is free to regulate.

FACTS: Smith (D) was fired from his job with a private drug rehabilitation organization because he ingested peyote for sacramental purposes during a ceremony of the Native American Church. Oregon law classifies peyote as a controlled substance. Persons convicted of possessing peyote are guilty of a felony. Smith (D) was deemed ineligible for unemployment compensation benefits after it was determined that he was discharged for "misconduct." The Oregon Court of Appeals and the Oregon Supreme Court reversed that determination on the basis that the Oregon prohibition of the sacramental use of peyote violated Smith's (D) free exercise of religion. The United States Supreme Court granted certiorari.

ISSUE: Do an individual's religious beliefs excuse noncompliance with an otherwise valid law prohibiting conduct that the state is free to regulate?

HOLDING AND DECISION: (Scalia, J.) No. An individual's religious beliefs do not excuse noncompliance with an otherwise valid law prohibiting conduct that the state is free to regulate. The free exercise of religion means the right to believe and profess whatever religious doctrine one desires. The exercise of religion often involves not only belief and profession but the performance of physical acts. A state would be prohibiting the free exercise if it seeks to ban acts that are only engaged in for religious reasons. Smith (D) contends that his religious motivation for using peyote places its use beyond the reach of a criminal law not specifically directed at religious practice even though the law is constitutional when applied against nonreligious use of a controlled substance. This Court's decisions have consistently held that the right of free exercise does not relieve an individual of the obligation to comply with a valid and neutral law of general applicability on the ground that the law proscribes conduct that his religion prescribes. Smith (D) contends that rejection of his claim for religious exemption for peyote use may be

justified only by a balancing compelling state interest. The compelling state interest test is inapplicable to validate challenges to criminal prohibitions on a particular form of conduct. Application of the compelling interest standard in this context would open the prospect of constitutionally required religious exemptions from civic obligations of almost every conceivable kind—ranging from compulsory military service to the payment of taxes. Reversed.

CONCURRENCE: (O'Connor, J.) Oregon has a compelling state interest in regulating peyote use by its citizens, and accommodating Smith's (D) religiously motivated conduct will unduly interfere with the fulfillment of the government interest.

DISSENT: (Blackmun, J.) The critical question in this case is whether exempting Smith (D) from Oregon's general prohibition on peyote use will unduly interfere with fulfillment of the governmental interest. It is not Oregon's broad interest in fighting the critical war on drugs that must be weighed against Smith's (D) claim, but Oregon's narrow interest in refusing to make an exception for the religious, ceremonial use of peyote. The state's asserted interest amounts to the symbolic preservation of an unenforced prohibition. Almost half the states and the federal government have maintained an exemption for religious peyote use and have not found themselves overwhelmed by claims to other religious exemptions. Also, the courts should not turn a blind eye to the severe impact of a state's restrictions on the adherents of a minority religion. Oregon's interest in enforcing its drug laws against religious use of peyote is not sufficiently compelling to outweigh Smith's (D) right to the free exercise of religion.

▶ ANALYSIS

Selective service laws have traditionally exempted from military service conscientious objectors opposed to war in any form on religious grounds. However, the Court has traditionally held that the exemption is a product of the legislature rather than compelled by the constitutional prohibition on the free exercise of religion. See, for example, the *Selective Draft Law Cases*, 245 U.S. 366 (1918).

Quicknotes

COMPELLING STATE INTEREST Defense to an alleged Equal Protection Clause violation that a state action was necessary in order to protect an interest the government is under a duty to protect.

Continued on next page.

FELONY A criminal offense of greater seriousness than a misdemeanor; felonies are generally defined pursuant to statute as any crime that is punishable by death or by a term of imprisonment exceeding one year.

FREE EXERCISE OF RELIGION The right to practice one's religious beliefs free from governmental conduct or interference.

SACRAMENTAL USE (referring to ingestion of peyote during church ceremonies—native Amer.) Use pertaining to church ceremonies.

Everson v. Board of Education

Taxpayer (P) v. School board (D)

330 U.S. 1 (1947).

NATURE OF CASE: Certiorari review of taxpayer's suit challenging the constitutionality of a state statute.

FACT SUMMARY: Acting pursuant to a state statute authorizing local boards to make rules and contracts for the transportation of school children, a Board of Education (D) authorized the reimbursement to parents of money spent on their children's transportation to school, including parochial schools.

🏛 **RULE OF LAW**
A state statute authorizing that parents be reimbursed for money spent on their children's transportation to parochial schools does not violate the First Amendment.

FACTS: A state statute authorizes local school boards to make rules and contracts for the transportation of school children. A Board of Education (D), acting pursuant to this statute, authorized reimbursement to parents of money spent on their children's transportation to school on the public transportation system. Part of this money was for the payment of transportation of children to Catholic parochial schools. At these schools, the children received religious instruction, as well as a secular education. Everson (P) brought this taxpayer's suit challenging the statute's constitutionality. He contended that the statute violated the First Amendment in that it forced its citizens to pay taxes to help support and maintain schools that taught the Catholic faith.

ISSUE: Does a state statute authorizing that parents be reimbursed for money spent on their children's transportation to parochial schools violate the First Amendment?

HOLDING AND DECISION: (Black, J.) No. A state statute authorizing that parents be reimbursed for money spent on their children's transportation to parochial schools does not violate the First Amendment. The First Amendment forbids a state to exclude any of its citizens, because of their religious faith, or lack of it, from receiving the benefits of public welfare legislation. A statute authorizing the spending of tax-raised funds to pay the bus fares of parochial school children as part of a general program under which it pays the fares of children attending public and other schools is public welfare legislation. The First Amendment, which is made applicable to the states by the Fourteenth Amendment, commands that a state shall make no law respecting an establishment of religion, or prohibiting the free exercise thereof. A state cannot, consistent with the First Amendment, contribute tax-raised funds to any institution that teaches the tenets and faith of any church.

On the other hand, neither can a state hamper its citizens in the free exercise of their own religion. Hence, it cannot exclude members of any faith, because of their faith or lack of it, from receiving the benefits of public welfare legislation. State power is no more to be used so as to handicap religions than it is to favor them. Parents would be less willing to send their children to parochial schools if such children were not to be protected by police employed to protect them from traffic dangers, or if such schools were cut off from government services such as police and fire protection, sewage disposal, highways and sidewalks. Likewise, such parents might be less willing to permit their children to attend parochial schools if they were thereby cut off from state reimbursement for their children's school transportation. A statute authorizing the spending of tax-raised funds to pay the bus fares of parochial school children as a part of a general program under which it pays the fares of children attending public and other schools is public welfare legislation and does not violate the First Amendment. Affirmed.

DISSENT: (Jackson, J.) There are no good grounds on which to support this legislation. The undertones of the opinion which advocate complete and uncompromising separation of Church and State seem discordant with its conclusion yielding support to their commingling in educational matters.

DISSENT: (Rutledge, J.) The purpose of the First Amendment was the creation of a permanent and complete separation of the spheres of civil authority and religious activity by "comprehensively forbidding" every form of public aid or support for religion. Money taken by taxation (in this case by New Jersey) from one person is not to be used or given to support another's religious training or belief, or indeed even one's own. The prohibition is absolute.

▍ *ANALYSIS*

The First Amendment guarantees that neither the federal nor any state government may establish an official religion and that every person is free to practice his faith as he chooses. The former involves the Establishment Clause and the latter the Free Exercise Clause. These clauses protect overlapping values but they may exert conflicting pressures. Under the Establishment Clause, the Supreme Court has ruled against the giving of any state assistance to religious causes, even though it may be nondiscriminatory as between different faiths. Although the Court's

Continued on next page.

attention to financial assistance involving religious groups is longstanding, it did not become intense and controversial until recently with the increasing demand for federal spending for education.

■■■

Quicknotes

ESTABLISHMENT CLAUSE The constitutional provision prohibiting the government from favoring any one religion over others, or engaging in religious activities or advocacy.

FREE EXERCISE OF RELIGION The right to practice one's religious beliefs free from governmental conduct or interference.

PAROCHIAL SCHOOLS Schools affiliated with a parish or other religious body.

■■■

Mueller v. Allen

Taxpayer (P) v. State (D)

463 U.S. 388 (1983).

NATURE OF CASE: Certiorari review of the constitutionality of a state tax deduction law.

FACT SUMMARY: Mueller (P) instituted suit challenging the constitutionality of a Minnesota law allowing taxpayers, in computing their state income tax, to deduct certain expenses incurred in providing for their children's education, whether or not the children attended public schools or private parochial schools.

🏛 **RULE OF LAW**
The three-prong test for determining whether a program aiding parochial schools violates the Establishment Clause is: (1) Does it have a secular purpose? (2) Does it have "the primary effect of advancing the sectarian aims of the nonpublic schools"? and (3) Does it "excessively entangle" the state in religion?

FACTS: Minnesota passed a law allowing taxpayers, in figuring their state income tax, to deduct actual expenses incurred for the "tuition, textbooks and transportation" of dependents attending elementary or secondary schools," whether or not they are nonsectarian or sectarian. A maximum of $500 deduction for each dependent in grades K through 6 and $700 for each dependent in grades 7 through 12 was permitted. Mueller (P) brought suit challenging the validity of the law under the Establishment Clause. The court of appeals held that the Clause was not offended by this argument.

ISSUE: In order to decide whether a program aiding parochial schools (directly or indirectly) violates the Establishment Clause, must the following three-part test be applied: (1) Does it have a secular purpose? (2) Does it have "the primary effect of advancing the sectarian aims of the nonpublic schools?" and (3) Does it "excessively entangle" the state in religion?

HOLDING AND DECISION: (Rehnquist, J.) Yes. A three-part test was laid down in *Lemon*, 403 U.S. 602, and is the means by which it can be ascertained whether a particular program that in some manner aids parochial schools (either directly or indirectly) violates the Establishment Clause. The three-prong test for determining if a program aiding parochial schools violates the Establishment Clause is as follows: (1) Does it have a secular purpose? (2) Does it have "the primary effect of advancing the sectarian aims of the nonpublic schools?" and (3) Does it "excessively entangle" the state in religion? The first part inquires whether the program has a secular purpose. In this case, the answer is yes. The tax deduction attempts to give parents an incentive to educate their children and this

serves the secular purpose of ensuring a well-educated citizenry. The second part of the test asks the related question of whether the program has "the primary effect of advancing the sectarian aims of the nonpublic schools." Here, the answer is no. The deduction is available to all parents, including those sending their children to public schools and it channels whatever funds available to such schools only as a result of numerous, private choices of individual parents of school-age children. The third part of the test to which this program must be put inquires whether or not the program "excessively entangles" the state in religion. It does not. The only decision that might remotely involve state officials in state surveillance of religious-type issues would be the decisions state officials have to make in determining whether particular textbooks qualify for the deduction. In making this decision, they must disallow deductions taken from "instructional materials used in the teaching of religious tenets, doctrines or worship, the purpose of which is to inculcate such tenets, doctrines or worship." Making this type of decision does not differ substantially from making the types of decisions approved in early opinions of this Court. Thus, the program at issue here must be considered constitutional, as it has passed the three parts of the appropriate test. Affirmed.

DISSENT: (Marshall, J.) As this Court requoted in *Nyquist*, 413 U.S. 756 (1973), indirect assistance in the form of financial aid to parents for tuition payments is impermissible because it is not "subject to . . . restrictions" that "guarantee the separation between secular and religious educational functions and . . . ensure that state financial aid supports only the former." The Minnesota statute at hand here is little more than a subsidy of tuition masquerading as a subsidy of general education expenses. While tax deductions are ostensibly available to parents sending their children to public schools, most such parents have no tuition payments to make and would be able to deduct only what they pay for such things as gym clothes, pencils, notebooks, etc. These deductible expenses are de minimis in comparison to tuition expenses paid by most parents sending their children to parochial schools. Thus, the parochial schools are the ones benefited. In this case, the Court for the first time approves a program providing financial support for religious schools without any reason at all to assume that the support will be restricted to the secular functions of those schools and will not be used to support religious instruction. This result is flatly at odds with the fundamental principle that a state may provide no financial support whatsoever to promote religion.

Continued on next page.

▶ *ANALYSIS*

In the previously decided *Nyquist* case, on which the constitutional challenge to this tax deduction program relied
heavily, New York had passed a statute that gave the
parents of children attending private schools thinly disguised "tax benefits" that actually amounted to tuition
grants. This was found to violate the Establishment Clause.
By simply providing in its tax deduction statute that all
parents could take such tuition deductions, Minnesota
kept its tax deduction scheme from being declared unconstitutional. Yet, it is really a change in form more than
substance, for most public school parents do not have to
pay tuition. So, giving them the opportunity to deduct
tuition expenses is of little practical consequence and
does little to change the effect of the program in providing
indirect aid mostly to parochial schools.

■■■

Quicknotes

ESTABLISHMENT CLAUSE The constitutional provision prohibiting the government from favoring any one religion
over others, or engaging in religious activities or advocacy.

■■■

Zelman v. Simmons-Harris

School superintendent (D) v. Taxpayers (P)

536 U.S. 639 (2002).

NATURE OF CASE: Certiorari review of constitutionality of school voucher program.

FACT SUMMARY: To address the dismal performance of the Cleveland public school system, Ohio enacted a school voucher program that enabled parents to choose to send their children to participating private schools. An overwhelming number of the private schools participating in the program had a religious affiliation, and Ohio taxpayers (P) challenged the voucher program as a violation of the Establishment Clause.

RULE OF LAW
A school voucher program that gives parents the choice to send their children to a private school does not violate the Establishment Clause where the overwhelming number of participating private schools is comprised of religiously affiliated parochial schools.

FACTS: Ohio's Pilot Project Scholarship Program gave educational choices to families in any Ohio school district that was under state control pursuant to a federal court order. The program provided tuition aid for certain students in the Cleveland City School District, the only covered district because of its poor performance as compared to most other districts in the nation, to attend participating public or private schools of their parents' choosing and tutorial aid for students who chose to remain enrolled in public school. Both religious and nonreligious schools in the district could participate, as could public schools in adjacent school districts. Tuition aid was distributed to parents according to financial need, and where the aid was spent depended solely upon where parents chose to enroll their children. The number of tutorial assistance grants provided to students remaining in public school had to equal the number of tuition aid scholarships. In the 1999–2000 school year 82 percent of the participating private schools had a religious affiliation, none of the adjacent public schools participated, and 96 percent of the students participating in the scholarship program were enrolled in religiously affiliated schools. Sixty percent of the students were from families at or below the poverty line. Cleveland schoolchildren also had the option of enrolling in community schools, which were funded under state law but run by their own school boards and received twice the per-student funding as participating private schools, or magnet schools (public schools emphasizing a particular subject area, teaching method, or service). Ohio taxpayers (P) sought to enjoin the program on the ground that it violated the Establishment Clause. The district court

granted them summary judgment, and the court of appeals affirmed. The Supreme Court granted review.

ISSUE: Does a school voucher program that gives parents the choice to send their children to a private school violate the Establishment Clause where the overwhelming number of participating private schools is comprised of religiously affiliated parochial schools?

HOLDING AND DECISION: (Rehnquist, C.J.) No. A school voucher program that gives parents the choice to send their children to a private school does not violate the Establishment Clause where the overwhelming number of participating private schools is comprised of religiously affiliated parochial schools. Because the program here was undisputedly enacted for the valid secular purpose of providing educational assistance to poor children in a demonstrably failing public school system, the question is whether the program nonetheless has the forbidden effect of advancing or inhibiting religion. The Court's jurisprudence (see, e.g., *Mueller v. Allen*, 463 U.S. 388 [1983] and its progeny) makes clear that a government aid program is not readily subject to challenge under the Establishment Clause if it is neutral with respect to religion and provides assistance directly to a broad class of citizens who, in turn, direct government aid to religious schools wholly as a result of their own genuine and independent private choice. The instant program is one of true private choice, and is thus constitutional. It is neutral in all respects toward religion, and is part of Ohio's general and multifaceted undertaking to provide educational opportunities to children in a failed school district. It confers educational assistance directly to a broad class of individuals defined without reference to religion and permits participation of all district schools—religious or nonreligious—and adjacent public schools. The only preference in the program is for low-income families, who receive greater assistance and have priority for admission. Rather than creating financial incentives that skew it toward religious schools, the program creates financial disincentives: private schools receive only half the government assistance given to community schools and one-third that given to magnet schools, and adjacent public schools would receive two to three times that given to private schools. Families, too, have a financial disincentive, for they have to copay a portion of private school tuition, but pay nothing at a community, magnet, or traditional public school. Thus, no reasonable observer would think that such a neutral private choice program carries with it the imprimatur of government endorsement. Nor is there evidence that the

Continued on next page.

program fails to provide genuine opportunities for Cleveland parents to select secular educational options: their children may remain in public school as before, remain in public school with funded tutoring aid, obtain a scholarship and choose to attend a religious school, obtain a scholarship and choose to attend a nonreligious private school, enroll in a community school, or enroll in a magnet school. The Establishment Clause question whether Ohio is coercing parents into sending their children to religious schools must be answered by evaluating all options Ohio provides to Cleveland schoolchildren, only one of which is to obtain a scholarship and then choose a religious school. The taxpayers' (P) additional argument that constitutional significance should be attached to the fact that 96 percent of the scholarship recipients have enrolled in religious schools was flatly rejected in *Mueller*. The constitutionality of a neutral educational aid program simply does not turn on whether and why, in a particular area, at a particular time, most private schools are religious, or most recipients choose to use the aid at a religious school. In sum, the Ohio program is entirely neutral with respect to religion. It provides benefits directly to a wide spectrum of individuals, defined only by financial need and residence in a particular school district. It permits such individuals to exercise genuine choice among options public and private, secular and religious. The program is therefore a program of true private choice. Reversed.

CONCURRENCE: (O'Connor, J.) Here, it is clear that the voucher program is neutral as between religious and nonreligious schools. Nonreligious schools provide parents reasonable alternatives to religious schools in the voucher program, competing effectively with the parochial schools. Many parents sent their children to nonreligious private, magnet, and community schools. The parents have a genuine choice when all the choices available are considered, and, therefore, the voucher program is consistent with the Establishment Clause.

CONCURRENCE: (Thomas, J.) The use of the Fourteenth Amendment to protect religious liberty rights is acceptable, but to oppose neutral programs of school choice through the incorporation of the Establishment Clause is unacceptable. Without education, one cannot exercise the freedoms protected by the Fourteenth Amendment. Thus, the voucher program's importance for improving educational opportunities for minority children is consistent with the Establishment Clause.

DISSENT: (Souter, J.) Under the voucher program, public tax money will be used to pay not only for instruction in secular subjects but also for religious indoctrination. The Court's unrepudiated precedent in *Everson v. Board of Education*, 330 U.S. 1 (1947), makes it clear that no tax may be used to support religious activities or institutions. However, in Cleveland, the overwhelming proportion of large appropriations for voucher money must be spent on religious schools if it is to be spent at

all, and will be spent in amounts that cover almost all of tuition. The money will thus pay for eligible students' instruction not only in secular subjects but in religion as well, in schools that can fairly be characterized as founded to teach religious doctrine. Thus, tax money will pay for teaching religion. The Court cannot leave *Everson* on the books and approve the vouchers unless it ignores *Everson* and ignores the meaning of neutrality and private choice. From a historical perspective, the majority is creating a new phase of Establishment Clause jurisprudence in which the substantial character of government aid is held to have no constitutional significance, and the espoused criteria of neutrality in offering aid, and private choice in directing it, are shown to be nothing but examples of verbal formalism. Thus, even though *Everson*'s rule is still the touchstone of sound law, the reality is that with regard to educational aid, given the majority opinion, the Establishment Clause has largely been read away.

DISSENT: (Breyer, J.) Voucher programs direct financing to a core function of the Church: the teaching of religious truths to young children. Parental choice cannot help the taxpayer who does not want to finance the religious education of children.

▶ ANALYSIS

The Court has traditionally been satisfied that a law has a neutral primary effect if the religious impact of the law is remote, indirect, and incidental. Here, the dissent seems to argue that the voucher program's impact was not remote or incidental because by its very design, given the demographic realities of the school district, it encouraged enrollment in religious schools. The case leaves several constitutional questions unanswered, including whether provisions in voucher programs that prohibit discrimination by recipient schools are now constitutionally mandated, and whether state laws that expressly prohibit the use of aid for religious schools are themselves unconstitutional.

▬▬■

Quicknotes

ESTABLISHMENT CLAUSE The constitutional provision prohibiting the government from favoring any one religion over others, or engaging in religious activities or advocacy.

FOURTEENTH AMENDMENT Declares that no state shall make or enforce any law which shall abridge the privileges and immunities of citizens of the United States.

INJUNCTION A court order requiring a person to do or prohibiting that person from doing a specific act.

▬▬■

Lee v. Weisman

School officials (D) v. Parent (P)

505 U.S. 577 (1992).

NATURE OF CASE: Certiorari review of permanent injunction against public school religious invocations and benedictions.

FACT SUMMARY: Daniel Weisman (P), father of student Deborah (P), sought a permanent injunction barring the Providence public school officials (D) from inviting clergy to deliver invocations and benedictions at graduation ceremonies.

🏛 RULE OF LAW
Religious invocations and benedictions may not be given at a public primary or secondary school graduation ceremony.

FACTS: As allowed by the Providence School Committee (D), Principal Lee (D) invited Rabbi Gutterman to give the invocation and benediction at Lee's (D) middle school's graduation. Attendance at graduation exercises at Providence public schools is voluntary. Following school procedure, Lee (D) gave Rabbi Gutterman written guidelines for nonsectarian prayers. David Weisman (P), on behalf of himself and his daughter Deborah (P), sought a temporary restraining order (TRO) against school officials (D) to prevent Rabbi Gutterman from delivering prayers at Deborah's (P) graduation. The TRO was denied, and Deborah (P) went through ceremonies. The students stood for a few minutes while Rabbi Gutterman delivered prayers. The Weismans' (P) suit continued since Deborah (P) was a student at a Providence public high school and would likely face the same situation at high school graduation. The district court held the prayers violated the Establishment Clause and permanently enjoined school officials (D) from inviting clergy to give invocations and benedictions at future graduations. The court of appeals affirmed.

ISSUE: May religious invocations and benedictions be given at a public primary or secondary school graduation ceremony?

HOLDING AND DECISION: (Kennedy, J.) No. Religious invocations and benedictions may not be given at a public primary or secondary school graduation ceremony. Here, state officials (D) directed the performance of a formal, explicit religious exercise at public school graduation. Principal Lee (D) decided which prayers should be given, selected the cleric, and gave written guidelines for the prayer. Even for students who objected to religious exercise, attendance and participation was in every practical sense obligatory. High school graduation is one of life's most significant occasions. To say that attendance is "voluntary" is formalistic in the extreme. Such prayers in public schools carry a particular risk of coercion. There is public and peer pressure on attending students to stand as a group, or maintain respectful silence. A dissenter is injured by his reasonable perception that others view his standing as approval, and that he is being forced by the state to pray. The First Amendment protects the objector from having to take unilateral, private action to avoid compromising religious principles at a state function. The fact that the prayer was "nonsectarian" does not make government involvement acceptable. Affirmed.

CONCURRENCE: (Blackmun, J.) The Establishment Clause not only prohibits government coercion, but also any government engagement in religious practices. The simple issue is whether the state placed a stamp of approval on a religious activity. Here, it did.

CONCURRENCE: (Souter, J.) The history of the First Amendment supports the settled principle that the Establishment Clause prohibits support for religion in general as much as support for a particular religion. A distinction between "sectarian" and "nonsectarian" prayers would involve courts in an unconstitutional inquiry as to whether particular prayers are ecumenical enough. A showing of coercion is not necessary to establish a violation of the Establishment Clause. Were coercion a requirement under the Establishment Clause, the Clause would be redundant. The Framers' writings and practices indicate a much broader reading than a mere ban on state coercion.

DISSENT: (Scalia, J.) Nonsectarian prayers at graduations and other public celebrations are a long-standing American tradition. From the Framers to our current President, Congress, and Supreme Court, government leaders have opened public functions with prayer. No one here was forced to pray. Standing is not necessarily a sign of approval; more likely it is a sign of respect for religious beliefs of others, a civic virtue that our schools should cultivate. The Establishment Clause bars only state religious activity backed by threat of penalty for nonparticipation.

▶ ANALYSIS

The dissent claimed that the Court's failure to apply the three-part test of *Lemon v. Kurtzman*, 403 U.S. 602 (1971), means the test is no longer good law. However, Justice Kennedy in his opinion for the Court expressly declined to reconsider *Lemon*. Justices Kennedy and Souter both cited *Lemon* with approval, though they did not apply the test. Justice Blackmun's concurrence, joined by Justices

Continued on next page.

Stevens and O'Connor, expressed the view that *Lemon* still applies in all Establishment Clause cases.

■═■

Quicknotes

ESTABLISHMENT CLAUSE The constitutional provision prohibiting the government from favoring any one religion over others, or engaging in religious activities or advocacy.

TEMPORARY RESTRAINING ORDER (TRO) An order issued without notice or hearing used to preserve the status quo preventing specific activity from being conducted.

■═■

Edwards v. Aguillard

[Parties not identified.]

482 U.S. 578 (1987).

NATURE OF CASE: Certiorari review of constitutionality of an education statute.

FACT SUMMARY: Louisiana (D) contended its statute, requiring the teaching of evolution and creationism together if either was taught, was constitutional.

> **🏛 RULE OF LAW**
> Any statute requiring the teaching of a religious theory whenever a scientific theory is taught violates the Establishment Clause.

FACTS: Louisiana (D) enacted the Creationism Act, which required the teaching of creationism if the theory of evolution was taught. The statute was challenged as contrary to the Establishment Clause. The state defended it, saying it promoted academic freedom. The trial court held the statute unconstitutional. The court of appeals affirmed and the Supreme Court granted certiorari.

ISSUE: Does the requirement that a religious theory be taught with scientific theory violate the Establishment Clause?

HOLDING AND DECISION: (Brennan, J.) Yes. Any statute requiring the teaching of religious theory along with scientific theory violates the Establishment Clause. This Act required public schools to advance a religious doctrine. It thus clearly had a nonsecular purpose and violated the Constitution. Affirmed.

CONCURRENCE: (Powell, J.) This Act was clearly passed to advance a religious purpose. It thus was invalid.

DISSENT: (Scalia, J.) There was no evidence this Act was primarily motivated by a desire to advance a particular religious theory.

▎ *ANALYSIS*

The Court pointed out that religious freedom was not advanced by this statute. Because this was the stated rationale for its passage, it could not survive. It did not promote religious freedom because it deterred the teaching of one theory by requiring the simultaneous teaching of the other.

◼▬◼

Quicknotes

ESTABLISHMENT CLAUSE The constitutional provision prohibiting the government from favoring any one religion over others, or engaging in religious activities or advocacy.

◼▬◼

Lynch v. Donnelly

Municipality (D) v. Union/residents (P)

465 U.S. 668 (1984).

NATURE OF CASE: Certiorari review of constitutionality of religious display.

FACT SUMMARY: The district court held that the City of Pawtucket's (D) display of a nativity scene on public property violated the Establishment Clause.

> ## 🏛 RULE OF LAW
> The Establishment Clause does not prohibit a municipality from including a religious display in its annual Christmas display.

FACTS: The City of Pawtucket (D), Rhode Island, included a nativity scene in its annual Christmas display. It had done so for over 40 years. The American Civil Liberties Union (ACLU) (P) and certain residents of Pawtucket sued, contending the inclusion of the scene violated the Establishment Clause. The district court found for the ACLU (P), holding the scene conferred a substantial benefit on religion. The court of appeals affirmed, and the City (D) appealed.

ISSUE: Does the Establishment Clause prohibit a municipality from including a religious display in its annual Christmas display?

HOLDING AND DECISION: (Burger, C.J.) No. The Establishment Clause does not prohibit a municipality from including a religious display in its annual Christmas display. The Establishment Clause has historically not been interpreted in a strict manner. The inclusion of the nativity scene conferred no discernible advantage on religion that exceeded that resulting from the inclusion of "In God We Trust" on money and other permissible religious references. As a result, the display did not violate the Establishment Clause. Reversed.

CONCURRENCE: (O'Connor, J.) In this case there was no impermissible government entanglement in religion and no municipal endorsement of religion. Therefore, it did not violate the Establishment Clause.

DISSENT: (Brennan, J.) This display is a re-creation of an event which lies at the heart of the Christian religion. As a result, it promotes that religion and religion in general and violated the Clause.

DISSENT: (Blackmun, J.) The Court ignored the established precedents in upholding the display.

▌ *ANALYSIS*

This case represents the trend in the Supreme Court's handling of Establishment Clause cases, in contrast to its

previous application of the three-prong analysis used in many cases, such as *Larkin v. Grendel's Den, Inc.*, 454 U.S. 116 (1982), where a statute or other governmental action is evaluated for its effect on religion and government. In *Marsh v. Chambers*, 463 U.S. 783 (1983), the Court, again with Chief Justice Burger writing for the majority, failed to apply the three-prong analysis and upheld a government prayer observance.

■═■

Quicknotes

ESTABLISHMENT CLAUSE The constitutional provision prohibiting the government from favoring any one religion over others, or engaging in religious activities or advocacy.

■═■

McCreary County v. ACLU of Kentucky

Kentucky county (D) v. Civil liberties group (P)

545 U.S. 844 (2005).

NATURE OF CASE: Certiorari review of constitutional challenges to postings of the Ten Commandments in county courthouses.

FACT SUMMARY: Two Kentucky counties posted the Ten Commandments in their respective courthouses.

🏛 RULE OF LAW

Government action that has the ostensible and predominant purpose of advancing religion violates the Establishment Clause.

FACTS: Two Kentucky counties, McCreary County (D) and Pulaski County (D) (Counties), placed gold-framed copies of the Ten Commandments in their respective courthouses; each display contained only the Ten Commandments and included a citation to the Book of Exodus. The American Civil Liberties Union of Kentucky (ACLU) (P) sued Counties (D), [seeking injunctive relief and] alleging violations of the Establishment Clause. Counties (D) then altered their displays to include a statement that the Ten Commandments served as a foundation for the civil and criminal codes of Kentucky. The trial court ordered that the displays be removed. Counties (D) then altered their displays a second time, this time putting up new displays in their respective courthouses that included the Ten Commandments within a group of documents presented under the title of "Foundations of American Law and Government." [The trial court granted the ACLU's (P) request to supplement the original injunction to include the third display, and the intermediate appellate court affirmed.] Counties (D) petitioned the Supreme Court for further review.

ISSUE: Does government action that has the ostensible and predominant purpose of advancing religion violate the Establishment Clause?

HOLDING AND DECISION: (Souter, J.) Yes. Government action that has the ostensible and predominant purpose of advancing religion violates the Establishment Clause. Government action for a predominant religious purpose violates the cardinal principle of Establishment Clause jurisprudence—that government must maintain neutrality toward religion, that is, between one religion and another and between religion and irreligion. In any given case, details in the record are crucial in determining the government's purpose in the Establishment Clause analysis. Here, the first display of the plainly religious Ten Commandments, with the Commandments standing apart from any secular context, clearly furthered a religious purpose. The second display also demonstrated a

religious purpose because the statement about the Commandments' foundational status for Kentucky law was based on the Commandments' religious content. The third display, with the Ten Commandments included in and among several other documents, still demonstrates a religious purpose in this case, given the full context of Counties' (D) repeated efforts to post the Ten Commandments. This holding should not be interpreted as prohibiting all integrated displays of the Ten Commandments; this decision is only that this particular integrated display violates the Establishment Clause on this case's specific facts. Affirmed.

CONCURRENCE: (O'Connor, J.) As a nation, we have no reason to trade a system based on government neutrality toward religion for a system like so many others around the world that cause so much strife. Counties' (D) displays in this case clearly violated the Establishment Clause because the displays unmistakably endorsed religion. The Framers did not foresee the multiplicity of religious belief in today's America. They did see, though, that choosing between religions is an enterprise that government should avoid.

DISSENT: (Scalia, J.) The Constitution has never required the complete exclusion of religion from public life. The founding generation made multiple official references to and recognitions of religion. That generation believed that morality was crucial for the social order, and that fostering religion promoted morality. In the United States, government can favor religion over irreligion. It also can favor one religion—specifically, monotheistic religion—over another. Today's opinion thus only increases this Court's hostility toward religion by now requiring that a secular purpose must "predominate" in government action. The displays in this case were constitutional, though, even under the majority's misguided analysis. The third, integrated "foundations" display served precisely the secular purpose that Counties (D) have advanced: to show that the Ten Commandments have influenced our system of law. The Court has no basis for conflating the purposes for the first two displays into the analysis of the purpose behind the third display.

▶ ANALYSIS

As the *McCreary County* majority notes, a government's purpose in actions involving religion is a firmly developed part of the Court's Establishment Clause jurisprudence. Regardless of the general understanding of the Establish-

Continued on next page.

ment Clause held by some individual members of the founding generation, it is worth noting that none of Justice Scalia's examples from the founding period arose in a specifically framed case or controversy in which a litigant sought to enforce the Establishment Clause against the actions that Justice Scalia recites. In the case or controversy in *McCreary County*, the majority correctly saw through Counties' (D) belated defenses of their efforts to do nothing more than to promote the plainly religious Ten Commandments.

■≡■

Quicknotes

ESTABLISHMENT CLAUSE The constitutional provision prohibiting the government from favoring any one religion over others, or engaging in religious activities or advocacy.

INJUNCTION A court order requiring a person to do, or prohibiting that person from doing, a specific act.

INJUNCTIVE RELIEF A court order issued as a remedy, requiring a person to do, or prohibiting that person from doing, a specific act.

■≡■

Van Orden v. Perry

User of state capitol grounds (P) v. Governor of Texas (D)

545 U.S. 677 (2005).

NATURE OF CASE: Certiorari review of constitutional challenge to the placement of a Ten Commandments monument in an integrated display of monuments and historical markers on the grounds of the Texas State Capitol.

FACT SUMMARY: The State of Texas (D) created a display, on the grounds of its State Capitol, of monuments and historical markers to commemorate "Texan identity." One of the monuments was a large monolith depicting the Ten Commandments.

🏛 RULE OF LAW
Government action that has religious content or that promotes a religious message does not necessarily violate the Establishment Clause.

FACTS: On the 22 acres surrounding the Texas State Capitol, the State of Texas (D) placed 17 monuments and 21 historical markers to honor various aspects of "Texan identity." One of the 17 monuments was a six-by-three-foot monolith of the Ten Commandments. Van Orden (P) was offended by the monolith when he had to walk past it to reach the Texas Supreme Court Library. He sued the State of Texas (D), alleging that the use of the Ten Commandments violated the Establishment Clause.

ISSUE: Does government action that has religious content or that promotes a religious message necessarily violate the Establishment Clause?

HOLDING AND DECISION: (Rehnquist, C.J.) No. Government action that has religious content or that promotes a religious message does not necessarily violate the Establishment Clause. The three-factor test announced in *Lemon v. Kurtzman*, 403 U.S. 602 (1971), does not apply here because the case is more appropriately analyzed by considering the nature of the Ten Commandments monument and American history. The Ten Commandments are religious, but the person whom Judeo-Christians believe to have delivered the Commandments, Moses, was also a lawgiver. Here, Texas (D) has treated the display involving the Ten Commandments as an expression of the State's (D) political and legal history. That display therefore does not violate the Establishment Clause. Affirmed.

CONCURRENCE: (Scalia, J.) This decision accurately represents the Court's Establishment Clause jurisprudence. Consistent with the Establishment Clause, government can promote religion in general, conduct public prayer, or neutrally respect the Ten Commandments.

CONCURRENCE: (Thomas, J.) The original understanding of the Establishment Clause means that the Clause should not be incorporated against the states at all. Even if it is incorporated, the Court should adopt the original meaning of "establishment," a term that the Framers understood to mean "necessarily [to] involve actual legal coercion." Under that correct understanding of establishment, Texas's (D) use of the Ten Commandments here clearly comports with the Establishment Clause because Texas (D) has not compelled Van Orden (P) in any way.

CONCURRENCE: (Breyer, J.) This borderline case requires an exercise of legal judgment more than it requires a legal test. The key inquiry here is how the Ten Commandments are used, and that consideration in turn requires the further consideration of the context in which the Commandments appear. The circumstances suggest that the State of Texas (D) intended a predominantly secular purpose. That no one has challenged the Commandments in 40 years, until this case, only buttresses the conclusion that visitors to the grounds themselves have seen a predominant secular purpose. Invalidating Texas's (D) use of the Ten Commandments in this case, merely because the Ten Commandments are religious, could well lead to the very religious strife that the Establishment Clause was adopted to avoid.

DISSENT: (Stevens, J.) Texas (D) has placed the Ten Commandments on its Capitol grounds solely for the Decalogue's religious content. The State's (D) message is therefore clear: Texas (D) endorses the "Judeo-Christian" God. Texas (D) can use secular means to legitimately combat juvenile delinquency (which was one purpose that informed the original decision to place the Ten Commandments on the grounds 40 years ago). The message in the monument, however, is a plainly religious text, indeed an inherently sectarian text, and Texas's (D) use of the monument is therefore unconstitutional. The beliefs of the individual members of the founding generation are irrelevant; it is also easy to contradict views of Founders who favored fusing church and state with, for example, the views of Jefferson and Madison, who advocated strictly separated church and state. Regardless of individual Framers' beliefs, though, this Court is bound, not by the Framers' individual expectations, but by the text of the Constitution that they adopted and ratified. That text prohibits Texas's (D) use of the Ten Commandments in this case.

DISSENT: (O'Connor, J.) The majority is incorrect for the reasons stated in Justice Souter's dissent in this case,

Continued on next page.

and stated in the concurrence in *McCreary County v. ACLU of Kentucky*, 545 U.S. 844 (2005).

DISSENT: (Souter, J.) Neutrality can be reconciled with a government's display of an indisputably religious text only if the display's predominant purpose is not to promote the religious message. The Ten Commandments can be depicted with a predominant secular purpose, as in their depiction, and the depictions of Moses, in and around this Court. In this case, though, people strolling through the Texas State Capitol grounds would be hard-pressed to find a non-religious reason for Texas's (D) use of the Ten Commandments: there is no readily discernible theme linking the Ten Commandments to the other displays scattered across the 22 acres of the grounds. A state's Capitol, however, should represent all the state's citizens, not only the ones who agree with a religious perspective promoted by the state.

▌*ANALYSIS*

An important point to note in this difficult, intensely fragmented decision is that five members of the Court applied some form of the "predominant purpose" test used in *McCreary County v. ACLU of Kentucky*, 545 U.S. 844 (2005). The four dissenters here use that test (with Justice O'Connor using the "endorsement" language that she long preferred in Establishment Clause cases). Despite his protestations that he favors legal judgment over a legal test in this case, Justice Breyer, in his concurrence, also examines Texas's (D) predominant purpose in its use of the Ten Commandments. Even after *Van Orden*, then, some form of the "predominant purpose" test still seems to be the law.

■━■

Quicknotes

ESTABLISHMENT CLAUSE The constitutional provision prohibiting the government from favoring any one religion over others, or engaging in religious activities or advocacy.

■━■

Glossary

Common Latin Words and Phrases Encountered in the Law

A FORTIORI: Because one fact exists or has been proven, therefore a second fact that is related to the first fact must also exist.

A PRIORI: From the cause to the effect. A term of logic used to denote that when one generally accepted truth is shown to be a cause, another particular effect must necessarily follow.

AB INITIO: From the beginning; a condition which has existed throughout, as in a marriage which was void ab initio.

ACTUS REUS: The wrongful act; in criminal law, such action sufficient to trigger criminal liability.

AD VALOREM: According to value; an ad valorem tax is imposed upon an item located within the taxing jurisdiction calculated by the value of such item.

AMICUS CURIAE: Friend of the court. Its most common usage takes the form of an amicus curiae brief, filed by a person who is not a party to an action but is nonetheless allowed to offer an argument supporting his legal interests.

ARGUENDO: In arguing. A statement, possibly hypothetical, made for the purpose of argument, is one made arguendo.

BILL QUIA TIMET: A bill to quiet title (establish ownership) to real property.

BONA FIDE: True, honest, or genuine. May refer to a person's legal position based on good faith or lacking notice of fraud (such as a bona fide purchaser for value) or to the authenticity of a particular document (such as a bona fide last will and testament).

CAUSA MORTIS: With approaching death in mind. A gift causa mortis is a gift given by a party who feels certain that death is imminent.

CAVEAT EMPTOR: Let the buyer beware. This maxim is reflected in the rule of law that a buyer purchases at his own risk because it is his responsibility to examine, judge, test, and otherwise inspect what he is buying.

CERTIORARI: A writ of review. Petitions for review of a case by the United States Supreme Court are most often done by means of a writ of certiorari.

CONTRA: On the other hand. Opposite. Contrary to.

CORAM NOBIS: Before us; writs of error directed to the court that originally rendered the judgment.

CORAM VOBIS: Before you; writs of error directed by an appellate court to a lower court to correct a factual error.

CORPUS DELICTI: The body of the crime; the requisite elements of a crime amounting to objective proof that a crime has been committed.

CUM TESTAMENTO ANNEXO, ADMINISTRATOR (ADMINISTRATOR C.T.A.): With will annexed; an administrator c.t.a. settles an estate pursuant to a will in which he is not appointed.

DE BONIS NON, ADMINISTRATOR (ADMINISTRATOR D.B.N.): Of goods not administered; an administrator d.b.n. settles a partially settled estate.

DE FACTO: In fact; in reality; actually. Existing in fact but not officially approved or engendered.

DE JURE: By right; lawful. Describes a condition that is legitimate "as a matter of law," in contrast to the term "de facto," which connotes something existing in fact but not legally sanctioned or authorized. For example, de facto segregation refers to segregation brought about by housing patterns, etc., whereas de jure segregation refers to segregation created by law.

DE MINIMIS: Of minimal importance; insignificant; a trifle; not worth bothering about.

DE NOVO: Anew; a second time; afresh. A trial de novo is a new trial held at the appellate level as if the case originated there and the trial at a lower level had not taken place.

DICTA: Generally used as an abbreviated form of obiter dicta, a term describing those portions of a judicial opinion incidental or not necessary to resolution of the specific question before the court. Such nonessential statements and remarks are not considered to be binding precedent.

DUCES TECUM: Refers to a particular type of writ or subpoena requesting a party or organization to produce certain documents in their possession.

EN BANC: Full bench. Where a court sits with all justices present rather than the usual quorum.

EX PARTE: For one side or one party only. An ex parte proceeding is one undertaken for the benefit of only one party, without notice to, or an appearance by, an adverse party.

EX POST FACTO: After the fact. An ex post facto law is a law that retroactively changes the consequences of a prior act.

EX REL.: Abbreviated form of the term "ex relatione," meaning upon relation or information. When the state brings an action in which it has no interest against an individual at the instigation of one who has a private interest in the matter.

FORUM NON CONVENIENS: Inconvenient forum. Although a court may have jurisdiction over the case, the action should be tried in a more conveniently located court, one to which parties and witnesses may more easily travel, for example.

GUARDIAN AD LITEM: A guardian of an infant as to litigation, appointed to represent the infant and pursue his/her rights.

HABEAS CORPUS: You have the body. The modern writ of habeas corpus is a writ directing that a person (body) being detained (such as a prisoner) be brought before the court so that the legality of his detention can be judicially ascertained.

IN CAMERA: In private, in chambers. When a hearing is held before a judge in his chambers or when all spectators are excluded from the courtroom.

IN FORMA PAUPERIS: In the manner of a pauper. A party who proceeds in forma pauperis because of his poverty is one who is allowed to bring suit without liability for costs.

INFRA: Below, under. A word referring the reader to a later part of a book. (The opposite of supra.)

IN LOCO PARENTIS: In the place of a parent.

IN PARI DELICTO: Equally wrong; a court of equity will not grant requested relief to an applicant who is in pari delicto, or as much at fault in the transactions giving rise to the controversy as is the opponent of the applicant.

IN PARI MATERIA: On like subject matter or upon the same matter. Statutes relating to the same person or things are said to be in pari materia. It is a general rule of statutory construction that such statutes should be construed together, i.e., looked at as if they together constituted one law.

IN PERSONAM: Against the person. Jurisdiction over the person of an individual.

IN RE: In the matter of. Used to designate a proceeding involving an estate or other property.

IN REM: A term that signifies an action against the res, or thing. An action in rem is basically one that is taken directly against property, as distinguished from an action in personam, i.e., against the person.

INTER ALIA: Among other things. Used to show that the whole of a statement, pleading, list, statute, etc., has not been set forth in its entirety.

INTER PARTES: Between the parties. May refer to contracts, conveyances or other transactions having legal significance.

INTER VIVOS: Between the living. An inter vivos gift is a gift made by a living grantor, as distinguished from bequests contained in a will, which pass upon the death of the testator.

IPSO FACTO: By the mere fact itself.

JUS: Law or the entire body of law.

LEX LOCI: The law of the place; the notion that the rights of parties to a legal proceeding are governed by the law of the place where those rights arose.

MALUM IN SE: Evil or wrong in and of itself; inherently wrong. This term describes an act that is wrong by its very nature, as opposed to one which would not be wrong but for the fact that there is a specific legal prohibition against it (malum prohibitum).

MALUM PROHIBITUM: Wrong because prohibited, but not inherently evil. Used to describe something that is wrong because it is expressly forbidden by law but that is not in and of itself evil, e.g., speeding.

MANDAMUS: We command. A writ directing an official to take a certain action.

MENS REA: A guilty mind; a criminal intent. A term used to signify the mental state that accompanies a crime or other prohibited act. Some crimes require only a general mens rea (general intent to do the prohibited act), but others, like assault with intent to murder, require the existence of a specific mens rea.

MODUS OPERANDI: Method of operating; generally refers to the manner or style of a criminal in committing crimes, admissible in appropriate cases as evidence of the identity of a defendant.

NEXUS: A connection to.

NISI PRIUS: A court of first impression. A nisi prius court is one where issues of fact are tried before a judge or jury.

N.O.V. (NON OBSTANTE VEREDICTO): Notwithstanding the verdict. A judgment n.o.v. is a judgment given in favor of one party despite the fact that a verdict was returned in favor of the other party, the justification being that the verdict either had no reasonable support in fact or was contrary to law.

NUNC PRO TUNC: Now for then. This phrase refers to actions that may be taken and will then have full retroactive effect.

PENDENTE LITE: Pending the suit; pending litigation under way.

PER CAPITA: By head; beneficiaries of an estate, if they take in equal shares, take per capita.

PER CURIAM: By the court; signifies an opinion ostensibly written "by the whole court" and with no identified author.

PER SE: By itself, in itself; inherently.

PER STIRPES: By representation. Used primarily in the law of wills to describe the method of distribution where a person, generally because of death, is unable to take that which is left to him by the will of another, and therefore his heirs divide such property between them rather than take under the will individually.

PRIMA FACIE: On its face, at first sight. A prima facie case is one that is sufficient on its face, meaning that the evidence supporting it is adequate to establish the case until contradicted or overcome by other evidence.

PRO TANTO: For so much; as far as it goes. Often used in eminent domain cases when a property owner receives partial payment for his land without prejudice to his right to bring suit for the full amount he claims his land to be worth.

QUANTUM MERUIT: As much as he deserves. Refers to recovery based on the doctrine of unjust enrichment in those cases in which a party has rendered valuable services or furnished materials that were accepted and enjoyed by another under circumstances that would reasonably notify the recipient that the rendering party expected to be paid. In essence, the law implies a contract to pay the reasonable value of the services or materials furnished.

QUASI: Almost like; as if; nearly. This term is essentially used to signify that one subject or thing is almost analogous to another but that material differences between them do exist. For example, a quasi-criminal proceeding is one that is not strictly criminal but shares enough of the same characteristics to require some of the same safeguards (e.g., procedural due process must be followed in a parole hearing).

QUID PRO QUO: Something for something. In contract law, the consideration, something of value, passed between the parties to render the contract binding.

RES GESTAE: Things done; in evidence law, this principle justifies the admission of a statement that would otherwise be hearsay when it is made so closely to the event in question as to be said to be a part of it, or with such spontaneity as not to have the possibility of falsehood.

RES IPSA LOQUITUR: The thing speaks for itself. This doctrine gives rise to a rebuttable presumption of negligence when the instrumentality causing the injury was within the exclusive control of the defendant, and the injury was one that does not normally occur unless a person has been negligent.

RES JUDICATA: A matter adjudged. Doctrine which provides that once a court of competent jurisdiction has rendered a final judgment or decree on the merits, that judgment or decree is conclusive upon the parties to the case and prevents them from engaging in any other litigation on the points and issues determined therein.

RESPONDEAT SUPERIOR: Let the master reply. This doctrine holds the master liable for the wrongful acts of his servant (or the principal for his agent) in those cases in which the servant (or agent) was acting within the scope of his authority at the time of the injury.

STARE DECISIS: To stand by or adhere to that which has been decided. The common law doctrine of stare decisis attempts to give security and certainty to the law by following the policy that once a principle of law as applicable to a certain set of facts has been set forth in a decision, it forms a precedent which will subsequently be followed, even though a different decision might be made were it the first time the question had arisen. Of course, stare decisis is not an inviolable principle and is departed from in instances where there is good cause (e.g., considerations of public policy led the Supreme Court to disregard prior decisions sanctioning segregation).

SUPRA: Above. A word referring a reader to an earlier part of a book.

ULTRA VIRES: Beyond the power. This phrase is most commonly used to refer to actions taken by a corporation that are beyond the power or legal authority of the corporation.

Addendum of French Derivatives

IN PAIS: Not pursuant to legal proceedings.

CHATTEL: Tangible personal property.

CY PRES: Doctrine permitting courts to apply trust funds to purposes not expressed in the trust but necessary to carry out the settlor's intent.

PER AUTRE VIE: For another's life; during another's life. In property law, an estate may be granted that will terminate upon the death of someone other than the grantee.

PROFIT A PRENDRE: A license to remove minerals or other produce from land.

VOIR DIRE: Process of questioning jurors as to their predispositions about the case or parties to a proceeding in order to identify those jurors displaying bias or prejudice.

Casenote® Legal Briefs